What Logics Mean

What do the rules of logic say about the meanings of the symbols they govern? In this book, James W. Garson examines the inferential roles of logical connectives (such as 'and', 'or', 'not', and 'if ... then'), whose behavior is defined by strict rules, and proves definitive results concerning exactly what those rules express about connective truth conditions. He explores the ways in which, depending on circumstances, a system of rules may provide no interpretation of a connective at all, or the interpretation we ordinarily expect for it, or an unfamiliar or novel interpretation. He also shows how the novel interpretations thus generated may be used to help analyze philosophical problems such as vagueness and the open future. His book will be valuable for graduates and specialists in logic, philosophy of logic, and philosophy of language.

JAMES W. GARSON is Professor of Philosophy at the University of Houston. He is the author of *Modal Logic for Philosophers*, 2nd edition (Cambridge, 2013).

What Logics Mean

From Proof Theory to Model-Theoretic Semantics

JAMES W. GARSON

CAMBRIDGE
UNIVERSITY PRESS

University Printing House, Cambridge CB2 8BS, United Kingdom

Published in the United States of America by Cambridge University Press, New York

Cambridge University Press is part of the University of Cambridge.

It furthers the University's mission by disseminating knowledge in the pursuit of education, learning, and research at the highest international levels of excellence.

www.cambridge.org
Information on this title: www.cambridge.org/9781107039100

© James W. Garson, 2013

First published 2013

A catalog record for this publication is available from the British Library

Library of Congress Cataloging in Publication data

ISBN 978-1-107-03910-0 Hardback
ISBN 978-1-107-61196-2 Paperback

For Connie – a valiant friend

Contents

Preface

Syntax all by itself doesn't determine semantics

D. Dennett (1984, p. 28)

Where does meaning come from? There is no more compelling question in the philosophy of language. Referentialists seek an answer in a correspondence between word and object, statement and reality. Inferentialists look to an expression's deductive role, its contribution to the web of relations that determine what follows from what. Logic is the perfect test bed for assessing the merits of inferentialism. The deductive role of the connectives for a given system is defined precisely by its rules. Whether the meanings of the connectives are determined by those roles is now a question with a rigorous answer. This book proves what some of those answers are, revealing both strengths and weaknesses in an inferentialist program for logic. The results reported here are only the tip of an iceberg, but they illustrate the important contribution that metalogic can play in resolving central puzzles in the philosophy of language.

To make headway on this project, we need to explore the options in syntax, in semantics, and in ways to plausibly bridge the two. On the syntactic side, we are faced with a rich variety in the systems of logic. This book examines only intuitionistic and classical rules for propositional logic, and then briefly, rules for quantified and modal systems. So this is just a start. A second important source of syntactic variation is rule format. The details about the way the rules of a logical system are formulated affect whether that system allows unintended interpretations of its connectives. In the same way that moving from first-order to second-order languages strengthens the expressive power of the logic, so does the move from axiomatic formulations, to natural deduction systems, and to sequent calculi with multiple conclusions. Answers to questions about what logics

mean depend crucially on which format is chosen. The moral is that inferentialists who claim that inferential roles fix meaning are duty bound to
specify what *kind* of rules undergird those roles.

On the semantics side, we are faced with a decision concerning conceptual foundations. Exactly what vocabulary is to be used in formulating the
meaning of a connective? There are two main choices: proof-theoretic
semantics and model-theoretic semantics. The latter tradition follows
Tarski in presuming that a semantics is a recursive definition of truth on a
model. That definition allows one to delineate a corresponding notion of
validity.

On the other hand, proof-theoretic semantics eschews "referential"
notions such as denotation and truth. It proposes to define meaning using
only syntactic concepts such as proof. It is natural for inferentialists who
view the referential/inferential divide as a battleground, to opt for proof-
theoretic (PT) semantics, for referential notions are perceived as the devices
of their enemy. The stance of this book, however, is pluralistic. There is
nothing wrong with PT semantics, but we choose to investigate model-
theoretic (MT) semantics instead, for there is ample room for a model-
theoretic inferentialism. Such a view holds that meaning is determined by
inferential role, but that the use of model-theoretic notions in characterizing the meaning so fixed is compatible with the inferentialist project, and
even useful to PT inferentialists who think of semantics entirely in proof-
theoretic terms. A main concern of this book is to demonstrate by example
that MT inferentialism is both interesting and viable. So henceforth by
'semantics' we will mean model-theoretic semantics, without intending to
indicate a prejudice against the proof-theoretic tradition.

A last source of variation must be mentioned. Definitive answers to
questions about the meanings rules express are not possible until a firm
bridge between syntax and semantics is in place. We need a mathematically
precise account of what a rule expresses. At least three different standards
for expressive power are found in the literature, so our job is to canvass
their strengths and weaknesses, and select the one that is best.

The idea of the expressive power of a rule is a generalization of an idea
that will be familiar from model theory. In the language of predicate logic,
there are well-formed formulas that express a variety of conditions on the
domain of quantification. For example, $\exists x \exists y \sim x = y$ expresses that there are at
least two objects in the domain. That means that a model satisfies that

formula iff its domain meets that condition. By analogy, a rule R should express a condition C on models exactly when a model satisfies R iff it obeys C. But what does it mean to say that a model satisfies a rule? A model satisfies a sentence iff it makes the sentence true. What is the corresponding honorific in the case of rules? This book argues that the correct choice is preservation of validity, and that alternative choices face serious problems.

What are the outcomes given the options chosen here? Given the very negative conclusions of the work of Quine (1960, Section 12) and Davidson (Lepore and Ludwig, 2005, Chapter 15) on underdetermination of meaning in natural languages, and Dennett's summary pronouncement that "syntax all by itself doesn't determine semantics" (Dennett, 1984, p. 28), one might expect that functional role radically underdetermines meaning in logic, and that rules never determine a semantics. This appraisal appears to be supported by a well-known collection of negative results for propositional logic (Carnap, 1943, pp. 81ff.; McCawley, 1993, pp. 107ff.; Shoesmith and Smiley, 1978, p. 3; Belnap and Massey, 1990). So it looks bad for model-theoretic inferentialism. However, it is argued here that this wholesale underdetermination is the result of poor choices in rule format and in the definition of what rules express. A more optimistic assessment plays out in the chapters of this book.

Chapter 1 lays out the whole project more intelligibly than this preface can manage. Chapters 2 and 3 examine and dismiss two alternative accounts of what rules express. Chapter 4 develops the notion of expression based on preservation of validity in detail, and defines natural semantics as the semantics so expressed. Since Kripke's intuitionistic semantics plays a central role in this book, Chapter 5 presents that semantics and illustrates how to define an isomorphism to a natural semantics. The next few chapters report results on natural semantics for conditionals (6), disjunction (7), and negation (8). We learn here that the rules for the conditional and for intuitionistic negation express exactly their readings in Kripke semantics. These results will hearten inferentialists of an intuitionistic persuasion. However, an unfamiliar condition is expressed by the rules for disjunction and worries about its legitimacy are explored in detail. Furthermore, there are concerns about classical negation to face as well, although in the classical setting some of the problems with disjunction are resolved. It is then argued that the classical natural deduction rules for propositional logic express a variant of an intuitionist semantics ‖PL‖ that is entirely acceptable.

The odd outcome, however, is that the classical rules for negation express an intuitionistic reading. Supervaluations and ‖PL‖ show interesting similarities and differences, which are explored in Chapter 9. Chapter 10 is a philosophical interlude, showing how ‖PL‖ may be deployed as a logic for an open future. Chapter 11 lays out results for logics in sequent format with multiple conclusions where classical rather than intuitionist semantics is expressed. Chapter 12 shows how completeness results may be obtained for systems with respect to their natural semantics. Chapter 13 demonstrates that natural semantics can be helpful in vindicating notions of harmony found in the proof-theoretic tradition. It also shows that natural semantics can be transformed into a useful proof-theoretic version. Chapter 14 describes the natural semantics for the quantifiers, which is essentially intensional, and differs from both the objectual and substitution interpretations. Furthermore, it fails to support the presumption that terms of the language denote objects. Chapter 15 applies natural semantics for standard predicate logic to the problem of vagueness. The final chapter provides a brief account of some results in modal logic. The book ends with a summary of what has been accomplished, and offers a defense of model-theoretic inferentialism in the face of some objections.

Acknowledgements

Even if I could remember what I have forgotten about their contributions, it would not be possible to acknowledge everyone who contributed to this book. But some people deserve special thanks as sources of inspiration:

to my wife, who supports me through thick and thin, and to whom the book is dedicated,

to my teacher Nuel Belnap, who showed me by example how much fun logic can be,

to Joshua D. K. Brown, whose kindness, support, and intellectual energy have brought me to life,

to Will Langley and Brandon Tinklenberg, who talked me into giving them a course on this book, which I profited from and thoroughly enjoyed,

to Jack Woods, who made many valuable suggestions and who always gets me thinking,

to Lloyd Humberstone, who read most of a first draft, headed off many errors, and made valuable suggestions,

to Thomas Wright, who spotted errors in a draft of Chapter 15,

to Hilary Gaskin at Cambridge University Press, who helped get this project on its way, and to anonymous readers who offered kind support and excellent suggestions for improvement.

1 Introduction to model-theoretic inferentialism

The purpose of this book is to explore what rules of logic express about the meanings of the logical symbols they govern. Suppose that the only thing you know about the symbol '*' is that the following rules govern its behavior. Given an English sentence of the form A*B, it follows that A, and it also follows that B. Given A and B together, it follows that A*B. Can you tell what the symbol '*' means? Did you think that '*' must mean what we mean by 'and' in English, and that the truth behavior of sentences involving '*' must conform to the standard truth table for conjunction? If you did, can you be certain that the same deductive role for '*' specified by these rules might not also allow some alternative (or unintended) interpretation for '*'?

1.1 The broader picture

Questions like this are special cases of a general concern in the philosophy of language. To what extent can the meanings of expressions of a language be defined by the roles they play in our reasoning? Does knowing the meaning of a sentence simply amount to knowledge of which sentences entail it and which ones it entails? Would it be possible at least in principle for alien anthropologists from a planet circling the star Alpha Centauri (who know initially nothing about our language) to learn what our sentences mean by simply investigating the way we reason from one to another in different circumstances?

The predominant research methodology for understanding natural language in the field of artificial intelligence assumes the answer is: Yes. It is presumed that the project of designing computers capable of understanding a natural language such as English amounts to the development of systems capable of drawing the conclusions humans typically draw from a body of available text. So if a computer program can summarize correctly articles from the *New York Times*, or cogently answer questions about a visit to a restaurant (Shank and Abelson, 1977), then the system counts as one that understands, and in fact models how understanding is possible in the natural world. If this research program is right, the problem of what sentences mean is reduced to resolving the issues involved in storing, efficiently retrieving, and drawing conclusions from relevant information found in a massive data-base incorporating knowledge of a typical human (Davis and Lenat, 1982).

Of course there is wide disagreement about the viability of such an answer to the problem of understanding meaning. Everyone from Fodor (1988, Chapter 2) to Searle (1980) objects, and for widely varying reasons. (See Cummins (1989, Chapters 4–6) for a useful discussion.) Among the many challenges that such a view faces is the complaint that the inferential roles of an expression are by themselves too weak to determine the semantical interpretations we intuitively assign to them. Worries about underdetermination of meaning motivate externalist strategies, such as covariance and causal role theories. These hold that part of what determines meaning is connections to the outside world mediated by our perceptual abilities. So to have a full understanding of what 'red' means, you would have to associate this word with the visual sensation you have when you see blood. Others point out the importance of connections to our actions as well as to our perceptions. If they are right, the aliens who wanted to know what we mean would have to study not only the logical relations between our utterances, but also the connections between those utterances and what we sense, and how we act.

Nevertheless, it is fairly widely held that inferential relations between sentences will contribute an important part of the answer about how meaning is determined. The idea is that at least part of what helps fix the meaning of a sentence like 'McKinley was assassinated' is the deductive connections it has with other sentences such as 'McKinley was killed', 'McKinley died', 'McKinley was shot', and even 'McKinley was president'. A person who does not understand how the truth of the latter sentences are inferentially related to the truth of 'McKinley was assassinated' doesn't really know what that sentence means.

One of the difficulties in trying to resolve questions about how inferential relations play a role in fixing meaning is that working out a theory in detail for a given language is such a massive project. If you are truly serious about supporting such an inferentialist account, the best plan would be to show in detail that it has the resources to determine the meanings of hundreds of thousands of words and billions of expressions. Unfortunately, that project is still far beyond us. In the meantime, a sensible research strategy for controlling some of the complexity starts by defining solvable "toy" problems. Once these are understood, the lessons learned can be applied to more complex cases. The question of how and whether the deductive roles of the logical symbols can determine their meanings is a good example of such a toy problem. Here it is less plausible to think that relations to perception and action are essential to the meanings of the logical symbols. If there is any hope for a theory that presumes that meaning can be defined by logical relations alone, the best place to look would be in a study of the meanings of the logical connectives. One of the purposes of this book is to explore that question in detail and to report on the lessons learned. The realm of logic is especially well chosen since here it is possible to give mathematical demonstrations that answer such questions as whether connective meaning is or is not underdetermined by a set of rules. So the question on the table will be whether the alien anthropologists, knowing what will be revealed in this book, can determine what our logical symbols mean from a study of the rules we use.

An important conclusion established here is that the answers depend on decisions about the format of the rules, and decisions about how to define what rules express about connective meaning. As different choices are made, the view that the patterns of inference set up by the rules of deduction are sufficient for determining connective meaning are in some cases vindicated and in others undermined. By noting the strategies that can be employed to resolve problems of meaning underdetermination for the logical connectives, new insights may be obtained about how one might resolve problems of meaning underdetermination for language in general.

1.2 Proof-theoretic and model-theoretic inferentialism

A quick way to summarize what this book is about is to say that it explores the viability of a brand of inferentialism in logic. A logical inferentialist, or inferentialist for short, is somebody who believes that the rules of logic alone determine the meanings of the logical connectives. (For an excellent review of inferentialism including comparisons with the work of Brandom

(1994, 2001), see Tennant (forthcoming, Section 2).) However, there are at least two rather different ways of identifying the foundational commitments of the view. One is to think of inference as the rival of reference for serving as the foundation for a theory of meaning. A referentialist theory of meaning takes the idea of denotation of an expression as basic. Names refer to objects, and in general, all words refer to something. In the model-theoretic tradition, the idea is fleshed out by taking the reference (extension) of predicate letters to be sets of n-tuples of objects and the reference of well-formed formulas to be the truth-values t and f. One can even go so far as to claim that the reference of a connective is its truth function.

St. Augustine advocates an idea like this in the famous quotation that opens Wittgenstein's *Investigations*. "Thus as I heard words repeatedly used in their proper places in various sentences, I gradually learnt to understand what objects they signified; and after I had trained my mouth to form these signs, I used them to express my own desires" (Wittgenstein, 1969, p. 2). Certainly this was Wittgenstein's doctrine on what explained the meaning of names in the *Tractatus Logico-Philosophicus* (Wittgenstein, 1961, 3.203). Wittgenstein's point in placing such a referential theory of language on the table was to launch an argument that a theory of meaning based on word reference accounts, at best, for a very limited set of cases. To fully understand how language works, one must appreciate the rich variety in the ways in which words have a *use* in the social activities. Even reference itself makes no sense apart from those wider concerns. For those who take this to heart in the case of logic, it is natural to found a theory of the use of logical connectives on their inferential roles, for it is the activity of assessing inferential relations that appears relevant to the social role of logic.

Inferential theories will be particularly attractive to those who have epistemological worries about reference, or about how reference can be fixed. Those theories will also attract people with anti-realist sympathies, and who advocate pragmatic or coherentist rather than correspondence theories of truth. Therefore it is no surprise that semantical theories for logic based on proof-theoretic role have historical roots in the work of intuitionists such as Brouwer. (See Sundholm (1986 especially Section 2) for a good discussion of the motives in this tradition.) Such proof-theoretic inferentialists reject model-theoretic semantics in the Tarskian tradition as misguided. Its truth conditions are non-constructive, and attempts to characterize the notion of truth without constructivist constraints leads to paradox. Therefore a tradition has grown up among logical inferentialists to develop proof-theoretical semantics, which strictly avoids any mention of concepts from model theory such as reference, truth, and validity as preservation of truth.

Strictly speaking, however, the demand that model-theoretic notions be laid aside is not part of the central inferentialist doctrine. Proof-theoretic inferentialists subscribe to two doctrines that can and should be distinguished.

> (Inferentialism) The connectives obtain their meanings from the proof-theoretic roles that are established by the rules that govern them.

> (Proof-Theoretic Semantics) The meanings determined for the connectives must be characterized using only concepts found in proof theory. In particular, notations like denotation and truth are not to be employed.

(Proof-Theoretic Semantics) is not essential to inferentialism, despite its centrality in the historical tradition going back to intuitionism. This book demonstrates that an inferentialism that investigates how proof-theoretic roles determine model-theoretic readings is of technical and philosophical interest. Sundholm (1986, p. 478) recommends a project of this kind. The idea is to find a way to "read off a [model-theoretic] semantics from the ... rules." He is describing what he takes to be a failed attempt by Hacking to carry this out in the case of classical logic, and goes on to say "the problem still remains open how to find a workable proposal along these lines." This book shows how to solve that problem.

Tennant (forthcoming, Section 2, note 7) notes that Brandom's views on inferentialism have evolved towards a kind of quietism with respect to epistemological and metaphysical commitments. Recognizing that inferentialism is orthogonal to those concerns opens room for brands of model-theoretic inferentialism. The model-theoretic tradition has important intuitions in its favor. The role of semantics in logic is to provide a definition of validity, and arguably validity amounts to the preservation of truth. Given this standard, proof-theoretic semantics, for all its technical interest, looks like an oxymoron. Although proof-theoretic notions of validity are in the offing (Schroeder-Heister, 2006) they are complex, and it is not clear how they meet the concerns for limning correctness of reasoning that motivated the concept of validity in the first place. From the model-theoretic side, however, defining validity is straightforward.

I do not wish to dwell on possible failings of proof-theoretic semantics here. It is sufficient for my purposes to argue for a pluralism in the style of semantics chosen, so that an inferentialism that uses model-theoretic notions counts as a live option. As we will see, such a view need not be a rival of proof-theoretic inferentialism. It is a way of thinking that can actually be of service to the proof-theoretic side. So a *model-theoretic inferentialist* subscribes to these two theses: (Inferentialism), of course, and (Model-Theoretic Semantics).

> (Inferentialism)   The connectives obtain their meanings from the proof-theoretic roles that are established by the rules that govern them.

> (Model-Theoretic Semantics)   When characterizing the meanings of the connectives, it is of interest (and even helpful to those in the proof-theoretic tradition) to employ concepts from model theory such as truth, reference, and validity understood as preservation of truth.

The purpose of this book will not be to argue for model-theoretic inferentialism. Although, some comfort for the view is found in the result that rules for most connectives can be proven to fix exactly one model-theoretic interpretation for the connectives, there are also reasons for worry. In some cases (notably disjunction (Section 7.3), and the failure of referentialism in predicate logic (Section 14.7)), it can be argued that inferential roles of the connectives fail to determine the expected model-theoretic counterparts. In those negative cases, proof-theoretic inferentialists may find some support for their view.

Results of this book can also be helpful to the proof-theoretic tradition in another way. One of the major challenges to inferentialism in logic is Prior's (1960) famous demonstration that there are sets of rules that do not define an acceptable logical operation. His example of *tonk* showed that not all logical systems determine corresponding meanings for the connectives they regulate. The response of those with inferentialist sympathies has been to invent harmony constraints on the rules designed to guarantee that the rules are successful in defining connective meaning. Many definitions of harmony have been proposed. One of the first was Belnap's (1962) requirement that the rules be conservative and unique. Notions involving inversion and normalization (Prawitz, 1965, p. 33; Dummett, 1978, pp. 220–222; Weir, 1986; Tennant, 1997, pp. 308ff. and forthcoming) have also been introduced as the missing constraint. The difficulty proof-theoretic inferentialists face in motivating these responses to Prior is to provide independent evidence that the constraints proposed are necessary conditions for defining connective meaning. Results found in this book will help inferentialists motivate such constraints. For example, it will be shown (in Sections 13.1 and 13.4) that any set of rules that determines a connective meaning from the model-theoretic point of view meets Belnap's conservation and uniqueness requirements. The approach taken here will also help us develop a new understanding of the inversion principle and normalization. (See Sections 13.5–13.7.)

A proof-theoretic inferentialist may still be uncomfortable with the model-theoretic project. Wasn't the whole point of inferentialism to avoid the realism and anti-verificationism that is implicit in the use of model-theoretic notions? There is a simple answer to that worry. It is to argue for metaphysical and epistemological quietism for model-theoretic notions of reference and truth. I submit that those notions, in themselves, commit us to nothing. This book shows that on very modest assumptions, the roles for the connectives set up by logical rules fix exactly certain corresponding truth conditions. These use the notation: '$v(A)=t$' (for valuation v assigns to wff A the value t). What should an inferentialist antecedently committed to a pragmatic or coherentist theory of truth make of '$v(A)=t$'? The answer is anything he or she likes, but in fairness, why not read 't' as coherence, or assertibility, rather than truth as correspondence? Model-theoretic inferentialism need not saddle one with any particular reading of the set theoretical machinery of model theory. As a matter of fact, as we will see in Section 13.9, '$v(A)=t$' has a provability reading, so that what initially looks like model-theoretic semantics is transformed into a proof-theoretic semantics that is new to the literature. The upshot is that the mere use of the notation of model theory is compatible with a very broad range of epistemological and metaphysical views, including those of the founders and followers of the inferentialist tradition.

1.3 Three rule formats

This book shows that the answer to the question: 'do rules fix the meanings of the connectives?' is that it depends. One source of variability in the answers is the format in which we frame the logical rules. A lot depends on the details concerning the way the rules are defined. Three main approaches will be explored here. The first is axiomatic. An *axiomatic system* lays down a set of axioms (or axiom forms) that serve as examples of logical truths, along with a collection of rules taking a formula or formulas into a new formula. For example, here is a economical axiomatic formulation for propositional logic in a language where → (if then) and ~ (not) are the only connectives.

⊢ A→(B→A)

⊢ A→(B→C) → ((A→B) → (A→C))

⊢ (~A→B) → ((~A→~B) → A)

(Modus Ponens)

⊢ A

$\dfrac{\vdash A{\to}B}{\vdash B}$

We use 'A', 'B', 'C', and 'D' as metavariables over well-formed formulas (wffs) of propositional logic. The notation '⊢ (~A→B) → ((~A→~B) → A)' indicates that any wff with the displayed form is provable. In presenting formal systems, we use '⊢' for 'is provable'. (We treat the logical symbols '~', '→', '&', etc. in the metalanguage as *used* to refer to symbols with similar shapes. It is also understood that '~A', for example, refers to the result of concatenating ~ with the wff A. This convention avoids the need to use corner quotes.)

As anyone who tries it knows, finding proofs of wffs in axiomatic systems can be difficult. For example, the shortest proof of A→A in the above system comes to six lines and requires the use of complex and non-obvious instances of the first two axioms.

The second tactic for defining a logic is to use *natural deduction* (ND) format. Here a pair of rules is provided for each connective showing how it is introduced into, and eliminated from inference. Proof finding in ND systems is greatly simplified because of an important innovation; one is allowed to make additional assumptions in the course of a deduction, which are then discharged by the application of the appropriate rules. For example, the rule (→ Introduction) asserts that when one is able to derive sentence B from having made an additional assumption A, then that derivation is a warrant for introducing the conditional A→B and eliminating A from the set of active assumptions. This innovation means that ND rules are defined over more complex structures than are axiomatic systems. An axiomatic proof is a sequence of wffs, each of which is an instance of an axiom or one that follows from previous steps by a rule. However, it is useful to take it that ND rules are defined over arguments, not wffs. For example, ($\rightarrow$ Introduction) takes the argument H, A / C (which asserts that C follows from the ancillary hypothesis A along with other hypotheses H) to the new argument H / A$\rightarrow$C (which asserts that the conditional A$\rightarrow$C follows from hypotheses H leaving aside the assumption A).

Here is an example of a ND system for a propositional logic with $\rightarrow$ and $\sim$ as its only connectives, using "horizontal" notation that makes apparent the idea that ND rules are defined over arguments.

($\rightarrow$ Introduction)   ($\rightarrow$ Elimination)

$$\frac{H, A \vdash B}{H \vdash A \rightarrow B}$$ $$\frac{H \vdash A \qquad H \vdash A \rightarrow B}{H \vdash B}$$

($\sim$ Introduction)   ($\sim$ Elimination)

$$\frac{H, A \vdash B \qquad H, A \vdash \sim B}{H \vdash \sim A}$$ $$\frac{H, \sim A \vdash B \qquad H, \sim A \vdash \sim B}{H \vdash A}$$

For ease of comparison with multiple conclusion sequent systems to be presented shortly, it will be assumed that H is a possibly infinite set of wffs. The notation 'H, A' is used as shorthand for $H \cup \{A\}$, and we sometimes omit set braces so that 'A, B' abbreviates '{A, B}'. In the case of ND systems, the symbol '/' is assumed to be in the object language, and a rule takes one from an argument or arguments to a new argument. The symbol '$\vdash$' is used in the metalanguage to indicate the provability of an argument in a system being discussed. Therefore 'H $\vdash$ C' abbreviates the claim that the object language argument H / C has a proof in that system. (See Hacking (1979, p. 292), who adopts this convention.)

Natural deduction systems will play an important role in this book because of their interesting expressive powers. The results developed for them will help vindicate inferentialist intuitions that natural deduction rules have a special role to play in defining connective meaning.

The third format for presenting rules of logic is multiple conclusion *sequent* notation. A (multiple conclusion) sequent H / G is a generalization of the notion of an argument H / C, where the "conclusion" G is now taken to be a set of wffs. In this book, we will always use 'sequent' to refer to such a multiple conclusion sequent. The sequent H / G is understood to express the idea that if all the wffs in the hypothesis set H are true, then at least one of the wffs in the conclusion set G is true. Sample rules G→~ for a sequent formulation for a propositional logic with → and ~ as its only connectives follow.

G→~:   (→Left)   (→Right)

$$\frac{G \vdash A, H \qquad G, B \vdash H}{G, A{\to}B \vdash H}$$ $$\frac{G, A \vdash B, H}{G \vdash A{\to}B, H}$$

(~Left)   (~Right)

$$\frac{G, \vdash A, H}{G, {\sim}A \vdash H}$$ $$\frac{G, A \vdash H}{G, \vdash {\sim}A, H}$$

It is useful for comparing systems in different formats to treat (multiple conclusion) sequent format as the most general case, and to define axiomatic and ND systems as special cases of sequent systems. So let an *argument* be defined as a sequent whose conclusion has a single member, and let an *assertion* be an argument with an empty set of hypotheses. Call the items to which a rule is applied the *inputs* to the rule, and let the result of applying the rule be called its *output*. Then a ND system is simply a set of sequent rules whose inputs and outputs are all arguments. Similarly, axiomatic systems are systems whose sequent rules have assertions as their inputs and outputs.

1.4 Expressive power and models of rules

This book is about the expressive power of the rules of logic. To what degree does acceptance of the principles of logic force a particular interpretation of its connectives? As we said, the answer depends on how the rules are formulated, but it will also depend on how we define expressive power. Let us explore some of the options.

It helps to start with an analogy from model theory. The idea of a sentence (or group of sentences) expressing a condition on a model should be familiar. For example, the sentence $\exists x \exists y {\sim} x{=}y$ expresses that the domain of a model contains at least two objects. The reason is that $\exists x \exists y {\sim} x{=}y$ is true on a model exactly when the domain of the model domain contains at least two objects. In general, wff A expresses a property P of models iff A is true on any model M exactly when M has property P. When A is true on a model, we say M is a model of A. So when we say that A expresses P, we mean that for every model

M, M is a model of A iff M has P. Similarly, we say that M is a model of a set of wffs H iff M is a model of every wff in H. So a set of wffs H express property P iff the models of H are exactly the models with property P.

How should this idea be generalized to the case of what is expressed by rules of logic? By analogy, we would want to say that a set of rules R expresses property P iff M is a model of R exactly when M has P. But what does it mean to say that M is a model of R, or that a set of rules R holds in a model? M is a model of a set of wffs when all its members are true on M; but what is the corresponding notion in the case of a rule, and what exactly counts as a model of rules in the first place?

A natural answer is to say that a model of rules should guarantee that all arguments provable from those rules be valid, in the sense that each provable argument whose hypotheses are true on a model has a true conclusion as well. This is, after all, the criterion we use in showing the soundness of rules. In the study of formal systems it is natural to define a semantics that gives the truth conditions for the logical constants, and then to explore which deductive system is adequate for it. There the notion of validity is used as a bridge to connect the semantical theory to a corresponding syntactic treatment. The present approach reverses that procedure. Like good inferentialists, we begin with a set of rules. Using validity again as a bridge to the semantics, we ask which truth conditions are determined by the deductive behavior those rules establish presuming the rules respect validity.

It is crucial to the MT inferentialists' strategy to provide a formal account of validity of an argument on a model. The intuition is that an argument is valid when every way of assigning semantical values to the primitive expressions of the language has the feature that when it makes the hypotheses of the argument true, it makes the conclusion true as well. So let us start with the idea of a valuation for propositional logic, that is, a way of assigning truth-values to the wffs. Since we will want to see what conditions on valuations are determined by the requirement that the rules preserve validity, we begin by saying (almost) nothing about how valuations must behave. A valuation is just any way of assigning truth-values to the wffs of propositional logic. It may completely disregard the truth conditions for the logical connectives. For example, it may assign both A and ~A the value f, and it may assign t to A&B even when A and B are both assigned f. The only requirement placed on a valuation is the minimal condition that it assign at least one wff the value f. This ensures that valuations be at least minimally consistent. (See for example, Belnap and Massey (1990) and McCawley (1993, p. 109) who calls this an "innocuous assumption." I note, sadly, that not everyone finds this innocuous; for example, Humberstone (2011, p. 458 note 7) objects. Adopting the "innocuous assumption" causes some feelings of guilt, since ideally one would say absolutely nothing about valuations. However, many of the pleasing results in this book depend on valuations being consistent.)

A more formal definition of a valuation for a language of propositional logic (PL) follows. Let us assume that L is a language for PL containing one or more of the connectives: &, →, ↔ (iff), ∨ (or), ~ (not), and possibly the symbol ⊥ for a contradiction. (For convenience, ⊥ is classified among the connectives of the language by the ruse of taking it to be zero place connective.)

> (Valuation for PL) A *valuation* v is *any* function from the set of wffs of L to the set {t, f} of truth-values such that it assigns f to at least one wff.

Although the definition of a valuation depends on the choice of the language L, mention of L will be omitted when it is clear from the context.

Since all systems in this book are treated as special cases of sequent systems, let us define what it means for a valuation v to satisfy a sequent. Let a *sequent* H / G be composed of (possibly empty) sets of wffs H (its hypotheses), and G (its conclusions). Valuation v satisfies a sequent H / G iff whenever v assigns t to all members of H, it assigns t to at least one of the member of G.

> (v satisfies H / G) *v satisfies H / G* iff if v(A)=t for each A in H, then v(B)=t for some B in G.

In the case that H / G is an argument (written: H / C, where C is the unique member of the set of conclusions G), it follows from this definition that v satisfies H / C iff whenever v assigns t to all members of H, v assigns t to C. When H / C is an assertion, with an empty hypothesis set H (written: / C), then v satisfies / C iff v assigns t to C.

1.5 Deductive models

With these ideas in hand, let us explore how the expressive power of a set of rules of logic should be defined. Three different approaches will be outlined, but here is the simplest version. Since validity of an argument amounts to the claim that every valuation satisfies the argument, it makes sense to think of a model as a set of valuations V.

(Model)   A *model* V (for language L) is any set of valuations for L.

You may think of the set V as akin to a set of possible worlds in a model for modal logic. Then an argument H / C would count as *V-valid* (abbreviation: H $\vDash_V$ C) iff every valuation in V satisfies it, that is every valuation in v that makes the hypotheses t also makes the conclusion t. More generally, a sequent H / G would be V-valid iff every valuation in V satisfies H / G.

(V-valid)   A sequent is *V-valid* iff it is satisfied by every valuation in V.

Now we are ready for a first pass at a definition of what a model of a set of rules is. Here is an example. Let PL be any set of ND rules for propositional logic with the rules defined over arguments. The rules of PL will serve to distinguish a set of arguments that are the deductive output of PL. Now imagine we have a set of valuations V, and that it turns out that all the arguments so proven in PL are V-valid. Then it is reasonable to think that the model V respects the system PL, or to put it another way, V should qualify as a model for the system PL. When this happens for a given system S, we will say that V is a deductive model for S. In general, a deductive model for sequents is defined the same way.

(Deductive Model)   V is a *deductive model* of S iff the provable sequents of S are all V-valid.

What does the fact that V is a deductive model of PL tell us about the behavior of the valuations in V? Can the requirement that the provable arguments of PL be V-valid guarantee any constraints on how the valuations in V assign truth-values to the wffs? For example, does that requirement entail that the connectives obey their standard truth tables?

In the case of & (conjunction) the answer is: Yes, and it is not difficult to see why. These three arguments are all provable in PL.

$$A\&B/A$$
$$A\&B/B$$
$$A, B/A\&B$$

If each of these is V-valid, then every valuation v in V satisfies them. But if v satisfies the first, we learn that if v(A&B)=t then v(A)=t. If v satisfies the second, we obtain that if v(A&B)=t then v(B)=t. Finally, if v satisfies the third, we have that if v(A)=t and v(B)=t then v(A&B)=t. Taken together these three claims entail ‖&‖, the content of the classical truth table for conjunction.

‖&‖ v(A&B)=t iff v(A)=t and v(B)=t.

To summarize, this means that the system PL expresses the truth condition ‖&‖, in the sense that V is a model of the system PL iff V obeys ‖&‖.

Unfortunately, that is as far as it goes. Long ago, Carnap (1943, pp. 81ff). showed that PL deductively underdetermines the classical truth tables for the other connectives. It is simple enough to manufacture sets of valuations V such that all the provable arguments of PL are all V-valid, but where the tables for ∼, →, ∨, and ↔ are all violated. (See Section 2.2.) Interestingly, all of the rows of the tables are fixed correctly save for the last one (where the input values for the propositional letter(s) are f). So there are deductively faithful models of PL that fail to determine the standard interpretation we give the connectives.

This outcome would appear to be a serious blow to a model-theoretic inferentialist. The rules of PL allow alternative interpretations for the connectives, and in fact, no one coherent set of truth conditions is compatible with what PL requires of sets of valuations. By this standard, propositional logic in ND format radically underdetermines the meanings of the logical symbols, for it fails to express coherent truth conditions. Sadly, the Alpha Centaurian anthropologists equipped only with information about which arguments are provable in a ND logic for PL will be unable to determine what our connectives (other than &) mean. The rules of PL do not express a unique interpretation for the connectives; they leave connective meaning underdetermined.

However, there is way to rescue inferentialism. It is to adopt sequent systems with multiple conclusions. Here the classical interpretations of the connectives are immediately enforced. To see why, consider the case of the G→∼ where the following sequents are all provable.

$$B \vdash A \to B$$
$$A, A \to B \vdash B$$
$$\vdash A, A \to B$$
$$\vdash A, \sim A$$
$$A, \sim A \vdash$$

Given that V is a deductive model of G→~, these sequents must all be V-valid. A quick calculation shows that the V-validity of each above sequent entails the condition to its right for any v in V.

$$B \vDash_V A{\to}B \qquad \text{If } v(B)=t, \text{ then } v(A{\to}B)=t.$$
$$A, A{\to}B \vDash_V B \qquad \text{If } v(A)=t \text{ and } v(B)=f, \text{ then } v(A{\to}B)=f.$$
$$\vDash_V A, A{\to}B \qquad \text{If } v(A)=f, \text{ then } v(A{\to}B)=t.$$
$$\vDash_V A, \sim A \qquad \text{If } v(A)=f, \text{ then } v(\sim A)=t.$$
$$A, \sim A \vDash_V \qquad \text{If } v(A)=t, \text{ then } v(\sim A)=f.$$

But that means that each member v of V must obey the truth tables for → and ~. Similar results can be shown for ∨ and ↔. It appears then, that the only hope for inferentialists who wish to avoid underdetermination is to employ sequent systems.

1.6 Global models

But that is not the end of the story. There are still other options to explore. The deductive benchmark we are using for what counts as a model of a system is completely insensitive to the rules that are used to formulate it. It has been assumed that all that matters for specifying the inferential relations set up by a logic are the arguments that qualify as provable in the system. However, this view is shortsighted, as we will soon see. Let us explore what it might mean for a set of valuations V to be a model of a *rule*.

Consider, for starters, the rule (→ Introduction).

(→ Introduction)

$$\frac{H, A \vdash B}{H \vdash A{\to}B}$$

What it says is that if you have a proof of the argument H, A / B, then you have a proof of H / A→B. Presuming that when we prove an argument we take it to be valid, then the view that (→ Introduction) is correct amounts to the claim that if H, A / B is valid then so is H / A→B. Therefore, V should be a model of (→ Introduction) iff (→ Introduction) preserves V-validity, that is, if H, A ⊢ B is V-valid then so is H ⊢ A→B.

> (Validity Preservation) A rule R *preserves V-validity* iff whenever all the inputs of R are V-valid, then so is R's output.

For reasons that will become clear later, when a rule R preserves V-validity, let us say that V is a global model of R. When S is a set of rules, V will be a global model of S when it is a global model of each of its rules.

(Global Model)   V is a *global model* of S iff each rule of S preserves V-validity.

Now a new set of questions is on the table. Suppose V is a global model of the ND rules ($\rightarrow$ Introduction) and ($\rightarrow$ Elimination). What does this say about the behavior of the valuations in V? Do the underdetermination results for deductive models persist for global models? They do for the axiomatic systems, but not for ND and sequent systems. Being a global model of ND rules places a stronger constraint on the valuations it contains. The requirement is that the valuations meet what amounts to the truth condition found in Kripke's semantics for intuitionistic logic. So oddly, the rules fix a semantical interpretation for $\rightarrow$, but it is not the one given by the standard material implication truth table. (See Section 6.1.) The results for negation and disjunction are somewhat more complex, but again, truth conditions are determined that are related to those found in intuitionistic semantics.

Is there some way to obtain the standard reading for $\rightarrow$? The answer is: Yes. We noted that sequent calculi are able to overcome the underdetermination results noted by Carnap. (See Shoesmith and Smiley (1978, p. 3) and Hacking (1979, p. 312).) In the present context, it is not difficult to show, for example, that if V is a model of both ($\rightarrow$Left) and ($\rightarrow$Right), then all the valuations in V must meet the material implication truth table. Furthermore the sequent rules for the other connectives enforce their standard truth tables. (See Section 11.1.)

So when we consider what rules express globally, rather than deductively, a variety of results emerge that depend on rule format. As we move from axiomatic, to ND, and then to sequent systems, we obtain underdetermination, a semantics related to intuitionistic logic, and finally the classical truth tables. The upshot of all of this is that there are deductively faithful models of systems of logic that are not models of the system's rules, and so being a global model of the rules of a system provides stronger information about the interpretation of the connectives.

Alpha Centaurian anthropologists who know this fact will do more than quiz the natives about which argument forms are acceptable. They will also ask higher-order questions about *relations between* acceptability of different argument forms such as these: Suppose you accept an argument with the form H, A / B. Would you be forced to also accept the argument with the form H / A→B? Given confidence in the idea that our acceptance of an argument form amounts to our finding it valid, the Alpha Centaurians will be able to use answers to their more complex queries to refine their understanding of which rules preserve validity from our point of view. Given they know the results in this book, they will be able to come to well-founded answers about what we must mean by our connectives (whether we realize what we mean or not).

There is an application of these ideas to solving problems of underdetermination of meaning in natural languages. In the Quine–Davidson tradition, the only data the non-native linguist has to go on in interpreting the language of the natives is which sentences are and are not accepted under certain conditions. (See Lepore and Ludwig (2005, Chapter 5) and Quine (1960, Section 12).) We are allowed to look only at what is or is not asserted. However, a whole host of higher-order questions about deductive relations between the native's sentence forms might also be explored. By looking at the intricate relations set up between patterns of argumentation involving a given expression, one might get a more nuanced picture of how that expression is *used*, in particular the role it plays in rules that allow deduction from one argument form to another. (Azzouni (2000, Part III) makes a related point. Thanks to Joshua D. K. Brown for the citation.)

This book is not the place to explore how answering such questions might provide data to narrow the range of interpretation; however, this is a promising place to look. It at least provides a new tactic for challenging the underdetermination thesis. Our intuitions about whether there is breathing room to holistically reinterpret one's whole language in a non-standard way are unreliable or at least moot in the domain of logic. The matter is rigorously determined rather than determined by intuition. Who would have intuited that interpretations of the connectives are intuitionistic in ND systems and classical in sequent systems? So why accept the idea that we can find a non-standard reinterpretation of 'gavagai' that conforms to all data that could in principle be collected about the native's linguistic practices – especially given that that data could include not only information on acceptability of sentences involving 'gavagai', but also higher-order information on the ways in which 'gavagai' is or could be used in the process of derivation?

There is another way in which the study of what rules of logic express might have implications for inferentialism in language in general. It is widely presumed that a use theory of language meaning must be holistic. Only by tracing all possible deductive relations between one expression and all the others could one know its complete meaning. However, as we will see, logic is a setting where the meaning of a connective can be fully determined by a small number of rules governing it alone. While the rules establish a holistic set of relationships between one connective and all the others, the means by which those deductive roles are specified are (for the most part) modular and local to a given connective. In that sense, meanings defined need not be holistic. The presence or absence of rules for one of the connectives does not affect the meanings of the others. So results on expressive power in logic can provide a more sophisticated understanding of issues surrounding holism. For example, it has the potential to undermine the presumption that use theories are always burdened with the unpalatable principle that change in the meaning of any one expression must in itself affect the meanings of all the others.

1.7 Local models

There is yet a third way to define what counts as a model of a rule. It generates a corresponding notion of what rules express. Instead of requiring that rules preserve validity, the idea is to require instead that they preserve satisfaction. Here are the relevant definitions.

> (Valuation v Satisfies Rule R)   v *satisfies* R iff whenever v satisfies the input(s) of R it satisfies the output of R.

> (Preservation of Satisfaction)   A rule R *preserves V-satisfaction* iff for each member v of V, v satisfies R.

> (Local Model of a Rule)   V is a *local model of rule* R iff R preserves V-satisfaction.

The terms 'local' and 'global' are used here on analogy with the way local and global consequence relations are defined in modal logic (Blackburn et al., 2002, pp. 31–32).

The difference between V being a local model of R and V being a global model of R matters. It amounts to a difference in the scope of the quantification over the members of V. When V is a global model of R, it follows that V-validity is preserved, and this means that if *for every valuation v in V*, v satisfies the inputs of R, then *for every member v of V*, v satisfies the output of R. Here we have two quantifications over V, each with narrow scope. In contrast, when V is a *local* model of R, it follows that for every v in V, if v satisfies the inputs of R, then v satisfies the output of R. Here quantification over V takes wide scope.

The choice of local over global models in the definition of what rules express about connective meaning makes no difference for axiomatic and sequent systems. When V is a local model of an axiomatic formulation of propositional logic, no determinate truth conditions for the connectives are chosen. (See Theorem 3.3.) When V is a local model of a sequent formulation of propositional logic, it follows that all its members must obey the classical truth tables for the connectives. This occurs because the whole distinction between local and global models collapses for sequent systems. (See Theorem 11.3.1.) The difference is preserved, however, for ND systems. Here choice of local models fixes the *classical* interpretation of the connectives, not the intuitionistic semantics mentioned above. For example, when V is a local model of the two ND rules ($\to$ Introduction) and ($\to$ Elimination), every member of V must obey the material implication truth table.

1.8 Three definitions of expressive power compared

Three different definitions for what qualifies as a model of a system of logic have been proposed. They form a hierarchy, since every local model of a system S is a global model of S, and every global model of S is a deductive model of S. These in turn generate three different benchmarks for what a system of rules expresses. The following definitions will make the three options explicit. They are identical save for the notion of a model of a system they employ. Here it is understood that a model V is a set of valuations over any language that contains the connectives mentioned by the rules of S.

(Deductive Expression) A system S *deductively expresses* property P iff for every model V, V is a deductive model of S exactly when V has property P.

(Global Expression) A system S *globally expresses* property P iff for every model V, V is a global model of the rules of S exactly when V has property P.

(Local Expression) A system S *locally expresses* property P iff, for every model V, V is a local model of the rules of S exactly when V has property P.

The results mentioned so far can be summarized in the following table, which indicates which semantics (if any) is determined given each choice of the definition of expression, and the format of the rules. The numerals in each box indicate the sections or chapters of this book where the results are obtained.

What PL rules express about readings of the connectives

Definition of expression	Rule format		
	Axiomatic	Natural deduction	Multiple conclusion sequent
Deductive	none 3.3	none 2.2	classical 1.5
Global	none 3.3	intuitionistic (6, 7, 8)	classical 11.1
Local	none 3.3	classical 3.3	classical 11.1

('None' in the above chart indicates that neither the classical nor the intuitionistic reading of the connectives is expressed. There is an outside possibility that some other semantics might be expressed in those cases. I conjecture that this is not the case.)

With so many options about the expressive powers of systems at hand, it is natural to want to simplify the situation by finding reasons to eliminate one or more of them. Those with an interest in the model-theoretic inferentialist project will want to eliminate options where no semantics is fixed, and so rule out deductive expression and the axiomatic approach to formulating rules. This book will take at least a short look at all the options. It will, however, exhibit what may appear to be an inferentialist bias by spending most of the time on global expression and natural deduction systems, the option in the dead center of the above chart.

But why, you may ask, shouldn't we give the options equal time, and explore local expression and sequent systems in a more balanced way? Local expression would appear more attractive than global in that the choice of the semantics expressed is invariant across the choice between ND and sequent systems. A further attraction is that when local models are used to define what rules express, the classical interpretations of the connectives are chosen, and this way of understanding them is presumably what we have intended all along. Global models would seem less apt a choice, since it is counterintuitive that we give our connectives a variant of an intuitionistic reading.

On the other hand, there are telling reasons for thinking that local expression is the wrong criterion for defining what a rule expresses. (See Section 3.6 for more details.) A simple objection, which I owe to Joshua D. K. Brown, is that local models get it wrong about how we actually evaluate arguments. A natural deduction rule presumably takes acceptable arguments into a new acceptable argument. But what should count as an acceptable argument? Surely not an argument that is satisfied, for we take pains to teach our students in elementary logic classes that an argument with a false premise or a true conclusion is not necessarily correct. What we aim for in arguments is validity, and therefore preservation of satisfaction is not the correct criterion for capturing what a rule is supposed to do, namely to take us from acceptable (valid) arguments to another acceptable (valid) one.

A second complaint against local expression is that according to this benchmark, there are many systems of logic that express a semantics for which they are not complete. For example the system composed of ($\rightarrow$ Introduction) and ($\rightarrow$ Elimination) locally expresses the classical material implication truth table, but that system does not prove all arguments that are classically valid. For example, it cannot prove Peirce's Law: $((A{\rightarrow}B){\rightarrow}A){\rightarrow}A$. Even more tellingly, it will be shown (Section 3.5) that the rules for *intuitionistic* negation locally express the *classical* truth table for negation, and so the semantics they locally express counts the Law of Double Negation as valid – this despite the fact that Double Negation is the paradigm of a rule unacceptable to intuitionists, and not deducible using the intuitionistic rules. It is bizarre in the extreme to claim that a system of rules expresses a semantics when that system cannot even prove some of the arguments that semantics deems valid.

As we will see (Theorem 3.5), this untoward behavior is a reflection of a deeper worry about the concept of local expression. The requirement that rules preserve satisfaction amounts to a covert requirement that the truth conditions for all the logical connectives be truth tabular. But this is not compatible with semantics for even standard predicate logic. The rules of predicate logic locally express a condition on models that is so strong that it validates At $\leftrightarrow$ ∀xAx, which would allow elimination of the quantifiers altogether. (See Section 3.5.) If we wish to explore any systems outside the realm of propositional logic, it will be essential that global and not local expression be used.

Another possible complaint about the emphasis in this book is its relatively short treatment of sequent systems with multiple conclusions (called 'sequent systems' for short in this book). Here there is no formal argument to rely on, but there are intuitive considerations for giving them second billing. Sequent rules, while elegant, appear to be a technical device unrelated to ordinary understanding of the concept of logical inference. To illustrate the worry, imagine that the Alpha Centaurian anthropologists come to Earth to determine which are the sequent rules our culture accepts for the logical connectives. They will be hard pressed to find more than a few thousand people in Earth who even have the concept of a (multiple conclusion) sequent. Even worse, it is fair to say that they will not find anyone who displays argumentation in the form of sequents in their deductive behavior in daily life. The notion of reasoning from a set of hypotheses to a set of conclusions interpreted disjunctively just is not part of the conceptual apparatus of our ordinary understanding of deductive inference. The Alpha Centaurians will appreciate the merit of an opinion of Gerhard Gentzen, the inventor of multiple conclusion sequent systems. Gentzen held (reported in Hacking, 1979, p. 291) that ND systems get at the heart of logical reasoning, while the very sequent notation he invented is a mere artifice, because its multiple conclusions interpreted as a *disjunction* are not part of the ordinary conception of reasoning. The only way Alpha Centaurians could collect data on which sequent rules we accept would be for them to learn enough of our language to successfully decode logic books that talk about sequents. In any case, they would not be finding out what our deductive behavior says about connective meaning directly, because they will not find any sequents to evaluate "in the wild." (See also Steinberger (2011) and Tennant (1997, p. 320) who argue that multiple conclusions are incompatible with the inferentialist project.)

While it should be admitted that sequent systems might have applications to other concerns, that does not show they are any more apt for serving as the centerpiece for an inferentialist project. For example, it has been argued (Restall, 2005, and Beall and Restall, 2006, pp. 46ff.) that multiple conclusion sequents are a good way to simultaneously represent the incoherence of joint assertions and denials, thus providing an attractive anti-realist semantics. However, while this "bilateralist" project is arguably interesting, it does not argue that sequent systems are better suited than are ND systems for characterizing the form of inferential relations found in human reasoning. For example, Steinberger (2011, Section 8, pp. 349ff.) argues convincingly that a true bilateralist would employ two sets of rules with *single* conclusions, one for assertion and the other for denial, and not rules for sequents with multiple conclusions.

Some may argue that the complaint that such sequents are not found "in the wild" is misguided or irrelevant. It has been suggested that sequent calculi, while unfamiliar, are nevertheless essential for our understanding of connective meaning. For example, Shoesmith and Smiley argue from the fact that propositional logic underdetermines meanings for the connectives and that sequents fix the classical interpretations, that those of us who give the connectives the standard readings have been "speaking multiple conclusions all their lives without knowing it" (1978, p. 4). Presumably Shoesmith and Smiley assume that neither axiomatic nor ND systems are capable of expressing the classical semantics. However results of this book show that the situation is more complex than they had realized.

If we consider local expression, both ND format and multiple conclusion sequent formats are capable of determining the classical interpretation of the connectives. So the latter format is not unique in this respect. Perhaps this point is moot because, as we have suggested, local expression is too strong a benchmark for what a system expresses. However, in the case of global expression, ND systems do not underdetermine the meanings of the connectives. They select an intuitionistic interpretation.

Does it follow from that result that those of us who are determined to select the classical semantics must adopt sequent format for their rules, since only those rules globally express classical semantics? Certainly not, for this suggestion has it backwards, at least from the point of view of inferentialism. For inferentialists, the formal system comes first, and the account of meaning emerges from it. An inferentialist does not argue from a given semantical choice to its matching formal system. Therefore, inferentialists should respond to Shoesmith and Smiley's preference for sequents in the following way. Given your choice, the classical semantics is determined, but that does not show that classicists have been speaking sequents all their lives. The soundness and completeness of ND and axiomatic systems of propositional logic shows that those wedded to classical semantics can operate perfectly well in any of the formats. The inferentialist, on the other hand, selects the system format first, on grounds that are independent of semantical considerations. If ND systems are more appealing than sequent systems in formalizing patterns found in the wild concerning about what follows from what, then this is decisive. Assuming ND format is preferred on these grounds, the conclusion should not be that classicists were speaking sequent format all their lives without knowing it, but that we were all speaking intuitionistically without knowing it.

1.9 What counts as a logical connective?

These results have important implications for perennial concerns about what counts as a logical connective. Traditionalists such as Hacking (1979) have tried to argue that only the rules of standard classical logic are capable of determining a logical connective, and that alternatives such as intuitionistic and modal logic are not up to the task. However, Hacking's arguments for the primacy of standard logic have centered on formal features of sequent systems. This is no accident, for as we have seen, the standard sequent rules fix the standard interpretation of the connectives.

The results of this book show that concentration on sequents begs the question against those who would argue the legitimacy of connectives in non-classical systems such as intuitionistic logic. For anyone who has an antecedent preference for ND systems, arguments based on the nature of sequent systems can be safely skirted. It is important to note that the effect of ND format can be achieved within sequent systems by restricting sequent rules to a single formula on the right-hand side. This throws light on a long-standing mystery: namely why intuitionistic sequent rules are obtained by imposing the single formula restriction on the rules for negation and the conditional. The answer is, of course, that the restriction simply amounts to choice of ND format, which globally expresses an intuitionistic interpretation of the connectives. (See Section 11.2.) Given independent reasons for preferring single over multiple conclusions in presentation of the rules of logic, connectives with non-classical readings emerge as the contenders to the claim for the "correct" logic.

The conclusion is that decisions about what counts as a correctly defined logical connective (and what counts as a genuine logic) depend on the format adopted for presenting the rules. In sequent notation, standard connectives are natural, but in ND format, intensional connectives are defined. This relativism suggests that a debate between a standard and an intensional logician for rights to the genuinely *logical* connectives ends in a draw at the very least. For those who consider multiple conclusions a technical device unrelated to our concerns for formalizing logical inference, a brand of intuitionistic logic may be the one that wins. The Alpha Centaurians, who of course are impartial in this debate, and who do not find multiple conclusion sequents in the wild, will agree.

2   Deductive expression

The purpose of this book is to rigorously explore the inferentialist thesis that the rules of logic determine the meanings of the connectives. The answer to what a logic expresses about the connectives it regulates depends on how expressive power is defined. The purpose of this chapter is to explore a criterion for expressive power that has been common in the literature, and which was dubbed 'deductive expression' in Section 1.8. According to this benchmark, the news is not good for the inferentialist. In the overwhelming majority of cases, systems of logic underdetermine the meanings of the connectives they regulate (Section 2.2). Many different interpretations are compatible with what the rules deductively express. This chapter illustrates the problem in the case of propositional logic, reviewing negative results that are well known. Then we will consider an idea that would eliminate the underdetermination. It is that if any one connective is given the classical interpretation, then classical interpretations are fixed for all the others (Section 2.3). Although that condition seems fairly modest, it does not resolve the fundamental problem. The moral of the story will be that what is wrong is not the inferentialist's thesis, but the benchmark we are using to adjudicate it. This will set the stage for better criteria that just happen to provide more optimistic answers.

2.1 Deductive expression defined

The main idea behind deductive expression is to ask what semantics is determined by the requirement that all the provable arguments of a system are valid. For example, suppose we have a set V of valuations, which, remember, are arbitrary (but consistent) functions from the wffs for propositional logic to the truth-values t and f. Assume that the arguments provable in a standard system for propositional logic are all V-valid.

What does this tell us about the members of V? In particular, we want to know whether the valuations in V obey the familiar truth tables, or if not, whether they satisfy some other truth conditions for the connectives.

Here is a sequence of formal definitions (drawn from Chapter 1) that make the idea more precise. Since we will not discuss sequent systems here, the definitions have been adjusted to focus on arguments only.

> (Valuation for L) A *valuation* v is *any* function from the set of wffs of L to the set {t, f} of truth-values such that it assigns f to at least one wff.

> (Satisfaction of an Argument)   v satisfies argument H / C iff whenever v assigns t to all members of H, v assigns t to C.

> (Model for L) A *model* V for L is any set of valuations for L.

> (V-valid) Argument is *V-valid* iff it is satisfied by every valuation in V.

> (Deductive Model)   V is a *deductive model* of S iff the provable arguments of S are all V-valid.

> (Deductive Expression) A system S *deductively expresses* property P iff for every model V, V is a model of the provable arguments of S exactly when V has property P.

2.2 Negative results for deductive expression

To begin, let us review a few technical details, some of which were mentioned in Section 1.3. A *language* for propositional logic is outfitted with parentheses, an infinite collection of propositional variables p, q, r, p′, q′, …, the propositional constant ⊥ (for a contradiction), and the connectives &, →, ↔, ~, and ∨. We presume the usual formation rules for well-formed formulas (wffs), and we drop the outermost set of parentheses to save eyestrain. We use 'A'–'E' as metavariables over wffs. We treat the logical symbols '~', '→', '&', etc. in the metalanguage as *used* to refer to symbols with similar shapes. It is also understood that '~A', for example, refers to the result of concatenating ~ with the wff A. (This convention will save us from the need to use corner quotes.)

We use the notation 'H ⊢$_S$ C' to indicate that the argument H / C is provable in the system S. When no confusion would arise, the subscript indicating the system at issue may be dropped. So for the moment '⊢'

indicates provability in (classical) propositional logic (PL). Since the present project is to consider the expressive power of PL taken as a whole, it will not matter how the rules are formulated as long as they are defined over arguments. So the reader may choose any axiomatic or ND system adequate for propositional logic to define '⊢'.

Now let V be a set of valuations and presume that all the provable arguments of PL are V-valid. What does this tell us about the semantical behavior of the connectives? It is easy to verify that any valuation in V assigns values to wffs of the form A&B according to the conjunction truth table. So the deductive structure set up by the symbol & entails that the connective & means conjunction exactly.

As we pointed out in Section 1.5, the proof of this is straightforward. In PL we have: A&B ⊢ A, A&B ⊢ A, and A, B ⊢ A&B. When v satisfies the first two arguments, the left to right portion of the standard truth condition ∥&∥ for & follows, while preservation of validity by v for the third argument guarantees the implication from right to left.

$\|\&\|$ v(A&B)=t iff v(A)=t and v(B)=t.

So the standard & table is determined completely.

A	B	A&B
t	t	t
t	f	f
f	t	f
f	f	f

Theorem 2.2.1 If V is a deductive model of PL, then every member of V obeys ∥&∥.

So far so good. PL has sufficient (deductive) expressive power to guarantee exactly the content of the & truth table.

A similar result is available for ⊥. The truth condition ∥⊥∥ we would expect for ⊥ is that v never assigns t to ⊥.

$\|\bot\|$ v(⊥)=f.

It is easy to see that if V is a (deductive) model of PL, then $\|\bot\|$ must hold for any valuation v in V. The reason is that $\bot / A$ is provable for any wff A, so if $v(\bot)=t$ then $v(A)=t$ for each wff A. Since valuations are consistent, they cannot assign t to all the wffs, and so $v(\bot)=f$.

Theorem 2.2.2 If V is a deductive model of PL, then every member v of V obeys $\|\bot\|$.

(To make mention of truth conditions more general, we treat $\bot$ as a (zero place) connective.)

On the other hand, PL does not enforce the truth tables for $\rightarrow$, $\leftrightarrow$, $\sim$, and $\vee$. These negative results are reported in many places (Carnap, 1943, pp. 81ff.; McCawley, 1993, pp. 107ff.; Shoesmith and Smiley, 1978, p. 3; Belnap and Massey, 1990).

Consider $\rightarrow$ first. In PL, we have $B \vdash A \rightarrow B$. So any valuation v belonging to a deductive model of PL will have to satisfy that argument. It follows that if $v(B)=t$ then $v(A \rightarrow B)=t$, so that the first and third rows of the truth table for $\rightarrow$ must have the output t.

A	B	A→B
t	t	t
t	f	
f	t	t
f	f	

We also have A, A→B $\vdash$ B in PL. So when v is in a model of PL, if $v(A)=t$, then $v(A \rightarrow B)=t$ only if $v(B)=t$. Therefore it follows that the output for the second row of the table, where $v(A)=t$ and $v(B)=f$, is set to f.

A	B	A→B
t	t	t
t	f	f
f	t	t
f	f	

Valuations in a model of PL may also assign the classical value t to the last row, but they need not do so. For example, the model V⊢ whose only member is the *provability valuation* $\mathbf{v}_\vdash$, defined so that $\mathbf{v}_\vdash$(A)=t iff A is a theorem of PL, is a model of PL, but none of p, q, p→q is provable in PL, and so $\mathbf{v}_\vdash$ assigns f to all of these wffs, thus violating the last row of the standard table. (To show V⊢ is a model of PL, demonstrate that if H ⊢ C, and $\mathbf{v}_\vdash$(H)=t, then $\mathbf{v}_\vdash$(C)=t. But this amounts to showing that if each member of H is provable in PL then so is C, and that follows directly from H ⊢ C.) Therefore deductive models of PL contain valuations that are non-classical in the sense that they violate the classical truth tables. Furthermore, since p→p is provable in PL, $\mathbf{v}_\vdash$(p→p)=t. Therefore, since $\mathbf{v}_\vdash$(p)=f, it follows that the provability valuation $\mathbf{v}_\vdash$ is not truth functional, since in some cases where A and B are f, A→B is f, while in others such as p→p, A→B is t. So PL has non-standard deductive models, that is, models whose valuations do not obey the classical truth tables. PL lacks the expressive power to force the intended interpretation of →.

Now consider negation. In light of A, ~A ⊢ B, it follows that when v is a valuation in a model of PL, then it must not assign both A and ~A the value t, for if it did, it would assign t to every wff, which is incompatible with its consistency. Therefore valuations that satisfy PL, assign f to ~A, when they assign t to A.

A	~A
t	f
f	

However, the second row of the truth table for ~, is not fixed by all valuations in models of PL. For example, the provability valuation assigns f to both p and ~p.

The situation for disjunction is similar. Although A ⊢ A∨B and B ⊢ A∨B guarantee the last three rows of the truth table for disjunction, the standard truth condition for disjunction is violated by the provability valuation, for we have that neither p nor ~p is provable, while p∨~p is, and so on some occasions the provability valuation $v_\vdash$ assigns t to A∨B, even when A and B are assigned f.

A	B	A∨B
t	t	t
t	f	t
f	t	t
f	f	

The connective ↔ suffers from exactly the same failing. The provability of the arguments (1) A, B ⊢ A↔B, (2) A↔B, A ⊢ B, (3) A↔B, B ⊢ A guarantee (respectively) the first three rows of the table for ↔.

A	B	A↔B
t	t	t
t	f	f
f	t	f
f	f	

However, the provability valuation does not satisfy the last row of the table, for neither p, nor q, nor p↔q is provable, with the result that the provability valuation assigns f to p, q, and p↔q.

To sum it up, PL does not deductively express the truth conditions for →, ~, ∨, and ↔. In fact, valuations in models for PL are not even truth functional. So the meaning of the connectives is underdetermined given this way of understanding expressive power.

Deductive Expression Theorem. The ND rules for PL do not deductively expresses the standard truth tables for the connectives other than & and ⊥.

As a side note, it is worth mentioning here that the model V⊢ may also be used to show the violation of the intuitionistic truth condition for → and ~. (See Sections 6.1 and 8.1.) Therefore axiomatic and ND systems also fail to express intuitionistic truth conditions. Whether they can express any truth conditions at all is still an open question, but it seems quite unlikely.

2.3 Semantic holism

The upshot of the previous section is that PL has weak deductive expressive power. None of the interpretations fixed for the connectives other than & is classical, and furthermore none of these is even truth functional. It seems that the conventional wisdom that deductive role underdetermines meaning holds at the very core of logic. This bodes ill for inferentialist accounts of meaning for language in general, for if the inferentialist strategy works at all, one would expect it to work in logic.

One response to these failures has been to investigate how the notion of a valuation can be strengthened to insure standard truth conditions. For example, by stipulating that valuations are standard for one of the connectives (even ∨ or ↔), the classical truth tables for all the other connectives emerge. So removing non-classical readings of any one of the connectives removes them from all the others. Belnap and Massey (1990) call this phenomenon: semantic holism, the idea being that the meaning of one connective is sensitive to the meanings of all the others. Another striking example of semantic holism, noticed by Hand (1993), is that when a symbol for classical negation is added to a system for intuitionistic negation, the intuitionistic negation symbol takes on the classical truth table. The mere presence of a symbol for classical negation in a system undermines an intuitionistic reading even of a different negation sign. This topic will be discussed further in Section 8.5.

It is not too surprising to learn that when ~ is given a classical interpretation, the other connectives follow suit. When ~ is classical, both & and ~ will be. This will fix classical meanings for the other connectives since their standard definitions in terms of & and ~ are provable equivalences. It is more surprising to learn that if any one of ∨, →, and ↔ is classical alone, then so are all the other connectives. This may be shown in each case by noting that when one of these connectives is classical so is negation. The details are given in the proof of the following theorem. The classical truth conditions $\|PL\|$ for PL are named and listed here for ease of reference.

$\|\&\|$ $v(A\&B)=t$ iff $v(A)=t$ and $v(A)=t$.

$\|C\sim\|$ $v(\sim A)=t$ iff $v(A)=f$.

$\|C\rightarrow\|$ $v(A\rightarrow B)=t$ iff $v(A)=f$ or $v(B)=t$.

||C∨|| v(A∨B)=t iff v(A)=t or v(B)=t.

||C↔|| v(A↔B)=t iff v(A)=v(B).

Holism Theorem. If V is a deductive model of PL and v is a valuation in V, and v obeys the classical truth condition for any one of ~, →, ∨ or ↔, then v obeys the classical truth conditions for all the other connectives.

Proof. Assume that V is a deductive model of PL and v∈V. Then all provable arguments of PL are V-valid, which means that v satisfies any provable argument of PL.

The Case for ~. Suppose that v obeys the truth condition ||C~||. By the reasoning presented in Section 2.2, we know that v conforms to classical values on all but the last row of the truth tables for →, ∨, and ↔. So to show that the truth conditions →, ∨, ↔ are met we need only show that the classical values are determined in the row where v (A)=v(B)=f. The following arguments are provable in PL: ~A&~B / A→B, ~A&~B / ~(A∨B), and ~A&~B / A↔B. If these arguments are satisfied by v, then v(~A&~B)=t, only if v(A)=v(B)=f. This entails in turn that v (A→B)=t, v(A∨B)=f, and v(A↔B)=t, which are the desired classical values.

The Case for ∨. In light of the case for ~, it is sufficient to show that if v obeys ||C∨||, then it also obeys ||C~||. Since A∨~A is a theorem of PL, the valuation v must satisfy the theorem A∨~A . If v obeys ||C∨||, it follows that either v(A)=t or v(~A)=t . It follows that it is impossible that v(~A)=v(A)=f. This fixes the bottom row of the truth table for ~ to the classical value, for if v(A)=f, then v(~A) must be t.

The Case for →. In light of the case for ~, it is sufficient to show that if v obeys ||C→||, then v obeys ||C~||. So suppose that v obeys ||C→||. Assume that v(A)=f, and show that v(~A)=t as follows. Since v obeys ||C→|| this means that v(A→~A)=t. But A→~A / ~A is provable in PL, and so v satisfies this argument. Therefore when v(A)=f, v(~A)=t which fixes the bottom row of the negation truth table as desired.

The Case for ↔. Similar to the previous case. Assume for reductio that v(A)=v(~A)=f and that v obeys ||C↔||, it follows that v(A↔~A)=t. But A↔~A / B. Therefore v(B)=t for each wff B, which is incompatible with the consistency of v.   □

Though semantic holism is an interesting phenomenon worth exploring further (see Massey, 1990 for example), the main concern here will be not to study methods to repair indeterminacies, but to explore what rules actually say about connective meaning. The addition of an *ad hoc* condition on valuations requiring that one of the connectives has a classical reading disguises a rule's true semantical import. If standard rules do not deductively express standard conditions, then we must define and motivate alternative notions of expressive power. One candidate for an alternative is local expression, a topic to which we turn in the next chapter.

3   Local expression

The last chapter shows that the rules of propositional logic underdetermine a meaning for the connectives, at least when deductive expression is the benchmark to be used for determining what the system says about how to interpret them. One diagnosis of the problem is that deductive expression is entirely insensitive to how the rules of a logic are formulated. All that matters to whether a set of valuations is a deductive model of a system is what arguments are distinguished as provable by its rules. However, rule format can have an effect on expressive power when the criterion for what a system expresses takes details concerning rule formulation into account. The most direct way of doing this is to define expression via the notion of a local model of a rule. A set of valuations V is a local model of a rule when every member of V that satisfies the input(s) of the rule also satisfies its output. The relevant definitions leading to the notion of local expression are listed here. Since we will discuss (multiple conclusion) sequent systems in this chapter, we will speak more generally of satisfaction of sequents rather than satisfaction of arguments.

(Valuation for L)   A *valuation* v is *any* function from the set of wffs of L to the set {t, f} of truth-values such that it assigns f to at least one wff.

(Model for L)   A *model* V is any set of valuations for L.

(Satisfaction of a Sequent)   Valuation v *satisfies sequent* H / G iff whenever v assigns t to all members of H, v assigns t to at least one of the members of G.

(V-valid)   A sequent is *V-valid* iff it is satisfied by every valuation in V.

(Valuation v Satisfies Rule R)   v *satisfies rule* R iff if v satisfies the inputs of R, then v satisfies the output of R.

(Local Model of a Rule)   V is a *local model of rule* R iff every member of V satisfies R.

(Local Expression)   A system S *locally expresses* property P iff for every model V, V is a local model of the rules of S exactly when V has property P.

Our concern in this chapter will be to show that although axiomatic systems are unable to locally express truth conditions for the connectives, the situation is quite different for ND systems and sequent systems. Systems of PL presented in these formats express exactly the classical interpretation of the connectives provided in their standard truth tables. This chapter will provide independent evidence for the special place of ND format in determining meanings for the connectives. Though it has been well known that (multiple conclusion) sequent rules for PL fix the standard truth tables, it has only been relatively recently that Humberstone (1996) showed that ND rules locally express the classical readings as well. Theorem 3.3 will show that the result does not apply to axiomatic formulations of propositional logic, so this vindicates the intuition that ND rules have a special role in defining connective meaning.

Local expression results for ND systems entail a strange and potentially worrisome behavior. As we will see, systems of ND rules that locally express the standard truth conditions are nevertheless incomplete for those very conditions. Analogies with incompleteness results in modal logic, discussed in Section 3.4, will help make better sense of this. Nevertheless, it will be argued in Section 3.5 that incompleteness is a major obstacle to accepting local expression as an acceptable benchmark for model-theoretic inferentialism. In the following chapter, we will move on to global expression, the criterion we prefer for the remainder of this book.

3.1 Natural deduction rules

Since local expression is a criterion that is sensitive to rule format, it will be important to provide details here on natural deduction (ND) systems, and to present such systems for propositional logic (PL). Here are the details. As we explained in Section 1.2, horizontal or sequent style notation will be used for better comparison with (multiple conclusion) sequent systems.

Natural deduction systems are based on the structural rules S⊢.

System S⊢: The structural rules for natural deduction

(Hypothesis)	H ⊢ C, provided C is in H.
(Weakening)	$\dfrac{H \vdash C}{H, H' \vdash C}$

(Restricted Cut) $H \vdash A$

$\underline{H', A \vdash C}$

$H, H' \vdash C$

(Restricted Cut) is a derived rule in all the systems we will consider in this book. However, it would be an annoyance to have to show that it is derivable for every conceivable choice of rules. So we will adopt it explicitly as a structural rule.

Pairs of natural deduction rules are given here for each of the connectives &, $\rightarrow$, $\sim$, and $\vee$ in turn. The system S& is formed by adding the following to the structural rules.

S&:   (& Introduction)   (& Elimination)

$H \vdash A$ $\underline{H \vdash A\&B}$ $\underline{H \vdash A\&B}$

$\underline{H \vdash B}$ $H \vdash A$ $H \vdash B$

$H \vdash A\&B$

Although S& is a fragment of propositional logic, exactly the reasoning presented in Section 2.2 will show that any valuation that satisfies S& is classical.

The system S$\rightarrow$ is formed by adding the following pair to the structural rules.

S$\rightarrow$:   ($\rightarrow$ Introduction)   ($\rightarrow$ Elimination)

$\underline{H, A \vdash B}$ $H \vdash A$

$H \vdash A{\rightarrow}B$ $\underline{H \vdash A{\rightarrow}B}$

$H \vdash B$

Similarly, the systems S$\sim$, S$\leftrightarrow$, and S$\vee$ are formed by adding the following pairs of rules to the structural rules.

S$\sim$:   ($\sim$ Introduction)   ($\sim$ Elimination)

$H, A \vdash B$ $H, \sim A \vdash B$

$\underline{H, A \vdash \sim B}$ $\underline{H, \sim A \vdash \sim B}$

$H \vdash \sim A$ $H \vdash A$

S$\leftrightarrow$:   ($\leftrightarrow$ Elimination)   ($\leftrightarrow$ Introduction)

$H \vdash A$ $H \vdash B$ $H, A \vdash B$

$\underline{H \vdash A{\leftrightarrow}B}$ $\underline{H \vdash A{\leftrightarrow}B}$ $\underline{H, B \vdash A}$

$H \vdash B$ $H \vdash A$ $H \vdash A{\leftrightarrow}B$

S$\vee$:   ($\vee$ Introduction)   ($\vee$ Elimination)

$\underline{H \vdash A}$ $\underline{H \vdash B}$ $H \vdash A{\vee}B$

$H \vdash A{\vee}B$ $H \vdash A{\vee}B$ $H, A \vdash C$

$H, B \vdash C$

$\overline{H \vdash C}$

3.2 ND rules and sequent calculi for the conditional

The reasoning of Section 2.2 shows that the system for →, ~, ↔, and ∨ fails to deductively express the classical interpretation of its connectives. This indeterminacy is removed when sequent rules with multiple conclusions are adopted. As Hacking (1979, p. 312) points out, truth conditions for a connective can be read directly from its sequent rules, and those conditions are the classical ones. (See Section 11.1 for the full details.)

That the standard interpretation is fixed by sequent rules is reflected in a corresponding feature of the proof theory. It has been long known that the ND rules for →, along with the structural rules, form the implication fragment of intuitionistic, not classical logic. These rules are incomplete for the classical interpretation, since they cannot prove tautologies with the shape of Peirce's Law: $((A{\to}B){\to}A){\to}A$. On the other hand, sequent rules for → do not suffer from this defect. That they generate all the classical theorems is the proof-theoretic correlate of the fact that they determine classical truth conditions.

Shoesmith and Smiley (1978, p. 4) cite this as a motivation for interest in sequent systems with multiple conclusions. The suggestion is that the connectives do not even count as properly logical when formulated in ND rules with single conclusions. Since sequent rules are the only ones known to force their models to obey their intended logical interpretations, nothing less than sequent rules will do for classical logic. However, Shoesmith and Smiley are mistaken, since they presume that multiple sequent format is the only way to obtain this effect. In the next section, it is shown that ND systems also locally express the classical tables, so they too are up to the task for those with classical sympathies.

3.3 The Local Expression Theorem

Let Sc be the ND system that results from adding to the structural rules given at the end of Section 3.1, the ND rules for connectives on any list c drawn from these connectives: &, →, ↔, ~, ∨.

Local Expression Theorem. Sc locally expresses the classical truth tables for the connectives on list c.

Proof. It must be shown that V is a local model of the rules of Sc iff every member of V obeys the classical truth tables. It is easy to see that Sc is sound for the classical tables, that is, when V obeys the classical tables, V is a model of Sc. For the proof of the reverse, suppose V is a local model of the rules of Sc, and let v be a member of V, and demonstrate that v obeys the classical truth tables as follows. It is easy to check that v satisfies the structural rules. Since v satisfies each rule of Sc, v satisfies any argument that Sc can prove – including all of the following that contain connectives of Sc:

$$A, B / A\&B$$
$$A\&B / A$$
$$A\&B / B$$
$$A, A{\rightarrow}B / B$$
$$B / A{\rightarrow}B$$
$$A, A{\leftrightarrow}B / B$$
$$B, A{\leftrightarrow}B / A$$
$$A, {\sim}A / B$$
$$A / A{\vee}B$$
$$B / A{\vee}B$$

In Section 2.2 it was shown that when v satisfies these arguments, it assigns classical values to & and the classical values for all rows of the truth tables other than the last ones for the remaining connectives. So the only remaining cases are where $v(A)=f$ in case of $\sim$, and $v(A)=v(B)=f$ for $\rightarrow$, $\leftrightarrow$, and $\vee$.

The Case for $\rightarrow$. Assume that $v(A)=v(B)=f$. Then v satisfies A / B. Since v satisfies ($\rightarrow$ Introduction), v also satisfies / A$\rightarrow$B, and $v(A{\rightarrow}B)=t$.

The Case for $\leftrightarrow$. Assuming $v(A)=v(B)=f$, v satisfies the arguments A / B and B / A. By v's satisfying ($\leftrightarrow$ Introduction), v satisfies / A$\leftrightarrow$B, and so $v(A{\leftrightarrow}B)=t$.

The Case for $\sim$. Assume that $v(A)=f$. Then v satisfies the arguments A /A and A / $\sim$A. By ($\sim$ Introduction), v satisfies / $\sim$A and $v({\sim}A)=t$.

The Case for $\vee$. Assume that $v(A)=v(B)=f$, and show $v(A{\vee}B)=f$ as follows. By definition, valuation v assigns f to at least one wff D. Since v satisfies ($\vee$ Elimination), we have that if v satisfies the arguments: / A$\vee$B, A/D, and B/D, then v satisfies / D. But $v(D)=f$, so v cannot satisfy / D, with the result that v must fail to satisfy one of the arguments: / A$\vee$B, A / D, and B / D. However, $v(A)=v(B)=f$, and so v satisfies both A / D and B / D. So v fails to satisfy / A$\vee$B, and $v(A{\vee}B)=f$ as desired.   □

The proof of the Local Expression Theorem illustrates why being a *local* model, a model of the *rules* of Sc is a stronger condition than being a *deductive* model – a model of the provable *arguments* of Sc. The expressive content of rules such as ($\rightarrow$ Introduction), ($\leftrightarrow$ Introduction), ($\sim$ Introduction), and ($\vee$ Elimination) cannot be formulated in terms of the acceptability of arguments alone, and it is exactly these rules that impose stronger conditions on how the connectives are to be interpreted. They manage to fix the formerly missing last row of the truth table for a connective c because a subformula (A and/or B) of the wff AcB appears as a hypothesis in some input. When v is a local model of such an rule, a condition of the form: 'if $v(A)=f$ then $\ldots$' is enforced on v. For example, consider what satisfaction of ($\rightarrow$ Introduction) entails. One obtains: $v(A\rightarrow B)=t$ provided that if $v(A)=t$ then $v(B)=t$. But when $v(A)=f$, it follows that if $v(A)=f$ then $v(B)=t$, and hence $v(A)=f$ entails $v(A\rightarrow B)=t$. So such rules are able to obtain control over rows of a truth table where subformulas have the value f. Defining rules over arguments with subformulas in their hypotheses is the secret to success.

The upshot is that what a system locally expresses is heavily dependent on exactly how the rules are formulated. For example, consider the axiomatic system S$\rightarrow$ax consisting of the axioms $\vdash$ A$\rightarrow$(B$\rightarrow$A) and $\vdash$ (A$\rightarrow$(B$\rightarrow$C))$\rightarrow$ ((A$\rightarrow$B)$\rightarrow$(A$\rightarrow$C)), along with Modus Ponens as its only rule. The Local Expression Theorem does not hold for S$\rightarrow$ax, because the non-classical provability valuation $v_\vdash$ for S$\rightarrow$ax *does* satisfy the axioms and rule of S$\rightarrow$ax.

Theorem 3.3 S$\rightarrow$ax allows non-classical local models.

Proof. Consider V$\vdash$, the model whose only valuation is the provability valuation $v\vdash$ such that $v\vdash(A) = t$ iff A is a theorem of PL. The valuation $v\vdash$ clearly satisfies the axioms and rule of S$\rightarrow$ax, so V$\vdash$ is a local model of S$\rightarrow$ax. However $v\vdash(p) = v\vdash(q) = v\vdash(p\rightarrow q) = f$, violating the material implication truth table. Therefore V$\vdash$ is a non-classical local model of S$\rightarrow$ax. $\square$

It is a simple matter to verify that every local model of a system is also a global model of it (and a deductive model as well). Therefore the last theorem shows that axiomatic systems have non-classical global and deductive models. This goes part of the way towards establishing that axiomatic systems fail to express a semantics in any of the three senses of expression we have defined. The possibility that some axiomatic system might express a non-classical set of truth conditions has not been ruled out. However, it is easy to see that V⊢ also violates the intuitionistic truth condition ‖→‖ for → to be presented in Section 5.2. So if there are any axiomatic systems that locally express a semantics, it will be an unfamiliar one. My guess is that axiomatic rules for propositional logic fail to locally express any readings at all for connectives other than & and ⊥.

3.4 Local expressive power and completeness

One might have thought (as I once did) that if a system of rules has sufficient expressive power to force its models to obey a semantics, then the system must be complete for that semantics. That is true of global expression, as we will see in Section 12.1. However, things are quite different in the present setting. S→ is incomplete for classical semantics, because it is unable to prove Peirce's Law. Yet the Local Expression Theorem (Section 3.3) says that it locally expresses classical truth conditions. Oddly, S→ has the (local) expressive power to force the validity of a formula it cannot even prove!

The system S→ is not the only incomplete propositional logic of this kind. For example, an examination of the proof of the Local Expression Theorem (Section 3.3) reveals that the proof for negation requires only (∼Introduction) and the derivability of A, ∼A / B. So the system S¬ that results from adding structural rules to the following two principles allows only classical models of negation.

S¬:   (∼ Introduction)   (Contradiction)
           H, A ⊢ B   H ⊢ B
           H, A ⊢ ∼B   H ⊢ ∼B
           ─────────   ─────────
           H ⊢ ∼A   H ⊢ A

However, S¬ is a formulation of a system for *intuitionistic* negation, and incapable of proving the classical law of Double Negation. So S¬ is another incomplete propositional logic.

It is surprising that local models of rules for *intuitionistic* negation force the *classical* interpretation of ∼. Such a strong outcome may lead one to suspect that we have committed some fundamental mistake. The analogy with incompleteness in modal logic will help allay these fears, and provide better insight into what is happening here (Garson, 2010). Let us briefly review an incompleteness result in provability logic that will illustrate the relevant ideas. (See Boolos, 1993 pp. 148ff.) A standard provability logic GL is formulated by adding the axiom $\Box(\Box A \rightarrow A) \rightarrow \Box A$ to the basic modal logic K. The system H results from adding to K the weaker axiom: $\Box(\Box A \leftrightarrow A) \rightarrow \Box A$. GL is stronger than H because it is able to prove the standard axiom for S4: $\Box A \rightarrow \Box\Box A$, and H is not.

Now let us consider which wffs of these logics are valid on frames of various kinds, where a wff A is *valid on frame* <W, R> iff it is true in every world in any model with that frame. Validity on frames selects a benchmark that individuates less finely than does validity on models. For while there are models of $\Box(\Box A \leftrightarrow A) \rightarrow \Box A$ that are not models of $\Box(\Box A \rightarrow A) \rightarrow \Box A$, there is no frame where $\Box(\Box A \leftrightarrow A) \rightarrow \Box A$ is valid and $\Box(\Box A \rightarrow A) \rightarrow \Box A$ is not. Frames are insensitive to structure that can be captured in models, with the result that the two axioms express the same conditions on frames. As a result, H is essentially incomplete. It cannot prove $\Box A \rightarrow \Box\Box A$, which is valid on every frame that accepts its axiom $\Box(\Box A \leftrightarrow A) \rightarrow \Box A$ as valid. As a result, it follows that there is no class of frames for which H is sound and complete. H lies outside the class of systems that are adequate for conditions on frames.

The same phenomenon explains the results reported here. The propositional logics S→ and S¬ are essentially incomplete in the same way. Being a local model of a rule is a stronger condition than being a global or deductive model of a rule, which means that the local model benchmark for expressive power individuates less finely. For example, there is no way within the class of local models to discriminate between being a model of S→ and being a model SP→, the system that adds Peirce's Law to S→. The local models of one set of rules are exactly the local models of the other. The only local models of S→ must be classical and so must validate Peirce's Law – a formula that cannot be proven in S→. As a result S→ is essentially incomplete in exactly the same way as was the modal logic H.

The first incompleteness results in modal logic came as a surprise, but now the phenomenon is considered natural. The condition that a modal axiom be valid for a frame is essentially second-order. If a semantics for modal logic were chosen so that the condition on models that corresponded to an axiom would be its second-order condition on models, then completeness would be a matter of course. However, our interest in finding corresponding conditions on frames (such as reflexivity, transitivity, symmetry, and the like) amounts to the requirement that those conditions be first-order. So the realm of complete modal logics for conditions on frames is demarcated by cases where second-order conditions collapse to first-order ones. Since this will be relatively rare, incompleteness is the norm. (See Salqvist (1975) for classic work on how reduction of second-order conditions to first-order frame conditions is related to completeness.)

There is a parallel explanation for the incomplete propositional logics. As we will show in the next section, local models of rules are essentially extensional, and so rules (such as those for conjunction) whose intensional truth conditions collapse to extensional ones are safe from incompleteness. However, incompleteness will be a distinct possibility otherwise. In the same way that there are modal logics too weak to correspond to any set of conditions on frames, there are propositional logics too weak to correspond to any extensional truth conditions. The moral is that incompleteness of propositional logics is what should be expected.

3.5 Local expression evaluated

The claim that ND rules define the classical meanings of the connectives can be justified in the present setting. There is an end run around the problem that models of propositional logic underdetermine the standard truth tables. Simply define expressive power using local models. When this is done, ND systems, but not axiomatic systems, fix exactly the classical account of their connectives' truth conditions.

While this may seem pleasing to a champion of the expressive power of ND systems, the question to be resolved for the purposes of this book is whether local expression is a viable benchmark for what rules express about connective meaning. I believe it is not, for the incompleteness results pose a serious obstacle to the inferentialist project. According to local expression, the rules of S$\rightarrow$ express more about the meaning of the connective $\rightarrow$ than they can prove. S$\rightarrow$ determines a classical semantics but cannot prove Peirce's Law, which is validated by that very semantics. So in this sense, there is a massive mismatch between the deductive role of $\rightarrow$ and the meaning fixed by the $\rightarrow$ rules. While the Local Expression Theorem will be of some comfort for those who hoped that natural deduction rules would define the standard semantics for classical logic, the fact that expressive power defined via satisfaction of rules does not entail completeness undermines one's confidence in the idea that deductive role corresponds to meaning, the very idea that prompted natural deduction rules in the first place.

This problem is related to a simple and fundamental objection to local expression discussed in Section 1.8. In using the idea of a local model, one is committed to the idea that it is *satisfaction* of arguments that must be preserved by members of V for V to be a model of the rules. However, every teacher of elementary logic takes care to emphasize that the correct criterion for acceptability of an argument is not satisfaction. Surely the truth of the conclusion (or the falsity of the premises) are insufficient for showing that the argument is correct. What we need for argument correctness is validity, and therefore what rules ought to preserve is this form of correctness. The loss of completeness, then, is a symptom of a poor choice of a standard for the acceptability of arguments.

There are other serious problems with local expression. Many systems of logic contain rules that do not preserve satisfaction. Both modal logic and predicate logic are systems of this kind. For example, the rule of Universal Generalization for the quantifier ∀ has it that from H / At, one may derive H / ∀xAx as long as the term t does not appear in H or ∀xAx. However a valuation that satisfies the argument H / At need not satisfy H / ∀xAx, even when the term t is missing from H or ∀xAx. Therefore, the classical valuations for predicate logic do not satisfy Universal Generalization. So the requirement that a valuation satisfy this rule is too strong. It would demand more of a rule than what is required to establish its soundness: namely preservation of validity.

Not only is predicate logic not complete with respect to the notion of validity defined by local models, the system that *is* complete for local models is bizarre. The requirement that a valuation v satisfy both Universal Introduction and Elimination rules would entail that v(Ax)=t iff v(∀xAx)=t. The result is collapse of quantification. Any set V that is a local model of the quantifier rules will have the feature that Ax↔∀xAx, is V-valid. So every wff containing a quantifier would have to be semantically equivalent to the result of deleting it, and it would be pointless to introduce quantifiers into such a logic in the first place. To put it another way, local models render the quantifier meaningless.

Modal logics also employ rules that do not preserve truth. For example, the rule of Necessitation says that one may prefix theorems with the modal operator □. From ⊢ A one obtains ⊢ □A. However, when a valuation v satisfies the argument / A (i.e. v(A)=t), it does not follow that v satisfies / □A (i.e. v(□A)=t). Requiring that a model V preserve satisfaction, as local models require, results in modal collapse, where introduction of □ is pointless.

This collapsing behavior is related to another disturbing feature of local expression, namely that it incorporates a covert prejudice against truth conditions that are not truth tabular. It automatically eliminates intensional truth clauses that define truth of a wff in terms of truth behavior over a whole set of valuations (possible worlds). Even in predicate logic, one needs the flexibility to define the truth condition for the quantified wff ∀xAx in terms of the truth behavior of Ax for *alternative* valuations of the variable x. The requirement that the rules preserve satisfaction does not provide this needed flexibility.

To make this point precise, it is helpful to define what we mean by extensional truth conditions. With the concept in place, it can be shown that the local model criterion for expressive power oversteps its bounds by allowing only extensional truth conditions. You may think of a truth condition for a connective c as a requirement on models V that says about every valuation v in V something of the following form. (We have assumed the connective is a binary one, but the reader can adjust the schema below to connectives of 1 or more than 2 places.)

(Form of a Truth Condition)   v(AcB)=t iff ...

Here the dots indicate a definiens that makes some stipulation concerning the values that A and B have across the various valuations that are members of V. So in general, a truth condition may mention anything it likes about truth behavior of the subformulas of AcB not only for v, but also for all the valuations in V. However an extensional truth condition has a form where the definiens mentions only the behavior of A and B *at v*. Therefore an extensional truth condition is one with the following form.

(Form of an Extensional Truth Condition)   v(AcB)=t iff f(v(A), v(B)).

Here f indicates some feature defined over the values v(A) and v(B), and nothing more.

Now imagine that some set of rules R locally expresses a truth condition C. Then it is not hard to show that C must be extensional.

Theorem 3.5 If a system locally expresses a truth condition for a connective, then it must be an extensional one.

Proof. Suppose S locally expresses a truth condition C for connective c. Then we know that every model V has the feature that V is a local model of S iff C holds of V. This means that condition C is equivalent to the requirement that V be a local model of S, that is, that each valuation v in V satisfies each rule of S. Therefore C is equivalent to a conjunction of conditions for each rule having the form:

(F) If v satisfies inputs $I_1, \ldots, I_n$ then v satisfies output O.

In the most general case, $I_1, \ldots, I_n$, and O are all sequents. Now the claim that v satisfies a sequent makes a claim only about the truth-values on v of the formulas in the sequent. Therefore the conditional (F) above contains only mention of values that valuation v assigns to wffs, and not to any values assigned by any other valuations in V. It follows that C is an extensional truth condition. □

The last theorem makes clear that local expression essentially incorporates a prejudice against any logic that might have intensional truth conditions. This explains why local expression cannot even accommodate a meaningful introduction of quantifiers or modal operators. This is a serious failing. The more general way to characterize what a set of rules expresses requires instead that the rule preserves *validity*, not satisfaction. Therefore, global expression will be the benchmark employed in the rest of this book.

4   Global expression

Of the accounts of expressive power examined so far, one definition is too weak and the other too strong. The Deductive Expression Theorem of Section 2.2 showed that indeterminacy of connective meaning affects all symbols other than & and ⊥ when deductive expression is chosen as the criterion for what rules express. However, when local expression is chosen in its place, the Local Expression Theorem of Section 3.3 applies, and so natural deduction rules determine classical interpretations of all the connectives. Unfortunately, this has the bizarre consequence that systems of rules locally express semantical conditions for which they are incomplete. Furthermore, the use of local expression is simply incompatible with predicate logic or modal logic, and it flies in the face of the fact that it is validity, not satisfaction, that serves as our criterion for the correctness of arguments. (See the objections discussed in Section 3.5.)

In this chapter, we will define global expression, the notion of expression that gets it just right. It is neither too strong nor too weak, and it fits nicely with an interest in systems stronger than propositional logic. Here preservation of validity is taken as the appropriate benchmark for what counts as a model of a rule. Therefore system S globally expresses property P of models iff for every model V, the rules of S preserve V-validity exactly when V obeys P. The interesting thing about global expression is that natural deduction (ND) rules express intuitionistic truth conditions. The present chapter will set the stage for discussing these results by defining global expression and exploring its features. We will first show (Section 4.1) that the natural deduction rules for & and ⊥ globally express the standard interpretations for & and ⊥. In Section 4.2, we will define and explore the notion of a natural semantics for a system of rules S, that is, a condition on models that is globally expressed by S, and that provides a recursive account of the truth behavior of the connectives that S regulates. After that, it will be shown (Section 4.4) that the natural semantics for the natural deduction systems regulating $\rightarrow$, $\leftrightarrow$, and $\vee$ is not classical, by exploiting results in Section 4.3 concerning what is called the canonical model. The end of Section 4.4 rounds out the discussion by proving an analog of the Lowenheim–Skolem Theorem. The upshot is that the language of propositional logic is incapable of expressing the difference between classical and non-classical models. Not only do the rules of PL fail to express the classical conditions for the connectives, there is no consistent set of sentences of PL that forces models of PL to become classical.

This may appear to be a blow for a model-theoretic (MT) inferentialist, since it appears that connective meaning is radically underdetermined. However, that is the wrong conclusion to draw. The proper way to understand the role of this chapter for the MT inferentialist is that it clears the way for showing that natural deduction rules exactly express intuitionistic readings for the connectives. Alien anthropologists who understand the facts reported in this chapter will know that it is pointless to try to attribute classical readings for the connectives based on evidence that we adopt natural deduction rules for $\rightarrow$, $\leftrightarrow$, $\vee$, and $\sim$. They will also know that when it comes to the question of whether we adopt the classical readings for these connectives, it is pointless to gather any further evidence about what we assert in the language of propositional logic, for nothing that we could say in that language is even relevant for establishing that we adopt classical readings. They will conclude that if the natural deduction rules say anything at all about the meanings of $\rightarrow$, $\leftrightarrow$, and $\vee$, those meanings will have to be non-classical. In subsequent chapters, we will show what those non-classical meanings are.

4.1 Global expression and preservation of validity

Here is a review of the basic technical machinery needed for defining global expression.

> (Valuation for L) A *valuation* v is *any* function from the set of wffs of language L to the set {t, f} of truth-values such that it assigns f to at least one wff.

> (Model for L) A *model* V is any set of valuations for L.

> (v satisfies H / G) v *satisfies H / G* iff if v(A)=t for each A in H, then v(B)=t for some B in G. (Therefore in the special case when H / G is an argument H / C, v satisfies H / C iff whenever v(H)=t, v(C)=t.)

(V-valid) A sequent is *V-valid* iff it is satisfied by every valuation in V.

(Preservation of Validity) Rule R *preserves V-validity* iff whenever the inputs of R are all V-valid, the output of R is also V-valid.

(Global Model of a Rule) V is a *global model* of rule R iff R preserves V-validity.

(Global Expression) A system S *globally expresses* property P iff for all models V for a language L for S, V is a global model of the rules of S exactly when V has property P.

For concreteness, the main ideas presented here will be illustrated for the case of S&, the natural deduction system for conjunction consisting of the structural rules (& Introduction) and (& Elimination).

S&:   (& Introduction)   (& Elimination)

$$\frac{H \vdash A \quad H \vdash B}{H \vdash A\&B}$$ $$\frac{H \vdash A\&B}{H \vdash A} \qquad \frac{H \vdash A\&B}{H \vdash B}$$

Suppose that V is a global model of S&, that is, V is a set of valuations (over formulas of a language L containing &) such that the S& rules preserve V-validity. What does this tell us about V? It turns out that the system S& forces V to obey the truth table for conjunction.

(Forces) System S *forces* condition P iff every global model of S obeys P.

This can be proven by noting that every global model V of S& preserves the V-validity of the rules of S&, and that entails that the provable arguments of S& are all V-valid. That means in turn that V is a deductive model of S&. But we showed in Theorem 2.2.1 that any deductive model of a system that can prove the below three arguments obeys the classical truth condition ‖&‖.

$$A\&B \mid A$$
$$A\&B \mid B$$
$$A, B \mid A\&B$$
$$\|\&\| \ v(A\&B)=t \text{ iff } v(A)=t \text{ and } v(B)=t.$$

So the classical truth condition for conjunction is forced by S&. However, we also know that S& is sound for ‖&‖, which means that when V obeys ‖&‖, the rules of S& are V-valid, i.e. V is a global model of S&.

(Sound for) System S *is sound for* condition P iff if every model that obeys P is a global model of S.

Since S& both forces and is sound for ‖&‖, it follows that V is a global model of S& iff V obeys ‖&‖, for any model V for a language containing &, and that amounts to saying that S& globally expresses ‖&‖. So S& (globally) expresses the classical meaning for &.

S& Expression Theorem. S& globally expresses ‖&‖.

Since global expression is the topic of the rest of this book, we will drop the term 'global'. Unless we say otherwise, by 'model' we mean global model, and by 'expresses' we will mean globally expresses.

4.2 Natural semantics

Let us call a model V *standard* (for a language) when it meets the intended truth conditions for the logical symbols (of that language). There is no attempt to give a formal account of what the intended truth conditions for a symbol are, but the idea should be clear enough in the case of propositional logic, where the connectives &, →, ↔, ∨, and ~ are given their well-known truth tables. The S& Expression Theorem entails that any model of the system S& defined over a language containing & is standard with respect to &.

In mathematical logic, we call a system categorical when all of its models are standard. When individuation conditions for models are chosen so that isomorphic models are treated as identical, one would say that a categorical system has the standard model as its only model. It is easy to import the notion of categoricity in the present context. Here again, a system will be said to be *categorical* just in case every model of S is standard. So another way to express the contents of the & Expression Theorem is to say that S& is categorical.

When a system S expresses a condition P on models, it does not necessarily follow that P provides a viable account of connective meaning. Every system of rules S trivially expresses at least one corresponding condition ‖S‖ on V, namely that V is a model of S (i.e. the rules of S preserve V-validity). However, condition ‖S‖ does not always provide truth conditions for its logical vocabulary. The idea can be illustrated by considering alternative sets of rules for &.

For example, when system S- consists of (& Elimination) *alone*, ‖S-‖ expresses that whenever H / A&B is V-valid, so are H / A and H / B. This is too weak to provide the equivalence needed for a complete recursive account of truth conditions for the wffs with the shape A&B. From $\|S\text{-}\|$ one may derive that any valuation v in V must obey the first three rows of the truth table for conjunction, but this does not uniquely determine a value for A&B on the last row, so the value of A&B is not determined by values of its subformulas as one would desire.

On the other hand, when S+ consists of (& Elimination) plus the following rule:

$$\frac{H \vdash A}{H \vdash A\&B}$$

the condition expressed by S+ is too strong to count as a truth condition. The system S+ is Prior's famous example given in (1960) to show that not every set of rules defines a meaning for a connective. The problem is that A / B is provable in S+, and so a valuation v in a model of S+ must assign all wffs t if *any* wff is assigned t. Therefore, v(p&q)=t if (say) v(r&s)=t; but then the value of A&B is not determined solely by values given to its subformulas A and B.

The system S&, however, is neither too strong nor too weak, because the condition it expresses is equivalent to $\|\&\|$, which uniquely fixes that values of A&B given the values of its subformulas A and B. (By *equivalence of two conditions* we mean that models that obey one are exactly the models that obey the other.)

A *semantics* $\|Sc\|$ for a connective c is a condition on models V that allows one to calculate a unique value for a wff AcB with c as its main connective given the values of the subformulas A and B across the various valuations in V. In short, $\|S\|$ gives a recursive truth condition for c. A semantics $\|S\|$ for a language L is a condition on models V that is the conjunction of a semantics $\|Sc\|$ for each connective of L. When a system S expresses a semantics for a language defined for the connectives that occur in the rules of S, we call $\|S\|$ the natural semantics for S.

(Natural Semantics) Condition $\|S\|$ on models is a *natural semantics* for S iff S expresses $\|S\|$, and $\|S\|$ is a semantics for a language defined over the connectives that occur in the rules of S.

This definition depends on what counts as a semantics. For the moment, we may think of a semantics as a set of truth conditions for the connectives.

However, the idea will be a fluid one. At the beginning of Section 5.5, we will propose a slightly more liberal criterion, allowing conditions that are "isomorphic" to a standard model-theoretic definition of validity using recursive truth conditions. (Furthermore, in Section 8.9, we explicitly allow a semantics to impose side constraints on how valuations assign values to the propositional variables, and in Section 7.4, we even contemplate the idea that those constraints could concern values of complex wffs.)

The classical truth condition $\|\&\|$ is clearly a semantics for &, and the S& Expression Theorem (Section 4.1) tells us that S& expresses $\|\&\|$, so it follows that S& is a natural semantics for S&.

S& Theorem. $\|\&\|$ is a natural semantics for S&.

Now let us turn to $\bot$. Let $S\bot$ consist of the structural rules $S\vdash$ plus a single rule ($\bot$ Elimination) to govern the behavior of the symbol $\bot$ (for a contradiction).

$S\bot$:   ($\bot$ Elimination)

$$\frac{H \vdash \bot}{H \vdash A}$$

It is a simple matter to show that $S\bot$ forces $\|\bot\|$, and that $S\bot$ is sound for $\|\bot\|$, the truth condition for $\bot$. So $S\bot$ expresses $\|\bot\|$, and $\|\bot\|$ is a natural semantics for $S\bot$.

$\|\bot\|$ For each v in V, $v(\bot)=f$.

To prepare for the theorem, it is useful to introduce the notation: '$v(H)=t$' which means that $v(A)=t$ for every member of H.

($v(H)=t$) *v(H)=t* iff for each member A of H, $v(A)=t$.

$S\bot$ Theorem. $\|\bot\|$ is a natural semantics for $S\bot$.

Proof. $\|\bot\|$ fixes the truth-value for $\bot$, so it is a semantics for $\bot$. We must show that $S\bot$ expresses $\|\bot\|$, that is, $S\bot$ is sound for, and forces $\|\bot\|$.

For soundness, assume that V obeys $\|\bot\|$ and demonstrate that ($\bot$ Elimination) preserves V-validity by assuming $H \vDash_V \bot$ and deriving a contradiction from $H \nvDash_V A$. From $H \nvDash_V A$, we have that there is a valuation v in V such that $v(H)=t$ and $v(A)=f$. But then by $H \vDash_V \bot$ and $v(H)=t$, we would have $v(\bot)=t$ which conflicts with $\|\bot\|$.

To show $S\perp$ forces $\|\perp\|$, suppose that V is a model of $S\perp$. $\perp \vdash A$ is provable in $S\perp$ for any wff A. Since V is a model of $S\perp$, $\perp \vDash_V A$. Let v be any member of V. Suppose for reductio that $v(\perp)=t$. Then $v(A)=t$ for every wff A which conflicts with the consistency of v. So $v(\perp)=f$ as desired. $\qquad\square$

Now consider $S\&\perp$, the system whose language contains only the symbols & and $\perp$, and whose rules consist of the rules for $S\&$, $S\perp$, and the structural rules. This system is sound for $\|S\&\perp\|$, the conjunction of $\|\&\|$ with $\|\perp\|$, and the $S\perp$ and $S\&$ Theorems together show that $S\&\perp$ forces $\|S\&\perp\|$. Therefore the natural semantics for $S\&\perp$ is $\|S\&\perp\|$.

In the rest of this book, we will simply assume that a system of rules defines the meaning of its connectives iff it has a natural semantics. The next section demonstrates that the meanings for the connectives expressed by the natural deduction systems for $\rightarrow$, $\leftrightarrow$, $\lor$, and $\sim$ are non-classical. In the following chapters, we will show that natural semantics for these systems exists, but it is intensional, and related to the semantics for intuitionistic logic.

4.3 The canonical model

In Section 2.2, it was shown that systems for propositional logic fail to deductively express meanings for the connectives. In the case of global expression, where preservation of validity is taken to be the standard for expressive power, it is somewhat more difficult to demonstrate that the natural deduction (ND) systems for $\rightarrow$, $\leftrightarrow$, $\lor$, and $\sim$ fail to express classical truth conditions. To show this, it will be helpful to define a special kind of model that will be useful at many points in this book. Let S be any system of ND rules presented in Section 3.1 that also includes the structural rules. A valuation v satisfies system S iff it satisfies its provable arguments.

(Satisfaction of a System)   v *satisfies* S iff if $H \vdash_S C$ and $v(H)=t$, then $v(C)=t$.

For a given language L of propositional logic that includes the symbols of a system S, let [S] be the set of all valuations over the wffs of L that satisfy S. We will call [S] the canonical model (for L and S) because it will play a central role in proving relationships between expressive power and completeness.

(Canonical Model)   The *canonical model* for S is the set [S] of all valuations that satisfy S.

For the moment, two fundamental features of the canonical model will be shown. S is adequate (both sound and complete) with respect to its canonical model [S], from which it follows that [S] is always a model of S. In light of the fact that (Hypothesis) and (Restricted Cut) are structural rules of S, the following lemmas hold, for (possibly) infinite sets of wffs H and G. Let us say an argument form H / C is *finitary* for system S iff whenever $H \vdash_S C$, there is a finite subset H^* of H, such that $H^* \vdash_S C$.

Finitary Lemma. All arguments are finitary for S.

Proof. Any argument introduced by (Hypothesis) is clearly finitary, and inspection of all the ND rules shows that they preserve the property of being finitary. So every provable argument in S is finitary.   □

Cut Lemma. If $H \vdash_S A$ for each A in G, and $G \vdash_S C$, then $H \vdash_S C$.

Proof. Suppose $H \vdash_S A$ for each A in G, and $G \vdash_S C$. By the Finitary Lemma, G / C is finitary. Therefore it follows that there is a finite subset $\{B_1, \ldots, B_n\}$ of G such that $\{B_1, \ldots, B_n\} \vdash_S C$. The initial assumption yields $H \vdash_S B_1, \ldots, H \vdash_S B_n$. Application of (Restricted Cut) n times yields $H \vdash_S C$ as desired.   □

When an argument H / C is V-valid, we write: $H \vDash_V C$.

$(H \vDash_V C)$ $H \vDash_V C$ iff H / C is V-valid.

So the adequacy (soundness and completeness) of S for its canonical model [S] may be expressed as follows: $H \vdash_S C$ iff $H \vDash_{[S]} C$.

[S] Adequacy Theorem. $H \vdash_S C$ iff $H \vDash_{[S]} C$.

Proof. The proof of soundness (the proof from left to right) follows immediately since members of [S] satisfy S.

For the proof of completeness (the proof from right to left), it is sufficient to prove the contrapositive: if $H \nvdash_S C$, then $H \nvDash_{[S]} C$, so suppose that $H \nvdash_S C$ and find a member v of [S] such that $v(H)=t$ and $v(C)=f$ as follows. Define v_H so that $v_H(B)=t$ iff $H \vdash B$, for every wff B. So we have $v_H(H)=t$ and $v_H(C)=f$, and all that remains to show that v_H is the desired valuation is to show that v_H satisfies S, and hence qualifies as a member of [S]. So assume that $v_H(G)=t$ and $G \vdash_S B$, and demonstrate that $v_H(B)=t$ as follows. From $v_H(G)=t$, it follows that $H \vdash_S A$, for each A in G. This with $G \vdash_S B$ and the Cut Lemma entails $H \vdash_S B$ and so $v_H(B)=t$ as desired. □

You may remember (from Section 2.2) that the provability valuation $v_\vdash$ (for S) was defined so that $v_\vdash(A)=t$ iff $\vdash_S A$. It is easy to show that [S] is a model of S, and $v_\vdash$ is a member of [S].

Theorem 4.3 [S] is a model of S and $v_\vdash$ is a member of [S].

Proof. To show that [S] is a model of S, use the [S] Adequacy Theorem, to replace '$H \vdash_S C$' with '$H \vDash_{[S]} C$' in the statement of each rule of S to show that it preserves [S]-validity.

To show $v_\vdash$ is a member of [S], assume $G \vdash_S C$ and $v_\vdash(G)=t$ and show that $v_\vdash(C)=t$ as follows. Given $v_\vdash(G)=t$, it follows that $\vdash_S A$ for every A in G. By the Cut Lemma, it follows that $\vdash_S C$, and so $v_\vdash(C)=t$ as desired. □

4.4 Negative results for global expression

The provability valuation played a central role in showing that there are non-classical valuations that respect the deductive consequences of PL. (See Section 2.2.) The fact that $v_\vdash$ is in [PL] (the canonical model for PL) can be exploited to show that negative results previously obtained in the case of deductive models transfer to the case of preservation of validity. As a result, [PL] will serve as a non-classical (global) model for PL, and this will establish that PL does not (globally) express the classical truth conditions for connectives other than & and ⊥.

Now let PL be any system of propositional logic that includes the natural deduction rules for the logical symbols. It will not matter whether the rules for classical or intuitionistic negation or chosen. Using the results on the provability valuation for PL given at the end of the last section, negative results on the expressive power of PL follow immediately from Theorem 4.3.

Theorem 4.4.1 PL expresses neither $\|C{\to}\|$, nor $\|C{\leftrightarrow}\|$, nor $\|C{\sim}\|$, nor $\|C{\vee}\|$.

Proof. Theorem 4.3 guarantees that [PL] is a model of S, and that the provability valuation $v_\vdash$ is a member of [PL]. Note that none of p, ~p, q, p→q, p↔q is provable in PL, and p∨~p is. Therefore $v_\vdash(p)$=f, $v_\vdash(q)$=f, and $v_\vdash(p{\to}q)$=f, which violates $\|C{\to}\|$; $v_\vdash(p)$=f, $v_\vdash(q)$=f, and $v_\vdash(p{\leftrightarrow}q)$=f which violates $\|C{\leftrightarrow}\|$; $v_\vdash(p)$=f and $v_\vdash({\sim}p)$=f, which violates $\|C{\sim}\|$, and $v_\vdash(p{\vee}{\sim}p)$=t while $v_\vdash(p)$=f and $v_\vdash({\sim}p)$=f, which violates $\|C\vee\|$. So [PL] is a model of PL that violates these conditions. Hence it does not express them.   □

It follows from this theorem that PL does not have a classical natural semantics. The conclusion will be that propositional logic expresses a non-classical reading for the connectives →, ↔, ∨, and ~.

It is worth remarking that the last theorem entails an analog of the Lowenheim–Skolem Theorem. Remember that a model V is any set of consistent valuations. A model V is *classical* when every valuation v in V satisfies the classical truth tables. Let us say that V is a model of H, or H *has model* V iff there is a member v of V that satisfies all the wffs in H, that is, v(H)=t. Then the last theorem entails that whenever a set of wffs H of PL has a classical model, it also has a non-classical model.

Theorem 4.4.2 If a set of wffs H of PL has a classical model, then it has a non-classical model.

Proof. Suppose H has a classical model. That means that there is a set V of classical valuations over wffs of PL and a member v of V such that v(H)=t. By the soundness of PL with respect to classical semantics it follows that $H \nvdash_{PL} \bot$. It follows from the [S] Adequacy Theorem (Section 4.3) that $H \nvDash_{[PL]} \bot$. But we have learned in the course of proving Theorem 4.4.1 that [PL] is not classical. So [PL] is the desired non-classical model of H.   □

The last theorem tells us something important about expressive power, namely that wffs of PL cannot express the condition that their models are classical. It is not just that the classical conditions are not expressed by the rules of PL. No additional (consistent) set of wffs of PL is capable of forcing the models of PL to be classical. Let us flesh out this idea by defining the notion of what a language can express, where P is some condition on models.

(H expresses P) A set of wffs H *expresses condition* P iff H has at least one model, and every model of H obeys P.

(L can express P)   A language L *can express condition* P iff some set H of the wffs of L expresses P.

The last theorem guarantees that no set H of the wffs of PL can express that its models are classical, so the language of propositional logic cannot express that either.

Theorem 4.4.3 The language of PL cannot express that its models are classical.

Proof. It will be sufficient to show that if H has at least one model, then it has a non-classical model. So suppose that H has a model. If it is non-classical we are done. If it is classical, use Theorem 4.4.2 to obtain a non-classical one.   □

As we will see throughout this book, the reasoning used in the last two theorems generalizes to all situations where we are able to show that a system of rules cannot express a certain condition on models. An upshot of that result will be that no set of wffs in the language can express the same condition.

What are the proper conclusions to draw from these results? Well, as we said at the beginning of this chapter, they mean that if the natural deduction rules for →, ↔, ∨, and ~ express any semantical conditions at all, they cannot be classical. The coming chapters will flesh this out by showing how the conditions that are expressed by those rules are related to the semantics for intuitionistic logic.

5   Intuitionistic semantics

In this chapter, we will lay the groundwork for showing that the natural semantics for natural deduction formulations of propositional logic is intuitionistic. In Section 5.1, we present Kripke's semantics for intuitionistic logic, which is a variant of the semantics for the modal logic S4 (van Dalen, 1986, pp. 243ff.). In Section 5.2, intuitionistic models are introduced. Intuitionistic models are sets of valuations V that satisfy conditions for each of the connectives that resemble the corresponding truth conditions for Kripke models. Intuitionistic models, being sets of valuations of a certain kind, lack the structure found in Kripke models, notably the accessibility relation $\subseteq$. In intuitionistic models, the analog $\leq$ of $\subseteq$ has to be defined by the way valuations in V assign values to the wffs. Section 5.3 discusses the objection that the conditions that mention $\leq$ are therefore circular or fail to meet other standards for a successful account of recursive truth conditions. The proof that there is an isomorphism between structures generated by intuitionistic models and Kripke models (Section 5.4) helps respond to those objections. A further constraint for successful truth conditions is defined (Section 5.5), and it is shown that intuitionistic models meet it. This supports the contention that intuitionistic models count as a legitimate account of connective meaning, and prepares the way for the results on natural semantics that are proven in later chapters.

5.1 Kripke semantics for intuitionistic logic

Kripke's semantics (1963) is a simplification of the topological semantics developed in the 1930s by Heyting and refined by Kreisel. The main idea is to define truth relative to the history of discovery of an idealized mathematician (or community of mathematicians). At each point in that history, a body of mathematical results has been developed. Since perfect memory of past results is presumed, that body of knowledge grows as time proceeds. At each stage in the history, the mathematician has choices concerning which topics should be investigated next. The collection of choices for future research can be modeled as a branching structure with forks representing the choice points.

This idea can be captured by introducing a *Kripke frame* $<W, \subseteq>$ (for a given propositional language L) consisting of a non-empty set W (containing the possible stages or worlds of the history) and a binary, reflexive, and transitive relation $\subseteq$ on W (for 'later than'). Let us assume that the language L contains any of the propositional connectives &, $\perp$, $\rightarrow$, $\leftrightarrow$, $\vee$, and ~, with the standard formation rules. Then an *assignment function* u for a language L is introduced which assigns to each propositional variable p of L, and each world w in W a truth-value subject to the condition ($\subseteq$) that when w' is later than w, all propositional variables assigned true in w by u, are still true in w'.

($\subseteq$) If $w \subseteq w'$ and u(w, p)=t then u(w', p)=t.

A Kripke model U=$<W, \subseteq, u>$ for L consists of a frame $<W, \subseteq>$ along with its assignment function u for L. The relation $\vDash^U$ is then defined to provide a recursive definition of truth for complex formulas of L on a Kripke model U=$<W, \subseteq, u>$. Here 'w $\vDash^U$ A' indicates that A is true at world w in W on U, and 'w $\nvDash^U$ A' indicates that it is false. (We suppress the superscript 'U' where it can be recovered from the context, and we assume that w ranges over arbitrarily chosen members of W.)

(Kp) $w \vDash p$ iff u(w, p)=t, for propositional variables p.

(K$\perp$) $w \nvDash \perp$.

(K&) $w \vDash A\&B$ iff $w \vDash A$ and $w \vDash B$.

(K$\rightarrow$) $w \vDash A\rightarrow B$ iff for every w' in W, if $w \subseteq w'$, then $w' \nvDash A$ or $w' \vDash B$.

(K$\leftrightarrow$) $w \vDash A\leftrightarrow B$ iff for every w' in W, if $w \subseteq w'$, then $w' \vDash A$ iff $w' \vDash B$.

(K$\vee$) $w \vDash A\vee B$ iff $w \vDash A$ or $w \vDash B$.

(K¬) $w \vDash {\sim} A$ iff for every w' in W, if $w \subseteq w'$, then $w' \nvDash A$.

Conditions (K&) and (K$\vee$) are the standard classical ones. The idea behind the condition (K$\rightarrow$) for $\rightarrow$ is that to verify A$\rightarrow$B at stage w one needs to know not only that A$\rightarrow$B meets the classical truth condition at w, but that A$\rightarrow$B meets it in all lines of research in the future of w. In the same way, (K¬) has it that for the truth of ~A at w, it is required that A is false at w and remains false in the entire future of w. The relation $\vDash^U$ is also called forcing. This idea has been central in the study of models for set theory. More details on forcing appear in Section 5.6 below.

Notions of satisfaction, counterexample, and validity for Kripke models can be defined in the usual way, as follows. For convenience, we will use the notion 'w ⊨ H' for sets of wffs H, so that w ⊨ H iff w ⊨ A for every wff A in H. <W, ⊆, u> *satisfies wff* A iff for some w in W, w ⊨ A. <W, ⊆, u> *satisfies set* of wffs H iff for some w in W, w ⊨ H. Argument H / C has a *K-counterexample* (abbreviated H ⊭$_K$ C) iff there is a Kripke model <W, ⊆, u> (for a language containing at least the symbols of H / C) and member w of W, such that w ⊨ H and w ⊭ C. Argument H / C is *K-valid* (abbreviated H ⊨$_K$ A) iff H / C has no K-counterexample.

It is not necessary to include ↔ and ~ in the language because these connectives can be defined in a standard way as follows.

$$A \leftrightarrow B =_{df} (A \rightarrow B) \& (B \rightarrow A)$$
$$\sim A =_{df} A \rightarrow \bot$$

It is a simple exercise to verify that the truth conditions (K¬) and (K↔) follow from these definitions along with (K⊥), (K&), and (K→). (See the ~ Definition Theorem of Section 6.4 and the ↔ Definition Theorem of Section 6.3.) Later on, we will explore systems where ↔ (Section 6.3) and ~ (Chapter 8) are primitive symbols of the language, but it will not matter for the present purposes whether ↔ and ~ are defined or primitive.

5.2 Intuitionistic models

The next project will be to show how conditions on sets of valuations can mimic the truth conditions for Kripke models. Let V be a set of valuations over all the wffs of a language L for propositional logic. A V-frame <V, <> consists of a set of valuations V and a binary relation ≤ on V called the *extension relation*, which is intended to mimic the relation ⊆ of a Kripke model. Now intuitionistic truth conditions for the logical symbols may be defined for the structure <V, ≤> as follows.

||⊥|| v(⊥)=f.

||&|| v(A&B)=t   iff v(A)=t and v(B)=t.

$\|\rightarrow\|$ $v(A\rightarrow B)=t$ iff for all v' in V, if $v\leq v'$, then v'(A)=f or v'(B)=t.

$\|\leftrightarrow\|$ $v(A\leftrightarrow B)=t$ iff for all v' in V, if $v\leq v'$, then v'(A)=v'(B).

$\|C\vee\|$ $v(A\vee B)$ iff v(A)=t or v(B)=t.

$\|\neg\|$ $v(\sim A)=t$ iff for all v' in V, if $v\leq v'$, then v'(A)=f.

As you can see, these conditions are simply their Kripke model versions written in the notation of V and $\leq$. Now consider any language L that has as its connectives one or more of these: &, $\bot$, $\rightarrow$, $\leftrightarrow$, $\vee$, and $\sim$. Let $\|KI\|$ be the conjunction of whichever of the above conditions govern the connectives of L. A V-frame for L that satisfies the clauses of $\|KI\|$ for the connectives of L is called an intuitionistic frame.

(Intuitionistic Frame) $<V, \leq>$ is an *intuitionistic frame* for language L iff $<V, \leq>$ is a frame for L that satisfies the clauses of $\|KI\|$ for the connectives of L.

So far we have said nothing about the extension relation $\leq$. However, when $\leq$ obeys $\|\leq\|$, $\leq$ is defined by V alone. (Again v and v', are arbitrary members of V.)

$\|\leq\|$ $v\leq v'$ iff for all wffs A of L, if v(A)=t then v'(A)=t.

When we say that V (alone) obeys $\|KI\|$ (or any other set of conditions $\|S\|$ for the connectives), we mean that $<V, \leq>$ obeys $\|KI\|$ where $\leq$ is defined by $\|\leq\|$.

(V obeys $\|S\|$)   *V obeys* $\|S\|$ iff $\leq$ obeys $\|\leq\|$ and $<V, \leq>$ obeys $\|S\|$.

With the exception of $\|C\vee\|$, the classical condition for $\vee$, it is possible to show that the set of natural deduction rules for each connective expresses the corresponding truth condition from the above list, presuming that $\|\leq\|$ holds. (See Chapters 6 and 8.) So in languages without $\vee$, models of the natural deduction rules are intuitionistic. However, this is not quite the same as proving that those rules express Kripke semantics. A Kripke model $<W, \subseteq, u>$ has considerably more structure than does a model V, for it consists of a set of possible worlds W, a binary relation $\subseteq$ over W, and an assignment function u. While this kind of structure is not explicitly generated by conditions on sets of valuations V, those conditions do at least guarantee that the structure $<V, \leq>$ implicit in V, with $\leq$ defined by $\|\leq\|$, is isomorphic to a corresponding Kripke model $<W, \subseteq, u>$, in a sense to be defined in the next section. This is the most we could expect by way of showing a connection between conditions on sets of valuations expressed by systems of rules and Kripke semantics. Proving that any model of a system of natural deduction rules generates a structure isomorphic to a Kripke semantics will help establish that that system expresses intuitionistic semantics.

5.3 Complaints against intuitionistic models

The isomorphism results to be shown in the next section are important because they can be used to head off complaints about the conditions used in intuitionistic models. Given reasonable scruples concerning the standards for defining truth conditions, one might argue that the conditions $\|\rightarrow\|$, $\|\leftrightarrow\|$, and $\|\neg\|$, which are the ones that mention $\leq$, do not really count as properly constructed given that $\leq$ is defined by $\|\leq\|$. For example, an intuitionist who requires that definitions be constructive will complain that $\|\rightarrow\|$ is impredicative, and so is not a well-formed definition of anything. In the course of trying to calculate the truth-value of A→B at v, one will need to know which are the valuations v′ such that v≤v′. But according to $\|\leq\|$, that will depend on whether every wff assigned t at v is also assigned t at v′. To know this, one needs to already have in place the values of all the wffs on all the valuations in V, and that would include already knowing the value of A→B at v. Therefore $\|KI\|$ does not really qualify as a semantics for a language. Call this the *circularity objection*.

Those who take a more liberal attitude may not be worried by the circularity objection. If one is already "given" a model V, each member v of V must assign a value to each wff. So the frame <V, ≤> will already be given by the nature of the valuations themselves, and given that frame, $\|\rightarrow\|$ corresponds to a condition that explains the truth behavior of the wffs.

On the other hand, most people have higher standards for what counts as a truth condition for a connective. They will object that truth conditions have not been established unless one is given a recursive recipe that allows one to calculate the truth-value of each wff given only the truth-values assigned to the propositional variables by the various valuations. A direct response to this objection is to show that $\|KI\|$, for all the complaints one might have about its circularity, is still a viable recursive definition of truth because any model V that obeys $\|KI\|$ sets up a structure isomorphic to a Kripke model, where circularity objections do not arise. The next section is devoted to showing how this is done.

There is a second worry with $\|{\rightarrow}\|$ that prompts interest in the isomorphism results. Ordinarily, we expect the truth conditions for a complex wff to depend only on the values of its subformulas across the valuations in a model. However, according to $\|{\rightarrow}\|$, the value of $v(A{\rightarrow}B)$ depends on which valuations bear the relation $\leq$, and this in turn may depend on the values of wffs that are not subformulas of $A{\rightarrow}B$. So the value of $A{\rightarrow}B$ is not local to its subformulas, and a form of compositionality appears to be violated. Call this the *non-locality objection*. The coming isomorphism result responds to both the circularity and locality objections.

5.4 The Isomorphism Theorem

Let L be a language that contains one or more of the symbols: $\&$, $\bot$, $\rightarrow$, $\leftrightarrow$, $\vee$, and $\sim$. Let us define the relevant notion of an isomorphism between frames $<V, \leq>$ for L and Kripke models for the same language.

> (Isomorphic) $<V, \leq>$ is *isomorphic* to Kripke model $<W, \subseteq, u>$ iff there is a 1–1 mapping $*$ from V into W such that $(\leq\subseteq)$ and (vu) hold.
>
> $(\leq\subseteq)$ $v\leq v'$ iff $v^*\subseteq v'^*$
>
> (vu) $v(A)=t$ iff $v^* \models^U A$

Strictly speaking, this definition does not define an isomorphism, because frames $<V, \leq>$ and Kripke models $<W, \subseteq, u>$ are structures of different types. Furthermore, the definition makes mention of $\models^U$, which is not really part of a Kripke model itself. Therefore the mapping does not actually go between two kinds of models. Our concern, however, is to show a correspondence between two models *along with their truth conditions*, and so the isomorphism as defined must take $\models^U$ into consideration, not just u. To clarify the situation, the reader may take it that the isomorphism in question is actually being defined between a Kripke structure $<W, \subseteq, \models^U>$, and an intuitionistic model structure $<V, \subseteq, \models^V>$, where $<V, \leq>$ is an intuitionistic frame, and the truth relation $\models^V$ is defined by $v\models^V A$ iff $v(A)=t$, for all v in V. Then (vu) above would be modified to read: $v \models^V A$ iff $v^* \models^U A$. For ease of exposition, however, we will leave the definition of an isomorphism as it stands, here and in the future.

Let $\|KI\|$ be the conjunction of whichever semantical conditions $\|\bot\|$, $\|\&\|$, $\|\rightarrow\|$, $\|\leftrightarrow\|$, $\|C\lor\|$, and $\|\neg\|$ govern the logical symbols of L. Remember that when we say that V obeys $\|KI\|$, it is understood that the relation $\leq$ mentioned in those conditions is defined by $\|\leq\|$.

$\|\leq\|$ $v \leq v'$ iff for all wffs A of L, if $v(A)$=t, then $v'(A)$=t.

The next project will be to show that V obeys $\|KI\|$ iff $<V, \leq>$ is isomorphic to a Kripke model. However, first we will need a lemma that reminds one of so-called persistence results for Kripke semantics. (See van Dalen (1986, 3.4 Lemma, p. 250).) Consider the condition $\|p\leq\|$ that defines $\leq$ via behavior of the propositional variables.

$\|p\leq\|$ $v \leq v'$ iff for all propositional variables p, if $v(p)$=t then $v'(p)$=t.

Then the lemma shows that given $\|KI\|$, the choice between $\|p\leq\|$ and $\|\leq\|$ makes no difference.

$\leq$ **Lemma.** If $<V, \leq>$ obeys $\|KI\|$, then it obeys $\|p\leq\|$ iff it obeys $\|\leq\|$.

Proof. Assume V obeys $\|KI\|$. To show $\|p\leq\|$ iff $\|\leq\|$, demonstrate the equivalence of their right-hand sides (p) and (A).

(A) For all wffs A, if $v(A)$=t then $v'(A)$=t.

(p) For all propositional variables p, if $v(p)$=t then $v'(p)$=t.

(A) entails (p) trivially, so what remains is to show that (p) entails (A). So assume (p) and demonstrate (A) by mathematical induction on the length of A. For the base case, when A is $\bot$ or a propositional variable p, is trivial. The inductive cases follow.

A has the form B&C. Assume $v(B\&C)$=t. From $\|\&\|$, it follows that $v(B)$=t and $v(C)$=t. By the inductive hypothesis, $v'(B)$=t and $v'(C)$=t, and so $v'(B\&C)$=t by $\|\&\|$.

A has the form B∨C. The proof is similar to the previous case.

A has the form B→C. Assume $v(B\rightarrow C)$=t, and establish $v'(B\rightarrow C)$=t using $\|\rightarrow\|$. Assume that v'' is an arbitrary member of V such that $v' \leq v''$ and show that $v''(B)$=f or $v''(C)$=t as follows. From $v \leq v'$, $v' \leq v''$ and the transitivity of $\leq$, it follows that $v \leq v''$. Given $v(B\rightarrow C)$=t, it follows by $\|\rightarrow\|$ that either $v''(B)$=f or $v''(C)$=t as desired.

A has the form B↔C or ~B. The proofs are similar to the previous case. $\square$

Now we are ready to prove the isomorphism theorem.

Isomorphism Theorem. V obeys $\|KI\|$ iff $<V, \leq>$ is isomorphic to some Kripke model.

Proof. (Left to Right). Assume V obeys $\|KI\|$, which means that $\leq$ is defined by $\|\leq\|$. Show $<V, \leq>$ is isomorphic to a Kripke model as follows. $<V, \leq>$ is a Kripke frame, for $\leq$ is reflexive and transitive. Define u so that $u(v, p)=v(p)$. In light of $\|\leq\|$, u obeys $(\subseteq)$. Therefore model $U = <V, \leq, u>$ qualifies as a Kripke model. Show that $<V, \leq>$ is isomorphic to $U = <V, \leq, u>$, by letting $*$ be the identity mapping. Prove $v(A)=t$ iff $v \vDash^{U} A$ by induction on the length of A. The base case is trivial, and the inductive cases are also easy given the relation $\subseteq$ of U is identical to $\leq$.

Proof. (Right to Left). Assume $<V, \leq>$ is isomorphic to a Kripke model $<W, \subseteq, u>$, and show V obeys $\|KI\|$ as follows. There is a 1–1 mapping $*$ from V into W such that $v \leq v'$ iff $v^* \subseteq v'^*$, and $v(A)=t$ iff $v^* \vDash A$. Given $(\subseteq)$, it follows that $<V, \leq>$ obeys $\|p \leq\|$, and by the $\leq$ Lemma, it follows that $<V, \leq>$ obeys $\|\leq\|$. To show V obeys $\|KI\|$, we demonstrate each of the truth conditions of $\|KI\|$ as follows. Let w be any member of W. Since $*$ is 1–1 there is a unique member v of V such that $w=v^*$. Now let us consider the cases one by one.

$\|\bot\|$. From $(K\bot)$ we have $v^* \nvDash \bot$, and so $v(\bot)=f$, by $v(A)=t$ iff $v^* \vDash A$.

$\|\&\|$. From $\|\&\|$ we obtain:

$w \vDash A\&B$ iff $w \vDash A$ and $w \vDash B$.

But $v^*=w$ so:

$v^* \vDash A\&B$ iff $v^* \vDash A$ and $v^* \vDash B$.

But in light of $v(A)=t$ iff $v^* \vDash A$, this comes to $\|\&\|$ as desired.

$v(A\&B)=t$ iff $v(A)=t$ and $v(B)=t$.

$\|\rightarrow\|$. From $(K\rightarrow)$ we obtain:

$w \vDash A\rightarrow B$ iff for all w' in W, if $w \subseteq w'$, then $w' \nvDash A$ or $w' \vDash B$.

Since $w=v^*$ and $*$ is 1–1, it follows that:

$v^* \vDash A\rightarrow B$ iff for all v'^* in W, if $v^* \subseteq v'^*$, then $v'^* \nvDash A$ or $v'^* \vDash B$.

But in light of $v(A)=t$ iff $v^* \vDash A$, $v(B)=t$ iff $v^* \vDash B$, and $v \leq v'$ iff $v^* \subseteq v'^*$, we have $\|\rightarrow\|$ as desired.

$||\rightarrow||$ v(A→B)=t iff for each v′ in V, if v≤v′ then v′(A)=f or v′(B)=t.

The demonstrations for the remaining truth conditions follow exactly the same pattern.   □

While the last theorem shows that every set of valuations V that obeys ‖KI‖ is such that the frame <V, ≤> is isomorphic to *some* Kripke model, it must be admitted that it does not follow from this that every Kripke model is isomorphic to a set V that obeys ‖KI‖. So we have not shown that when V obeys ‖KI‖, every Kripke model is isomorphic to V. The reason is that there are Kripke models with "excessive" structure such that the condition that v≤v′ iff v*⊆v′* cannot be met. This occurs because the identity conditions for valuations require that v and v′ be identical provided that v and v′ assign the same values to all the formulas. However, worlds in Kripke models may be distinct even when they count as true exactly the same wffs, as the next theorem notes.

Theorem 5.4 There is a Kripke model <W, ⊆, u> which is not isomorphic to any model V obeying ‖KI‖.

Proof. Define a Kripke model <W, ⊆, u> with W={w, w′} such that u(w, p)= u(w′, p)=t for each propositional variable p and ⊆ is an equivalence relation on W. It is easy to see that w ⊨ A iff w′ ⊨ A, for each wff A. When one attempts to define a 1–1 mapping * from V into W, * must satisfy (vu): v(A)=t iff v* ⊨^{U} A. That means that if v*=w and v′*=w′, then v=v′, and so * is not 1–1.   □

This difference between Kripke models and the structures set up by intuitionistic models V reflects unavoidable differences in the way that worlds in Kripke models and valuations are individuated. Fortunately the difference will not affect any result needed in this book.

5.5 Intuitionistic models and functional semantics

The view of this book is that the isomorphism result of the previous section is sufficient for establishing that ‖KI‖ is a viable semantics. The following will make that position official. A formal definition of what counts as a *standard semantics* is not attempted here, but the idea is that it provides a definition of validity for sequents (or arguments) of the language, using the notion of a model (which includes an assignment of values to the non-logical vocabulary) and a recursive definition of truth on a model. So Kripke semantics clearly qualifies as a standard semantics. The next definition tells us which conditions on sets of valuations qualify as a semantics.

> (Semantics) Condition ∥S∥ on models is a *semantics* for S iff every model V obeying ∥S∥ is isomorphic to a model of a standard semantics (for a language defined over the connectives that occur in the rules of S).

Since models obeying ∥KI∥ are isomorphic to models of Kripke semantics, ∥KI∥ officially qualifies as a semantics.

Some readers will object that their conception of truth conditions requires that models be defined for valuations over the non-logical vocabulary, in our case the propositional variables, and that valuations over complex wffs should be determined from those recursively in a separate stage of the definition. Only when this is shown will the objectors feel that the circularity and non-locality objections have been fully addressed.

Unfortunately, there is no way for sets of rules to express a semantics that separates truth evaluation in two stages in this way. However, the isomorphism result for ∥KI∥ can still be deployed to help show that were we to decide to define a semantics in two stages, the conditions ∥KI∥ would be sufficient to fix unique values for all the formulas. That result should motivate the view that a set of conditions C on models counts as correctly defined provided we can show that every model V obeying C is isomorphic to a semantics that clearly provides a standard two-stage account of truth for the formulas.

Our idea is to show directly that ∥KI∥ behaves as a recursive definition of truth ought to do, namely to provide a unique account of the truth-values of the complex formulas given an assignment of values to the propositional variables. Consider sets W of *atomic valuations*, that is, valuations over propositional variables only. Given such a set of valuations W, it will be shown that there is a unique model obeying ∥KI∥ that extends W to the complex wffs.

We need to develop a few definitions. Let an *atomic model* W for L be a set of *atomic valuations*, that is, valuations over *propositional variables of L only*. A model V (for language L) counts as an *extension* of W when it agrees with the values for the propositional variables and extends values to all the wffs of L in some way. More technically, a model V is an *extension* of W iff there is a

1–1 function from W into V such that for each member w of W, there is a unique member v_w of V such that $w(p) = v_w(p)$, for all propositional variables p. The project is to show that each atomic model W has a unique extension obeying ‖KI‖. This property is important enough to give a name.

(Functional) Condition ‖S‖ is *functional* for L iff for each atomic model W for L, there exists one and only one extension of W obeying ‖S‖.

Surely a functional condition qualifies as a properly defined recursive account of the truth conditions for a system's connectives. So we can certify ‖KI‖ provides a recursive set of truth conditions by showing it is functional.

‖KI‖ Theorem. ‖KI‖ is functional.

Proof. To show that ‖KI‖ is functional, assume that W is any set of atomic valuations, and show that there is exactly one model V obeying ‖KI‖ that extends W. Given any choice of W, define the Kripke model $<W, \leq, u>$ so that $\leq$ obeys the analog of ‖p≤‖, that is, for any members w and w' of W, $w \leq w'$ iff if $w(p)=t$, then $w'(p)=t$. Let u be defined by $u(w, p)=w(p)$. Now consider the truth relation ⊨ defined for this Kripke model by clauses (Kp), (K⊥), (K&), (K→), (K↔), (K∨), and (K¬) of Section 5.1. To define a model V obeying ‖KI‖, let ^ be the function that takes each atomic valuation w in W to w^, the valuation over wffs defined by $w^\wedge(A)=t$ iff $w \models A$. Let V be the set of all w^ for each w in W. Note that $w^\wedge(p)=t$ iff $w \models p$ iff $u(w, p)=t$ iff $w(p)=t$. So $w^\wedge(p)=w(p)$, and V is an extension of W. Therefore $w \leq w'$ iff $w^\wedge \leq w'^\wedge$. Since ^ is clearly 1–1, $<V, \leq>$ is isomorphic to the Kripke model $<W, \leq, u>$. By the Isomorphism Theorem of Section 5.4, V obeys ‖KI‖.

   To show that V is the only extension of W, consider the possibility that there are two models V and Y that are extensions of W and obey ‖KI‖. Since V is an extension of W, there is a 1–1 function that maps each member w of W into a unique member v_w of V such that $v_w(p) = w(p)$ for all propositional variables p. Similarly for Y, each member of w is mapped to a unique member y_w such that $y_w(p) = w(p)$. So we may assume that $V = \{v_w: w \in W\}$ and $Y = \{y_w: w \in W\}$. We prove by structural induction on the wffs that $v_{w^*}(A) = y_{w^*}(A)$ for any w^* in W, for every wff A. When that proof is complete, it will follow that $v_{w^*}=y_{w^*}$ for each w^* in W, with the result that V=Y as desired. The base case of the induction is easy because $v_w(p) = w(p) = y_w(p)$. This entails that for any w, w' in W, $v_w \leq v_{w'}$ iff $y_w \leq y_{w'}$. So the inductive cases are straightforward, as is illustrated in the case for →. Given the hypothesis of the induction, we have $v_{w^*}(A) = y_{w^*}(A)$ and $v_{w^*}(B) = y_{w^*}(B)$ for all w^* in W. The task is to show $v_w(A{\rightarrow}B) = y_w(A{\rightarrow}B)$ for a given w in W as follows. Since V and Y obey ‖KI‖, we have by ‖$\rightarrow$‖ and V={v_w: $w \in$ W} and Y={y_w: $w \in$ W} the following two conditions for $\rightarrow$.

$v_w(A{\rightarrow}B)$=t iff for all $w' {\in} W$, if $v_w {\leq} v_{w'}$, then $v_{w'}(A)$=f or $v_{w'}(B)$=t.

and

$y_w(A{\rightarrow}B)$=t iff for all $w' {\in} W$, if $y_w {\leq} y_{w'}$, then $y_{w'}(A)$=f or $y_{w'}(B)$=t.

But in light of $v_w {\leq} v_{w'}$ iff $y_w {\leq} y_{w'}$, and the hypothesis of the induction, the right-hand sides of the above two truth conditions are equivalent, and hence $v_w(A{\rightarrow}B)$=t iff $y_w(A{\rightarrow}B)$=t, as desired. The cases for the other connectives are similar.   □

The last theorem demonstrates that intuitionistic models meet all the conditions we could hope for in providing a recursive set of truth conditions for the connectives. Note that the proof depended on the $\leq$ Lemma, for we had to appeal to the Isomorphism Theorem, which depends on that result. This point will be important when we turn to problems raised by disjunction, where the $\leq$ Lemma fails. (See Theorem 7.3.2 and Section 7.6.) There we will be unable to show that the condition expressed by the disjunction rules is functional.

Now that we have established that ‖KI‖ qualifies as a functional set of semantical truth conditions, we may turn to the task of showing that the intuitionistic conditions found in ‖KI‖ (or their variants in the case of disjunction) are expressed by the ND rules. This in turn will allow us to identify the natural semantics for various collections of PL rules. That project is taken up in Chapters 6, 7, and 8.

5.6 Forcing and intuitionistic models of set theory (an aside)

The truth relation in Kripke semantics for intuitionistic logic is the inspiration for forcing – a set of powerful techniques in mathematics that have been useful, most notably, for providing independence results for postulates of set theory. The concept of forcing has been exploited to create models for set theory where certain sentences are satisfied, thus showing that they are consistent with the rest of set theory. When consistency holds for both sentence S and its negation ~S, we know that S is independent from the other principles, that is, neither S nor ~S is provable from them. The most celebrated use of forcing is Cohen's proof of the independence of the Continuum Hypothesis.

The Continuum Hypothesis concerns Cantor's famous demonstration that some infinite sets are larger than others, and there is, in fact, a hierarchy $\omega_0, \omega_1, \omega_2, \ldots$ of the sizes (or cardinalities) of infinite sets, where ω_0 is the size of the set of all integers N. Cantor showed, for example, that the power set P(N) of the set of integers N is larger than N. A natural question to ask is whether there is any infinite set whose size falls between the size of N and P(N), or is the size of P(N) the next size in the sequence. The Continuum Hypothesis states that there is no intervening infinite cardinality. Cohen's result that this hypothesis is independent from set theory is quite disturbing. Given the commonly accepted principles of set theory, this intuitively substantive question about sets simply has no answer. The successful use of forcing to obtain this spectacular conclusion has sparked its widespread and fruitful deployment ever since.

Smullyan and Fitting (1996, p. 189) admit that it is hard to say exactly what forcing is, as there are many variations on the theme, and the relationships one to another are not immediately transparent. However, a common thread is a connection with the intuitionistic truth conditions presented in Section 5.1 of this chapter. Fitting (1969) makes the connection between Cohen's result and that semantics quite explicit, while Smullyan and Fitting (1996) take a syntactic turn, using transformations to sentences of a modal logic with the strength of S4.

Whatever viewpoint one takes on forcing, there is a moral to be drawn from the study of natural semantics. The fundamental idea that Cohen employed was to find intuitionistic models that satisfied the axioms of set theory along with the negation of the Continuum Hypothesis. Those so-called "non-standard" models are the close cousins of the natural semantics expressed by the rules of predicate logic – the foundation on which set theory rests. I say 'close cousins' because the intuitionistic interpretation at the core of Cohen's method takes a somewhat stronger treatment of disjunction and the quantifiers than the natural semantics provides. (See Chapters 7 and 14.) Still, the message for those who think of forcing as a novelty is that the concept is actually built right into the very foundation of predicate logic, for it is a variant of the interpretation expressed by its rules.

Alpha Centaurian anthropologists are puzzled that we think of forcing as a discovery. They know it was under our noses all along, for it is what predicate logic really means. Now that we appreciate the point as well, it is worth asking whether the additional flexibility found in natural semantics' weaker treatment of disjunction and quantification might also one day find a use.

6 Conditionals

The last chapter has paved the way for showing that natural deduction systems for propositional logics express intuitionistic semantics. It is now time to lay out the results connective by connective. We already proved that the natural semantics for S& and S⊥ is classical (Sections 4.1 and 4.2); but intuitionistic semantics agrees with these interpretations of & and ⊥. So it is time to turn to cases where classical and intuitionistic readings differ. We begin with the rules for the conditional → and the biconditional ↔. It is shown that the natural deduction rules S→ for → express the corresponding intuitionistic truth condition ‖→‖ (Section 6.1). So alien anthropologists who learn that S→ describes our deductive behavior must conclude that we assign → the intuitionistic reading (whether we know it or not). In fairness to those who claim that our interpretation of → must be classical, systems that strengthen S→ with Peirce's Law are then considered (Section 6.2). However, the result of that investigation will be to show that those stronger systems express conditions that are neither classical nor appropriate for defining connective truth conditions. Section 6.3 deals with ↔, and 6.4 provides a summary. These results will supply the basic understanding necessary for handling disjunction (Chapter 7) and negation (Chapter 8) where the situation is more complicated.

6.1 Intuitionistic truth conditions for the conditional

We know from Theorem 4.4.1 that the system S→ of natural deduction rules for → does not express the classical truth conditions for →

S→:   (→ Introduction)   (→ Elimination)

$$\frac{H, A \vdash B}{H \vdash A {\rightarrow} B} \qquad \frac{H \vdash A \qquad H \vdash A {\rightarrow} B}{H \vdash B}$$

The requirement that V be a model for S→ does entail that members of V obey the first three rows of the material implication table, but it does not rule out the possibility that V contains valuations that assign A, B, and A→B the value f. The failure of S→ to express classical truth conditions was predictable. As is well known (see Theorem 6.2.1 below), (Peirce's Law): ((A→B)→A)→A cannot be proven from S→ alone.

(Peirce's Law) ((A→B)→A)→A

Although it is possible to prove Peirce's Law in PL, that proof makes essential use of the classical rules for negation, which are missing from S→. Therefore the provability valuation $v_⊢$ for S must assign f to ((p→q)→p)→p, and so the canonical model [S] for S is a non-classical model of S.

Nevertheless S→ does have a natural semantics, namely the intuitionistic truth condition $\|→\|$, where the relation ≤ is defined by $\|≤\|$.

$\|→\|$ v(A→B)=t iff for all v' in V, if v≤v', then either v'(A)=f or v'(B)=t.

$\|≤\|$ v≤v' iff for all wffs A, if v(A)=t, then v'(A)=t.

The next project will be to establish that $\|→\|$ is a natural semantics for S→. Two things must be shown. First, we must verify that $\|→\|$ is a semantics for →; but this follows from the $\|KI\|$ Theorem of Section 5.5, in the special case where L is a language with → as its only connective. Second, it must be shown that S→ (globally) expresses $\|→\|$, that is, that V is a model of S→ iff V obeys $\|→\|$.

S→ Expression Theorem. S→ expresses $\|→\|$.

Proof. It is sufficient to show for any model V for L that V is a model of S→ iff V obeys $\|→\|$.

For the proof that S→ is sound for $\|→\|$ (the proof from right to left), assume V obeys $\|→\|$. To show that V is a model of S→, we must show that (→ Introduction) and (→ Elimination) preserve V-validity as follows.

(→ Introduction). Assume H, A ⊨$_V$ B and show H ⊨$_V$ A→B by reductio. From H ⊭$_V$ A→B it follows that for some v in V, v(H)=t and v(A→B)=f. This with $\|→\|$ entails that for some v' in V, v≤v', v'(A)=t and v'(B)=f. From v(H)=t and v≤v', it follows by $\|≤\|$ that v'(H)=t. So given H, A ⊨$_V$ B, it follows immediately that v'(B)=t, which contradicts v'(B)=f.

($\rightarrow$ Elimination) Assume $H \vDash_V A$ and $H \vDash_V A \rightarrow B$ and show $H \vDash_V B$, by assuming for an arbitrary member v of V that v(H)=t and proving v(B)=t as follows. From $H \vDash_V A$ and $H \vDash_V A \rightarrow B$ we have that v(A)=t and v(A→B)=t. By $\|\rightarrow\|$ and the reflexivity of $\leq$, v(A)=f or v(B)=t. From v(A)=t, we have v(B)=t as desired.

For the proof that S→ forces $\|\rightarrow\|$ (the proof from left to right), assume the rules of S→ preserve V-validity and show that V obeys $\|\rightarrow\|$. For the proof of $\|\rightarrow\|$ left to right, assume v(A→B)=t and v≤v', and show that v'(A)=f or v'(B)=t by assuming v'(A)=t and proving v'(B)=t as follows. We know that (→ Elimination) preserves V-validity. Choosing H = A, A→B in the premises of that rule, and noting that A, A→B / A and A, A→B / A→B are clearly V-valid, we establish that A, A→B / B is V-valid. In light of v≤v' and v(A→B)=t, we have v'(A→B)=t and so v'(A, A→B)=t. By the V-validity of A, A→B / B, it follows immediately that v'(B)=t.

For the proof of $\|\rightarrow\|$ from right to left, assume v(A→B)=f and prove that there is a member v' of V such that v≤v', v'(A)=t and v'(B)=f. Let H_v be the set of all wffs assigned t by v. From the contrapositive of the statement that (→ Introduction) preserves V-validity, we obtain:

If $v(H_v)$=t and v(A→B)=f,
then for some v' in V, $v'(H_v, A)$=t and v'(B)=f.

The antecedent of this conditional holds, and so it follows that for some v' in V:

$v'(H_v, A)$=t and v'(B)=f.

But $v'(H_v)$=t insures v≤v', hence v' is the desired valuation such that v≤v', v'(A)=t, and v'(B)=f.   □

The S→ Expression Theorem is significant, because the fact that S→ expresses $\|\rightarrow\|$ entails that $\|\rightarrow\|$ is the weakest possible condition consistent with the requirement that S→ preserves validity. Although stronger readings of → are consistent with S→, for example the classical one, they do not conform to what is actually expressed by S→. Such stronger interpretations are dangerous because completeness may fail in languages where differences between stronger and natural interpretations affect the definition of validity. For example, because Peirce's Law cannot be proven in S→, S→ is incomplete for classical semantics. Therefore, a model-theoretic inferentialist cannot accept any readings for → other than $\|\rightarrow\|$.

Given the S→ Expression Theorem, it follows immediately from the ∥KI∥ Theorem that ∥→∥ is the natural semantics for S→.

S→ Theorem. ∥→∥ is a natural semantics for S→.

6.2 Peirce's Law and Peirce's Rule

The S→ Theorem is useful. For one thing, it provides a quick way to show that Peirce's Law is not provable in S→.

Theorem 6.2.1 $\nvdash_{S\to} ((p{\to}q){\to}p){\to}p$.

Proof. Simply construct a set of valuations V* that obeys ∥→∥ and invalidates $((p{\to}q){\to}p){\to}p$ as follows. Let W be the atomic model {w, w'}, and let w(q) =w'(q)=f and w(p)=f and w'(p)=t. The ∥KI∥ Theorem of Section 5.5 assures us that there is an extension V*={v, v'} of W with v(q)=v'(q)=f and v(p)=f and v'(p)=t that obeys ∥→∥ and ∥≤∥. It follows by the S→ Theorem of the previous section that the rules of S→ preserve V*-validity, and hence that any theorem of S→ is V*-valid. But $((p{\to}q){\to}p){\to}p$ is V*-invalid by the following reasoning. From ∥≤∥ and the ≤ Lemma of Section 5.4, ≤ obeys ∥p≤∥, so by inspection of V* we have v≤v'. Since v'(p)=t and v'(q)=f, and v'≤v', and v≤v', it follows that v'(p→q)=v(p→q)=f. Therefore v'(p→q)=f for every v' such that v≤v', and by ∥→∥, v((p→q)→p)=t. But v(p)=f and v≤v, so by ∥→∥ again, v(((p→q)→p)→p)=f as desired. □

One might wonder whether adding Peirce's Law as an axiom to S∼ might create a system that expresses the standard material implication truth condition ∥C→∥ for →.

∥C→∥ v(A→B)=t iff v(A)=f or v(B)=t.

However, Theorem 4.4.1 reports that even all of PL does not express ∥C→∥, so there is a non-classical interpretation for → even in systems where all the classical principles for → are provable.

We know from previous experience with what S→ expresses that natural deduction rules have stronger expressive powers than do axioms. Perhaps the situation might change were we to add to S→ the following natural deduction rule (PR) (for Peirce's Rule) that captures the spirit of Peirce's Law:

(PR)

H, A→B ⊢ A
―――――――
H ⊢ A

Could this rule do what the axiom did not? The answer is that (PR) does no better at fixing the classical interpretation. Peirce's Rule does force an additional condition on models V, but this condition does not entail that valuations in V are classical. The next theorem shows that (PR) expresses the following condition ‖PR‖.

‖PR‖ If v(A)=f, then for each wff B, there is a v′ in V, such that v≤v′, v′(A)=f and v′(A→B)=t.

‖PR‖ entails that when a valuation is non-classical by assigning v(A)=v(B) =v(A→B)=f, then for each consequent B, the value of A→B is "corrected" to t in some extension of v, thereby meeting the material implication truth table. This condition does not entail that there is an extension of v where all the conditionals of the form A→B behave classically, but only that for each formula B, there is an extension where *that* formula behaves. The next theorem shows that ‖PR‖ is exactly what (PR) expresses.

Theorem 6.2.2 (PR) expresses ‖PR‖.

Proof. We must demonstrate that V is a model of (PR) iff V obeys ‖PR‖.

For the proof from right to left (that (PR) is sound for ‖PR‖) assume that V obeys ‖≤‖ and ‖PR‖, and show that (PR) preserves V-validity, by assuming H, A→B ⊨$_V$ A and showing H ⊨$_V$ A by reductio. So assume that H ⊭$_V$ A. Then for some v∈V, v(H)=t and v(A)=f. By ‖PR‖, it follows that for some member v′ of V, v≤v′, v′(A)=f, and v′(A→B)=t. By v(H)=t and ‖≤‖, we have v′(H)=t, and so by H, A→B ⊨$_V$ A, it follows that v′(A)=t which contradicts v′(A)=f.

For the proof from left to right (that (PR) forces ‖PR‖), assume that V is a model of (PR), and that v is any member of V such that v(A)=f for a given wff A. Let B be any wff, and show that there is a v′∈V such that v′(A)=f, and v′(A→B)=t as follows. Let H$_v$ = {A: v(A)=t}. Then H$_v$ ⊭$_V$ A. By the contrapositive of the statement that (PR) preserves V-validity one obtains: H$_v$, A→B ⊭$_V$ A. So for some v′∈V, v′(H$_v$)=t, v′(A)=f and v′(A→B)=t. Since v′(H$_v$)=t, we have v≤v′, and so v′ is the desired valuation.   □

It was claimed that the system S→PR that results from adding (PR) to S→ does not force the classical interpretation of →. The last theorem is helpful in this regard, since it may be used to show that the canonical model [S→PR] for S→PR obeys ‖S→PR‖, the conjunction of ‖→‖ with ‖PR‖ (what (PR) expresses) but contains a valuation that violates the material implication truth table.

Theorem 6.2.3 There are non-classical models that obey ‖S→PR‖.

Proof. By Theorem 4.3, [S→PR] is a model of S→PR and $v_\vdash$ is a member of [S→PR], where $v_\vdash$ is defined by $v_\vdash(A)$=t iff $\vdash_{S\to PR}$ A. Theorem 6.2.2 with the S→ Theorem of Section 6.1 shows that any model of S→PR meets the condition ‖S→PR‖, so [S→PR] obeys it as well. Show that $v_\vdash$ is non-classical by noting that none of p, q, nor p→q are classical tautologies, so $\nvdash_{S\to PR}$ p, $\nvdash_{S\to PR}$ q, and $\nvdash_{S\to PR}$ p→q, with the result that $v_\vdash(p)$=$v_\vdash(q)$= $v_\vdash(p\to q)$=f.   □

In languages that contain either ⊥ or ~ and in models that obey ‖⊥‖ or ‖¬‖ (the intuitionistic account of negation), ‖PR‖ can be recast in an equivalent form ‖LL′‖ that does not mention any connective.

‖LL′‖ If v(A)=f, then for some v′ in V, v≤v′ and for any v″ in V, if v′≤v″, then v″(A)=f.

‖LL′‖ says that once v(A)=f, there is an extension v′ of v where A is "determined" false, that is, where A is f in all further extensions of v′.

Theorem 6.2.4 If V obeys either ‖⊥‖ or ‖¬‖, then V obeys ‖PR‖ iff V obeys ‖LL′‖.

Proof. Suppose V obeys ‖⊥‖ or ‖¬‖. It must be shown that V obeys ‖PR‖ iff V obeys ‖LL′‖.

For the proof from left to right, assume V obeys ‖PR‖, and prove ‖LL′‖ as follows. Assume v(A)=f. From ‖PR‖, it follows that for any wff B, there is a member v′ of V such that v≤v′, v′(A)=f and v′(A→B)=t. In case V obeys ‖⊥‖, let B be ⊥, and note that v′(A→⊥)=t together with ‖→‖ entails that A is f in every extension of v′. Hence ‖LL′‖ holds. In case V obeys ‖¬‖, let B be ~A, and note that v′(A→~A)=t together with ‖→‖ and ‖¬‖ entails that v″(A)=f for every extension v″ of v′ as well.

For the proof from right to left, assume that V obeys ‖LL′‖, and show ‖PR‖ by assuming that v(A)=f, and that B is any wff, and finding an extension of v where A is f and A→B is t. From v(A)=f and ‖LL′‖ we have that there is an extension v' of v where for all v" such that v'≤v", v"(A)=f. By v'≤v', v'(A)=f, and by ‖→‖, v'(A→B)=t, so v' is the desired extension of v.   □

Our interest in ‖LL'‖ is motivated by the role it plays in the discussion of classical negation. (See Section 8.5.) We learn there that ‖LL'‖ is exactly what is expressed by the intuitionistically unacceptable form of (Double Negation): ~~A / A. In that section, it will be argued that ‖LL'‖ "exceeds its authority" as a truth condition because it affects the readings of all the connectives that mention ≤ in their natural truth conditions. This is the explanation for why the classical rules for negation form a non-conservative extension of S→ by proving Peirce's Law. ‖LL'‖ affects the interpretation for → given by ‖→‖ by adding further constraints on the behavior of ≤ that validate all the classical theorems for → written with → only.

A similar interference occurs in the other direction. Suppose we have a language containing →, and a primitive negation symbol ¬. Consider the system S→PR¬, regulated by S→PR, the structural rules, and the *intuitionistic* rules S¬ for ¬.

S¬:   (¬ Introduction)   (Contradiction)

        H, A ⊢ B   H ⊢ B

        $\dfrac{\text{H, A} \vdash \neg \text{B}}{\text{H} \vdash \neg \text{A}}$ $\dfrac{\text{H} \vdash \neg \text{B}}{\text{H} \vdash \text{A}}$

Then the presence of (PR) in the system S→PR regulating → oversteps its bounds by creating a non-conservative extension of the system S¬. Even though the S→PR rules do not mention ¬, their presence converts the formerly intuitionistic ¬ into classical negation. The reason is that (Double Negation) is provable in S→PR¬. That result can be obtained from general considerations concerning natural semantics. In Section 12.1, it will be shown that systems of rules that express a condition are automatically complete for that condition. Since ‖LL'‖ with ‖¬‖ guarantees the V-validity of (Double Negation), any system (such as S→PR¬) that expresses those conditions will be able to prove (Double Negation). However, there is no need to appeal to that abstract reasoning, since it is easy enough to show (Double Negation) in S→PR¬ directly. Here is a sketch of the proof.

    1.   ¬¬A, ¬A ⊢ A   use (Contradiction)

    2.   ¬¬A, A→¬A, A ⊢ A   (Hypothesis)

3. $\neg\neg A, A \rightarrow \neg A, A \vdash \neg A$ use ($\rightarrow$ Elimination)
4. $\neg\neg A, A \rightarrow \neg A \vdash \neg A$ 2, 3 ($\neg$ Introduction)
5. $\neg\neg A, A \rightarrow \neg A \vdash \neg A \rightarrow A$ 1, ($\rightarrow$ Introduction) then (Weakening)
6. $\neg\neg A, A \rightarrow \neg A \vdash A$ 4, 5 ($\rightarrow$ Elimination)
7. $\neg\neg A \vdash A$ 6, (PR).

This violation of conservativity underscores a deep worry about classical connectives. Whether a system for classical negation or the classical conditional is chosen, the rules express conditions on models that violate the etiquette expected of a definition of meaning: that it should not be unacceptably creative. Establishing the interpretation of one connective using rules that mention that connective only should not undermine what other rules say about their connectives. The upshot of these considerations is that what (PR) expresses does not qualify as a legitimate contribution to a definition of the meaning of $\rightarrow$. (See Section 8.9 for further reflections on this matter.)

6.3 Intuitionistic natural semantics for equivalence

It is easy to establish that if $\leftrightarrow$ is defined in terms of $\rightarrow$ and & in the usual way by (Def$\leftrightarrow$), then S&$\rightarrow$ the system consisting of S& and S$\rightarrow$ expresses $\|\leftrightarrow\|$.

(Def$\leftrightarrow$) $A \leftrightarrow B =_{df} (A \rightarrow B)\&(B \rightarrow A)$

$\|\leftrightarrow\|$ $v(A \leftrightarrow B)=t$ iff for all v' in V, if $v \leq v'$ then $v'(A)=v'(B)$.

One simply uses the truth conditions for & and $\rightarrow$ to verify that $\|\leftrightarrow\|$ holds in any model that obeys $\|\&\|$ and $\|\rightarrow\|$, and the S& and S$\rightarrow$ Theorems do the rest.

$\leftrightarrow$ **Definition Theorem.** If V obeys $\|\&\|$ and $\|\rightarrow\|$, and $\leftrightarrow$ is defined by (Def$\leftrightarrow$) then V obeys $\|\leftrightarrow\|$.

However, it is also worth showing that a similar result can be obtained without taking a route through & and $\rightarrow$. Even when $\leftrightarrow$ is primitive, and one or more of the connectives & and $\rightarrow$ are missing, $\|\leftrightarrow\|$ is a natural semantics for S$\leftrightarrow$. Here are the rules of S$\leftrightarrow$.

S$\leftrightarrow$:	($\leftrightarrow$ Elimination)		($\leftrightarrow$ Introduction)
	$H \vdash A$	$H \vdash B$	$H, A \vdash B$
	$H \vdash A \leftrightarrow B$	$H \vdash A \leftrightarrow B$	$H, B \vdash A$
	$H \vdash B$	$H \vdash A$	$H \vdash A \leftrightarrow B$

The reader may easily verify the next theorem using the S→ Expression Theorem as a guide to the strategy.

S↔ Theorem. The natural semantics for S↔ is ‖↔‖.

6.4 Summary: natural semantics for intuitionistic logic

We will close this chapter by summarizing the results on natural semantics obtained so far, and extend them to systems that contain more than one connective. Let SI be the system for intuitionist logic that is defined over a language L that includes any of the symbols &, ⊥, →, ↔, ~ (but not ∨). The rules of SI are all rules in the natural deduction systems S&, S⊥, S→, and S↔ that govern the connectives of L. If ~ is present, SI introduces it by definition (Def~).

(Def~) ~A =_{df} A→⊥

It is easy to verify that (Def~) ensures that every model V that satisfies the truth conditions ‖⊥‖, and ‖→‖, must also satisfy ‖¬‖ as well.

‖¬‖ v(~A)=t iff for all v' in V, if v≤v', then v'(A)=f.

~ Definition Theorem. If V obeys ‖⊥‖ and ‖→‖ and ~ is defined by (Def~), then V obeys ‖¬‖.

Let the condition ‖SI‖ be the conjunction of whichever of these conditions govern the connectives of the language L: ‖&‖, ‖⊥‖, ‖→‖, ‖↔‖, and ‖¬‖. Note ‖SI‖ differs from ‖KI‖ in that it lacks the classical truth condition ‖C∨‖. In light of Theorem 4.4.1, it will not be possible to show that every model of SI obeys the classical condition ‖C∨‖ even if we were to add the rules S∨ to SI. However, we can prove a result for SI, where ∨ is not in L. By "pasting together" expression results gained so far, it is easy to show that SI has ‖SI‖ as its natural semantics.

SI Theorem. ‖SI‖ is a functional natural semantics for SI.

Proof. The ‖KI‖ Theorem (Section 5.5) (in the special case where ∨, and possibly other connectives are missing from the language L) guarantees that ‖SI‖ is functional. What remains to show is that SI expresses ‖SI‖, that is, V is a model of SI iff V obeys ‖SI‖.

For the proof that **SI** forces ‖**SI**‖ (the proof from left to right), assume V is a model of **SI** and note that this means that V is a model of whichever of these rules S&, S⊥, S→, and S↔ concern connectives of L. So the corresponding conditions from this list: ‖&‖, ‖⊥‖, ‖→‖, and ‖↔‖ all hold by the S&, S⊥, S→, and S↔ Theorems. (See Sections 4.1, 4.2, 6.1, and 6.3.) The ∼ Definition Theorem guarantees that ‖¬‖ holds, and so V obeys ‖**SI**‖ as desired.

The proof that **SI** is sound for ‖**SI**‖ (the proof from right to left), is equally easy using the same theorems.   □

An interesting corollary of this theorem follows from the Isomorphism Theorem of Section 5.4. Since **SI** expresses ‖**SI**‖, and the Isomorphism Theorem shows that obeying ‖**SI**‖ is equivalent to being isomorphic to a Kripke model, we have the following.

SI Expression Theorem. SI expresses being isomorphic to a Kripke semantics.

It is hard to imagine more convincing evidence that the meanings for the connectives &, ⊥, →, ↔, and ∼ determined by SI are those given by Kripke semantics for intuitionistic logic. Anyone who thinks that the rules of SI fix a different interpretation of the connectives is simply mistaken.

Of course alien anthropologists who study our deductive practices might determine that we use a stronger logic than SI, a logic, for example that accepts the intuitionistically unacceptable form of the Law of Double Negation. However, as we will see in Chapter 8, systems for classical negation suffer from the failings that emerged in Section 6.2, where Peirce's Rule was discussed. As we will see, such logics do not qualify as having a functional natural semantics. (See Section 8.6.) Therefore, those alien anthropologists with higher standards for what counts as a definition of meaning may conclude that classical logic simply fails to assign a meaning to ∼. The discussion found in Section 8.9, however, may persuade them (or you) otherwise.

7 Disjunction

It has been relatively easy to locate a natural semantics for propositional logics that involve connectives other than disjunction. Discussion of disjunction has been postponed because the situation here is more complicated. It is possible to locate a condition $\|\vee\|$ on models that the rules for disjunction express (Section 7.2). However, it is unfamiliar; $\|\vee\|$ is neither the classical condition nor the intuitionistic reading of $\vee$ that was introduced by Beth (Section 7.1). Furthermore, there is reason to worry whether $\|\vee\|$ qualifies as a recursive characterization of truth conditions (Section 7.3). So it will be necessary to try to rescue $\|\vee\|$ (if we can) with a new isomorphism result. In Section 7.4, a variant of the Kripke semantics will be introduced (called path semantics) that includes an additional structure used in the disjunction truth condition. An isomorphism is shown to exist between the models in path semantics and models that obey $\|\vee\|$ (Section 7.5). This goes part of the way towards legitimizing the condition expressed by the disjunction rules as qualifying as a semantics. However Section 7.6 demonstrates that neither functionality nor a desirable form of compositionality holds for $\|\vee\|$. So whether the isomorphism result goes far enough to offset this pathology is in doubt. Whether we should accept $\|\vee\|$ as a legitimate reading for $\vee$ will be something left for the reader to judge.

7.1 Beth's intuitionistic truth condition for disjunction

Remember the system $S\vee$ consisted of the following natural deduction rules.

$S\vee$:   ($\vee$ Introduction)   ($\vee$ Elimination)

$$\frac{H \vdash A}{H \vdash A \vee B} \qquad \frac{H \vdash B}{H \vdash A \vee B} \qquad \frac{H \vdash A \vee B \quad H, A \vdash C \quad H, B \vdash C}{H \vdash C}$$

Unfortunately we cannot show that a natural semantics for S∨ is the truth condition ‖C∨‖ for Kripke semantics, because that condition is classical.

‖C∨‖ v(A∨B)=t iff v(A)=t or v(B)=t.

Theorem 4.4.1 guarantees that propositional logic has models that violate ‖C∨‖ by allowing v(A∨B)=t even when v(A)=f and v(B)=f.

An alternative way of treating intuitionistic disjunction was proposed by Beth (van Dalen, 1986, p. 249). Beth's truth condition is based on the following intuition. We imagine a valuation v that rules true the sentences that have been established under our present state of knowledge, and we imagine possible future extensions of our knowledge as an infinite tree with v at the base. Each branch on the tree represents a possible pathway for improving our knowledge, depending on which decisions we make about what to investigate next. So a path through v amounts to a set of valuations including v, linearly ordered by ≤ and containing an extension of each of its members whenever possible. The bar condition for disjunction says that v (A∨B)=t iff either A or B is assigned t somewhere on every path through v, that is, along every path for improving our knowledge (van Dalen, 1986, p. 249). The relevant definitions follow.

(Path) P *is a path through* v iff the conditions (i), (ii), and (iii) are met, for all v' v" in V.

(i)   v∈P.
(ii)   (P is connected) If v'∈P and v"∈P, then v'≤v" or v"≤v'.
(iii) (P is maximal) If v'∈P, v'≠v" and v'≤v", then there is a valuation u∈P such that v'≤u and v'≠u.

In semantics for an open future, paths are also known as histories (Belnap, Perloff, and Xu, 2001, p. 30).

(Bar) A *bar for* v is a set 𝔹 such that for each path P through v there is member of P in 𝔹.

Beth's truth condition for ∨ can now be expressed as follows.

‖B∨‖ v(A∨B)=t iff there is a bar 𝔹 for v such that
              for all v' in 𝔹, either v'(A)=t or v'(B)=t.

Unfortunately there are models of S∨ that violate Beth's condition, as the next theorem demonstrates. (Many proofs in this chapter are lengthy, so proofs for theorems marked with a star (*) are found at the end of this chapter in Section 7.8, where they will not interrupt the flow of the narrative. In the remainder of this book, proofs for starred theorems appear at the end of each chapter.)

Theorem 7.1* S∨ does not express ‖B∨‖.

This result is disappointing, for it entails that whenever we have a model of S∨ that obeys the Beth condition, as it certainly might, there is another model of S∨ that violates the condition. So S∨ is not strong enough to force its models to be classical, nor to obey Beth's condition. As far as S∨ is concerned, neither classical nor Beth truth conditions are fixed.

7.2 What disjunction rules express

Is there any hope for finding a condition expressed by S∨ that does qualify as the natural semantics for those rules? The answer is: perhaps. There is a condition weaker than Beth's that is exactly expressed by S∨, although it is rather complicated (Garson, 2001, p. 124). The issue to face is whether it should qualify as a properly constructed truth condition for a connective. It is ‖∨‖.

‖∨‖ v(A∨B)=t iff for every path bundle P though v,
there is a v′ in P such that v′(A)=t or v′(B)=t.

A set of valuations P counts as a path bundle through v iff there is some wff D such that v(D) is false, and P contains exactly those extensions of v that keep D false.

(Path Bundle)   P is a *path bundle through* v iff for some wff D, v(D)=f, and P = {v′: v≤v′ and v′(D)=f}, where ≤ is defined by ‖≤‖.

‖≤‖ v≤v′ iff for all wffs A, if v(A)=t, then v′(A)=t.

Notice that valuations in a path bundle through v extend our knowledge in a certain way, since they are extensions of v that all agree with v on some false wff. This wff might be a very long disjunction, thus insuring all its many disjuncts are false along the path bundle. (‖∨‖ insures that all disjuncts of a false disjunction are also false, because it guarantees the first three rows of the classical disjunction truth table.) Though this does not delimit a path completely, it does enforce a requirement on how knowledge must be extended on the path bundle. So ‖∨‖ reflects something of the spirit of the bar condition in requiring that disjunctions are true only if one disjunct or the other will eventually be true along many different ways of extending our knowledge.

On the other hand, a path bundle through v is *not* a path through v because the valuations in the path bundle need not be linearly ordered. Instead, the structure in the path could resemble a tree. Though finitely many wffs may be forced false along a path bundle, there is always the possibility that two valuations in the path bundle extend v in incompatible ways. The bar condition is stronger than the right-hand side of ‖∨‖ because it demands that at some point along every path for extending our knowledge one or other disjunct be true. Condition ‖∨‖, on the other hand, only insures that a disjunct be true at some point in every *group* of paths that all preserve the false value of some wff.

The next theorem asserts that S∨ expresses ‖∨‖, that is, the models of S∨ are exactly the models that obey ‖∨‖.

S∨ Expression Theorem*. S∨ expresses ‖∨‖.

This result may be extended to systems that include S∨ and rules for other connectives. Let I∨ be the system for intuitionist logic that is defined over a language L that includes any of the symbols &, ⊥, →, ↔, ~, ∨. The rules of I∨ are all rules in the natural deduction systems S&, S⊥, S→, S↔, S∨ that govern the connectives of L. If ~ is present, I∨ introduces it by definition: ~A =_df A→⊥. Let ‖I∨‖ be the conjunction of ‖∨‖ with the intuitionistic semantics ‖SI‖ that gave truth conditions for connectives other than ∨. The S∨ Expression Theorem along with the SI Theorem of Section 6.4, entails that I∨ expresses ‖I∨‖.

I∨ Expression Theorem. I∨ expresses ‖I∨‖.

7.3 Do the disjunction rules express a semantics?

In light of the last theorem, ‖I∨‖ might appear to be a good candidate for a natural semantics for I∨. However, it is not entirely clear that ‖∨‖ should count as a recursive characterization of the truth conditions for ∨. Determining the truth-value of A∨B at v requires determining which sets of valuations count as path bundles through v. This in turn requires that we already know which valuations stand in the relation ≤, and to know that we need to know the truth-values of all the complex wffs (including A∨B!). So the condition is circular.

The breadth of the problem may be appreciated by considering ‖W∨‖, an equivalent (and somewhat simpler) way of formulating ‖∨‖.

‖W∨‖ v(A∨B)=t iff for every wff C, if v(C)=f, then there is a v' in V
such that v≤v', v'(C)=f, and either v'(A)=t or v'(B)=t.

Theorem 7.3.1* ‖W∨‖ is equivalent to ‖∨‖.

‖W∨‖ reveals a second objection to ‖∨‖. In it, there is explicit reference to the truth-values of wffs C other than the subformulas A and B of A∨B. (The label '‖W∨‖' is chosen to remind us that ‖W∨‖ mentions wffs.) Therefore, the truth-value of A∨B is not local; it does not depend upon the values of its subformulas alone. Note that mention of path bundles in ‖∨‖ entails the same objection, for what counts as a path bundle depends again on the values of formulas other than the subformulas of A∨B.

One might hope to resolve the circularity problems with ‖∨‖ and ‖W∨‖ on analogy with the case of the conditional. Let ≤ be the relation defined by ‖≤‖, and ≤ₚ the relation defined by ‖p≤‖.

‖≤‖ v≤v' iff for all wffs A, if v(A)=t, then v'(A)=t.

‖p≤‖ v≤ₚv' iff for all propositional variables p, if v(p)=t, then v'(p)=t.

Perhaps we can prove a version of the ≤ Lemma and show that it does not matter whether ≤ or ≤ₚ is employed. Then we could hope to reformulate ‖W∨‖ as ‖pW∨‖ where mention of the values of complex wffs C no longer occurs.

‖pW∨‖ v(A∨B)=t iff for every propositional variable p, if v(p)=f, then
there is a v' in V such that v≤ₚv', v'(p)=f, and
either v'(A)=t or v'(B)=t.

But attempts along these lines are foiled by the sad fact that the ≤ Lemma fails for any condition that S∨ expresses.

Theorem 7.3.2* S∨ does not force the content of the ≤ Lemma, in fact, there is a set of valuations V* that is a model of S∨ such that for some v and v′ in V*, $v \leq_p v'$, and not $v \leq v'$.

The failure of the ≤ Lemma is related to the fact that path bundles are not linear structures. Disjunctions that are t at v need not remain t at extensions of v when $\|p \leq\|$ rather than $\|\leq\|$ defines what counts as an extension. Inspection of the proof of the S∨ Expression Theorem reveals that replacing ≤ with $\leq_p$ in that proof would block the argument given there. In particular, cases involving (∨ Elimination) for both forcing and soundness depend on ≤ being used in the definition of a path bundle.

Given that there is no obvious way to save $\|\vee\|$ from circularity objections, it is important to show that $\|\vee\|$ is well defined by establishing an isomorphism result. However, we cannot show that models of S∨ are isomorphic to Kripke models (where disjunction is classical), or even to models that use Beth's condition for disjunction, since models of S∨ do not meet those conditions. To obtain the desired isomorphism theorem, we will need to construct a variant of Kripke semantics that introduces structures that play the role of path bundles.

7.4 Path semantics for disjunction

The purpose of this section is to develop a Kripke-style semantics for ∨ called path semantics that qualifies as a recursively defined semantics. Then $\|\vee\|$ may be certified as a semantics by demonstrating that models that obey $\|\vee\|$ are isomorphic to the models of path semantics. That would calm our fears about $\|\vee\|$, for it would show that even though $\|\vee\|$ appears circular and non-local, the structure set up by models V obeying $\|\vee\|$ can always be "unraveled" into well-behaved recursively defined models.

Path semantics proves an alternative treatment of ∨ that is isomorphic to what S∨ expresses. It is interesting in its own right, since results given here will show that intuitionistic logic is sound and complete when disjunction is interpreted according to path semantics. The main idea is a variant of Beth's semantics where path bundles are used instead of paths.

Let us introduce a neighborhood relation N, which is defined over pairs <v, P> where the second item P (called the neighborhood for v) is a subset of (rather than a member of) V.

> (Neighborhood Relation) A *neighborhood relation* for V is a set of pairs <v, P> such that v∈V and P⊆V.

The intuitive idea will be that vNP holds just in case P is a path bundle through v. A neighborhood model will be a Kripke model that also contains a neighborhood relation N.

> (Neighborhood Model) U is a *neighborhood model* iff U=<W, ⊆, N, u>, N is a neighborhood relation, and <W, ⊆, u> is a Kripke model.

The truth relation $\models^U$ (for U) is then defined for neighborhood models using the conditions (Kp), (K⊥), (K&), (K→), (K↔), and (K¬), along with (P∨). (Again, the superscript 'U' is suppressed.)

> (Kp) $w \models p$ iff u(w, p)=t, for propositional variables p.
> (K⊥) $w \not\models \bot$.
> (K&) $w \models A\&B$ iff $w \models A$ and $w \models B$.
> (K→) $w \models A{\to}B$ iff for every w′ in W, if w⊆w′, then w′ $\not\models$ A or w′ $\models$ B.
> (K↔) $w \models A{\leftrightarrow}B$ iff for every w′ in W, if w⊆w′, then w′ $\models$ A iff w′ $\models$ B.
> (K¬) $w \models {\sim}A$ iff for every w′ in W, if w⊆w′, then w′ $\not\models$ A.
> (P∨) $w \models A{\vee}B$ iff for every subset P of W such that wNP, there is a w′∈P such that w′ $\models$ A or w′ $\models$ B.

It is clear that these conditions recursively determine the values of all the wffs on a given neighborhood model. However, neighborhood models are not the models we desire. It will be necessary to narrow the class of neighborhood models to the ones we seek by enforcing side conditions in a definition of validity. Note this narrowing down of the class of models occurs after an account of truth conditions has been given. The side conditions play the role of constraints one places on frames in models for modal logic (such as reflexivity and transitivity) in order to select an appropriate notion of validity for a given conception of necessity. A path model will be any neighborhood model such that ⊆ is an extension relation over wffs, and its neighborhood relation N holds for <w, P> exactly when P "looks like" a path bundle through w.

> (Path Model) A *path model* U=<W, ⊆, N, u> is any neighborhood model that obeys (⊆) and (N).

($\subseteq$) w$\subseteq$w' iff for all wffs A, if w $\vDash$ A, then w' $\vDash$ A.

(N) wNP iff there is some wff D such that w $\nvDash$ D, and P = {w': w$\subseteq$w' and w' $\nvDash$ D}.

Argument H / C is *path-valid* (abbreviated: H $\vDash_p$ C) iff for every path model U=<W, $\subseteq$, N, u> and every w in W, if w $\vDash$ H, then w $\vDash$ C.

By adding the side conditions ($\subseteq$) and (N) *after* the definition of truth on a neighborhood model, one leaves the recursive definition of truth uncontaminated by circularity worries. Note however, that both conditions ($\subseteq$) and (N) involve mention of the truth relation, and are not defined on the structure of the model as originally defined. Therefore, although an isomorphism result for path semantics of this kind will help support the view that $\|\lor\|$ is free of blatant circularity problems, we will not be able to show that $\|\lor\|$ is functional. Further worries about whether $\|\lor\|$ is compositional emerge in Section 7.6.

7.5 Isomorphism for path models

We are ready to show that models obeying the truth condition expressed by S$\lor$ are isomorphic to path models. Consider a language L that introduces ~ by definition (~Def) and contains one or more of the primitive connectives &, $\bot$, $\rightarrow$, $\leftrightarrow$, and $\lor$. Let $\|$I$\lor\|$ be the conjunction of whichever of these conditions governs connectives in L: $\|$&$\|$, $\|\bot\|$, $\|\rightarrow\|$, $\|\leftrightarrow\|$, $\|\dashv\|$, and $\|\lor\|$. Our task will be to show that V obeys $\|$I$\lor\|$ iff <V, $\leq$> with $\leq$ defined by $\|\leq\|$ is isomorphic to a path model.

A frame <V, $\leq$> will be said to be *isomorphic* to U=<W, $\subseteq$, N, u> iff there is a 1–1 mapping * from V into W such that v$\leq$v' iff v*$\subseteq$v'* and u fixes values of the propositional variables so that v*(A)=t iff v* $\vDash^U$ A. When we say V obeys $\|$I$\lor\|$, it will be understood that we mean that $\leq$ is defined by $\|\leq\|$.

Path Isomorphism Theorem*. V obeys $\|$I$\lor\|$ iff <V, $\leq$> is isomorphic to some path model.

Note that the isomorphism result does not go both ways, for there are path models with w and w' in W where w and w' agree on all the values of the wffs, and this defeats an attempt to secure a 1–1 function to a corresponding set of valuations. We discussed the same feature for systems without $\lor$ in Section 5.4. This is unfortunate because it would have yielded a quick proof that $I\vee$ is also sound for path semantics. Instead, the soundness will be shown directly (Theorem 12.2.2). As we will see in the same chapter (Theorem 12.2.1), the Path Isomorphism Theorem is sufficient for showing that $I\vee$ is complete for path semantics, for in general, any system is complete for a semantics isomorphic to a condition it expresses. So path semantics can be added to the list of semantics for which intuitionistic logic is adequate.

7.6 The failure of functionality and compositionality

The Path Isomorphism Theorem (Section 7.5) goes a good way towards allaying fears that $\|\vee\|$ does not qualify as a legitimate truth condition. However, in Section 5.5 a stronger result was obtained for systems without disjunction. There it was shown that every atomic set of valuations can be extended to a unique model that obeyed the condition for intuitionistic models. Will the same functionality result extend to systems that use $\|\vee\|$? The condition $\|I\vee\|$ is the semantics that results from replacing the classical truth condition $\|C\vee\|$ in $\|KI\|$ with $\|\vee\|$. We would hope to justify the legitimacy of $\|I\vee\|$ by showing it is functional.

Howerver an example of J. Woods (forthcoming) puts an end to these hopes, for it shows that functionality fails for $\|\vee\|$.

Theorem 7.6.1* There is an atomic model W with member w and two extensions V and V′ of W that obey $\|\vee\|$, but disagree on the value of $p\vee q$ at the valuation that extends w.

The upshot of this theorem is that while an isomorphism result for $\|I\vee\|$ exists, it does not follow that extensions of atomic models that obey $\|I\vee\|$ are unique, and so it is questionable whether $\|I\vee\|$ provides a legitimate semantics.

Woods (forthcoming) gives us a second reason to worry, for he also shows that a desirable form of compositionality fails for $\|\vee\|$. We noted in Section 5.3 that the truth condition $\|\rightarrow\|$ for the conditional is non-local, which means that the value of A→B at v may depend on the values of variables that do not appear in the subformulas A or B. The reason is that values of such wffs can affect the extension relation $\leq$ which figures in the truth condition $\|\rightarrow\|$. The proof that $\|\rightarrow\|$ is functional puts those worries to rest. However, Woods shows that even in case of two models with *exactly the same extension relation*, the value of A∨B may depend on variables that do not appear in A∨B. This is a surprising failure to meet what we could reasonably expect of a compositional semantics.

Theorem 7.6.2* There are two models $V=\{v_0, v_{pr}, v_{qr}\}$ and $V'=\{v'_r, v_{pr}, v_{qr}\}$ obeying $\|V\|$ that are identical in every respect, including which valuations bear the $\leq$ relation defined by $\|\leq\|$, with the exception that $v_0(r)\neq v'_r(r)$ for only one variable r, and where $v_0(p\lor q)=f$ and $v'_r(p\lor q)=t$.

The Path Isomorphism Theorem takes some of the sting out of the last result, for we know that for V and V' as described in the last theorem there are corresponding path models were the truth-value of the wffs are uniquely determined by their neighborhood structures. However, it is only fair to admit that path models are semantically odd, since the condition (⊆) on ⊆ and (N) on the neighborhood relation N mention the truth relation ⊨. Therefore, path models cannot be defined unless ⊨ has been fixed by some neighborhood model. This is not the normal procedure in defining a semantical structure, so suspicions about $\|V\|$ remain. We will leave it to the reader to decide how serious these objections to $\|V\|$ should be.

7.7 Converting natural into classical models

Those who believe that $\|V\|$ is illegitimate will be motivated to find an alternative account of disjunction. Kripke's (and Beth's) semantics for intuitionistic logic are stronger than what is actually expressed by the rules of intuitionistic logic. There is a gap between what the disjunction rules do express (namely $\|V\|$) and Kripke's treatment embodied in $\|CV\|$.

$\|V\|$ v(A∨B)=t iff for every path bundle P though v,
there is a v'∈P such that v'(A)=t or v'(B)=t.

$\|CV\|$ v(A∨B)=t iff v(A)=t or v(B)=t.

Although S∨ does not express $\|CV\|$, $\|CV\|$ has the advantage of being clearly functional. Perhaps there is some way to justify the idea that $\|CV\|$ qualifies as a semantics for S∨ even though it is not expressed by S∨. One way to argue for that idea is to show that using $\|CV\|$ in place of $\|V\|$ does not affect the class of arguments defined as valid. So the "gap" between the two ways of interpreting ∨ does not matter if validity is our concern. While this would not show that ‖C∨‖ is expressed by S∨, it would at least motivate the use of ‖C∨‖ in place of ‖∨‖.

There are at least two ways to demonstrate such a result. One is to prove that the intuitionistic logic I∨ is adequate for both path semantics and Kripke semantics. Hence the two semantics must identify as valid exactly the same arguments. The strategy given here will be more direct. It is to show how to convert a model that obeys the natural condition ‖∨‖ into one that obeys ‖C∨‖, the classical one. Although this demonstration parallels standard results in intuitionistic logic, it is interesting to view the reasoning as a series of results about expressive power. It will also be useful for showing completeness of multiple conclusion sequent systems in Section 12.3.

Let a valuation v be called *prime* for system S (or S-prime) when v satisfies S and the classical truth condition ‖C∨‖ for ∨ holds.

(Satisfies S) Valuation v satisfies system S iff whenever $H \vdash_S C$, and
$v(H)=t$, then $v(C)=t$.

(Prime) v is *prime* for S iff v satisfies S and v obeys ‖C∨‖.

Here we will prove an analog of the Prime Filter Theorem. (See van Dalen, 1986, pp. 252 ff.) We will show that the natural truth condition ‖∨‖ (or equivalently ‖W∨‖) contains the seeds of the classical one by establishing that any valuation in a model V of S where ‖W∨‖ holds has an S-prime extension.

‖W∨‖ $v(A \lor B) = t$ iff for every wff C, if $v(C)=f$, then there is a v' in V
such that $v \leq v'$, $v'(C)=f$, and either $v'(A)=t$ or $v'(B)=t$.

Note that although we will show there is such a prime extension, we will not be able to show that this extension is a member of V.

Theorem 7.7.1* If V is a model of a system S that includes S∨, and v is a member of V such that $v(C)=f$, then there is a S-prime extension v^* of v such that $v^*(C)=f$.

Let S be a system that includes the rules of I∨ that has a model V. By the previous theorem, there is at least one S-prime extension v^* for each member v of V. Let Vp be the set that contains all the S-prime extensions of the members of V. The next theorem demonstrates the adequacy of S with respect to [S]p, the result of "priming" the canonical model, that is, taking all S-prime extensions of members of [S].

[S]p Adequacy Theorem*. H ⊢$_S$ C iff H ⊨$_{[S]p}$ C. Furthermore, [S]p is a model of S.

The [S]p Adequacy Theorem will be central to understanding why the classical treatment of disjunction provides a complete and sound semantics for I∨. Let ‖S‖ be any semantics for an extension S of S∨ that includes ‖W∨‖ (or in light of Theorem 7.3.1, ‖∨‖), and let ‖KS‖ be the Kripke-style semantics that results from replacing the truth clause for disjunction in ‖S‖ with the classical truth condition ‖C∨‖.

‖W∨‖ $v(A{\lor}B)=t$ iff for every wff C, if $v(C)=f$, then there is a v' in V
such that $v{\le}v'$, $v'(C)=f$, and either $v'(A)=t$ or $v'(B)=t$.

‖C∨‖ $v(A{\lor}B)=t$ iff $v(A)=t$ or $v(B)=t$.

Under what circumstances does this replacement leave the resulting notion of validity unaffected? In others words, when is it true that arguments valid using ‖S‖ are exactly those valid using ‖KS‖? The next theorem shows that all that is required is that ‖S‖ be a natural semantics for S. So the following theorem will apply not only when S=I∨, but for a variety of systems that will be discussed in this book. Let us say that argument H / C is ‖S‖-valid (written: H ⊨$_{‖S‖}$ C) iff H ⊨$_V$ C for every model V that obeys ‖S‖. Then the following holds.

Theorem 7.7.2* When ‖KS‖ is the result of replacing ‖W∨‖ (or ‖∨‖) with ‖C∨‖ in a natural semantics ‖S‖ for a system that includes S∨, the replacement does not affect the notion of validity so defined, that is, H ⊨$_{‖S‖}$ C iff H ⊨$_{‖KS‖}$ C.

The last result may be viewed as a reflection on the expressive weakness of I∨. When H is a set of wffs, and V is a model of system S, and there is a member v of V such that $v(H)=t$, we will say that H *has an S-model*.

Theorem 7.7.3* If H has an I∨-model that disobeys ‖C∨‖, then H has a model that obeys ‖C∨‖, the classical truth condition for ∨.

In Theorem 4.4.2, an analog of the Lowenheim–Skolem Theorem was proven to the effect that whenever a set of sentences has a classical model it has a non-classical one as well. The last theorem is intended to remind the reader again of the Lowenheim–Skolem Theorem in the case of intuitionistic logic, but this time in the reverse direction. It says that every set of wffs with a non-classical I∨ model has a classical model. Therefore I∨ lacks the expressive power to force models to be non-classical with respect to disjunction.

This expressive weakness is reflected in results concerning the adequacy of I∨ that will be examined in detail in Section 12.1. There we will present a very easy proof that any system must be adequate for conditions it expresses, and so I∨ is adequate for ‖I∨‖. It is also well known that I∨ is adequate for Kripke semantics, and we will prove as well that it is also adequate for ‖KI‖ (its close cousin which gives ∨ a classical reading). So even though ‖KI‖ is stronger than ‖I∨‖, I∨ remains complete for ‖KI‖. (The fact that ‖KI‖ is stronger than ‖I∨‖ explains the extra complications in the completeness proof such as the need for the prime extension construction, which is embodied in Theorem 7.7.1.) Whenever a system is adequate for a semantics stronger than its natural semantics in this way, the resulting gap corresponds to a weakness in the expressive resources of the system. The system is blind to the differences between its natural semantics and any other semantics for which it is adequate, and so no set of sentences of the language can force a model to obey conditions that reflect those differences. The upshot of this is that alien anthropologists who discover that we employ intuitionistic logic can gather no evidence that would verify that our reading of disjunction is classical.

7.8 Proofs of theorems in Chapter 7

Theorem 7.1 S∨ does not express ‖B∨‖.

‖B∨‖ v(A∨B)=t iff there is a bar B for v such that
for all v' in B, either v'(A)=t or v'(B)=t.

Proof. Let V={v, u} be a model of a language with ∨ the only connective such that v(B)=f for all wffs B, and u(B)=t iff B contains some variable other than p.

Both v and u are consistent (u(p)=f), and so count as valuations. Furthermore V is a model of S∨ by the following reasoning.

To show (∨ Introduction) preserves V-validity, assume H ⊨ᵥ A and v'(H)=t and show v'(A∨B)=t for v' a member of V. From H ⊨ᵥ A it follows that v'(A)=t and valuation v' cannot be v. So v'=u, u(A)=t and A contains some variable other than p. Therefore A∨B contains some variable other than p, and u(A∨B)=t as desired. The proof that if H ⊨ᵥ B, then H ⊨ᵥ A∨B is similar.

To show (∨ Elimination) preserves V-validity, assume (1) H ⊨ᵥ A∨B, (2) H, A ⊨ᵥ C, and (3) H, B ⊨ᵥ C, and prove H ⊨ᵥ C, by reductio. From H ⊭ᵥ C, it follows that for some v' in V, v'(H)=t and v'(C)=f. From (1), H ⊨ᵥ A∨B, and v'(H)=t, it follows that v'(A∨B)=t, and so v' cannot be v. Therefore v' is u, and we have u(C)=f and u(A∨B)=t. Therefore A∨B contains some variable other than p. But this means that either A or B contains some variable other than p. If it is A, u(A)=t, and by (2), H, A ⊨ᵥ C, we have u(C)=t, which conflicts with u(C)=f. If it is B, the proof is similar using (3).

It follows then that V is a model of S∨. But ‖B∨‖ is violated by V, for v(q∨r)=f. If V were to obey ‖B∨‖, then every bar B through v would be such that for some member v' of B, v'(q)=f and v'(r)=f. But {u} is a bar through v, because there is only one path through v, namely v followed by u, and u(q)=u(r)=t.

We have found a model of S∨ that violates ‖B∨‖ so S∨ does not express ‖B∨‖.   □

S∨ Expression Theorem. S∨ expresses ‖∨‖.
‖∨‖ v(A∨B)=t iff for every path bundle P though v,
    there is a v' in P such that v'(A)=t or v'(B)=t.

Proof. To show S∨ expresses ‖∨‖, prove V is a model of S∨ iff V obeys ‖∨‖.

S∨ **is sound for** ‖∨‖ (the proof from right to left). Assume that V obeys ‖∨‖ and show that (∨ Introduction) and (∨ Elimination) preserve V-validity as follows.

(∨ Introduction). Assume H ⊨ᵥ A and show that H ⊨ᵥ A∨B by assuming that v is any member of V such that v(H)=t and proving that v(A∨B)=t as follows. In light of ‖∨‖, v(A∨B)=t will follow if we demonstrate that for any path bundle P through v, there is a member v' of P such that either v'(A)=t or v'(B)=t. So assume that P is a path bundle through v. In light of v≤v and v(D)=f, v must be a member of P. From H ⊨ᵥ A and v(H)=t, it follows that v(A)=t. So v is a member of P such that v(A)=t or v(B)=t as desired. The proof that if H ⊨ᵥ A then H ⊨ᵥ A∨B is similar.

(∨ Elimination) Assume (1) H ⊨$_V$ A∨B, (2) H, A ⊨$_V$ C, and (3) H, B ⊨$_V$ C, and show that H ⊨$_V$ C, by reductio. From H ⊭$_V$ C it follows that for some v in V, v(H)=t and v(C)=f. Given (1), it follows that v(A∨B)=t. Let P′={v″: v≤v″ and v″(C)=f}. Since v(C)=f, P′ is a path bundle through v. So by ‖∨‖ there is a member v′ of P such that v′(A)=t or v′(B)=t. If it is A, we have v≤v′, v′(H)=t, and given (2), it follows that v′(C)=t which contradicts v′(C)=f. Similarly if v′(B)=t, the contradiction follows from (3).

S∨ forces‖∨‖ (the proof from left to right). Assume that V is a model of S∨ and prove V obeys ‖∨‖ as follows.

To show V obeys ‖∨‖ from left to right, assume that v(A∨B)=t, and that P is a path bundle through v, and show that there is a v′ in P such that v′(A)=t or v′(B)=t as follows. By the definition of a path bundle P, there must be a wff D such that v(D)=f and for all v′ in V, v′ is in P iff v≤v′ and v′(D)=f. Let H$_v$ be the set of wffs assigned t by v. It follows that H$_v$ ⊨$_V$ A∨B. To see why, let v′ be any member of V such that v′(H$_v$)=t and show v′(A∨B)=t as follows. Since v′(H$_v$)=t, it follows by ‖≤‖ that v≤v′. But we had that v(A∨B)=t, so v′(A∨B)=t as desired. So we have H$_v$ ⊨$_V$ A∨B; but we also have v(H$_v$)=t and v(D)=f, so H$_v$ ⊭$_V$ D. It follows from the fact that (∨ Elimination) preserves V-validity that either H$_v$, A ⊭$_V$ D or H$_v$, B ⊭$_V$ D. In the first case we have a valuation v′ such that v′(H$_v$, A)=t and v′(D)=f. Because v′(H$_v$)=t, v≤v′. By the definition of a path bundle, v′ is in P, and since v′(A)=t, either v′(A)=t or v′(B)=t as desired. The second case, where H$_v$, B ⊭$_V$ C, is similar.

To show V obeys ‖∨‖ from right to left, assume v(A∨B)=f and find a path bundle P through v, where v′(A)=f and v′(B)=f for every v′ in P. Let P = {v′: v<v′ and v′(A∨B)=f}. Since v(A∨B)=f, P is a path bundle through v. To show that v′(A)=v′(B)=f for every member v′ of P, note that from the fact that (∨ Introduction) preserves V-validity and the provability of A / A∨B and B / A∨B in S∨, that A ⊨$_V$ A∨B and B ⊨$_V$ A∨B. Hence from v′(A∨B)=f we have v′(A)=v′(B)=f. ☐

Theorem 7.3.1 ‖W∨‖ is equivalent to ‖∨‖.

Proof. We must show that V obeys ‖W∨‖ iff V obeys ‖∨‖. To do this it will suffice to show that the right-hand sides ‖W∨R‖ and ‖∨R‖ of ‖W∨‖ and ‖∨‖ are equivalent.

‖W∨R‖ For every wff C, if v(C)=f, then there is a v′ in V
        such that v≤v′, v′(C)=f, and either v′(A)=t or v′(B)=t.

‖∨R‖ For every path bundle P though v,
     there is a v′ in P such that v′(A)=t or v′(B)=t.

So assume $\|W \vee R\|$ and prove $\|\vee R\|$ as follows. Assume that P is any path bundle through v, and show that there is a v′ in P such that v′(A)=t or v′(B)=t as follows. By the definition of a path bundle, we have there is some wff D such that v(D)=f, and P contains exactly those valuations v′ such that v≤v′ and v′(D)=f. From $\|W \vee R\|$, and v(D)=f we have that there is a member v″ of V such that v≤v″, v″(D)=f, and either v″(A)=t or v″(B)=t. Therefore, in light of v≤v″ and v″(D)=f, v″ is a member of P, so v″ qualifies as the member of P such that v″(A)=t or v″(B)=t as desired.

Now assume $\|\vee R\|$ and prove $\|W \vee v R\|$ as follows. Let C be any wff such that v(C)=f and show that there is a member v′ of V such that v≤v′, v′(C)=f, and either v′(A)=t or v′(B)=t. Let P = {u: v≤u and u(C)=f}. P is a path bundle through v. According to $\|\vee R\|$, there is a v″ in P such that v″(A)=t or v″(B)=t. So v≤v″, v″(C)=f and either v″(A)=t or v″(B)=t as desired.   □

Theorem 7.3.2 S∨ does not force the content of the ≤ Lemma, in fact, there is a set of valuations V* that is a model of S∨ such that for some v and v′ in V*, $v \leq_p v'$, and not v≤v′.

Proof. For simplicity, consider a language L where p, q, and r are the only propositional variables, and ∨ the only connective. Let V* be defined over L so that $V^* = \{v_{pq}, v_p, v_q, v_r\}$, where v_i for i=p, q, r is defined so that $v_i(A)=t$ iff A contains the variable i, and $v_{pq}(A)=t$ iff A contains both variables p and q. Note that $v_{pq}(p \vee q)=t$ but $v_r(p \vee q)=f$, so $v_{pq} \leq v_r$ fails. Note that $v_{pq}(p)=v_{pq}(q)=v_{pq}(r)=f$, and $v_r(p)=v_r(q)=f$, so $v_{pq} \leq_p v_r$ holds. To demonstrate the theorem, all that remains is to show that V* is a model of S∨. To do this, show that (∨ Introduction) and (∨ Elimination) preserve V*-validity.

(∨ Introduction) Presume $H \vDash_{V^*} A$ and demonstrate $H \vDash_{V^*} A \vee B$, by assuming that v is any member of V* such that v(H)=t and showing that v(A∨B)=t as follows. Given $H \vDash_{V^*} A$, it follows that v(A)=t. If v is v_{pq}, then $v_{pq}(A)=t$, which means that A contains both p and q. It follows that A∨B contains both p and q and so $v_{pq}(A \vee B)=t$. In case v is any of the v_i for i=p, q, r, the reasoning is similar. $H \vDash_{V^*} A \vee B$ follows from $H \vDash_{V^*} B$ in the same way.

(∨ Elimination). Presume (1) $H \vDash_{V^*} A \vee B$, (2) H, A $\vDash_{V^*}$ C, (3) H, B $\vDash_{V^*}$ C, and $H \nvDash_{V^*}$ C for reductio. We have that there is a member v of V* such that v(H)=t and v(C)=f. In light of (1), it follows that v(A∨B)=t. Suppose that v is one of the v_i for i=p, q, r. We have $v_i(A \vee B)=t$. So A∨B contains variable i, and so either A or B must contain i. In the first case we have $v_i(A)=t$. Given $v_i(H)=t$ and (2) it follows that $v_i(C)=t$, which conflicts with $v(C)=f$, and similarly for B by (3). The remaining possibility is that $v=v_{pq}$. In light of $v_{pq}(A \lor B)=t$ we know that both p and q appear in $A \lor B$. In case both p and q are in A or in B, the reasoning resembles previous cases. Only two cases remain, the first where A contains p and B contains q, and the second where A contains q and B contains p. In the first case, we have $v_p(A)=t$ and $v_q(B)=t$. We have that $v_{pq}(H)=t$, which means that all members of H contain both the variable p and the variable q. Therefore $v_p(H)=t$ and $v_q(H)=t$. Given H, A $\vDash_{V^\bullet}$ C and H, B $\vDash_{V^\bullet}$ C, it follows that $v_p(C)=t$ and $v_q(C)=t$. But this means that C contains both p and q, so that $v_{pq}(C)=t$, which conflicts with $v(C)=f$. The second case is similar.   □

Path Isomorphism Theorem. V obeys $\|I \lor\|$ iff $<V, \le>$ is isomorphic to some path model.

Proof. The proof follows the strategy of the Isomorphism Theorem of Section 5.4.

Proof from left to right. Assume V obeys $\|I \lor\|$, and show that $<V, \le>$ is isomorphic to a path model as follows. We have that $<V, \le>$ (where $\le$ obeys $\|\le\|$) is a Kripke frame, so define u so that $u(v, p)=t$ iff $v(p)=t$. Now define N so that vNP iff P is a path bundle through v, that is, there is a wff D such that $v(D)$ $=f$ and P = $\{v': v \le v'$ and $v'(D)=f\}$. Clearly U=$<V, \le, N, u>$ is a neighborhood model. Once the isomorphism between U and V is proven, it will follow that U is the desired path model isomorphic to V. To show that $<V, \le>$ is isomorphic to the model U=$<V, \le, N, u>$, we must show that $v(A)=t$ iff $v \vDash^U$ A. This is proven by induction on the length of A. Cases other than the one for $\lor$ are easy given that $\subset$ has been set to $\le$. To prove the case for $\lor$, show

$v(B \lor C)=t$ iff $v \vDash B \lor C$,

which follows if the right-hand sides of $(P \lor)$ and $\| \lor \|$ are equivalent.

$(P \lor)$ $v \vDash B \lor C$ iff for every P such that vNP,
                       there is a v' in P such that $v' \vDash B$ or $v' \vDash C$.

$\| \lor \|$ $v(B \lor C)=t$ iff for every path bundle P though v,
                       there is a v' in P such that $v'(B)=t$ or $v'(C)=t$.

But this follows immediately in light of the hypothesis of the induction and the definition of N: vNP iff P is a path bundle through v.

It remains to show that U=$<V, \le, N, u>$ is a path model. That requires we prove two things for all v and v' in V:

($\subseteq$) $v \leq v'$ iff all wffs A, if $v \vDash A$, then $v' \vDash A$.

(N) vNP iff there is some wff D such that $v \nvDash D$, and

$P = \{v': v \subseteq v'$ and $v' \nvDash D\}$.

($\subseteq$) follows immediately from v(A)=t iff $v \vDash A$, and the definition $\|\leq\|$ of $\leq$. (N) holds because by the definition of N, vNP iff P is a path bundle through v. So vNP iff there is a wff D such that v(D)=f and $P = \{v': v \leq v'$ and v'(D)=f\}. But we proved v(A)=t iff $v \vDash A$, for all $v \in V$, and so we may replace 'v(D)=f' with '$v \nvDash D$' and 'v'(D)=f' with '$v' \nvDash D$' in the last result to obtain (N).

Proof from right to left. What is needed is to show that when V is isomorphic to a path model, V obeys $\|\mathbf{I}\vee\|$, that is $<V, \leq>$ obeys $\|\mathbf{I}\vee\|$ and $\|\leq\|$. So assume that V is isomorphic to a path model $<W, \subseteq, N, u>$. That means there is a 1–1 mapping * from V into W such that * is *faithful*, which means that $v \leq v'$ iff $v^* \subseteq v'^*$, and v(A)=t iff $v^* \vDash A$, for any wff A. From ($\subseteq$) it follows immediately that $\|\leq\|$. We demonstrate each of the truth conditions $\|\bot\|$, $\|\&\|$, $\|\leftrightarrow\|$, and $\|\neg\|$ of $\|\mathbf{I}\vee\|$ as in the Isomorphism Theorem of Section 5.4. The remaining case is $\|\vee\|$, which is dealt with as follows.

From (P$\vee$) we obtain:

w $\vDash$ A$\vee$B iff for every P such that wNP,

there is a $w' \in P$ such that $w' \vDash A$ or $w' \vDash B$.

Since * is 1–1, this comes to the following for all $v \in V$:

$v^* \vDash$ A$\vee$B iff for every P such that v^*NP,

there is a $w' \in P$ such that $w' \vDash A$ or $w' \vDash B$.

To establish $\|\vee\|$, it will be easier to prove $\|W\vee\|$, which is equivalent in light of Theorem 7.3.1.

$\|W\vee\|$ v(A$\vee$B)=t iff for every wff C, if v(C)=f, then for some $v' \in V$, $v \leq v'$, v'(C)=f, and either v'(A)=t or v'(B)=t.

To prove $\|W\vee\|$ from left to right, assume v(A$\vee$B)=t. Now let C be any wff such that v(C)=f and show that there is a $v' \in V$ such that v'(C)=f, $v \leq v'$, and either v'(A)=t or v'(B)=t as follows. By v(A$\vee$B)=t, and the fact that * is faithful, we have $v^* \vDash$ A$\vee$B, and by (P$\vee$) it follows that:

For all P, if v^*NP then $w' \vDash$ A or $w' \vDash$ B, for some $w' \in P$.   (1)

Now define the subset P^* of W such that: $P^* = \{v'^*: v'(C)=f$ and $v \leq v'\}$. Since * is 1–1, this definition is well-founded. Now prove (2) as follows.

For all $w' \in W$, $w' \in P^*$ iff both $v^* \subseteq w'$ and $w' \nvDash C$.   (2)

Let w′ be any member of W. Then w′ is v′* for some v′∈V. We have v′*∈P* iff v′∈P. By the fact that * is faithful, the definition P* comes to: v′*∈P* iff v′* ⊬ C and v*⊆v′*. Since w′ is v′* we have w′∈P* iff both v*⊆w′ and w′ ⊬ C, which completes the proof of (2). Since * is faithful, we also know from v(C)=f that v* ⊬ C. Since <W, ⊆, N, u> is a path model, we know that N obeys (N).

(N*) v*NP* iff there is some wff D such that v* ⊬ D, and P* = {w′: v*⊆w′ and w′ ⊬ D}.

By v* ⊬ C and (2), it follows that the right-hand side of (N*) holds, and hence v*NP*. Using (1), it follows that w′ ⊨ A or w′ ⊨ B for some w′∈P*. But w′ must be v′* for some v′ in V, and so we have v′* ⊨ A or v′* ⊨ B, and v′*∈P*. By the fact that * is faithful, and the definition (P*) of P*, we have v′(C)=f and v≤v′ and v′(A)=t or v′(B)=t, which is the desired result. This completes the proof of ‖W∨‖ from left to right.

To prove ‖W∨‖ from right to left, assume (3) and prove v(A∨B)=t as follows.

For every wff C, if v(C)=f, then for some v′∈V,

v≤v′, v′(C)=f, and either v′(A)=t or v′(B)=t.   (3)

Since * is faithful, and (P∨) holds, demonstrating (4) will be sufficient for proving v* ⊨ A∨B and hence v(A∨B)=t as desired.

For every P, if v*NP, there is a w′∈P such that w′ ⊨ A or w′ ⊨ B.   (4)

So assume v*NP and find a w′ in P such that w′ ⊨ A or w′ ⊨ B as follows. Since <W, ⊆, N, u> is a path model, (N) holds, with the result that there is a wff D such that v* ⊬ D, and for all w′∈W, w′∈P iff both v*⊆w′ and w′ ⊬ D. Therefore (5).

For all v′∈V, v′*∈P iff both v*⊆v′* and v′* ⊬ D.   (5)

Since * is faithful, it follows from v* ⊬ D that v(D)=f. From (3), it follows for some v′∈V that:

v≤v′, v′(D)=f, and either v′(A)=t or v′(B)=t.

Therefore by the fact that * is faithful, it follows that:

v*⊆v′*, v′* ⊬ D, and either v′* ⊬ A or v′* ⊬ B.

By (5), v′*∈P iff both v*⊆v′* and v′* ⊬ D, so v′*∈P. It follows that v′* is the desired member w′ of W such that: w′∈P and either w′ ⊨ A or w′ ⊨ B. This completes the proof from right to left, hence the theorem as a whole. □

Theorem 7.6.1 There is an atomic model W with member w and two extensions V and V′ of W that obey $\|\vee\|$, but disagree on the value of $p\vee q$ at the valuation that extends w.

Proof. Consider a language with p, q, and r the only variables, and $\vee$ the only connective, and let atomic model W={w_r, w_{pr}, w_{qr}}, where for the list l of propositional variables and when s is one of p, q, r, $w_l(s)$=t iff s is in l. (For example $w_{pr}(s)$=t exactly when s is p or r.) Then there are two extensions V and V′ of W where v_r and v'_r are the extensions of w_r, and where $v_r(p\vee q)$=f and $v'_r(p\vee q)$=t in V′. For each list of propositional variables l, define v_l, so that $v_l(A)$=t iff one of the variables in l occurs in A. Let v'_r be defined so that $v'_r(A)$=t iff either r occurs in A or both p and q occur in A. Therefore, $v_r(p\vee q)$=f and $v'_r(p\vee q)$=t. To show that both V and V′ obey $\|W\vee\|$ for $\leq$ defined by $\|\leq\|$, show that V and V′ are models of $S\vee$. Then appeal to the $S\vee$ Expression Theorem of Section 7.2 to show that $\|\vee\|$ holds of V and V′. The proof that ($\vee$ Introduction) preserves V-validity and V′-validity is easy. (See the ($\vee$ Introduction) case of Theorem 7.3.2.)

To show that ($\vee$ Elimination) preserves V-validity and V′-validity, consider V first. We are given: (1) H $\vDash_V$ A$\vee$B, (2) H, A $\vDash_V$ C, and (3) H, B $\vDash_V$ C. We show H $\vDash_V$ C, by assuming v(H)=t for any v$\in$V and proving v(C)=t. By (1) H $\vDash_V$ A$\vee$B, (2) H, A $\vDash_V$ C, and (3) H, B $\vDash_V$ C, we have

$$v(A\vee B)=t, \text{ and} \tag{4}$$

$$\text{if } v(A)=t \text{ or } v(B)=t \text{ then } v(C)=t. \tag{5}$$

Since v$\in$V we have v is one of the v_l. Given (4), one of the variables of l occurs in A$\vee$B. So that variable appears in either A or B. Therefore $v_l(A)$=t or $v_l(B)$=t. By (5), $v_l(C)$=t and so v(C)=t as desired.

The case of V′ is similar, except a special argument must be given in the case where v is v'_r. For this we need a quick lemma.

$\leq'$ **Lemma.** Given $\|\leq\|$, $v'_r\leq v_{pr}$ and $v'_r\leq v_{qr}$.

Proof. By induction on the form of A, demonstrate that if $v'_r(A)$=t then $v_{pr}(A)$=t. (The case for v_{qr} will be similar.) The base case is easy. For the inductive case, assume $v'_r(B\vee D)$=t, and show that $v_{pr}(B\vee D)$=t as follows. From $v'_r(B\vee D)$=t we have that either B$\vee$D contains r or it contains both p and q. So B$\vee$D contains either r or p, and $v_{pr}(B\vee D)$=t. So the Lemma is proven.

Now let v=v'$_r$. By (4), A∨B either contains r or both p and q occur in A∨B. When A∨B contains r, the reasoning is the same as for v$_r$. When both p and q occur in A∨B, it follows that (6) both occur in A or both in B, or (7) one occurs in A and the other in B. In case (6), v'$_r$(A)=t or v'$_r$(B)=t. By (5), v'$_r$(C)=t and v(C)=t as in the previous cases. The hard case is (7), which we illustrate by assuming p is in A and q is in B. Then v$_{pr}$(A)=t and v$_{qr}$(B)=t. By the ≤' Lemma, v'$_r$≤v$_{pr}$ and v'$_r$≤v$_{qr}$, and so by v=v'$_r$ and v(H)=t, we have v$_{pr}$(H)=t and v$_{qr}$(H)=t. Then H, A ⊨$_V$ C and H, B ⊨$_V$ C yield v$_{pr}$(C)=t and v$_{qr}$(C)=t. But that means that both p is in C or r is in C and q is in C or r is in C, that is, either both p and q are in C or r is in C. Hence v'$_r$ (C)=t and v(C)=t as desired.   □

Theorem 7.6.2 There are two models V={v$_0$, v$_{pr}$, v$_{qr}$} and V'={v'$_r$, v$_{pr}$, v$_{qr}$} obeying ‖V‖ that are identical in every respect, including which valuations bear the ≤ relation defined by ‖≤‖, with the exception that v$_0$(r)≠v'$_r$(r) for only one variable r, and where v$_0$(p∨q)=f and v'$_r$(p∨q)=t.

Proof. Define V={v$_0$, v$_{pr}$, v$_{qr}$} and V'={v'$_r$, v$_{pr}$, v$_{qr}$} so that v$_0$(A)=f for each wff A, v$_{pr}$(A)=t iff either p or r occurs in A, v$_{qr}$ (A)=t iff q or r occurs in A, and v'$_r$(A) =t iff r occurs in A or both p and q occur in A. Then V' is defined as it was in the previous theorem, and can be shown to obey ‖V‖ in the same way. V resembles the V of the previous theorem with the exception of valuation v$_0$. To show it obeys ‖V‖ show that the V-validity of (∨ Introduction) and (∨ Elimination) is preserved, and use the S∨ Expression Theorem of Section 7.2. For (∨ Introduction) we assume H ⊨$_V$ A, and that v is any member of V such that v(H)=t and show v(A∨B)=t. Cases where v is v$_{pr}$ or v$_{qr}$, are easy. In case v=v$_0$, assume v(A∨B)=f for reductio. From H ⊨$_V$ A, and v(H)=t we obtain v$_0$(A)=t, from H ⊨$_V$ A, which is a contradiction since v$_0$ assigns f to all wffs. For (∨ Elimination), we are given: H ⊨$_V$ A∨B; H, A ⊨$_V$ C; and H, B ⊨$_V$ C. We show H ⊨ C, by assuming v(H)=t for any v∈V and proving v(C)=t. Cases where v is not v$_0$ follow the strategy of the previous theorem. When v is v$_0$, assume v(C)=f for reductio. From v$_0$(H)=t, and H ⊨$_V$ A∨B it follows that v$_0$(A∨B)=t, which contradicts the definition of v$_0$.   □

Theorem 7.7.1 If V is a model of a system S that includes S∨, and v is a member of V such that v(C)=f, then there is a S-prime extension v* of v such that v*(C)=f.

Proof. Assume the antecedent of the theorem. By the S∨ Expression Theorem of Section 7.2 and Theorem 7.3.1, V obeys ‖W∨‖. Construct a prime extension v^* of v such that $v^*(C)=f$ by the following recipe. Construct a series of ordered lists $L_0, L_1 \ldots, L_k, \ldots$ of wffs of the language and let L_0 be the list of all disjunctions. Construct a series of valuations $v=v_0, v_1, v_2, \ldots,$ $v_k, \ldots$ as follows. Given v_{k-1}, consider the first disjunction A∨B in the ordering L_{k-1} such that $v_{k-1}(A∨B)=t$. (If there is no such disjunction the series terminates at v_{k-1}.) By ‖W∨‖, there is a $v'∈V$ such that $v_{k-1}≤v'$, $v'(C)=f$, and where either $v'(A)=t$ or $v'(B)=t$. So let v_k be this v', and remove A∨B from the ordered list of wffs L_{k-1} to form L_k. Now define v^* by $v^*(A)=t$ iff $v_i(A)=t$ for some v_i in the series. Since each of the v_i assigns f to C, it follows that $v^*(C)=f$, and so v^* is consistent and qualifies as a valuation. (Note, however, there is no guarantee that v^* is a member of V.)

To show that v^* is prime, let A∨B be any disjunction such that $v^*(A∨B)=t$ and show that $v^*(A)=t$ or $v^*(B)=t$ as follows. Since $v^*(A∨B)=t$, it follows that $v_i(A∨B)=t$ for some i. Let k be the first index where $v_k(A∨B)=t$. In the construction of the series of valuations, $v_n(A∨B)=t$ for each $n≥k$, because each valuation in the series is an extension of its predecessor. Since there are only finitely many wffs between the beginning of the list L_k and the location of A∨B in it, there are only finitely many wffs of the form C∨D such that $v_n(C∨D)=t$ for any n such that $k<n$. Since one of these finitely many wffs is always removed from the lists L_i there must be a point j-1 such that A∨B is the first member of L_{j-1} where $v_{j-1}(A∨B)=t$. By the construction of the series, either $v_j(A)=t$ or $v_j(B)=t$, and so either $v^*(A)=t$ or $v^*(B)=t$.

The valuation v^* satisfies S because assuming that $H ⊢_S C$ and $v^*(H)=t$, we may argue that $v^*(C)=t$ as follows. Given $H ⊢_S C$, the Finitary Lemma of Section 4.3 guarantees that there is a finite subset H' of H such that $H' ⊢_S C$. Since $v^*(H)=t$ it follows that $v^*(H')=t$. Therefore for each wff A in H' there is a v_i which is a member of V such that $v_i(A)=t$. Since there are only finitely many members of H', there must be a largest i such that $v_i(A)=t$ for any of the A in H'. Call this largest index h. Since each v_i is an extension of its predecessor, $v_h(A)=t$ for each member A of H'. Therefore $v_h(H')=t$. But V was a model of S, so every provable argument in S is V-valid. Since v_h is a member of V, $H' ⊢_S C$, and $v_h(H')=t$, it follows that $v_h(C)=t$ with the result that $v^*(C)=t$.   □

[S]p Adequacy Theorem. When S contains S∨, $H ⊢_S C$ iff $H ⊨_{[S]p} C$. Furthermore, [S]p is a model of S.

Proof. Assume S contains the rules S∨. For the proof of soundness (the proof from left to right), assume H ⊢$_S$ C, and let v be any member of [S]p such that v (H)=t. Since v is a member of [S]p, v is S-prime, and so satisfies S. Since H ⊢$_S$ C, and v(H)=t it follows that v(C)=t. Therefore, H ⊨$_{[S]p}$ C as desired.

For the proof of completeness (the proof from right to left), assume H ⊬$_S$ C and find a member v of [S]p such that v(H)=t and v(C)=f as follows. Define v$_H$ so that v$_H$(B)=t iff H ⊢$_S$ B. So we have v$_H$(H)=t and v$_H$(C)=f. We may show that v$_H$ satisfies S so that it qualifies as a member of [S] as follows. Assume that v$_H$(G)=t and G ⊢$_S$ B and demonstrate that v$_H$(B)=t as follows. From v$_H$(G)=t, it follows that H ⊢$_S$ A for each member A of G. This with G ⊢$_S$ B and the Cut Lemma (Section 4.3) entails H ⊢$_S$ B and so v$_H$(B)=t as desired. We know by Theorem 4.3 that [S], (the canonical model for S), is a model of S, so by Theorem 7.7.1 there is an S-prime extension v* of v$_H$ such that v*(C)=f. Since v* is an extension of v$_H$, we also have v*(H)=t. Clearly v* is a member of [S]p, for it is a prime extension of a member v$_H$ of [S]. Therefore H ⊭$_{[S]p}$ C as desired.

To show that [S]p is a model of S, simply use H ⊢$_S$ C iff H ⊨$_{[S]p}$ C, to replace '⊨$_{[S]p}$' for '⊢$_S$' in the statement of the rules to show each rule preserves [S]p-validity.   □

Theorem 7.7.2 When ‖KS‖ is the result of replacing ‖W∨‖ (or ‖∨‖) with ‖C∨‖ in a natural semantics ‖S‖ for a system that includes S∨, the replacement does not affect the notion of validity so defined, that is, H ⊨$_{‖S‖}$ C iff H ⊨$_{‖KS‖}$ C.

Proof. Assume ‖KS‖ and ‖S‖ are as described in the theorem. We must show H ⊨$_{‖S‖}$ C iff H ⊨$_{‖KS‖}$ C.

The proof from left to right follows from the fact that any model that obeys ‖C∨‖ already obeys ‖W∨‖. To see why that holds, assume ‖C∨‖ and show ‖W∨‖ from left to right as follows. Assume v(A∨B)=t and note that v≤v. So by ‖C∨‖, v (A)=t or v(B)=t, hence, if v(C)=f there is a v' in V (namely v) where v'(C)=f and either v'(A)=t or v'(B)=t. For the other direction, assume the right-hand side of ‖W∨‖ and that v(A∨B)=f for reductio. Setting C to A∨B, it follows that there is a member v' of V where v'(A∨B)=f, and either v(A)=t or v(B)=t. But this is incompatible with ‖C∨‖. So any model that obeys ‖KS‖ must obey ‖S‖. So it follows that whenever H ⊨$_{‖S‖}$ C, H ⊨$_{‖KS‖}$ C.

For the proof from right to left, assume H ⊭$_{‖S‖}$ C and prove H ⊭$_{‖KS‖}$ C as follows. From H ⊭$_{‖S‖}$ C, there must be a model V obeying ‖S‖ such that H ⊭$_V$ C. Since ‖S‖ is a natural semantics, V is a model of S. Therefore the rules preserve V-validity with the result that if H ⊢$_S$ C, then H ⊨$_V$ C. Given that, and H $\nvDash_V$ C, it follows that H $\nvdash_S$ C, and so by the [S]p Adequacy Theorem, H $\nvdash_{[S]p}$ C. The [S]p Adequacy Theorem also tells us that [S]p is a model of S, and so since ‖S‖ is a natural semantics for S, it follows that [S]p obeys ‖S‖. [S]p also obeys ‖C∨‖, so it obeys ‖KS‖. Therefore [Sp] is a ‖KS‖-model V such that H $\vDash_V$ C, and H $\nvDash_{‖KS‖}$ C as desired.   □

Theorem 7.7.3 If H has an **I**∨-model that disobeys ‖C∨‖, then it has a model that obeys ‖C∨‖, the classical truth condition for ∨.

Proof. Assume that H has a **I**∨-model V. Then V is a model of **I**∨, and there is a valuation v in V such that v(H)=t. Since v is consistent so that v(C)=f for some C, it follows that H $\nvDash_V$ C for this wff C. By The **I**∨ Expression Theorem of Section 7.2, and the fact that V is a model of **I**, V obeys ‖**I**∨‖, and so H $\nvDash_{‖\mathbf{I}∨‖}$ C. **I**∨ contains S∨, so by Theorem 7.7.2 H $\nvDash_{‖KI‖}$ C, and hence there is a model V* that obeys ‖C∨‖ and a v* in V* such that v*(H)=t as desired.   □

8   Negation

We have already discussed intuitionistic logics that define ~ by ~$A =_{df} A \rightarrow \bot$. However, let us now consider the possibility that ~ is a primitive symbol of the language. In light of the ~ Definition Theorem of Section 6.4, it will come as no surprise that the natural deduction (ND) rules for intuitionistic negation express the intuitionistic truth condition $\|\neg\|$ (Section 8.1). More interesting results surface when we ask what is expressed by S~, the classical ND rules for negation (Section 8.2). It turns out that the condition $\|S\sim\|$ that S~ expresses is intuitionistic, but it also includes a side condition $\|LL\|$ corresponding to the requirement that (Double Negation) preserves validity. Sections 8.3–8.4 will explore the content of $\|LL\|$. In Section 8.5, $\|LL\|$ is recast in a form $\|LL'\|$ that mentions no connective. Questions are raised about whether $\|S\sim\|$ is a legitimate semantics for ~. The idea that $\|S\sim\|$ is not acceptable is supported in Section 8.6, where it is shown that $\|S\sim\|$ is not functional. That negative opinion of $\|S\sim\|$ is tempered somewhat in Section 8.7, where it is shown that $\|LL'\|$ makes a positive contribution to resolving the serious problems (discussed in Section 7.3) that bedevil the condition $\|\vee\|$ expressed by the disjunction rules S$\vee$. Section 8.8 shows that despite the non-functionality of $\|S\sim\|$, the condition $\|PL\|$ expressed by the classical rules PL for negation and the other connectives is isomorphic to a perfectly respectable semantics, one that has already appeared in the literature. In light of that result, the situation is reassessed (Section 8.9). $\|PL\|$ is defended by arguing that $\|LL\|$ has nothing to do with the truth conditions for negation, and that therefore the meaning for negation expressed by the classical rules is intuitionistic.

Chapters to come will underscore the virtues of $\|PL\|$. Chapter 10 deploys $\|PL\|$ as a logic for an open future, and a foundation for systems that can handle human agency. Chapter 15 shows that $\|PL\|$ is especially well suited for solving serious problems faced by supervaluation accounts of vagueness.

Alien anthropologists who discover that we employ classical natural deduction rules for our reasoning will conclude that ‖PL‖ tells us what we mean by the connectives (if anything does). The upshot is that whether we adopt intuitionistic or classical ND rules, what we mean by ∼ is intuitionistic.

8.1 Negation and intuitionistic semantics

A system S¬ for intuitionistic negation is formulated by adding the following pair of rules to the structural rules for ⊢.

S¬:   (∼ Introduction)   (Contradiction)

     H, A ⊢ B   H ⊢ B

     H, A ⊢ ∼B   H ⊢ ∼B

     ——————   ——————

     H ⊢ ∼A   H ⊢ A

A system for classical negation S∼ results from replacing (Contradiction) with (∼ Elimination).

S∼:   (∼ Introduction)   (∼ Elimination)

     H, A ⊢ B   H, ∼A ⊢ B

     H, A ⊢ ∼B   H, ∼A ⊢ ∼B

     ——————   ——————

     H ⊢ ∼A   H ⊢ A

A system for classical negation S∼ may also be equivalently formulated by simply adding (Double Negation) to S¬.

(Double Negation)

∼∼A ⊢ A

The classical truth condition for negation is, of course, ‖C∼‖.

‖C∼‖ v(∼A)=t iff v(A)=f.

Notice that from the provability of A, ∼A / A, and A, ∼A / ∼A it follows from (Contradiction) that A, ∼A / B, is provable in S¬. So if the rules of S¬ preserve V-validity, it will follow that A, ∼A ⊨ᵥ B, and hence for any v in V, if v({A, ∼A}) =t then v(B)=t for every wff B. Since all valuations are consistent, they may not assign t to every wff B, and it follows that v cannot assign t to both A and ∼A. So S¬ expresses ‖C∼‖ltr, the left-to-right portion of the classical truth condition ‖C∼‖.

‖C∼‖ltr If v(∼A)=t, then v(A)=f.

Of course S¬ is too weak to guarantee ‖C∼‖rtl, the truth clause in the other direction, for it cannot prove (Double Negation), a principle that is classically valid.

‖C∼‖rtl If v(A)=f, then v(∼A)=t.

It does not help to add (Double Negation) to S¬ because classical systems based on S∼ exhibit exactly the same failing. When PL is any propositional logic that includes S→ and S∼, Theorem 4.4.1 guarantees that PL has a non-classical interpretation where v(A)=v(∼A)=f.

We know by the ∼ Definition Theorem that ‖¬‖ holds when negation is introduced by definition.

‖¬‖ v(∼A)=t iff for all v′ in V, if v≤v′, then v′ (A)=f.

So one would expect that if ∼ is a primitive symbol, then ‖¬‖ is a natural semantics for the intuitionistic system S¬.

S¬ Expression Theorem. ‖¬‖ is a natural semantics for S¬.

Proof. By the ‖KI‖ Theorem of Section 5.5, ‖¬‖ qualifies as a semantics. The proof that V is a model of S¬ iff V obeys ‖¬‖ follows easily given one follows the strategies of the S→ Expression Theorem of Section 6.1. □

The SI Theorem of Section 6.4 showed that the system SI that defines ∼ and lacks ∨ has ‖SI‖ as its natural semantics, where ‖SI‖ included those of the conditions ‖&‖, ‖⊥‖, ‖→‖, ‖↔‖, and ‖¬‖ that govern the connectives of SI. It follows immediately from the S¬ Expression Theorem that when **I** is like SI save that it takes ∼ to be primitive, then it has the same conditions ‖SI‖ as its natural semantics.

I Theorem. ‖SI‖ is a natural semantics for **I**.

Proof. The ‖KI‖ Theorem of Section 5.5 guarantees that ‖SI‖ is a semantics. The SI Theorem of Section 6.4 shows that **I** expresses ‖⊥‖, ‖&‖, ‖→‖, and ‖↔‖ for the connectives it contains, and the S¬ Expression Theorem tells us that **I** expresses ‖¬‖, since S¬ does. So **I** expresses ‖SI‖. □

In case the Path Isomorphism Theorem of Section 7.5 persuades you that the condition ‖∨‖ expressed by S∨ qualifies as a semantics, then the S∨

Expression Theorem of Section 7.2 can be used to obtain the stronger result that the system $\mathbf{I}\vee$ (that is, $\mathbf{I}$ plus S$\vee$) has $\|\mathbf{I}\vee\|$ as a natural semantics, where $\|\mathbf{I}\vee\|$ is the conjunction $\|\mathbf{SI}\|$ with $\|\vee\|$.

I$\vee$ Theorem. Presuming $\|\vee\|$ qualifies as a semantics, $\|\mathbf{I}\vee\|$ is a natural semantics for $\mathbf{I}\vee$.

All of this is unremarkable. More interesting results emerge when we turn to systems incorporating the classical rules S$\sim$. So classical negation will be the topic for the rest of this chapter.

8.2 Intuitionistic truth conditions for classical negation

Of course the classical system S$\sim$ cannot have the intuitionistic truth condition $\|\neg\|$ as a natural semantics because (Double Negation) is intuitionistically invalid. However, one may create an "intuitionistic" condition $\|S\sim\|$ for S$\sim$ nonetheless by letting $\|S\sim\|$ be the conjunction of $\|\neg\|$ with an extra requirement $\|LL\|$ that validates (Double Negation).

$\|S\sim\| = \|\neg\|$ conjoined with $\|LL\|$.

$\|LL\|$ If $v(A)=f$, then for some v' in V, $v \leq v'$ and $v'(\sim A)=t$.

$\|LL\|$ is named for the Lindenbaum Lemma, for reasons that will become apparent in Section 8.3 below. Special care must be taken to investigate whether $\|S\sim\|$ qualifies as a semantics. Worries about $\|S\sim\|$ and possible solutions will be discussed in Sections 8.6–8.9 below. In the meantime, we may still prove that the system S$\sim$ for classical negation expresses $\|S\sim\|$.

S$\sim$ Expression Theorem. S$\sim$ expresses $\|S\sim\|$.

Proof. We must demonstrate V is a model of S$\sim$ iff V obeys $\|S\sim\|$.

To show S$\sim$ is sound for $\|S\sim\|$ (the proof from right to left), assume that V obeys $\|S\sim\|$. The S$\neg$ Expression Theorem established that ($\sim$ Introduction) and (Contradiction) preserve V-validity, so all that remains is to show (Double Negation) is V-valid. For arbitrary member v of V, assume $v(\sim\sim A)=t$, and show that $v(A)=t$ by reductio. From $v(A)=f$ and $\|LL\|$, there is a valuation v' in V such that $v \leq v'$ and $v'(\sim A)=t$. But from $\|\neg\|$ and $v(\sim\sim A)=t$ we have $v'(\sim\sim A)=f$, a contradiction.

To show S~ forces ‖S~‖ (the proof from left to right), assume V is a model of S~, and show that ‖⊣‖ and ‖LL‖ both hold. To show that V obeys ‖⊣‖, note that since V is a model of S~, and (Contradiction) is derivable in S~, V must be a model of S¬, and so by the S¬ Expression Theorem (Section 8.1), V obeys ‖⊣‖. To show that V obeys ‖LL‖ as well, assume that v(A)=f and show that for some v′, v≤v′ and v′ (~A)=t as follows. Since V is a model of S~, (Double Negation) is V-valid. Since v(A)=f, it follows that v(~~A)=f as well. By ‖⊣‖, there is a valuation v′ such that v≤v′ and v′ (~A)=t as desired.   □

Now let ‖PL‖ be the semantics that results from adding ‖LL‖ to the semantics ‖IV‖ for an intuitionistic logic that includes disjunction. (Remember that ‖IV‖ is the conjunction of ‖⊥‖, ‖&‖, ‖→‖, ‖↔‖, ‖∨‖, and ‖⊣‖.) Let PL be the classical system consisting of S⊥, S&, S→, S↔, S∨, and S~. Then PL expresses ‖PL‖.

PL Expression Theorem. PL expresses ‖PL‖.

Proof. Show that V is a model of PL iff V obeys ‖PL‖ as follows.

The soundness of PL for ‖PL‖ is guaranteed by the IV Expression Theorem of Section 7.2, and the S~ Expression Theorem. By the IV Expression Theorem, PL forces all conditions in ‖IV‖, and by the S~ Expression Theorem, it also expresses ‖LL‖, so PL expresses ‖PL‖.   □

8.3 ‖LL‖: what double negation expresses

The classical stipulation ‖LL‖ has an interesting interpretation from the point of view of intuitionistic semantics. Let us view ≤ as representing the process of extending our knowledge as new information becomes available. Suppose v(A)=f is taken to mean that we have no evidence that A is true. For the intuitionist, v(A)=f is compatible with v(~A)=f, which expresses that we also have no evidence for ~A as well. When this happens, neither A, nor ~A is determined to be true by our state of knowledge. So let us say that a wff A is *undetermined* at v when v(A)=v(~A)=f. A is *determined* at v when v(A)=t or v(~A)=t, which entails (given ‖⊣‖) that the classical truth condition holds for A.

(Determined)   Wff Λ is *determined* by v iff v(A)=t or v(~A)=t.

So $\|S\sim\|$ entails that every undetermined wff becomes determined in some possible extension of our knowledge. This is exactly the bone of contention between classical and intuitionistic accounts of truth.

Theorem 8.3.1 If V obeys $\|LL\|$ and A is not determined at v, then there is an extension of v in V where A is determined.

Proof. Suppose that A is not determined at v, that is $v(A)=v(\sim A)=f$. From $v(A)=f$ and $\|LL\|$, it follows that for some v' in V, $v\leq v'$ and $v'(\sim A)=t$. So A is determined at v' which is an extension of v as desired. $\qquad\Box$

The condition $\|LL\|$ was named in honor of Lindenbaum's Lemma, for it expresses the idea that lies at the core of the result that every consistent set has a maximally consistent extension. If we associate each set of wffs with the valuation that assigns t to its members, the Lindenbaum Lemma would say that every (consistent) valuation v can be extended to one that obeys the classical truth condition $\|C\sim\|$, so it determines all the wffs by assigning either A or $\sim A$ the value t.

$\|LL\|$ does not say this exactly, but it comes close. When $v(A)=f$, there is, of course, no guarantee that $v(\sim A)=t$ as $\|C\sim\|$ demands, for as we showed in Theorem 4.4.1, the provability valuation $v_{\vdash}$ is a member of a model of $S\sim$ such that $v_{\vdash}(p)=v_{\vdash}(\sim p)=f$. However, $\|LL\|$ entails that if $v(A)=v(\sim A)=f$, then there is an extension v' of v in V such that the value of $\sim A$ is "corrected," that is, where $v'(\sim A)=t$ as $\|C\sim\|$ requires. The resulting extension v' may not be classical, since there may be other wffs B where $v'(B)=v'(\sim B)=f$ that still need to be corrected. If there are only finitely many wffs that need fixing, then $\|LL\|$ guarantees that V will contain an extension v^* of v that obeys $\|C\sim\|$, because starting from v, one may apply $\|LL\|$ finitely many times to obtain a valuation that corrects all the offending wffs. However, if there are infinitely many wffs B where $v(B)=v(\sim B)=f$, then although there must be an extension v^* of v that obeys $\|C\sim\|$, there is no guarantee that v^* will be a member of V. However, this feature is sufficient, nonetheless, to guarantee that the concept of validity is not affected as one moves from $\|PL\|$ models to those that also obey $\|C\sim\|$.

8.4 Using $\|LL\|$ to generate classical models

When the language of PL has infinitely many propositional variables, $\|LL\|$ does not guarantee that all of its members have classical extensions in

V. However the strategy of the Lindenbaum Lemma can still be used to show that ||LL|| entails that such classical valuations exist, and that the set Vc of those classical valuations satisfies exactly the sets of wffs satisfied by V. This result can be seen from two points of view. On one hand it is a recapitulation (in semantical rather than proof-theoretic language) of the core of the proof of the completeness of PL using the Lindenbaum strategy. On the other hand, it reflects a fundamental underdetermination in the expressive resources of PL. There is no sentence or set of sentences of PL that forces models of PL to be classical. The language of PL cannot express the difference between its intuitionistic natural semantics and the classical semantics. This behavior illustrates a lesson we have seen before. When a system is complete for a semantics stronger than its natural semantics, the "reason" is that it lacks the expressive resources to tell the difference between the two.

We call a model *classical* when all its valuations are classical.

(Classical Model)   Model V is *classical* (for language L) iff each member v of V is classical for L.

When H is a set of wffs, and V is a model of system S, and there is a member v of V such that v(H)=t, we will say that H *has an S-model*.

Theorem 8.4.1 If H has a PL-model, then H has a PL-model that is classical.

Proof. Suppose that H has a PL model. Then for some model V of PL and member v of V, v(H)=t. Since V is a model of PL it follows by the S~ Theorem that ||S~|| holds which means that V obeys ||LL||. Let us mimic the Lindenbaum procedure by letting B_1, ..., B_n, ... be a list of all wffs undefined at v, and constructing a sequence of valuations v, v_1, ..., v_n, ..., in V by the following strategy. Given v_i, let v_{i+1} be an extension of v_i such that $v_{i+1}(B_{i+1})$=t. ||LL|| guarantees that there is such a v_{i+1} in V for each v_i. Now define a new valuation v* by v*(A)=t iff v_i(A)=t for some i. Since each of the v_i is an extension of v, so is v*, and v*(H)=t. If we can show that v* satisfies PL and obeys ||C~||, then by the Holism Theorem of Section 2.3, v* is classical, and the set of all classical valuations for PL is the desired classical PL model of H. The demonstration that v* obeys ||C~|| and satisfies PL are easy exercises using the strategies found in the proof of the Lindenbaum Lemma.   □

The last theorem may be viewed as an analog of the (downward) Lowenheim–Skolem Theorem, for it claims that every set with a non-classical (non-denumerable) model has a classical (denumerable) one. This demonstrates the expressive weakness of PL. PL lacks the expressive power to force models to be non-classical. Since every classical model determines every sentence, it also follows that PL cannot express that any of its sentences is undetermined. Remember that Theorem 4.4.3, like the upward Lowenheim–Skolem Theorem, established that every set with a classical model has a non-classical one. So PL can express neither that its models are classical nor that they are non-classical. Similarly PL is unable to express that its sentences are determinate nor can it express that they are indeterminate.

8.5 A structural version of ‖LL‖

The project for this section is to determine the role of ‖LL‖, if any, in providing an interpretation for the connective ~. One might think of ‖LL‖ as analogous to conditions on frames for modal logic such as reflexivity and transitivity. Such structural conditions are not part of the truth conditions for the connectives, but stipulations used to narrow down the class of models to be considered in defining validity. However, ‖LL‖ appears not to function in the same way, for while conditions on frames such as reflexivity and transitivity mention the structure of a frame only, and so are connective neutral, ‖LL‖ explicitly mentions the truth behavior of wffs involving ~.

‖LL‖ If v(A)=f, then for some v' in V, v≤v' and v' (~A)=t.

However, it is possible to reformulate ‖LL‖ so that no mention of any symbols of the object language is involved. The revised condition ‖LL'‖ follows. Humberstone (2011, p. 900) calls a condition related to this one (Refinability).

‖LL'‖ If v(A)=f, then for some v' in V, v≤v' and for any v'' in V,
        if v'≤v'', then v'' (A)=f.

‖LL'‖ says that once v(A)=f there is a later point v' where A is f in all extensions of v'. This entails that once A is f at v, it is false all along some path through v. Furthermore, at some point v' along that path, it is false at every extension of v'. When ‖⊣‖ holds, ‖LL'‖ is clearly equivalent to ‖LL‖, because ‖LL'‖ results from applying ‖⊣‖ to 'v' (~A)=t' in ‖LL‖.

The fact that ‖LL‖, the condition expressing the "essence" of classical negation, can be equivalently stated in a form that does not mention negation has important consequences for the behavior of the other connectives. The requirement that a model V meets ‖LL′‖ may validate new formulas, including ones that do not contain ~. That is exactly what occurs with Peirce's Law, and it explains why that principle is valid on classical semantics, while invalid on the natural semantics ‖→‖ for S→. We were able to demonstrate the independence of Peirce's Law in Theorem 6.2 by constructing a counterexample. However, once ‖LL′‖ is imposed, Peirce's Law becomes valid, as is clear from the next theorem.

Theorem 8.5.1 If V obeys ‖→‖ and ‖LL′‖, then $\vDash_V ((A{\to}B){\to}A){\to}A$.

Proof. Suppose that V obeys ‖→‖ and ‖LL′‖ and that $v(((A{\to}B){\to}A){\to}A)$=f for some v in V for reductio. By ‖→‖, there is a member v′ of V, such that v≤v′, v (($(A{\to}B){\to}A$)=t and v′ (A)=f. By ‖LL′‖ it follows from v′(A)=f that for some v″ in V, v′≤v″ and for every u in V, if v″≤u then u(A)=f. So v″(A)=f, since v′≤v″. In light of v′(($(A{\to}B){\to}A$)=t, v′≤v″ and ‖→‖, either v″(A→B)=f or v″(A)=t. But we established that v″(A)=f, so it follows that v″(A→B)=f. By ‖→‖ there must be some valuation v* in V such that v″≤v*, v*(A)=t and v*(B)=f. But we had that for every u in V, if v″≤u then u(A)=f. So since v″≤v*, v*(A)=f, which yields the desired contradiction. ☐

This result provides a semantical explanation for why the classical negation rules S~ do not form a conservative extension of the classical conditional fragment S→. The fact that there are wffs (like instances of Peirce's Law) provable in system S→ + S~ but not in S→ is a reflection of the fact that the natural semantics ‖→‖ for S→ becomes "contaminated" by the condition ‖LL′‖ expressed by S~. ‖LL′‖ says something new about ≤; and that validates new wffs involving →.

The fact that the classical negation rules S~ do not form a conservative extension of the classical fragment S→ has been cited in the past as reason for thinking that S~ does not define a connective. The idea is that in defining one connective, a system of rules should not change the deductive behavior of any others. Therefore a properly defined connective must meet Belnap's (1962) conservation requirement. Since S~ does not, it does not define a meaning for ~. (See, for example, the discussion in Prawitz (1971), Dummett (1991, pp. 297ff.), and Hand (1993, pp. 125ff.).) Natural semantics provides better insight into this pathology. Here the failure of conservation is a symptom of a deeper problem with $\|LL'\|$. Not only does $\|LL'\|$ disturb the semantical behavior of $\to$, it affects the truth behavior of all the other connectives. The ultimate example of this interference occurs when a language already containing $\sim$ is supplemented by adding a separate intuitionistic negation symbol $\neg$ governed by intuitionistic rules S$\neg$. Since $\leq$ appears in the natural truth condition $\|\neg\|$ for the symbol $\neg$, and $\|LL'\|$ governs $\leq$, the rule (Double Negation) is validated for $\neg$, and $\neg$ becomes classical.

Theorem 8.5.2 If V obeys $\|LL'\|$, and $\|\neg\|$ holds for the connective $\neg$, then $\neg\neg A \vDash_V A$.

Proof. Suppose V obeys $\|LL'\|$ and $\|\neg\|$, and let v be any member of V such that $v(\neg\neg A)=t$. Suppose for reductio that $v(A)=f$. From $\|LL'\|$ it follows that there is a member v' of V such that $v \leq v'$ and for all v'' if $v' \leq v''$, then $v''(A)=f$. By $\|\neg\|$, $v'(\neg A)=t$. But that cannot be, since by $v(\neg\neg A)=t$, $v \leq v'$ and $\|\neg\|$, it follows that $v'(\neg A)=f$. $\square$

The last theorem explains Hand's (1993) observation that classical and intuitionistic negations conflict. He notes that the mere presence of classical rules S$\sim$ in a system with a separate intuitionistic symbol for negation $\neg$ entails classical theorems for $\neg$. The fact that $\|LL'\|$ contaminates the behavior of $\leq$ in $\|\neg\|$ is the reason that $\|\neg\|$ collapses to the classical truth condition. Given the adequacy of systems with respect to their natural semantics (see Section 12.1), the conversion of an intuitionistic connective to its classical counterpart in the semantics is inherited by the proof theory.

This suggests that a general explanation for why S$\to$+S$\sim$ is not a conservative extension of S$\to$, is the presence of a structural side condition like $\|LL'\|$ in the condition expressed by S$\sim$. However, that would be wrong, because the classical truth condition for negation involves no side condition, and it too causes failure of conservation in the same way. The insistence that the connective $\sim$ have the standard classical reading $\|C\sim\|$ profoundly disturbs formerly non-classical behavior of the other connectives.

$\|C\sim\|$ $v(\sim A)=t$ iff $v(A)=f$.

The reason is that ‖C~‖ entails (≤=), which is yet another structural (or connective free) condition on ≤. (Restall (1999, section 5) makes a similar point in the context of the semantics for relevance logics.)

(≤=) v≤v' iff v=v'.

Theorem 8.5.3 If V obeys ‖C~‖, then V obeys (≤=).

Proof. Assume V obeys ‖C~‖, and prove that V obeys (≤=) as follows. The proof of (≤=) is trivial from right to left. For the left to right direction, assume v≤v', and prove v=v' by showing that v(A)=t iff v'(A)=t, for any wff A as follows. The proof of this from left to right is guaranteed by v≤v'. For the proof from right to left, assume v'(A)=t and v(A)=f for reductio. By ‖C~‖, v(~A)=t, and so by v≤v', v'(~A)=t. But this conflicts v'(A)=t and ‖C~‖.   □

The upshot of the last theorem is that ‖C~‖ entails that all valuations in V are maximal, in the sense that they have no extensions other than themselves. But this means, for example, that the natural truth condition ‖→‖ collapses to the standard truth condition ‖C→‖.

‖→‖ v(A→B)=t iff for every v' in V, if v≤v', then v' (A)=f or v' (B)=t.

‖C→‖ v(A→B)=t iff v(A)=f or v(B)=t.

(Use the last theorem to justify replacing '=' for '≤' in ‖→‖, and simplify to obtain ‖C→‖.) The same is true for all the connectives: ↔, ∨, ~, and even the symbol ¬ for intuitionistic negation. This provides deeper insight into the Holism Theorem of Section 2.3, which reported that when ~ is classical, all the other connectives must obey the classical truth conditions. That result follows directly from the fact that ‖C~‖ entails that the intuitionistic truth conditions collapse to their classical counterparts.

8.6 Why classical negation has no functional semantics

The disruptive behavior of ‖LL'‖ raises worries about whether ‖S~‖ could possibly qualify as a functional condition. As a matter of fact, it does not. To help see why, consider the model V* that was used to show (in Theorem 6.2.1) that Peirce's Law is independent from S→. We know from Theorem 8.5.1 that ‖LL'‖ validates Peirce's Law. But Theorem 6.2.1 tells us that Peirce's Law is V*-invalid. So V* can not obey ‖LL'‖. By considering the atomic portion of V*, it is possible to construct an atomic model that has no extension obeying ||LL′||, hence none that obeys ||S~||.

Theorem 8.6 ||S~|| is not functional.

Proof. We show that ||S~|| is not functional by proving that there is an atomic model that has no extension obeying ||S~||. For simplicity, we assume the language L contains ~ only. Consider the atomic model W*={v, u}, v(p)=v(q)= u(q)=f and u(p)=t. Now let V* be any extension of W*. Then V* contains two valuations v^ and u^ such that v^(p)=v(p) and u^(p)=u(p). Let $\leq_p$ be the relation defined by ||p≤||. Note that v^$\leq_p$u^, but not u^$\leq_p$v^. We show that V* cannot obey ||S~|| by reductio. If V* does obey ||S~||, it obeys ||LL′|| and the intuitionistic truth condition ||⊢||. By the ||KI|| Theorem of Section 5.5 in the special case where the language L contains ~ only, it follows that there is a unique extension of W* obeying ||⊢||, and so this extension must be V*. By the fact that V* obeys ||⊢|| and the ≤ Lemma of Section 5.4 (restricted to the language L), we have that v$\leq_p$v′ iff v≤v′, for all v and v′ in V*. So from v^$\leq_p$u^ we have v^≤u^. Since v^(p)=f, ||LL′|| would guarantee that either v^ or u^ is a valuation v′ such that for all v″∈V*, if v′≤v″, v″(p)=f. But v^ cannot be such a valuation v′ because v^≤u^ and u^(p)=t, and u^ cannot be such a v′ because u^≤u^ and u^(p)=t. So V* does not obey ||LL′|| which contradicts the assumption that V* obeys ||S~||.   □

The last theorem may viewed as further support for the idea that S~ defines no meaning for ~, and that classical negation does not qualify as a logical connective. (See Dummett, 1991, pp. 297ff., for proof-theoretic arguments to the same conclusion.) ||LL′|| requires that we throw away perfectly good atomic models. However, in the beginning of Section 5.5, we took the position that ||S|| qualifies as a semantics provided ||S|| is isomorphic to a standard semantical account with recursive truth conditions. It was only later that we considered the requirement that ||S|| be functional. So it is still an open question whether the non-functionality of ||S~|| is a serious defect. The next sections provide reasons for thinking that the failure of functionality is something we might learn to live with.

8.7 Disjunction with classical negation

The last section brought the disturbing news that ||S~|| is not a functional condition. There are some atomic models that cannot be extended to full models obeying ‖S~‖. In Theorem 7.6.1, we showed that the condition ‖∨‖ expressed by the disjunction rules S∨ is also not functional, this time because of the failure of uniqueness.

> ‖∨‖ v(A∨B)=t iff for every path bundle P through v,
>   there is a v′ in P such that v′(A)=t or v′(B)=t.

> (Path Bundle) P is a *path bundle through* v iff for some wff D,
>   v(D)=f, and P = {v′: both v≤v′ and v′(D)=f}.

Since the condition ‖PL‖ expressed by classical propositional logic includes ‖∨‖ and ‖S~‖ (along with ‖&‖, ‖⊥‖, ‖→‖, and ‖↔‖), it would be reasonable to expect that ‖PL‖ is doubly bad. However, the situation is better than it looks, for ‖∨‖ and ‖S~‖ offset each other's failings. In fact, we will be able to establish a pleasing isomorphism result with which to rescue ‖PL‖. The basis for success is that given ‖S~‖, the condition for disjunction ‖∨‖ (or equivalently ‖W∨‖, by Theorem 7.3.1) can be simplified so that the mention of the truth behavior of complex formulas C in ‖W∨‖ disappears.

> ‖W∨‖ v(A∨B)=t iff for every wff C, if v(C)=f, then there is a v′ in V
>   such that v≤v′, v′(C)=f, and either v′(A)=t or v′(B)=t.

As a result, an isomorphism can be established for models obeying ‖PL‖ to a version of Kripke models for intuitionistic semantics that does not require extra structure such as path neighborhoods introduced in Section 7.4. Furthermore, the ≤ Lemma is restored in this semantics, so that the use of ‖p≤‖ in place of ‖≤‖ is warranted, and circularity worries are nipped in the bud.

To help explain the new condition for ∨, it helps to employ the idea of determination first mentioned in Section 8.3. There we said that A is determined at v exactly when v(A)=t or v(~A)=t. Here it is better to define the idea equivalently without mention of ~.

> (Determined) A is *determined* at v iff A has the same value in every
>   extension of v.

When wff A is determined and false at v, we write: v(A)=F.

> (F) v(A)=F iff A is determined at v and v(A)=f.

This notation is useful in providing a more compact definition of ‖LL′‖.

> ‖LF‖ If v(A)=f, then for some v′∈V, v≤v′ and v′(A)=F.

A wff is quasi-true at v iff it is true whenever it is determined, or to put it another way when v(A)≠F.

(Quasi-true) A is *quasi-true* at v iff v(A)≠F.

When A is quasi-true at v, let us write: 'v(A)=qT'. Note that when v(A)=qT, it follows that either v(A)=t, or v(A) is not determined. Either way, this entails that A is t in some extension of v.

---

qT Lemma. v(A)=qT iff for some v'∈V, v≤v' and v'(A)=t.

The new condition ‖q∨‖ for disjunction is the requirement that a disjunction is true at v exactly when each of its extensions rates one of the disjuncts quasi-true.

‖q∨‖ v(A∨B)=t iff for all v' in V, if v≤v', then v'(A)=qT or v'(B)=qT.

Now let ‖qPL‖ be ‖PL‖ save that ‖∨‖ in ‖PL‖ is replaced with ‖q∨‖. The next project will be to show that PL expresses ‖qPL‖, and so models obeying ‖PL‖, (that is, the models of PL), are exactly the models that obey ‖qPL‖.

Although the result may be obtained indirectly by citing the equivalence of A∨B with ~(~A&~B), and reading the truth condition from ‖&‖ and ‖¬‖, it is important to find a proof that rests on the semantical behavior of ∨ alone. Not only will the demonstration given here be direct, it will be general, by treating ‖q∨‖ and ‖∨‖ as variants of one truth schema. The advantage of looking at things this way will be that isomorphism results for intuitionistic semantics to be presented in coming chapters will automatically apply to classical semantics as a special case. So classical and intuitionistic logics may be dealt with together as variations on the same theorem. The following truth schema ‖N∨‖ for ∨ is inspired by the neighborhood semantics used in KR-models (Section 7.4). Here we let N be an arbitrary relation between valuations v and subsets P of V.

‖N∨‖ v(A∨B)=t iff for every subset P of V such that vNP,
            there is a v'∈P such that v'(A)=t or v'(B)=t.

Each of the readings for disjunction discussed in this book: ‖C∨‖ (classical), ‖B∨‖ (Beth's), ‖∨‖ (path bundle), and ‖q∨‖ (quasi-truth) may be captured in schema ‖N∨‖ by defining N by (Def N∨), (Def NB∨), (Def NP∨), and (Def Nq∨) (respectively):

(Def N∨)   vNP iff P={v}. (classical)
(Def NB∨)   vNP iff P is the set of all paths through v. (Beth's)
(Def NP∨)   vNP iff P is the set of all path bundles through v.
(Def Nq∨)   vNP iff for some v′ in V, v≤v′ and P={v″: v′≤v″}. (qT)

Now let ‖NP∨‖ and ‖Nq∨‖ be special cases of the general truth condition ‖N∨‖ where N is defined by (Def NP∨) and (Def Nq∨) respectively. It should be clear that ‖NP∨‖ is just a restatement of ‖∨‖, the path bundle truth condition expressed by S∨. The following simple lemma makes it clear that ‖Nq∨‖ amounts to the quasi-truth condition ‖q∨‖ as well.

---

q∨ Lemma. V obeys ‖Nq∨‖ iff V obeys ‖q∨‖.

Proof. Show the right-hand sides (Nqr) of ‖Nq∨‖ and (qr) of ‖q∨‖ are equivalent, where N in (Nqr) is defined by (Def Nq∨).

(qr) For all v′ in V, if v≤v′, then v′(A)=qT or v′(B)=qT.

(Nqr) For all P, if vNP, then for some v′∈P, v′(A)=t or v′(B)=t.

Assume (qr) and demonstrate (Nqr) by assuming vNP, and finding a v′ in P such that v′(A)=t or v′(B)=t as follows. By vNP and (Def Nq∨), there is a v* in V such that v≤v* and P={v″: v*≤v″}. By v≤v* and (Nqr), v*(A)=qT or v*(B)=qT. By the qT Lemma, there must be a v′ in V such that v*≤v′ and v′(A)=t or v′(B)=t. Since v*≤v′, v′∈P, so v′ is the desired member of P.

Assume (Nqr) and demonstrate (qr) by supposing v≤v′ and showing v′(A)=qT or v′(B)=qT as follows. Let P*={v″: v′≤v″}. Then by v≤v′ and (Def Nq∨) we have vNP*, so (qr) yields that v*(A)=t or v*(B)=t, for some v*∈P*. Since v*∈P, v′≤v*, so the qT Lemma entails that v′(A)=qT or v′(B)=qT as desired. □

Now that ‖∨‖ and ‖q∨‖ have been recast as special cases ‖NP∨‖ and ‖Nq∨‖ of the general schema ‖N∨‖, we are ready to show that the path bundle condition ‖∨‖ is equivalent to the quasi-truth condition ‖q∨‖ in the presence of ‖LF‖. Given the last lemma, we need only show that ‖NP∨‖ and ‖Nq∨‖ are equivalent. The proof is given at the end of this chapter in Section 8.11.

Theorem 8.7* If V obeys ‖LF‖, then V obeys ‖NP∨‖ iff V obeys ‖Nq∨‖.

The last theorem entails that ‖∨‖ is equivalent to ‖q∨‖ when V obeys ‖LF‖. Remember that ‖qPL‖ is identical to ‖PL‖ save that the quasi-truth reading ‖q∨‖ is used in place of the path bundle reading ‖∨‖. Furthermore, ‖PL‖

includes ‖LF‖, the condition expressed by the classical version of (Double Negation). The PL Expression Theorem of Section 8.2 showed that PL expresses ‖PL‖, so it follows immediately that PL expresses ‖qPL‖.

---

qPL Expression Theorem. PL expresses ‖qPL‖.

It is a simple matter to verify that the ≤ Lemma holds for ‖qPL‖, hence ‖PL‖. This is a good sign, since it means that any circularity introduced by the use of ‖≤‖ in conditions of ‖PL‖ such as ‖∨‖ may be eliminated by using ‖p≤‖ in its place.

≤ **Lemma (for ‖PL‖).** If V obeys ‖PL‖, then V obeys ‖≤‖ iff it obeys ‖p≤‖.

Proof. Assume that V obeys ‖PL‖. Therefore V is a model of PL by the I∨ Expression Theorem of Section 7.2. By the last theorem, V obeys ‖qPL‖. At this point, the proof is identical to the proof of the ≤ Lemma of Section 5.4, save that a new argument is required in the inductive case for disjunction using ‖q∨‖.

   A has the form B∨C. Assume v(B∨C)=t and establish that v′(B∨C)=t with the help of ‖q∨‖. Assume that v″ is any member of V such that v′≤v″ and show that v″(B)=qT or v″(C)=qT as follows. From v≤v′ and v′≤v″ and the transitivity of ≤ it follows that v≤v″. Given ‖q∨‖ and v(B∨C)=t, it follows immediately that v″(B)=qT or v″(C)=qT as desired.   □

It is a pleasing discovery that the condition ‖LF‖ also has an equivalent form ‖pLF‖, which quantifies over propositional variables p only.

   ‖LF‖ If v(A)=f, then for some v′∈V, v≤v′ and v′(A)=F.

   ‖pLF‖ If v(p)=f, then for some v′∈V, v≤v′ and v′(p)=F.

As a result, ‖qPL‖ may be written as a set of truth conditions for the connectives along with two side conditions ‖p≤‖ and ‖pLF‖ on the behavior of propositional variables. (This result is essentially the analog of Humberstone's Lemma 6.44.2 (2011, p. 902).) The proof is in Section 8.11.

LF Lemma*. When ‖pPL‖ is the result of replacing ‖LF‖ in ‖qPL‖ with ‖pLF‖, V obeys ‖pPL‖ iff V obeys ‖qPL‖.

The LF Lemma will play an important role in our defense of ‖PL‖ in Section 8.9. (It is crucial to the proof of the LF Lemma that the quasi-truth interpretation ‖q∨‖ of disjunction was available in ‖qPL‖. Jack Woods notes (personal communication) that the model used in the proof of Theorem 7.6.1 obeys ‖pLF‖ and the path bundle condition ‖∨‖, but both ‖LF‖ and ‖q∨‖ fail. Therefore, when ‖∨‖ is the disjunction truth condition, the replacement of ‖pLF‖ for ‖LF‖ makes a difference. Note however, that the difference cannot arise in the context of ‖PL‖, since ‖PL‖ entails ‖q∨‖ by the qPL Expression Theorem.)

8.8 Possibilities semantics for classical propositional logic

The last theorems inspire the thought that ‖qPL‖ (hence ‖PL‖) can be shown to qualify as a legitimate semantics by proving an isomorphism theorem for a simple variant of Kripke semantics. The idea is to modify Kripke semantics in two ways: (1) adopt the analog of the quasi-truth condition ‖q∨‖ in place of (K∨), the classical condition for ∨, and (2) enforce an analog of ‖pLF‖ as a side condition on Kripke models so as to validate the classical principles for negation. The resulting semantics has already appeared in the literature. It is essentially the propositional portion of the possibilities semantics for modal logic described in Humberstone (2011, pp. 899ff.) and Humberstone, (1981). Possibilities semantics introduces a set W of possibilities rather than possible worlds. While possible worlds completely describe how everything is, a possibility provides only partial information about the ways things might be. The relation $\leq$ is introduced over possibilities to indicate that one possibility includes all information found in another. The parallel with valuations and our extension relation is striking.

Here are the formal details. A *KR-model* is a Kripke model U=<W, $\subseteq$, u> that meets ($\subseteq$) and (Refinability) for each propositional variable p.

($\subseteq$) If w$\subseteq$w′ and u(w, p)=t, then u(w′, p)=t.

(Refinability) If u(w, p)=f, then for some w′ in W, w$\subseteq$w′ and
                for any w″ in W, if w′$\subseteq$w″, then u(w″, p)=f.

('KR' stands for 'Kripke model with Refinability'.) The (Refinability) condition is simply the analog of ‖pLF‖. In KR-semantics, the definition of the truth relation $\vDash$ is revised so that the classical truth condition (K∨) is replaced by the analog of the quasi-truth condition (Kq∨). So $\vDash$ is defined as follows.

(Kp) $w \vDash p$ iff $u(w, p)=t$, for propositional variables p.

(K⊥) $w \nvDash \perp$.

(K&) $w \vDash A\&B$ iff $w \vDash A$ and $w \vDash B$.

(K→) $w \vDash A{\rightarrow}B$ iff for every w' in W, if $w{\subseteq}w'$, then $w' \nvDash A$ or $w' \vDash B$.

(K↔) $w \vDash A{\leftrightarrow}B$ iff for every w' in W, if $w{\subseteq}w'$, then $w' \vDash A$ iff $w' \vDash B$.

(K¬) $w \vDash {\sim}A$ iff for every w' in W, if $w{\subseteq}w'$, then $w' \nvDash A$.

(Kq∨) $w \vDash A{\vee}B$ iff for every w' in W, if $w{\subseteq}w'$, then there is a w'' in W
                         such that $w'{\subseteq}w''$ and $w'' \vDash A$ or $w'' \vDash B$.

The notion of KR-validity is defined as you would expect. $H \vDash_{KR} C$ iff for each KR-model $U=<W, \subseteq, u>$ and w in W, if $w \vDash A$ for each A in H, then $w \vDash C$.

The next project will be to show that any model V obeying ‖PL‖ is isomorphic to a KR-model, where the notion of an isomorphism is exactly the one used in Section 5.4.

(Isomorphic) $<V, \leq>$ is isomorphic to Kripke model $<W, \subseteq, u>$ iff there is a 1–1 mapping * from V into W such that (≤⊆) and (vu) hold.

(≤⊆) $v{\leq}v'$ iff $v^*{\subseteq}v'^*$

(vu) $v(A)=t$ iff $v^* \vDash^U A$

To produce a general result for future applications, we will show the isomorphism by exploiting the Path Isomorphism Theorem of Section 7.5.

Path Isomorphism Theorem. V obeys ‖I∨‖ iff $<V, \leq>$ is isomorphic to some path model, where ≤ is defined by ‖≤‖.

(Path Model) A path model $U=<W, \subseteq, N, u>$ is any neighborhood model that obeys (⊆) and (N).

(⊆) $w{\subseteq}w'$ iff for all wffs A, if $w \vDash A$ then $w' \vDash A$.

(N) wNP iff for some wff D, $w \nvDash D$, and $P = \{w': w{\subseteq}w'$ and $w' \nvDash D\}$.

Remember that a neighborhood model satisfies the intuitionistic truth conditions with the exception that the clause for ∨ goes as follows.

(P∨) $w \vDash A{\vee}B$ iff for every subset P of W such that wNP,
                     there is a $w'{\in}P$ such that $w' \vDash A$ or $w' \vDash B$.

However (P∨) and (N) are just the analogs of our generalized truth condition ‖N∨‖ with N defined by (Def NPv).

||N∨|| v(A∨B)=t iff for every subset P of V such that vNP,
        there is a v'∈P such that v'(A)=t or v'(B)=t.

(Def NP∨) vNP iff for some wff D, v(D)=f, and P = {v': v≤v' and
        v'(D)=f}.

That means that the reasoning used in Theorem 8.7 to show that ||NP∨|| is equivalent to ||Nq∨|| in the presence of ||LF|| may be exploited to show the analogous conclusion for path models. Let us introduce the abbreviation: 'w(A)=F' as follows.

w(A)=F =_df for any w' in W, if w⊆w', then w' ⊭A.

Now define (KR) as the analog of ||LF||, the condition like (Refinability) save that quantification is over wffs A.

(KR) If w ⊭A, then for some w' in W, w⊆w' and w'(A)=F.

The next theorem is proven transcribing the steps of Theorem 8.7 into the notation appropriate for path models.

KR Theorem. If a path model obeys (KR), then the path bundle truth condition (P∨) holds iff the quasi-truth condition (Kq∨) holds.

Furthermore, the reasoning of the LF Lemma of the previous section may also be used to show that (Refinability) entails (KR).

KR Lemma. If a path model obeys (Refinability), it obeys (KR).

These results allow us to exploit the Path Isomorphism Theorem to establish an isomorphism between ||PL|| and KR-models.

PL Isomorphism Theorem. V obeys ||PL|| iff <V, ≤> is isomorphic to some KR-model.

Proof. (Proof Left to Right). Assume V obeys ||PL||. Then it obeys ||I∨|| and ||LL|| or equivalently ||LF||. By the Path Isomorphism Theorem, there is a path model U = <W, ⊆, N, u> isomorphic to <V, ≤>. Since <V, ≤> obeys ||LF||, the isomorphism guarantees that (KR) holds of U. The KR Theorem tells us that the path bundle truth condition (P∨) may be replaced by the quasi-truth reading (Kq∨). But (Kq∨) makes no mention of the neighborhood relation N. So N may be dropped from the path model U to create a KR-model isomorphic to<V, ≤>.

(Proof Right to Left). Assume$<V, \subseteq>$ is isomorphic to a KR-model U = $<W, \subseteq, u>$ and show V obeys ||PL|| as follows. Since (Refinability) holds for U, the KR Lemma entails that (KR) also holds. Let us construct a path model U' = $<W, \subseteq, N, u>$ from U, where N is defined by (N) and the path truth condition (Pv) is employed in the place of (Kq∨). By the KR Theorem, the truth values determined for the wffs in all worlds of U and U' are identical, and so U' is isomorphic to V. The Path Isomorphism Theorem tells us that V obeys ||I∨||. Since the path model U' also obeys (KR), the isomorphism entails that $<V, \subseteq>$ must obey ||LF||, that is ||LL||, and so ||PL|| holds as desired. □

8.9 Does classical logic have a natural semantics?

The upshot of the last result is that ||PL|| is better behaved than expected. The classical natural deduction system PL for propositional logic expresses the property of being isomorphic to a KR-model. In other words, the constraint that V be a model of PL amounts to the claim that V maps into an intuitionistic model that meets the side condition (Refinability), presuming the quasi-truth condition (Kq∨) for disjunction is adopted.

(Refinability) If u(w, p)=f, then for some w' in W, w⊆w' and
               for any w" in W, if w'⊆w" then u(w", p)=f.

Therefore, what PL expresses is KR-semantics (at least up to isomorphism). Since KR-semantics is no worse behaved than standard Kripke semantics for intuitionistic logic, new confidence in ||PL|| is gained. We have good reason to consider ||qPL|| = ||PL|| to be the natural semantics for PL.

In Section 12.1, it will be shown that systems that express the property of being isomorphic to a semantics are complete for that semantics. Therefore it will be straightforward to show that PL is adequate (both sound and complete) for ||PL||. However, there is a deeper connection to stress. It is that the interpretation of the connectives given by ||PL|| is natural, in the sense that this interpretation and no other corresponds exactly to what PL expresses. Although the classical semantics is also adequate for PL, it is demonstrably stronger than the interpretation that is demanded by the PL rules. So whether we know it or not, ||PL|| tells us what our connectives have been meaning all along. In Chapter 10, ||PL|| will be deployed as a semantics for an open future. It will be argued that ||PL|| provides a good account of the way we actually understand the connectives in natural language, and in particular what we mean by 'or'. This will provide new tools to head off arguments for fatalistic conclusions based on the Law of Excluded Middle.

However, the liberal attitude we have just taken towards ‖PL‖ faces objections. One may assert that ‖PL‖ is a natural semantics by fiat, but the fact remains that ‖PL‖ is not a functional condition. We learned in Theorem 8.6 that it is not possible to extend the atomic model W* to one that obeys ‖PL‖. This is disturbing, for W* was defined over the *non-logical* vocabulary (the propositional variables) only, without reference to the truth behavior of any connective. The fact that ‖LF‖ rules out such atomic models appears to violate an important semantic principle, namely that the truth conditions for a connective should provide a recursive recipe for extending *any* atomic model to values for the complex wffs. Truth conditions should not be incompatible with interpretations of the non-logical vocabulary that they are supposed to extend.

It is exactly this elimination of certain atomic models that explains why S~ fails to form a conservative extension of S→ by proving Peirce's Law. It also explains the failure of conservation of the classical system S→PR for → that adopts Peirce's Rule. (See Section 6.2.) It seems then that anyone who requires that the semantics for a connective should not influence the interpretations of any other connectives must conclude that ‖S~‖ (and hence ‖PL‖) does not qualify as a semantics. By these lights, classical negation has no coherent interpretation, and any symbol governed by the classical rules S~ simply does not qualify as a bona fide connective in the first place. That would provide strengthened support for intuitionist's claims that classical negation is defective.

While this reasoning may seem persuasive, it is mistaken. There is a way to defend the view that ‖PL‖ qualifies as a semantics nevertheless. The isomorphism result to KR-semantics makes it apparent that ‖LF‖, which for KR-models amounts to (Refinability), in no way undermines one's ability to provide truth conditions for ~. In KR-semantics, the truth conditions for ~ are those for intuitionistic logic, and these clearly count as properly recursive. So the complaint against what PL expresses cannot be that it fails to provide truth conditions for ~. The problems of non-conservation and non-functionality arise not because of a defect in *truth conditions* for any connective, but because of the decision to accept (Refinability), a condition on models having to do with how values should be assigned to *propositional variables*.

To bring this point into focus in the case of ‖PL‖, remember that the LF Lemma (of Section 8.7) demonstrated that ‖LF‖ is equivalent to ‖pLF‖, a condition on the truth behavior of propositional variables only.

‖pLF‖ If v(p)=f, then for some v′∈V, v≤v′ and v′(p)=F.

So the characteristic classical constraint ‖LL‖, that is ‖LF‖, can be recast in a form ‖pLF‖ that says nothing at all about the truth-values of any complex wffs. Therefore, ‖LL‖ cannot possibly be involved in fixing or failing to fix the truth conditions for negation. This is supported by the fact that Peirce's Rule also forces ‖LL‖. (See Theorem 6.2.4 of Section 6.2.) So ‖LL‖ is not "about" negation in any case. While the presence of ‖LL‖ may be "disruptive" to the truth behavior of complex wffs by validating some that would not otherwise be valid, that does not interfere with the cogency of any connective's truth conditions. If we identify a connective's meaning with its truth conditions, then the meaning for ~ expressed by the classical rules S~ must be ‖¬‖, the intuitionistic reading.

The mistake in the above objection to ‖PL‖ was to identify ‖LL‖ with part of the *truth conditions* for ~. As is obvious in the reformulation ‖pLF‖, the role of ‖LL‖ is entirely analogous to side constraints on frames for tense logic. For example, the requirement that tense logic frames be dense validates wffs of the form FA→FFA, where F is the future tense operator read 'it will be the case that'. Surely whether we accept the idea that time is dense is not part of the meaning of 'it will be the case that', for whatever meaning is, it does not depend on contingent physical facts about the structure of time. Furthermore, adopting denseness for tense logic frames does not undermine the coherence of the standard truth condition for the temporal operator F. Although denseness restricts the models that we attend to in defining validity, thus validating FA→FFA, that restriction does not change the meaning of F. Similarly, the presence of ‖pLF‖ validates wffs with the forms ((A→B)→A)→A, and ~~A→A, but its presence does not disqualify intuitionistic models from providing recursive truth conditions for ~. In the same way that it is implausible to think that denseness is part of the meaning of F, it is implausible to count ‖LF‖ as part of the meaning of ~, for our acceptance or rejection of ‖LF‖ depends on contingent facts about the extension relation, such as whether each false atomic sentence is determinately false in the future. Whether that holds or does not is another contingent matter about the future, and so not part of the meaning of anything. (I am indebted to J. Woods for pressing objections that prompted the thoughts in the previous two paragraphs.)

It must be granted that the intuitionistic interpretation $\|\dashv\|$ is not the natural semantics for S~, since S~ proves arguments that are not sound given $\|\dashv\|$. But insofar as $\|PL\|$ provides any interpretation for ~ at all, the condition $\|LL\|=\|pLF\|$ fails to do that work, and so $\|\dashv\|$ is left to perform that job by default. One might reply that there is no reason to think that $\|PL\|$ might not be recast in a form where the effect of $\|pLF\|$ is incorporated into a (somewhat different) truth condition without side constraints. However this cannot happen, for suppose there were a truth condition of the form $\|\sim?\|$, that S~ expressed exactly.

$\|\sim?\|$ v(~A)=t iff P.

We know already that S~ forces $\|\dashv\|$.

$\|\dashv\|$ v(~A)=t iff v(A)=F.

Putting $\|\sim?\|$ and $\|\dashv\|$, end to end, we learn that S~ forces v(A)=F iff P, and that entails that the two conditions are equivalent. Since S~ does not express $\|\dashv\|$, because $\|LF\|$ is needed as well, S~ could not express $\|\sim?\|$ either. So the fact that S~ expresses a side condition is inescapable.

The lesson of Prior's (1960) connective *tonk* was that not all rules determine a connective meaning. It should come as no surprise, then, that Double Negation also fails to do so. For this reason, it is crucial to distinguish conditions expressed by a set of rules from the *truth* conditions expressed by those rules. While S~ expresses the conjunction of $\|\dashv\|$ with $\|pLF\|$, the latter is not part of the *truth* conditions expressed by S~. While S~ brings with it failures of conservation and functionality, those failures are not to be blamed on the *truth* conditions expressed by S~. They are a result of a side condition $\|pLF\|$ that is not involved in the business of defining connective meaning in any way.

It is worth taking a moment to explain how the definition of a semantics given in Section 5.5 makes room for $\|pLF\|$ and hence $\|LL\|$.

(Semantics) Condition $\|S\|$ on models is a *semantics* for S iff every model V obeying $\|S\|$ is isomorphic to a model of a standard semantics (for a language defined over the connectives that occur in the rules of S).

This definition, along with the PL Isomorphism of Section 8.8, guarantees that ‖PL‖ is a semantics, even though it includes a side condition ‖pLF‖. The reason is that the KR-semantics (to which ‖PL‖ is isomorphic) is perfectly standard, even though it includes (Refinability), the analog of ‖pLF‖. That should make it clear that a semantics may include more than a set of truth conditions. So the presence of ‖pLF‖ and the resulting failure of functionality does not disqualify ‖PL‖ from being a semantics.

The conclusions just drawn have interesting implications for pluralism in logic (Beall and Restall, 2006). Is intuitionistic logic to be preferred over its classical rival? The answer is clear. It depends. Given the model-theoretic inferentialism that is explored in this book, the selection of a set of rules as a viable logic depends on whether it has a natural semantics. Therefore, at the syntactic level, we advocate a brand of quietism. Any set of rules is as good as any other, provided it has a natural semantics. Given that ‖PL‖ so qualifies, classical rules are as good as intuitionistic ones. However, the picture is different at the semantical level, where the interpretations selected by the rules are considered. Here an intuitionistic semantics is preferred, for even the classical rules for ~ express an *intuitionistic* reading.

Those working in the intuitionist tradition have argued that natural deduction rules PL for classical logic are defective because of the failure of conservativity, or properties related to harmony such as inversion (Dummett 1991, pp. 297ff. and Hand, 1993, pp. 125ff.) (For more on the matter, see Section 13.5.) The position taken here provides a defense of PL against such attacks. The idea is that failure of conservation does not always entail a failure to define the meaning of a connective. That failure might be the syntactic correlate of a decision to adopt ancillary conditions on models when defining *validity* (not truth conditions). So failure of conservation does not challenge the acceptability of ‖PL‖ or other conditions that qualify as a natural semantics on our revised definition. Nevertheless, the intuitionist can take some comfort in the result that, try as he will, the classicist who adopts natural deduction rules is saddled with intuitionistic accounts of connective meaning.

Alpha Centaurian anthropologists who are persuaded by this, and discover that we adopt the rules of PL in our reasoning, will conclude that a perfectly legitimate interpretation is expressed by ~. The surprise for some of us humans is that it is the intuitionistic reading.

8.10 The primacy of natural semantics

The purpose of this section is to try to convince you that ‖PL‖, rather than classical semantics, should be taken seriously as defining what the connectives actually mean, for anyone who adopts the system PL of classical propositional logic. There are positive arguments, and a defense from an objection.

The best support for the view, of course, is that ‖PL‖ is the natural semantics for PL. That means that, despite what you may have thought, the rules of PL fix exactly the semantics ‖PL‖, and not the stronger classical conditions. Although PL is complete for the classical truth tables, the fact that ‖PL‖ is the natural semantics entails that there is no way for any set of wffs of PL to express the classical treatment. Anyone who argues that the classical readings are the only ones is faced with a formal proof to the contrary. As to which is the correct reading, surely the natural semantics, being what the rules actually express, has pride of place for anyone who takes model-theoretic inferentialism to heart. Natural semantics ‖PL‖ is the unique interpretation expressed by PL, so the classical interpretation is artificial.

There is a second reason for preferring ‖PL‖. It helps resolve a puzzle about the interpretation of the conditional. Early in my own teaching, I wondered about the disparity between two features of classical logic. On one hand, we have the strongly counterintuitive semantical principle that a conditional is true when its antecedent is false. Whatever one's pedagogical practices, it is very difficult to motivate this view in face of copious counterexamples. For example, from the mere contingent falsity of 'Bush is 100 years old', I must conclude that the conditional 'If Bush is 100 years old, then Bush is an infant' is true. On the other hand, PL is easy to motivate on the syntactic side. For example, such rules as ($\rightarrow$ Elimination), ($\rightarrow$ Introduction), and principles for negation make intuitive sense to the vast majority of my (attentive) students, few of whom have intuitionist qualms about (Double Negation). The puzzle is how can there be such a disconnect between the largely intuitive proof-theoretic side, and the strongly counterintuitive semantical side?

One answer is to try to discredit the irenic attitude taken towards classical syntax by citing the provability of $\sim A / A \rightarrow B$. But the puzzle persists. The argument ~A / A→B is provable from intuitively acceptable deductive principles – principles that preserve validity. But the validity of ~A / A→B apparently requires accepting the strongly counterintuitive claim that A→B is true when A is false. Stating, or even proving the adequacy of PL for the classical semantics does not explain this away.

Now that we know that the correct semantics for PL is ‖PL‖ rather than the classical one, the puzzle can be resolved. ‖PL‖ does not claim that if 'Bush is 100 years old' is false, then 'If Bush is 100 years old, then Bush is an infant' must be true. The conditional is true only when its antecedent is false or its consequent is true in any extension of our situation. Conceivably there is an extension of the way things are now where Bush is 100 years old where he is not an infant, thus rendering the conditional false.

The validity of ~A / A→B is no longer a problem. If one insists on the classical reading of ~ and →, then the result is certainly counterintuitive. But that interpretation is not the correct one. When ‖PL‖ is adopted instead, the validity of ~A / A→B does not support the intuitively defective row of the truth table where a false antecedent entails a true conditional. Instead v(~A) =t entails that v(A)=F, that is, A is false in every extension of v. Intuitively that is incorrect in the case of 'Bush is 100 years old', and other contingently false sentences. Therefore ‖PL‖ does not saddle us with a counterintuitive semantical reading, and the validity of ~A / A→B can be made compatible with our intuitions.

I grant that this does not entirely solve the problem, for we still have to explain the validity of wffs like (A&~A)→B, where the antecedent is contradictory. However, I submit that intuitions against accepting this feature of classical logic are far less compelling than those that object to the idea that conditionals with *contingently* false antecedents are thereby true.

I turn now to an objection to granting that ‖PL‖ defines the preferred reading of the connectives. It comes in the form of a simple question. The vast majority thinks that the semantics for PL is classical, so how could so many people be wrong? There are two answers. The first is that the classical semantics for PL was historically first, and qualifies as simpler than ‖PL‖. But, of course that is no compelling reason for deciding that it ought to have been adopted. A second answer is to provide an explanation for how we could have gone wrong. In the next chapter, we will define the uppercase values T, F, and U as follows.

(DefT)   v(A)=T iff v(A)=t.

(DefF)   v(A)=F iff v(~A)=t.

(DefU)   v(A)=U iff neither v(A)=T nor v(A)=F.

Theorem 9.3 in the next chapter will display the partial three-valued truth tables that are induced by the above definitions in any model that obeys ‖PL‖. Inspection of the subset of those tables that concern T and F only generates exactly the classical tables. So the explanation for the historical accident that classical tables were developed first is simply that the people involved failed to leave room for the possibility of the third case where a wff remains undetermined. As we will see, leaving room for U is crucial for interesting applications of ‖PL‖ for resolving philosophical problems about vagueness (Chapter 15) and the open future (Chapter 10). The reader who remains unconvinced should see whether those chapters change his or her mind.

8.11 Proofs of some results in Section 8.7

Theorem 8.7 If V obeys ‖LF‖, then V obeys ‖NP∨‖ iff V obeys ‖Nq∨‖.

Two quick lemmas will be helpful.

∨**f Lemma.** For every valuation v in a model V, if V obeys either ‖NP∨‖ or ‖Nq∨‖, and v(A∨B)=f, then v(A)=v(B)=f.

Proof. Suppose V obeys ‖NP∨‖ and v(A∨B)=f. Unpacking ‖NP∨‖, there is a path bundle P through v such that v′(A)=v′(B)=f, for all v′∈P. That means that for some wff D, v(D)=f and P = {v′: v≤v′ and v′(D)=f}. In light of v≤v and v(D)=f, v∈P, and so v(A)=v(B)=f.

Suppose V obeys ‖Nq∨‖ and v(A∨B)=f. Then for some v′ such that v≤v′, v′(A) =v′(B)=F. Given v≤v, v(A)=v(B)=f.   □

∨**F Lemma.** If V obeys ‖LF‖ and ‖NP∨‖, and v(A∨B)=f, then for some v′ in V, v≤v′ and v′(A)=v′(B)=F.

Proof. Suppose V obeys ‖LF‖ and ‖NP∨‖ and let v(A∨B)=f. Then by ‖LF‖, there is a member v′ of V such that v′(A∨B)=F. That means that v″(A∨B)=f for every extension v″ of v′. By the vf Lemma, v″ (A)=v″ (B)=f for all these extensions v″ of v′, so v′(A)=v′(B)=F .   □

Proof of Theorem 8.7. Assume V obeys ‖LF‖ and show V obeys ‖NP∨‖ iff V. obeys ‖Nq∨‖.

Proof from left to right. Suppose V obeys ‖NP∨‖. To prove that V obeys ‖Nq∨‖ from left to right assume v(A∨B)=t and vNP, with N defined by (Def Nq∨) and prove there is a member v′ of P such that v′(A)=t or v′(B)=t. Given vNP and (Def Nq∨), there is a member v* of V such that v≤v* and P={v″: v*≤v″}. By the definition ‖≤‖ of ≤, and v≤v*, v*(A∨B)=t. Since valuations are consistent, we know there is a wff D such that v*(D)=f. So let P* be {v″: v*≤v″ and v″(D)=f}, and note that P*⊆P. P* qualifies as a path bundle through v, therefore by (Def NP∨), we have vNP*. Therefore, ‖N∨‖ guarantees that there is a member v′ of P* such that v′(A)=t or v′(B)=t. But P*⊆P, therefore v′ is the desired member of P such that v′(A)=t or v′(B)=t.

To prove ‖Nq∨‖ from right to left, assume that v(A∨B)=f, and find a P such that vNP and v′(A)=v′(B)=f for every v′∈P, where N is defined by (Def Nqv). Since v(A∨B)=f, we have by the ∨F Lemma that there is a member v* of V such that v≤v* and v*(A)=v*(B)=F. Let P={v′: v*≤v′}. In light of v≤v*, and (Def Nqv), vNP. All that remains is to show that v′(A)=v′(B)=f for all v′∈P. That follows from the fact that all members of P are extensions of v*, and v*(A)=v*(B)=F.

Proof from right to left. Suppose ‖Nq∨‖. To prove that V obeys ‖NP∨‖ from left to right, assume v(A∨B)=t, with N defined by (Def NP∨) and prove there is a member v′ of P such that v′(A)=t or v′(B)=t. Given vNP and (Def NP∨), P is a path bundle through v, so there is a wff D such that v(D)=f and P={v″: v≤v″ and v″(D) =f}. By ‖LF‖, there is a v* such that v≤v* and v*(D)=F. By the q∨ Lemma, ‖Nq∨‖ yields ‖q∨‖ so from v≤v*, it follows that v*(A)=qT or v*(B)=qT. By the qT Lemma, there is a v′ such that v*≤v′ and either v′(A)=t or v′(B)=t. Furthermore, v*(D)=F guarantees that v′(D)=f, hence v′∈P. So v′ is the desired member of P such that v′(A)=t or v′(B)=t.

To prove V obeys ‖NP∨‖ from right to left, assume v(A∨B)=f, and find a P such that vNP and for all v′ in P, v′(A)=v′(B)=f. Let P = {v*: v≤v* and v*(A∨B)=f}. By (Def NPv), vNP. To show that any member v′ of P is such that v′(A)=v′(B)=f, simply use the ∨f Lemma and the fact that v′(A∨B)=f for each member v′ of P.   □

LF Lemma. When ‖pPL‖ is the result of replacing ‖LF‖ in ‖qPL‖ with ‖pLF‖, V obeys ‖pPL‖ iff V obeys ‖qPL‖.

‖LF‖ If v(A)=f, then for some v′∈V, v≤v′ and v′(A)=F.

‖pLF‖ If v(p)=f, then for some v′∈V, v≤v′ and v′(p)=F.

Proof. ‖LF‖ entails ‖pLF‖, so all that remains is to show that if V obeys ‖pLF‖ and the truth conditions of ‖qPL‖, then V obeys ‖LF‖. So assume V obeys ‖pLF‖ and show ‖LF‖ by induction on the form of A. The base case is trivial, and the inductive cases for each connectives follow.

⊥. This is easy because ‖⊥‖ guarantees $v(\bot)=$F for every v in V.

&. Assume $v(A\&B)=$f. Then by ‖&‖, $v(A)=$f or $v(B)=$f. In the first case we obtain $v(A)=$F by the hypothesis of the induction, from which it follows by ‖&‖ that w $(A\&B)=$F. The second case is similar.

~. Assume $v(\sim A)=$f. Then for some v' in V, $v\leq v'$ and $v'(A)=$t, by ‖⌐‖. To show $v'(\sim A)=$F, assume that $v'\leq v''$ for any v'' in V, and show that $v''(\sim A)=$f as follows. From $v'\leq v''$ and ‖≤‖, $v''(A)=$t. But $v''(\sim A)$ cannot be t since if it were, it would follow by $v''\leq v''$ and ‖⌐‖, that $v''(A)=$f. Therefore, $v'(\sim A)=$F as desired.

→. Assume $v(A{\rightarrow}B)=$f. Then by ‖→‖, for some v' in V, $v\leq v'$, $v'(A)=$t and $v'(B)$ $=$f. By the hypothesis of the induction, we have that for some v'' in V, $v'\leq v''$ and $v''(B)=$F. By ‖≤‖, $v\leq v'$ and $v'\leq v''$, $v''(A)=$t, hence $v^*(A)=$t in any extension v^* of v''. This means that $v^*(A)=$t and $v^*(B)=$f for any extension v^* of v''. By ‖→‖, v'' $(A{\rightarrow}B)=$F. Transitivity of $\leq$ yields $v\leq v''$, and so v'' is the desired member of V such that $v\leq v''$ and $v''(A{\rightarrow}B)=$F.

↔. Proof similar to the previous case.

∨. Assume $v(A{\vee}B)=$f. Then by ‖q∨‖, for some v' in V, $v'(A)=$F and $v'(B)=$F, by the definition of quasi-truth. So $v'(A{\vee}B)=$F, because were this not so, there would be a v'' in V such that $v'\leq v''$ and $v''(A{\vee}B)=$t. By ‖q∨‖ and $v''\leq v''$, there must be an extension v^* of v'' where $v^*(A)=$t or $v^*(B)=$t, and that conflicts with $v'\leq v''$, $v''\leq v^*$, $v'(A)=$F and $v'(B)=$F. □

9 Supervaluations and natural semantics

In the last chapter, we established that classical propositional logic PL allows a non-classical interpretation of the connectives. In fact, the natural semantics ‖PL‖ for PL is a variant of an intuitionistic semantics, where (Refinability) is added as a side condition. The existence of non-classical interpretations for classical propositional logic is nothing new, for supervaluation semantics (van Fraassen, 1969) qualifies as another example. The purpose of this chapter is to compare ‖PL‖ with supervaluation semantics. There are interesting similarities. Section 9.3 shows that the partial truth tables for ‖PL‖ and supervaluations are identical. Furthermore, there is a way to map supervaluations in the canonical model of PL (Section 9.2). However, two differences will emerge that are decisive. Supervaluation semantics does not preserve the validity of the most basic rules of PL (Section 9.4). Furthermore, it will be argued in Section 9.5 that supervaluations do not really qualify as a semantics, for they do not provide truth conditions for the connectives of PL. The upshot of this discussion will be to recommend ‖PL‖ as better suited for philosophical applications where supervaluations have been popular. In coming chapters, we will demonstrate the point in detail by showing the value of ‖PL‖ for handling the open future (Chapter 10) and vagueness (Chapter 15).

9.1 Supervaluation semantics

Supervaluation semantics has many applications, but a seminal motivation was to provide for a Strawsonian theory of singular terms where some sentences lack truth-values because of the failure of the presupposition that their terms denote. Strawson (1967) argued that the value of 'the present King of France is bald' is not false as Russell would have thought. Instead it lacks a value because (presuming there is no present King of France) the sentence simply fails to make an evaluable statement.

The fundamental idea behind supervaluations is to allow some sentences to remain undetermined, but only as far as that would be compatible with truth-values fixed by classical truth tables. When the atomic constituents of a sentence A are not defined, the value of A is t if all ways of filling in the missing values using classical truth tables would assign A t, and the value of A is f if every way of filling the missing values yields f. Otherwise A is left undefined.

Let us present the idea more formally following McCawley (1993, pp. 334ff.). Let H be any consistent set of wffs. Let $H \vDash_c A$ mean that every classical valuation that satisfies H (assigns t to every member of H) also satisfies A (assigns t to A). Then *the supervaluation v_H induced by H* is the assignment of truth-values T, F, and U (undefined) such that a.-c. hold.

a. $v_H(A)$=T if $H \vDash_c A$

b. $v_H(A)$=F if $H \vDash_c \sim A$

c. $v_H(A)$=U otherwise

Furthermore a *supervaluation* is any supervaluation induced by a consistent set H. For example, consider the supervaluation v induced by {p, ~q}. Then v(p)=T, v(q)=F, and v(r)=U. Furthermore, v(p∨r)=T since whether r is t or f, classical truth tables assign t to p∨r. Similarly, v(r&q)=F since q's being F entails that r&q is F, regardless of the value of r. Finally, v(p&r)=U since the value of p&r may be t or f depending on the value of r.

The notation 'v(A)=U' suggests that a supervaluation is a function over the set of all wffs whose range is the set of three values T, F, and U. It will be convenient to think of supervaluations this way. However there is an important caveat. Supervaluation semantics does not truly qualify as a three-valued logic, because supervaluations are not truth functional. For example, the row of a three-valued table for A∨B where A and B are assigned U cannot be fixed, because for the supervaluation v induced by the null set, v(p∨q)=U when v(p)=v(q)=U, but v(p∨~p)=T when v(p)=v(~p)=U. Supervaluation semantics is essentially intensional, a point that will come into better focus when relationships between it and ||PL|| are made clear.

We are now in position to define the relation ⊨s of supervaluation validity. H ⊨s C holds iff every supervaluation induced by a consistent set of wffs that satisfies H (that is, makes T each member of H) also satisfies C (assigns C the value T). A well-known result concerning supervaluations is that the notion of validity defined by the class of supervaluations is equivalent to classical validity, and so this ensures that PL is sound and complete for supervaluation semantics.

Supervaluation Theorem. H ⊨s C iff H ⊨c C (Any argument is supervaluation valid iff it is classically valid.)

Proof. The proof from left to right is easy since classical valuations are supervaluations induced by maximally consistent sets. For the proof in the other direction, suppose that H ⊨c C, let v be any supervaluation that satisfies H, and show v(C)=T as follows. We know that v is the supervaluation induced by some set H'. By clause a. above, it will be sufficient for showing v(C)=T to demonstrate that H' ⊨c C. So assume v_c is any classical valuation such that v_c(H')=t and show that v_c(C)=t as follows. Note that a.–c. guarantee that for any wff B, v(B)=t only if H' ⊨c B because otherwise v(B) would be either F or undefined. We already said that v satisfies H, so it follows that H' ⊨c B for each B in H. In light of v_c(H')=t, it follows that v_c satisfies H, and so from H ⊨c C it follows that v_c(C)=t as desired. ☐

9.2 Supervaluations and the canonical model for PL

The next project is to explore the relationships between the set SV of all supervaluations, and models that satisfy ‖PL‖. One connection is that supervaluations in SV can be identified with members of the canonical model [PL], which, remember, is the set of all (ordinary or two-valued) valuations that satisfy PL. To simplify the presentation, consider the following definitions of determinate truth (T), determinate falsity (F), and underdetermination (U).

(DefT) v(A)=T iff v(A)=t.

(DefF) v(A)=F iff v(~A)=t.

(DefU) v(A)=U iff neither v(A)=T nor v(A)=F.

The notation 'v(A)=T' suggests that the valuation v actually assigns the value T to A. However, a valuation v only assigns A one of the two lower case truth-values t and f. Therefore, the notation 'v(A)=T' should be read as a unit, and not as a claim about what v actually assigns. In order to correctly introduce the notion of a three-valued valuation induced by v, it will be necessary to define a mapping that takes each two-valued valuation v into the corresponding three-valued valuation v_3 that meets the following conditions.

$$v_3(A)=T \text{ iff } v(A)=t \tag{3T}$$

$$v_3(A)=F \text{ iff } v(\sim A)=t \tag{3F}$$

$$v_3(A)=U \text{ iff otherwise, i.e. when } v(A)=(\sim A)=f \tag{3U}$$

The three conditions (3T), (3F), and (3U) determine uppercase truth-values for v_3 given any valuation v. The uppercase truth-values induced by (3T), (3F), and (3U) will allow us to identify supervaluations with each of the ordinary valuations in [PL]. What we intend to show is that the set SV of supervaluations and the set [PL] of valuations that satisfy PL are isomorphic in the sense that there is a 1–1 mapping * from [PL] into SV that preserves the uppercase truth-values. Preservation of those truth-values means in turn that for all v in V, $v^*(A) = v_3(A)$, for every wff A. Therefore the three-valued versions of the valuations in [PL] may be identified with supervaluations and vice versa. (Remember, the proof of starred theorems are found at the end of each chapter.)

Theorem 9.2* There is a 1–1 mapping from [PL] into SV that preserves the uppercase truth-values.

While this theorem shows that the supervaluations can be identified with members of [PL], and we know that every model V that obeys ||PL|| is a subset of [PL], it does not follow that for every model V that obeys ||PL|| is isomorphic to a corresponding set S of supervaluations. Were that to be the case, we would have by the purported isomorphism that the rules of PL would preserve S-validity. However, we will prove below (in Section 9.4) that there are sets of supervaluations for which preservation of validity fails.

9.3 Partial truth tables

It has been shown in the last section that supervaluations and models of PL are tied together by an isomorphism between the set of all supervaluations and the canonical model [PL]. There is another way in which a connection between supervaluations and models of PL can be established. Using the "truth conditions" a.–c. for supervaluations of Section 9.1, it is a straightforward matter to verify that the following "partial truth tables" govern the truth conditions for the various connectives on supervaluation semantics. (See, for example, Beaver (1997, p. 955) and McCawley (1993, pp. 335 and 336).) Notice that all the values are determined in the ~ table and they are also determined in each cell of the other tables except for the row A=B=U. However, the tables are partial since the value of a wff with a binary main connective is not determined in this case. (Here the columns are used for the values of A, and the rows are used for the values of B.)

A&B	T	F	U
T	T	F	U
F	F	F	F
U	U	F	F/U

A→B	T	F	U
T	T	F	U
F	T	T	T
U	T	U	T/U

A∨B	T	F	U
T	T	T	T
F	T	F	U
U	T	U	T/U

A↔B	T	F	U
T	T	F	U
F	F	T	U
U	U	U	T/U

A	~A
T	F
F	T
U	U

Table Theorem. Any supervaluation obeys the above partial truth tables.

We intend to show that any model V that obeys ‖PL‖ obeys exactly the same partial truth tables in the sense that for any member v of V the three-valued valuation v_3 determined by v obeys them.

Theorem 9.3* If V obeys ‖PL‖, then values assigned by v_3 for any valuation v in V obey the above partial tables.

So supervaluations agree with ‖PL‖ on the partial truth tables. However there is a crucial difference between them concerning *how* wffs are assigned the value U. For supervaluations, this is done by considering all classical valuations. For example, s(A)=U when both Hs ⊬c A and Hs ⊬c ~A, so we consider all classical valuations v to determine whether those that satisfy Hs also satisfy A and whether those that satisfy Hs satisfy ~A as well. However, ‖PL‖ uses a different way to determine the U value, as can be seen from the following, which falls out of the truth condition ‖¬‖, when v(~A)=f.

$$v_3(A)=U \text{ iff } v(A)=f \text{ and for some } v' \in V \text{ such that } v \leq v', v'(A)=t.$$

Note this condition makes reference to V, rather than the class of all valuations, or the class of all classical valuations. That reference is crucial for guaranteeing that the rules of PL preserve V-validity, so that V is a model of PL. On the other hand, the method used by supervaluations does not entail that property. As we will show in the next section, there are sets of supervaluations that are not models of PL because rules like ($\rightarrow$ Introduction) and (~ Introduction) fail to preserve supervaluation validity. This will be a strong reason for preferring natural semantics over supervaluations for many of the tasks for which supervaluations are used in the literature.

9.4 The failure of supervaluations to preserve validity

So far we have emphasized the kinships between supervaluations and ‖S~‖. However, there are important differences as well. In this book, we take it that a semantics is a condition on models that controls how truth-values are assigned. However Theorem 9.2 identifies the set SV of all supervaluations not with a condition on models but with a particular model, namely [PL]. One might take it that being identical with [PL] is a property of models that corresponds to supervaluation semantics, but that would trivialize an important concern and overlook a deeper issue.

From our point of view, supervaluations do not qualify as a genuine semantics for PL. It is a well-known early result that (CN) is unsound for some classes of supervaluations that are subsets of SV (van Fraassen, 1969, p. 81).

(CN) $\dfrac{A \vdash B}{\sim\!B \vdash \sim\!A}$

So there are sets of supervaluations that are not even models of PL. Since (CN) is also valid in intuitionistic semantics, supervaluations are also not models of intuitionistic logic **I**. Therefore, there is no hope of providing a *strong* adequacy result for PL or **I**, where provability of *arguments* must be shown to be equivalent to argument validity defined by supervaluations.

An intuition behind the failure of (CN) is reflected in a Strawsonian theory of presupposition. Suppose sentence p is a presupposition of q. For example, q might be 'The present King of France is bald.' And p might be 'The present King of France exists.' Then q should be undefined unless p is T. So supervaluations v that reflect that p is a presupposition of q, are such that if $v(q)=T$ then $v(p)=T$, with the result that when S^* is the class of all those supervaluations, $q \vDash_{S^*} p$. Now consider a valuation v^* in S^* where $\sim$p is T. Then the presupposition fails, and so both q and $\sim$q should be undefined at v^*. Summing up, $v^*(\sim p)=T$ and $v^*(\sim q)=U$, and so $\sim p \nvDash_{v^*} \sim q$. So we have the following theorem.

Theorem 9.4.1 There is a subset S^* of the set of all supervaluations SV such that $q \vDash_{S^*} p$ and $\sim p \nvDash_{S^*} \sim q$.

One might consider this a minor aberration. However, the failure of soundness goes deeper, for the strategy just used may also be deployed to show that ($\rightarrow$ Introduction) fails in the same way.

Theorem 9.4.2 There is a subset S^* of SV such that $q \vDash_{S^*} p$ and $\nvDash_{S^*} p \rightarrow q$.

Proof. Let $S^*=\{v^*\}$, where v^* is the supervaluation induced by the set $\{\sim p\}$. Because $v^*(q)=U$, we have for all $v \in V^*$, if $v(q)=T$, then $v(p)=T$. But $v^*(q \rightarrow p)=T$ iff $\sim p \vDash_c q \rightarrow p$, and the latter fails since the classical valuation v_c where $v_c(q)=t$ and $v_c(p)=f$ is a counterexample to $\sim p / q \rightarrow p$. So we have $q \vDash_{v^*} p$ but not $\vDash_{v^*} q \rightarrow p$. $\square$

Similar results apply to ($\sim$ Introduction) and ($\vee$ Elimination).

Theorem 9.4.3 There is a subset V^* of SV such that $q \vDash_{v^*} p$, $q \vDash_{v^*} \sim p$, and $\nvDash_{v^*} \sim q$. Furthermore, $\vDash_{v^*} p \vee \sim p$, $p \vDash_{v^*} q$, $\sim p \vDash_{v^*} q$, and $\nvDash_{v^*} q$.

Proof. Let $V^*=\{v_0\}$, where v_0 is the supervaluation induced by the empty set. Because $v_0(q)=U$, we have trivially that for all $v \in V^*$, if $v(q)=T$, then $v(p)=T$, and for all $v \in V^*$, if $v(q)=T$, then $v(\sim p)=T$. So both $q \vDash_{V^*} p$ and $q \vDash_{V^*} \sim p$. But $v_0(\sim q)=U$ so $q \nvDash_{V^*} \sim q$. Furthermore, $v_0(p \vee \sim p)=t$ and so $\vDash_{V^*} p \vee \sim p$. Because $v_0(p) = v_0(\sim p)=U$, we have trivially that both $p \vDash_{V^*} q$ and $\sim p \vDash_{V^*} q$; but $v_0(q)=U$ so $\nvDash_{V^*} q$. □

The upshot of this is that the pathological behavior of supervaluations is massive. While supervaluation semantics accepts as valid the valid *arguments* of PL, that is, the arguments PL *asserts*, it does not respect the deductive behavior of $\rightarrow$, $\sim$, and $\vee$ as embodied in their natural deduction rules. This underscores an important moral. A theory that attempts to define connective meaning by which arguments are accepted may face problems of underdetermination of connective meaning. Supervaluations fail because while they qualify as deductive models of PL, they do not qualify as global models. So they disagree fundamentally with the *use* to which the connectives are put. Therefore supervaluations and inferentialism do not mix.

9.5 Is supervaluation semantics a semantics?

In this book, we have presumed that preservation of validity is the foundation for determining what rules say about connective meaning. So we must conclude that supervaluations do not qualify as a semantics for PL. Alpha Centaurian anthropologists would have no reason to think that the interpretation provided by supervaluations gives an account of the connectives determined by the rules. In fact, it is also far from clear whether they or we would think that supervaluations qualify as any brand of semantics at all.

$\|PL\|$ provides an alternative semantics for PL by providing intensional truth conditions for the connectives with the help of the relation $\leq$. Supervaluation semantics simply fails to supply any alternative truth conditions for the connectives. Granted, a statement of connective truth conditions is implicit in the consequence relation $\vDash c$ where classical conditions are chosen. But that does not tell us what the connectives mean, for giving the connectives a classical treatment straight out would not provide any alternative truth conditions. Furthermore, it would not change the outcome in any way were we to define $\vDash c$ using $\|PL\|$ or even proof theoretically, so that $H \vDash c\ C$ iff $H \vdash_{PL} C$. All that matters for success of the supervaluation strategy is that the relation $\vDash c$ pick out the valid arguments of propositional logic, and this can be done with an alternative semantics or even using syntactic means. Therefore, supervaluation semantics underdetermines the meaning of the connectives, if it gives them any meanings at all. Again, we find that supervaluation "semantics" is not compatible with the inferentialist project. Alpha Centaurian anthropologists must believe that supervaluations are not even a contender for an account of what the connectives mean.

9.6 Proofs for theorems in Chapter 9

Theorem 9.2 There is a 1–1 mapping from [PL] into SV that preserves the uppercase truth-values.

We begin with a helpful Lemma.

V3 Lemma. If $v_3 = v'_3$ then $v = v'$.

Proof. Suppose $v_3 = v'_3$. Let B be any wff, and show that $v(B) = v'(B)$, as follows. Suppose that $v_3(B) = v'_3(B) = T$. Then by $v_3 = v'_3$ and (3T), $v(B) = t$ and $v'(B) = t$. Hence $v(B) = v'(B)$ in this case. Suppose $v_3(B) = v'_3(B) = F$ or $v_3(B) = v'_3(B) = U$. Then by (3F) or (3U), $v(B) = f$ and $v'(B) = f$, so $v(B) = v'(B)$ in this case as well.   □

Proof of Theorem 9.2. To show the isomorphism, let the desired 1–1 mapping * from [PL] to SV be defined by $v^*(A) = v_3(A)$. By definition, this preserves the uppercase truth-values. So what remains is to prove that * is 1–1. The V3 Lemma guarantees that * is unique. So what remains is to show (1) and (2).

$$\text{For every } v \text{ in [PL], } v^* \text{ is a member of SV.} \qquad (1)$$

$$\text{For every } s \text{ in SV, } s = v^* \text{ for some } v \text{ in [PL].} \qquad (2)$$

Proof of (1). Let v be any member of [PL]. To show that $v^* = v_3$ is a member of SV, we need to find an inducing set Hv_3 for the supervaluation v_3 such that the supervaluation truth conditions a.–c. hold. This is easy; simply let Hv_3 be the set of all wffs A such that $v(A) = t$. Since v must be consistent, it follows immediately that Hv_3 is a consistent set. To show that v_3 is in SV, we must verify the following, for every wff A.

$$v_3(A){=}T \text{ if } Hv_3 \vDash c \; A, \hspace{3cm} \text{a3.}$$

$$v_3(A){=}F \text{ if } Hv_3 \vDash c \; {\sim}A, \hspace{2.8cm} \text{b3.}$$

$$v_3(A){=}U \text{ otherwise.} \hspace{3.2cm} \text{c3.}$$

Proof of a3. Suppose $Hv_3 \vDash c$ A and verify that $v_3(A){=}T$, by demonstrating that $v(A){=}t$. Clearly $v(Hv_3){=}t$. In light of the completeness of PL, $Hv_3 \vDash c$ A entails $Hv_3 \vdash_{PL}$ A. But v is in [PL] so v must satisfy PL. Therefore v (A)=t as desired.

Proof of b3. Suppose $Hv_3 \vDash c \; {\sim}A$ and verify that $v_3(A){=}F$, by demonstrating that $v({\sim}A){=}t$. By the completeness of PL, $Hv_3 \vdash {\sim}A$. But v is in [PL] so v must be deductively closed for PL. Since $v(Hv_3){=}t$, $v({\sim}A){=}t$ as desired.

Proof of c3. Suppose neither $Hv_3 \vDash c$ A nor $Hv_3 \vDash c \; {\sim}A$ and verify that $v_3(A){=}U$, by demonstrating that $v(A){=}v({\sim}A){=}f$. From $Hv_3 \nvDash c$ A it follows that A cannot be a member of Hv_3, and so $v(A){=}f$. Similarly from $Hv_3 \nvDash c \; {\sim}A$, it follows that $v({\sim}A){=}f$. So $v(A){=}v({\sim}A){=}f$ as desired.

Proof of (2). We must show that every member s of SV is identical to v_3 for some v in [PL]. So let s be any supervaluation and define valuation v by v (A)=t iff s(A)=T. We must verify that v is a member of [PL] such that $v_3{=}s$. To show that v is in [PL] we must verify that v satisfies PL, that is, if $H \vdash_{PL}$ C and v (H)=t, then v(C)=t. So assume that $H \vdash_{PL}$ C and v(H)=t. From v(H)=t it follows by the definition of v that s(H)=T. By the soundness of PL, H / C is classically valid, so by the Supervaluation Theorem (Section 9.1), it must also be valid for the class of supervaluations. Therefore s(C)=T, and so v(C)=t by the definition of v. All that remains is to show that $s(A){=}v_3(A)$ for each wff A. This may be done by considering each of the uppercase truth-values in turn.

Suppose s(A)=T. By the definition of v, v(A)=t, and by (3T), $v_3(A){=}T$ as desired.

Suppose s(A)=F. It follows from the definition of v that v(A)=f. From condition b. for supervaluations, it follows that $Hs \vDash c \; {\sim}A$, where Hs is the set that induces s. So by the Supervaluation Theorem, $Hs \vDash s \; {\sim}A$. Since each member of Hs follows classically from Hs, s(Hs)=T. Hence s(~A)=T, and v(~A)=t by the definition of v. So v(~A)=t, hence $v_3(A){=}F$ by (3F).

Suppose that s(A)=U, that is, s is undetermined at A. It follows that s(A)≠T, so by the definition of v, v(A)=f. v(~A) must also be f, because otherwise we would have s(~A)=T, which entails $Hs \vDash c \; {\sim}A$ by condition a.

for supervaluations. However, by c. and s(A)=U we have that Hs ⊬c ~A, a contradiction. Therefore both v(A)=f and v(~A)=f and v_3(A)=U by (3U).   □

Theorem 9.3 If V obeys ‖PL‖, then values assigned by v_3 for any valuation v in V obey the partial tables given in Section 9.3.

Proof. Suppose that V obeys ‖PL‖, and let v be a member of V. Note that by the PL Expression Theorem of Section 8.2, V must be a model of PL. But that means that the rules of PL preserve V-validity with the result that any valuation v in V must satisfy any provable argument of PL. We examine each connective in turn. Let 'v(A)=T', 'v(A)=F', and 'v(A)=U', be shorthand for 'v_3(A)=T', 'v_3(A)=F', and 'v_3(A)=U' respectively.

&. In the following table, the parenthesized number in each cell indicates the fact used to establish the value in that cell. Proofs for facts (1)–(5) are found below.

A&B	T	F	U
T	(1) T	(2) F	(4) U
F	(2) F	(2) F	(2) F
U	(3) U	(2) F	(5) F/U

$$\text{If } v(A)=T \text{ and } v(B)=T, \text{ then } v(A\&B)=T. \qquad (1)$$

Proof. If v(A)=T and v(B)=T, we have by (3T) that v(A)=v(B)=t. By ‖&‖, it follows that v(A&B)=t, and hence v(A&B)=T by (3T).

$$\text{If } v(A)=F \text{ or } v(B)=F, \text{ then } v(A\&B)=F. \qquad (2)$$

Proof. Suppose v(A)=F or v(B)=F. Then by (3F), v(~A)=t or v(~B)=t. By ~A ⊢PL ~(A&B) and ~B ⊢PL ~(A&B), it follows from the fact that v satisfies PL-provable arguments that v(~(A&B))=t. So by (3F), v(A&B)=F as desired.

$$\text{If } v(A)=T \text{ and } v(B)=U, \text{ then } v(A\&B)=U. \qquad (3)$$

Proof. From v(A)=T, we have by (3T) that v(A)=t, and from v(B)=U we have by (3U) that v(B)=v(~B)=f. By A, ~(A&B) ⊢PL ~B, it follows from v(~B)=f and v(A)=t that v(~(A&B))=f. But v(A&B)=f since v(B)=f and ‖&‖ holds, so v(A&B)=U as desired.

$$\text{If } v(A)=U \text{ and } v(B)=T, \text{ then } v(A\&B)=U. \qquad (4)$$

Proof. Similar to (3) by B, ~(A&B) ⊢PL ~A.

$$\text{When } v(A)=v(B)=U, v(A\&B) \text{ could be either F or U, but not T.} \qquad (5)$$

Proof. Note that v(A&B) is clearly f in this case so v(A&B) cannot be T. So we need only show that both v(~(A&B))=t and v(~(A&B))=f are possible. Note that A&B could be p&~p, in which case $\vdash_{PL}$ ~(p&~p) ensures v(~(A&B))=t. So in this case v(A&B)=F. To show that it might be that v(A&B)=U, let A&B be p&q. Consider the possibility that V is [PL] and that v is $v_{\vdash}$. [PL] is a model of PL and $v_{\vdash}$ is in [PL] (Theorem 4.3) but $\nvdash_{PL}$ ~(p&q) and $\nvdash_{PL}$ p&q, so $v_{\vdash}$(p&q)= $v_{\vdash}$(~(p&q))=f and so $v_{\vdash}$(A&B)=U in this case.

→. The table indicating the facts used to establish the various values follows. We sketch the proofs indicating only the salient facts used.

A→B	T	F	U
T	(1) T	(2) F	(3) U
F	(1) T	(1) T	(1) T
N	(1) T	(4) U	(5) T/U

$$\text{If v(A)=F or v(B)=T, then v(A→B)=T.} \qquad (1)$$

Proof. By ~A $\vdash_{PL}$ A→B and B $\vdash_{PL}$ A→B.

$$\text{If v(A)=T and v(B)=F then v(A→B)=F.} \qquad (2)$$

Proof. By A, ~B $\vdash_{PL}$ ~(A→B).

$$\text{If v(A)=T and v(B)=U then v(A→B)=U.} \qquad (3)$$

Proof. Use ~(A→B) $\vdash_{PL}$ ~B to establish v(~(A→B))=f. Use ‖→‖ with v≤v, and v(A)=t and v(B)=f to show v(A→B)=f.

$$\text{If v(A)=U and v(B)=T then v(A→B)=U.} \qquad (4)$$

Proof. Similar to (3) using ~(A→B) $\vdash_{PL}$ A.

$$\text{When v(A)=v(B)=U, v(A→B) could be either T or U, but not F.} \qquad (5)$$

Proof. If v(A→B)=F, v(~(A→B)) would be t, so by ~(A→B) $\vdash$ A, we would have v(A)=t, which is incompatible with v(A)=U. So v(A→B) is not F. When A→B is p→p, v(A→B) must be t, and so by (3T) v(A→B)=T. When A→B is p→q, V is [PL], and v is $v_{\vdash}$, $v_{\vdash}$(p→q)=$v_{\vdash}$(~(p→q))=f, since $\nvdash_{PL}$ p→q and $\nvdash_{PL}$ ~(p→q). Therefore v(A→B)=U in this case.

∨. The table displaying the facts used for this case follows.

A∨B	T	F	U
T	(1) T	(1) T	(1) T
F	(1) T	(2) F	(3) U
U	(1) T	(4) U	(5) T/U

If $v(A)=T$ or $v(B)=T$ then $v(A\lor B)=T$. (1)

Proof. Use $A\vdash_{PL} A\lor B$ and $B\vdash_{PL} A\lor B$.

If $v(A)=F$ and $v(B)=F$ then $v(A\lor B)=F$. (2)

Proof. Use $\sim A, \sim B\vdash_{PL} \sim(A\lor B)$ to establish $v(\sim(A\lor B))=t$.

If $v(A)=F$ and $v(B)=U$ then $v(A\lor B)=U$. (3)

Proof. Use $\sim A, A\lor B\vdash_{PL} B$ and $\sim(A\lor B)\vdash_{PL} \sim B$.

If $v(A)=U$ and $v(B)=F$ then $v(A\lor B)=U$. (4)

Proof. Similar to (3) using $\sim B, A\lor B\vdash_{PL} A$ and $\sim(A\lor B)\vdash_{PL} \sim A$.

When $v(A)=v(B)=U$, $v(A\lor B)$ could be either T or U, but not F. (5)

Proof. Similar to (5) for $\rightarrow$.

$\leftrightarrow$. The table for $\leftrightarrow$ may be verified using the definition of $\leftrightarrow$ together with the & and $\rightarrow$ tables.

$\sim$. The table for $\sim$ may be established as follows. When $v(A)=T$, we have $v(A)=t$, hence by $A\vdash_{PL} \sim\sim A$, $v(\sim\sim A)=t$. So $v(\sim A)=F$ by (3F). When $v(A)=F$, $v(\sim A)=t$, so $v(\sim A)=T$ by (3T). When $v(A)=U$, $v(A)=v(\sim A)=f$. But $v(A)=f$ with $\sim\sim A\vdash_{PL} A$ yields $v(\sim\sim A)=f$. Hence $v(\sim A)=U$. □

10 Natural semantics for an open future

(This chapter draws heavily from Garson (2013) "Open Futures in the Foundations of Propositional Logic," in *Nuel Belnap on Indeterminism and Free Action*, T. Mueller (ed.), Springer, New York.)

The natural semantics ‖PL‖ for classical logic has a number of interesting applications. This chapter will discuss its merits as a semantics that takes seriously the notion that the future is open (Section 10.1). Here future possibilities are represented as a branching structure, with choice points at each node. The ‖PL‖ models developed in Chapter 8 are well suited to this idea, since the frame <V, ≤> sets up that kind of structure. Furthermore, as Sections 10.3 and 10.4 show, the side condition ‖LF‖ and the quasi-truth reading ‖q∨‖ of disjunction match well with our concerns to locate the propositions that express events over which one might have control.

‖LF‖ If v(A)=f, then for some v′, v≤v′ and v′(A)=F.

‖q∨‖ v(A∨B)=t iff for all v′∈V, if v≤v′, then v′(A)=qT or v′(B)=qT.

In Section 10.5, it is shown that ‖PL‖ can be used to refute arguments that purport to show the inescapability of fatalism. The frame <V, ≤> is not entirely apt for modeling an open future because it need not satisfy the condition that there be no branching of possibilities in the past. Section 10.6 shows how this problem can be repaired.

10.1 The open future

It is a fundamental presupposition of a theory of action that there are some things that lie within, and some that lie outside, our control. The events of the past are determined, and nothing we can do will change them. Therefore, the sentences that report those events are not the "targets" of agency. If sentence A reports an event in the past, then 'person p brings it about (now) that A' is automatically false. There are also sentences reporting future events that defy agency as well, for example tautologies and contradictions. However, within the class of future contingent sentences A, there are at least some over which one may have control, so that it would be true to say that 'person p brings it about that A'. There is a strong intuition that when I act to bring about A, whether A is true or not is up to me. Therefore both A and ~A must have been possible before I acted. So the future offers me a collection of possibilities, which we might represent in a tree, with my choices (or those of others) at each of the branch points. An essential intuition related to this vision is that some future contingent sentences are not yet determined, though they may be at a future time. Therefore, if I act in a way that determines A, then neither A nor ~A could have been determined before I act.

It has been claimed that the asymmetry between past and future reflected in our ideas about action is actually bogus, and there is only one temporal stream, where both past and future are fixed. Some insist that our freedom to choose is an illusion. But even if one had convincing evidence for the correctness of such a view, it wouldn't change the fact that a natural model for the way we *understand* agency treats future possibilities as a forward-facing tree with our choices at the branch points. Whatever the fate of the concept of agency, its pervasive use motivates the development of a semantics that does justice to its basic intuitions. The interesting point is that the natural semantics ‖PL‖ is ready made for this understanding. Alpha Centaurian anthropologists who discover that we adopt the rules of PL will conclude that the interpretations of our connectives, and notably that for disjunction, maps into semantics for an open future. One upshot of this recognition is that modality is fundamental to our conception of the future. This idea is woven into the very syntax of the future tense in Indo-European languages. As John Lyons (1968, p. 306) puts it: "Even in the analysis of Greek and Latin (where the 'future' like the 'present' and the 'past' is realized inflexionally), there is some reason to describe the 'future tense' as partly modal."

10.2 Determination in natural semantics for PL

Consider a language whose atomic wffs are temporally closed, that is, their truth-values are insensitive to their time of evaluation, because they report dated events. A possible world (or valuation) v assigns t to those wffs that report events that are so far determined, so when A reports a past event, or something in the future that is inescapable (for example, something tautologous), v ought to assign it the value t. The relation $\leq$ then keeps track of the way in which valuations are extended as the passage of time determines more and more wffs. So $v \leq v'$ indicates that v' is one of the ways that choices might be eventually determined given the choices available in v.

The notion of determination at a valuation has been defined in the previous chapter in Sections 8.3 and 8.7. Here we will introduce the main ideas with a series of definitions that are equivalent to those in Section 8.7. We will say that A is *determined true* at valuation v (given model V) iff A is true in every extension of v. Similarly, A is *determined false* at v (for V) iff A is false in every extension of v. If A is determined true or determined false at v in V, then we say A is *determined*, and if A is not determined we call it *undetermined*. So we have the following official definitions, where the relation $\leq$ is defined by $\|\leq\|$.

(DefT) $v(A)=T$ iff for all v' in V, if $v \leq v'$, then $v'(A)=t$.

(DefF) $v(A)=F$ iff for all v' in V, if $v \leq v'$, then $v'(A)=f$.

(DefU) $v(A)=U$ iff neither $v(A)=T$ nor $v(A)=F$.

$\|\leq\|$ $v \leq v'$ iff for all wffs A of L, if $v(A)=t$, then $v'(A)=t$.

Wffs that report an event at v are determined at v. So for these wffs A, $v(A)=T$ or $v(A)=F$, and forever after.

Presuming that $\|PL\|$ holds for a model V, some useful facts about these definitions are worth noting (for all valuations v in V).

(t=T) $v(A)=T$ iff $v(A)=t$.

The reader can easily check that (t=T) follows from the definition $\|\leq\|$ and the reflexivity of $\leq$. So being true (t) and determined true (T) are extensionally equivalent.

$\|{\sim}F\|$ $v({\sim}A)=t$ iff $v(A)=F$.

$\|{\sim}F\|$ follows from the definition of F and the truth condition $\|\neg\|$. This allows a quick calibration of the difference between classical negation and intuitionistic negation. For classical negation ${\sim}A$'s being true entails that

A is false, while in the intuitionistic semantics the truth of ~A entails the stronger claim that A is determined false.

(U) v(A)=U iff v(A)=f and v(~A)=f.

The proof of (U) follows from the definition of U, (t=T), and $\|\neg\|$. The idea is that an undetermined wff is simply one for which neither it nor its negation is true. In light of (t=T), this makes sense, for when A or ~A are true they are determined true, and by $\|\sim F\|$, when ~A is determined true A must be determined false. Therefore for A to be undetermined neither A nor ~A can be true. The upshot is that the intuitionistic semantics $\|PL\|$ has the resources to capture the idea that some sentences are undetermined and so count as possible "targets" for agency.

($\neq$F) v(A)$\neq$F iff v(A)=T, if A is determined at v.

($\neq$F) follows because determined true, determined false, and undetermined are exhaustive categories. Therefore, v(A) is not F if and only if it is U or T, or to put it another way, v(A)=T if A is determined at v. As we explained in Section 8.7, when v(A)$\neq$F we say that A is *quasi-true* at v, and write: 'v(A)=qT' to indicate that A is determined true at v if determined there at all. So we have (FqT).

(FqT) v(A)$\neq$F iff v(A)=qT.

10.3 The Lindenbaum Condition revisited

Remember from Section 8.7 that the condition $\|LL\|$, which induces classical logic, can be expressed using F notation as follows.

$\|LF\|$ If v(A)=f, then for some v', v$\leq$v' and v'(A)=F.

It is worth looking at what $\|LF\|$ says more carefully. Consider the sentence A→A, where A reports some future event over which one has control. So for example, A might say there is a sea battle at a date that happens to be in the future. Since one may have control over A, A is undetermined, and so at the present world v, v(A)=v(~A)=f. Though one can control A, it does not seem correct to assert that one has control over A→A. The reason is that A→A is inevitable, that is, it will turn out true no matter how A gets determined, and so my actions have nothing to do with determining it. Therefore, although A is undetermined, we want A→A to be determined true, since it is inevitable. This is exactly what ‖LF‖ entails, for it amounts to the claim that all inevitable sentences are true, and hence determined true.

To prove that, we will need an official definition of inevitability, the notion that a sentence is true at every point in the future where it is determined. Here it helps to deploy the concept of quasi-truth, for the inevitable sentences are simply those that are quasi-true at every possibility for the future. (Humberstone (2011, p. 896) calls this 'weak inevitability'.)

(Inevitable)   A is inevitable at v iff for all $v' \in V$, if $v \leq v'$, then $v'(A) = qT$.

It is now easy to prove that ‖LF‖ is equivalent to ‖IT‖, the claim that all inevitable sentences are determined true.

‖IT‖ If A is inevitable at v, then $v(A) = T$.

Theorem 10.3 When ‖PL‖ holds for V, V obeys ‖LF‖ iff V obeys ‖IT‖.

Proof. The contrapositive of ‖LF‖ amounts to ‖CLF‖, and when the definition of inevitability is unpacked in ‖IT‖ we have ‖IT'‖.

‖CLF‖ If for all $v' \in V$, if $v \leq v'$, then $v'(A) \neq F$, then $v(A) = t$.

‖IT'‖ If for all $v' \in V$, if $v \leq v'$, then $v(A) = qT$, then $v(A) = T$.

These are equivalent in light of (FqT) and (t=T).   □

The upshot of this theorem is that the semantic contribution of the law of double negation to the intuitionistic semantics amounts to exactly the requirement that inevitable sentences are determined true. This fits nicely with our intuitions about when agency is possible for situations described by sentences about the future.

10.4 Disjunction, choice, and Excluded Middle

It is natural to express our choices using disjunction. When I have a choice between bringing about events described by A and B, it is fair to say that A∨B is true. But how is the truth of this disjunction compatible with the possibility that my choice between A and B is as yet undecided? The answer given by the natural semantics ‖PL‖ for propositional logic is an easy one, for the reading ‖q∨‖ for disjunction allows that A∨B may be true even when neither disjunct is true as yet.

‖q∨‖ v(A∨B)=t iff for all v′∈V, if v≤v′, then v′(A)=qT or v′(B)=qT.

All that is necessary is that in every future, one of the disjuncts is quasi-true, that is, true wherever defined.

This matches intuitions about sentences of the form of Excluded Middle such as A∨~A, when A reads: 'there is a sea battle at t' and the referent of 't' is to a time in the future. We feel that this disjunction is determined true, and so lies outside the realm of our agency. The explanation is that in every possible future, either A is true if determined or ~A is true if determined. That follows directly from the fact that being determined true, being determined false, and being undetermined are exhaustive categories. So the truth condition ‖q∨‖ explains nicely how it can be that A∨~A is determined true at a time when both of its disjuncts are undetermined. To put it another way, the semantics is faithful to the dictum: "no choice before its time" (Belnap, 2005, Section 3.1), since disjuncts of A∨~A may remain undetermined at the present. However, some *disjunctions* may be determined well before the time their disjuncts are determined.

The reader may complain that ‖q∨‖ leaves no room for indeterminacy since ‖q∨‖ says v(A∨B)=t iff either A or B is inevitable at v.

(Inevitable) A is inevitable at v iff for all v′∈V, if v≤v′, then v(A)=qT.

From ‖IT‖ it would follow that ‖q∨‖ collapses to the classical truth condition ‖C∨‖.

‖IT‖ If A is inevitable at v, then v(A)=T.

However, ‖q∨‖ does not say that the truth of A∨B entails that one of its disjuncts is inevitable. (Pay attention to the relative scope of 'or' and the universal quantifier on the right-hand side of ‖q∨‖.) What it says is that in each future, one of the disjuncts is quasi-true. It does not say that one of the disjuncts is quasi-true in every future. Recognizing that difference is crucial to understanding the successful contribution of ‖q∨‖ to a semantics for the open future. Were ‖q∨‖ to collapse to the classical reading of ∨, the result would be a total disaster, for then the validity of A∨~A would entail that either A is determined true, or A is determined false. As we saw in the case for ∨ in the proof of the Holism Theorem of Section 2.3, this entails that negation, and hence all the connectives, are classical, and no sentence is undetermined.

10.5 Defeating fatalism

The reader may still have serious worries about $\|PL\|$. The condition (t=T) entails that truth and determined truth are the same thing.

(t=T) If $v(A)=t$ then $v(A)=T$.

Furthermore, since PL is classical, the Law of Excluded Middle is a theorem. The concern is that these two features do not leave room for undetermined values in the semantics. Arguments related to this concern have surfaced at many points in the literature. Two notable examples are Taylor's (1962) famous argument for fatalism, and Williamson's purported demonstration that supervaluation semantics has no room for undetermined values (1994, pp. 187ff. and 300ff.).

Here a basic argument form concerning $\|PL\|$ will be presented with an eye to uncovering the flaw in its reasoning. Once the defect is located, the same solution may be applied wherever arguments of this kind arise. Here is the basic argument form:

Ur Argument for Fatalism
A or not-A.   Excluded Middle
If A, then it is determined that A.   (t=T)
If not-A, then it is determined that not-A.   (t=T)
Therefore, either it is determined that A or determined that not-A.

The argument has the form of ($\vee$ Elimination), so it is classically valid. The premises appear indisputable since adopting classical logic yields Excluded Middle and (t=T) was proven for $\|PL\|$. It appears to follow that there is no room in $\|PL\|$ for any undetermined sentences, for when not-A is determined, that is, $v(\sim A)=T$, we have $v(A)=F$. Therefore, the conclusion of the argument asserts that A must be determined true or determined false, hence determined.

The problem with this reasoning is that it is presented in a form that is insensitive to the difference between the object language and the metalanguage. The English renderings of the premises are ambiguous. Let us attempt to rewrite the argument more accurately using the notation:

'v(A)=' in which (t=T) is actually written. Here we assume v is an arbitrary member of V.

v Argument for Fatalism

v(A∨~A)=t.	Excluded Middle is V-valid
If v(A)=t, then v(A)=T.	(t=T)
If v(~A)=t, then v(~A)=T.	(t=T)
Therefore v(A)=T or v(~A)=T.	

It should be clear right away that this argument is invalid. The problem is that we need (or ~) rather than what we see in the first premise: 'v(A∨~A)=t' in order for the argument to have the form of (∨ Elimination) in the metalanguage.

(or ~)   v(A)=t or v(~A)=t.

So let us replace the first premise with (or ~).

Or Argument for Fatalism

v(A)=t or v(~A)=t.	(or ~)
If v(A)=t, then v(A)=T.	(t=T)
If v(~A)=t, then v(~A)=T.	(t=T)
Therefore v(A)=T or v(~A)=T.	

This will not help matters, since there is no reason to accept (or ~). It does not have the form of Excluded Middle, so there is no classical argument in its favor. Furthermore, it begs the question, as (or ~) just amounts to the claim that there are no undetermined values. But worse, (or ~) is demonstrably false for ‖PL‖, for Theorem 4.4.1 showed there are models of ‖PL‖ containing non-classical valuations v where v(p)=v(~p)=f.

Perhaps a second variation on this argument form might work better. Let us change the first premise so that it has the form of Excluded Middle where the disjunction and negation are expressed in the metalanguage. The third premise then needs an adjustment to ensure that the argument has the form of (∨ Elimination):

Or Not Argument for Fatalism

v(A)=t or not v(A)=t.	Metalanguage Excluded Middle
If v(A)=t, then v(A)=T.	(t=T)
If not v(A)=t, then v(~A)=T.	?????
Therefore v(A)=T or v(~A)=T.	

However, the third premise no longer is supported by (t=T), and it is demonstrable that this claim is false for some valuations in models that obey ‖PL‖. If not v(A)=t, then v(A)=f. But this, as we have just argued, is compatible with v(~A)=f, thus undermining v(~A)=T.

The upshot of this is that (t=T), acceptance of Excluded Middle, and the existence of undetermined sentences are demonstrably compatible with each other. In fact ‖PL‖, the very semantics that tells us what is expressed by classical rules, shows how this is possible. The secret is that the quasi-truth interpretation of disjunction makes room for accepting A∨~A when the value of A is undetermined.

This realization has direct applications to a variety of arguments that purport to show that there cannot be an open future. Take a simplification of Taylor's well-known argument (Taylor, 1962, pp. 129ff.) for fatalism. Here 'Q' abbreviates 'A naval battle occurs at t', where t refers to a time in the future, and 'O' abbreviates 'I issue the order for the battle at t'. Presume that O is necessary and sufficient for Q.

Argument for Fatalism

Q is true or not-Q is true.

If Q, then O is out of my control.

If not-Q, then not-O is out of my control.

Therefore, O is out of my control or not-O is out of my control.

Given the strategy of ‖PL‖ semantics, it may appear that the argument has a valid form, and that all premises must be accepted. ‖PL‖ would apparently support the second premise because if Q is true, Q is determined true, and whatever is determined true entails the determined truth of any sentence (such as O) necessary for Q. Therefore O is determined and therefore not the subject of my control despite its being in the future. Similar reasoning can be given to support the third premise. It appears ‖PL‖ yields fatalist conclusions.

However, it is easy to see what has gone wrong when care is taken in presenting the argument with sufficient notational detail. If we take its form to be the analog of the v Fatalist argument, we have the following, which has a true first premise and an invalid form:

v Argument for Fatalism

v(Q∨~Q)=t.   Excluded Middle

If v(Q)=t, then v(O)=T.
If v(~Q)=t, then v(~O)=T.
Therefore v(O)=T or v(~O)=T.

Modifying the first premise yields a valid form:

Or Argument for Fatalism

v(Q)=t or ∨(~Q)=t.   *????*
If v(Q)=t, then v(O)=T.
If v(~Q)=t, then v(~O)=T.
Therefore v(O)=T or v(~O)=T.

However, the first premise no longer has the form of Excluded Middle, and in fact begs the question by claiming that Q is determined, something that can be refuted in ‖PL‖.

Suppose we attempt to fix this by expressing the negation in the object language and modifying the third premise to maintain the form of (∨ Elimination).

Or Not Argument for Fatalism

v(Q)=t or not v(Q)=t.   Metalanguage Excluded Middle
If v(Q)=t, then v(O)=T.
If not v(Q)=t, then v(~O)=T.   *????*
Therefore v(O)=T or v(~O)=T.

Now the third premise is the problem, for it is demonstrably false.

When v(Q) is not t, it is f. Since Q is necessary and sufficient for O, O is also f, and its being f is compatible with O's being undetermined. and hence a target for agency.

The irony of the situation is that because classical logic essentially takes on an open futures interpretation, it automatically has the resources to undermine arguments for fatalism, and this despite its acceptance of Excluded Middle and the seemingly fatalist proposal that truth amounts to determined truth. When one is wedded to a classical reading for the connectives, this solution is invisible.

10.6 The No Past Branching condition

The accessibility relation in an open future semantics is ordinarily taken to be reflexive, transitive, and antisymmetric.

(Antisymmetric)   For all v, v' in V, if v≤v' and v'≤v, then v=v'.

The relation ≤ of ‖PL‖ obeys these three properties. However, it is also presumed that the set of open possibilities has the structure of a forward facing tree, with branching towards the future, but none in the past. Belnap, Perloff, and Xu (2001, pp. 185ff.) argue that no branching in the past is essential to our concept of agency. So if ‖PL‖ were to count as a full-blooded open futures semantics, we would expect it to satisfy the following condition, for all v, v', and u in V.

(No Past Branching)   If v≤u and v'≤u then v≤v' or v'≤v.

However, there are models V that obey ‖PL‖ where (No Past Branching) fails. Nothing said so far rules out the possibility that two valuations v and v' might extend to the same valuation u even though the two are not comparable, that is, neither v≤v' nor v'≤v. So one might object that ‖PL‖ does not really qualify as a semantics of the open future since it does not treat the past properly. However, the problem can be repaired by constructing a finer individuation of the set of possibilities. Instead of taking the "moments" in our model to be valuations, think of them instead as pairs <c, v> where c is a *past* for v, that is, a connected set of valuations u that are earlier than v in the ordering ≤. Given any set of valuations V obeying ‖PL‖, it is possible to construct a *past model* P = <W, ⊆, u> for V by letting the members of W be pairs <c, v> (where c is a past for v in V), rather than the valuations themselves. (We could also require a past c to be a past *history* for v, where c must be a *maximal* connected set, but that complicates the result given below.) This idea matches the intuition that were there to be two moments where all the same sentences were true but with different pasts, we would count them non-identical. By defining the relation ⊆ and the assignment function u for P in the appropriate way, it will be possible to show that a past model for V has a relation ⊆ that obeys (No Past Branching), and P preserves the truth-values for valuations in V, in a sense to be made clear below. Therefore, a set of valuations V has the resources to set up a truth-preserving structure that qualifies as a full-fledged semantics for an open future.

Here are the relevant definitions, where it is presumed that ≤ is defined by (≤) above.

(Connected)   Relation $\leq$ is *connected* for set s iff for every v and v'$\in$s, v$\leq$v' or v'$\leq$v.

(Chain)   A *chain* c (for V) is a subset of V such that $\leq$ is connected for c.

(Past for v)   c is a *past for* v iff c is a chain for V, v$\in$c, and for every u$\in$c, u$\leq$v.

The *past model* P = <W, $\subseteq$, u> for V is defined as follows:

W = {<c, v>: c is a past for v and v $\in$ V}.

To save eyestrain, we abbreviate pairs '<c, v>' to 'cv'. Then the relation $\subseteq$ is defined for cv and c'v' $\in$ W, so that

($\subseteq$)   cv $\subseteq$ c'v' iff v$\leq$v' and c = {u: u$\in$c' and u$\leq$v}.

So cv $\subseteq$ c'v' holds when v<v' and c and c' agree on the past up to v.
The assignment function u is defined for cv $\in$ W, so that

u(cv, p)=v(p), for propositional variables p.

The function u is extended to the complex wffs by the following analogs of truth conditions in $\|PL\|$, for arbitrary w in W.

$\|u\&\|$ u(w, A&B)=t iff u(w, A)=t and u(w, B)=t.

$\|u{\rightarrow}\|$ u(w, A$\rightarrow$B)=t iff for all w'$\in$W, if w$\subseteq$w', then
$$u(w', A)=f \text{ or } u(w', B)=t.$$

$\|u\neg\|$ u(w, ~A)=t iff for all w'$\in$W, if w$\subseteq$w', then u(w', A)=f.

$\|uq\vee\|$ u(w, A$\vee$B)=t iff for all w'$\in$W, if w$\subseteq$w', then for some w"$\in$W,
$$w'\subseteq w" \text{ and either } u(w", A)=t \text{ or } u(w", B)=t.$$

Now that the past model for V is defined, it is possible to show that reflexivity, transitivity, antisymmetry, and (No Past Branching) all hold in this model. So in that sense, V generates a full-fledged open future semantics. We can also show that the past model for V is truth preserving in the sense that u(cv, A)=v(A) for all wffs A and any past c for v. The intuition behind this result is that the truth conditions "face the future" and so are insensitive to adjustments to past structure created by past models. The ability of V to generate past models is important because it shows that V has the resources for defining a frame <W, $\subseteq$> with the right structure for an open future. Furthermore, when any set of wffs H is satisfied by V, we know that it is also satisfied in the past model for V. As a result, any argument H / C is V-valid for all V obeying ‖PL‖ iff it is valid for all past models for V. The rest of this section is devoted to stating and proving that result.

Past Model Theorem. Let V be any set of valuations that obeys ‖PL‖. Then the past model H = <W, ⊆, u> for V is such that u(cv, A)=v(A) for all wffs A, and any past c for v. Furthermore, the frame <W, ⊆> is reflexive, transitive, antisymmetric, and obeys (No Past Branching).

We begin with two lemmas.

Lemma 1. If <W, ⊆, u> is a past model for V, then <W, ⊆> is reflexive, transitive, antisymmetric, and obeys (No Past Branching).

Proof. It is easy to verify that <W, ⊆> is reflexive, transitive, and antisymmetric. To show that it obeys (No Past Branching), let cv, c'v', and c"v" be any members of W, such that c'v' ⊆ cv and c"v" ⊆ cv and demonstrate that c'v' ⊆ c" v" or c"v" ⊆ c'v' as follows. We have from the definition of ⊆ that v'≤v, v"≤v, c' = {u: u∈c and u≤v'} and c" = {u: u∈c and u≤v"}. When c is a past for v, it follows that v∈c. Therefore, v'∈c' and v"∈c". It follows that v'∈c and v"∈c. Since c is connected, it follows that v'≤v" or v"≤v'. In the first case, it is possible to show that c'={u: u∈c" and u≤v'} from which it follows immediately that c'v' ⊆ c"v". To show that c'={u: u∈c" and u≤v'} simply show the following.

$$u \in c' \text{ iff } u \in c'' \text{ and } u \leq v'.$$

The proof of this from right to left follows from c' = {u: u∈c and u≤v'} and c" = {u: u∈c and u≤v"}. For the other direction, use the same two facts, and v'≤v". In case v"≤v', it follows that c"v" ⊆ c'v' by similar reasoning.   ☐

Lemma 2. If v≤v' and cv∈W, then for some c'v'∈W, cv ⊆ c'v'.

Proof. Suppose v≤v' and cv∈W. Then c is a past for v, hence v∈c, c is connected and for every u∈c, u≤v. Let c'=c∪{v'}. Then c' is a past for v', because v'∈c' and for every u∈c', u≤v', and c' is connected. The reason that c' is connected is that cv∈W entails c is connected. The only member of c' not in c is v'. But u≤v' for all u∈c'. Therefore adding v' to the connected set c results in a new connected set c'. Set c is clearly {u: u∈c' and u≤v}, so by the definition of ⊆, cv ⊆ c'v', and c'v' is the desired member of W such that cv ⊆ c'v'.   ☐

Now we are ready to prove the Past Model Theorem.

Proof of the Past Model Theorem. To show that the frame $<W,\subseteq>$ is reflexive, transitive, antisymmetric, and obeys (No Past Branching), simply appeal to Lemma 1. The proof that u(cv, A)=v(A) for all wffs A, and every past c for v is by structural induction on A. The base case and the case for & are straightforward.

In the case of negations ~B show u(cv,~B)=v(~B) by showing that the right-hand side of $\|\neg\|$ and the right-hand side of $\|u\neg\|$ are equivalent given the hypothesis of the induction: u(cv, B)=v(B), for any member cv of W. So we must show $\|\neg\|$r iff $\|u\neg\|$r.

$\|\neg\|$r   For all v'∈V if v≤v', then v'(B)=f.

$\|u\neg\|$r For all w'∈W if cv $\subseteq$ w', then u(w', B)=f.

For the proof from $\|\neg\|$r to $\|u\neg\|$r, assume cv $\subseteq$ w' for any w'∈W, and prove u(w', B)=f as follows. Since w'∈W, w'=c'v' for some v'∈V. Since cv $\subseteq$ c'v', v≤v'. Hence v'(B)=f by $\|\neg\|$r. By the hypothesis of the induction, we have u(c'v', B)=f as desired. For the other direction, assume v≤v' and prove v'(B)=f as follows. We know cv∈W and v≤v', so by Lemma 2, we have cv $\subseteq$ c'v' for some member c'v' of W. From $\|u\neg\|$r, it follows that u(c'v', B)=f. The hypothesis of the induction yields v'(B)=f as desired.

The case for → is similar.

The case for disjunctions B∨C will follow from showing that the following two conditions are equivalent, given the hypothesis of the induction.

$\|qv\|$r   For all v'∈V, if v≤v', then for some v"∈V, v'≤v" and either v"(B)=t or
            v"(C)=t.

$\|uqv\|$r For all w'∈W, if cv $\subseteq$ w', then for some w"∈W, w'$\subseteq$w" and either
            u(w", B)=t or u(w", C)=t.

For the proof from $\|qv\|$r to $\|uqv\|$r, assume cv $\subseteq$ w' for any w'∈W, and show that for some w" such that w'$\subseteq$w", either u(w", B)=t or u(w", C)=t as follows. By the definition of W, w'=c'v' for some v'∈V, and by cv $\subseteq$ c'v', we obtain v≤v'. From $\|qv\|$r, it follows that for some v"∈V, v'≤v" and v"(B)=t or v"(C)=t. By Lemma 2, there is a member c"v" of W such that c'v' $\subseteq$ c"v". By the hypothesis of the induction u(c"v", B)=t or u(c"v", C)=t. So c"v" is the desired w"∈W such that w'$\subseteq$w" and either u(w", B)=t or u(w", C)=t.

For the proof from $\|uqv\|$r to $\|qv\|$r, assume v≤v', and find a v" in V such that v'≤v" and either v"(B)=t or v"(C)=t as follows. Since cv∈W, it follows from v≤v' by Lemma 2 that for some c'v' in W, cv ⊂ c'v'. By ‖uq∨‖r, there is a member w" of W such that c'v' ⊆ w" and either u(w", B)=t or u(w", C)=t. Since w" must be c"v" for some v"∈V, we have by the hypothesis of the induction that v"(B)=t or v"(C)=t. We have c'v' ⊂ c"v", so v'≤v", hence v" is the desired valuation such that v'≤v" and v"(B)=t or v"(C)=t.   □

11 The expressive power of sequent calculi

We have shown that systems based on natural deduction rules do not (globally) express classical semantics; they select intensional rather than standard interpretations for the connectives. Although S& forces the classical reading, the rules for $\to$, $\leftrightarrow$, $\vee$, and $\sim$ (whether classical or intuitionistic) pick out intuitionistic interpretations that are weaker than their classical ones. (See Chapters 6, 7, and 8.) It is well known that when local expression is the criterion at issue, the same "failing" does not apply to Gentzen sequent calculi with multiple conclusions (or sequent systems for short), for they are strong enough to force classical readings of the connectives. (See Shoesmith and Smiley (1978, p. 3) and Hacking (1979, p. 312).) That result is far from surprising, as we learned in Chapter 3 that even the natural deduction rules locally express the classical interpretation.

However, this leaves open the question as to whether the sequent rules globally express the classical truth conditions. At the end of Section 1.5, we gave a simple argument that the system G$\to$$\sim$ deductively expresses the classical readings. Since every global model of a system is a deductive model of it, it follows that G$\to$$\sim$ forces the classical conditions and so expresses them. In Section 11.1, that result will shown for a full range of sequent systems using a more powerful line of proof. This result has interesting consequences for our understanding of the relationships between natural deduction and sequent systems. Section 11.2 shows that it explains the "magical fact" (Hacking, 1979, p. 293) that when one restricts sequent rules to a single formula on the right-hand side, one obtains exactly intuitionistic (and not classical) propositional logic. In Section 11.3 it is shown that the distinction between global and local expression collapses for sequent systems, so that classical conditions forced by local models are exactly the ones forced by global models. Since we have argued in Section 3.5 that local expression is incompatible with an inferentialist account of connective meaning, sequent calculi forfeit a role in the project of this book. Another untoward feature of sequent systems was shown in Theorem 3.5. The only truth conditions that sequent rules can express are extensional. The collapse of global to local validity corresponds to a prejudice for extensional over intensional truth conditions. Section 11.4 will deploy these results to help adjudicate claims that classical systems are the only logics.

11.1 Sequent calculi express classical truth conditions

We have shown that natural deduction rules for $\rightarrow$, $\leftrightarrow$, $\vee$, and $\sim$ express intensional rather than standard interpretations for the connectives. It is well known that multiple conclusion sequent systems (or sequent systems for short) are strong enough to force a classical reading of the connectives when local models are used as the criterion for expressive power. Here it is shown that the same holds for global expression. In sequent systems, both sides H and G of a sequent H / G are *sets* of wffs. A valuation v *satisfies* sequent H / G (written: $H \vDash_v G$) iff whenever v(A)=t for all members A of H, there is a member B of G such that v(B)=t. A sequent H / G *is V-valid* (written $H \vDash_V G$) iff any valuation v in V satisfies H / G.

Here are sequent calculi rules for a Gentzen version GPL of propositional logic. In formulating the rules we abbreviate 'H∪{A}' to 'H, A' and '{A}∪G' to 'A, G'. Similarly 'H, H'' abbreviates: 'H ∪ H''. The structural rules are the following.

Structural rules for sequent calculi

(Hypothesis) $H \vdash G$, where some wff A is in both H and G.

(Left Weakening)	$\dfrac{H \vdash G}{H, H' \vdash G}$	(Right Weakening)	$\dfrac{H \vdash G}{H \vdash G', G}$

(Cut) $\dfrac{H \vdash A, G \qquad H', A \vdash G'}{H, H' \vdash G, G'}$

(Cut) is an admissible rule in the sequent calculi we will consider, and so it could in principle be dispensed with.

Here are the sequent rules for each of the logical symbols. These with the structural rules form the system GPL for propositional logic.

G⊥   H, ⊥ ⊢ G (taken as an axiom)

G→:   (→Left)   (→Right)
        H ⊢ A, G   H, A ⊢ B, G
        H, B ⊢ G   H ⊢ A→B, G
        H, A→B ⊢ G

G&:   (&Left)   (&Right)
        H, A, B ⊢ G   H ⊢ A, G
        H, A&B ⊢ G   H ⊢ B, G
                                   H ⊢ A&B, G

G∨:   (∨Left)   (∨Right)
        H, A ⊢ G   H ⊢ A, B, G
        H, B ⊢ G   H ⊢ A∨B, G
        H, A∨B ⊢ G

G↔:   (↔Left)   (↔Right)
        H, A, B ⊢ G   H, A ⊢ B, G
        H, ⊢ A, B, G   H, B ⊢ A, G
        H, A↔B ⊢ G   H ⊢ A↔B, G

It is a simple exercise to verify that each of these sets of rules (globally) expresses the corresponding classical truth clauses. One way to do this is to establish a method for reading off truth conditions from sequent rules. (This method is similar to one presented in Hacking (1979, pp. 312ff.).) For any valuation, v let Hv={A: v(A)=t} and Gv={A: v(A)=f}. Let us write 'v(G)=f' when v assigns f to *all* members of G. (So when G is empty, v(G)=f holds by default.) It should be clear that v(Hv)=t and v(Gv)=f. Furthermore for any valuation v', if v'(Hv)=t and v'(Gv)=f, then the values v' assigns to the wffs agree with those of v, and so v'=v. Now let V be any set of valuations and v any member of v. Then H ⊨v G (v satisfies H / G) iff either v assigns f to one of the members of H (that is, v(H)≠t) or t to one of the members of G (v(G)≠f). Similarly H ⊨v G holds iff for each valuation v in V, either v(H)≠t or v(G)≠f. These definitions help us to establish the following theorem, which will show us how to read off values of members of a V-valid sequent that contains Hv and Gv. It will also make it clear that V-validity of such sequents (⊨v) and satisfaction by v (⊨v) are equivalent. This will help us prove (in Section 11.3) that global validity collapses to local validity.

Read Values Theorem. For any valuation v in V, H ⊨v G iff Hv, H ⊨$_V$ G, Gv.

Proof.

Right to Left. Assume Hv, H ⊨$_V$ G, Gv, and show v(H)≠t or v(G)≠f. From Hv, H ⊨$_V$ G, Gv, it follows that v must either assign f to one of the members of Hv, H, or t to one of the members of G, Gv. In the first case, it cannot assign f to any of the members of Hv, since v(Hv)=t. So it must assign f to one of the members of H. In the second case, by parallel reasoning, v must assign t to one of the members of G.

Left to Right. Assume Hv, H ⊭$_V$ G, Gv, and show v(H)=t and v(G)=f as follows. From Hv, H ⊭$_V$ G, Gv it follows that for some v' in V, v'(Hv, H)=t and v'(Gv, G) =f. Since v'(Hv)=t and v'(Gv)=f, v'=v, and so we have v(H)=t and v(G)=f as desired.   □

Call the metavariables 'A' and 'B' in the statement of the rules of GPL, the *parameters* of a rule. By taking the special case where H is Hv and G is Gv, it is possible to use the Read Values Theorem to obtain, for each sequent in a rule, a statement about the values of the parameters assigned by v. For example when G={A} and H={B}, we have that Hv, A ⊨$_V$ B, Gv iff v(A)=f or v(B)=t. In general, the statement for a sequent asserts a disjunctive claim where v assigns f to parameters to the left of '⊨', and t to parameters to the right of '⊨'. The claim that a rule preserves V-validity in the special case where H and G are set to Hv and Gv respectively, asserts a conditional with the parameter value statement(s) for the premise(s) as a (conjunctive) antecedent, and the statement for the conclusion of the rule as a consequent. For example, from such a special case of the claim that the rules of G→ preserve V-validity, one obtains two conditionals as follows.

G→:   (→Left)   (→Right)
         If Hv ⊨$_V$ A, Gv and   If Hv, A ⊨$_V$ B, Gv,
         Hv, B ⊨$_V$ Gv,   then Hv ⊨$_V$ A→B, Gv.
         then Hv, A→B ⊨$_V$ Gv.

Given the Read Values Theorem, one may remove 'Hv' and 'Gv' from these conditions and unpack the definition of satisfaction to obtain the classical truth condition for ⊃.

G→:   (→Left)   (→Right)
        If v(A)=t and   If v(A)=f or v(B)=t,
        v(B)=f,   then v(A→B)=t.
        then v(A→B)=f.

It follows immediately that G→ expresses the classical truth condition for →.

The reader will find it a simple exercise to read off the classical truth conditions for all the other connectives in the same way in order to establish the next theorem.

GPL Expression Theorem. Each pair of rules of GPL for a given connective (globally) expresses the classical truth conditions for that connective.

It is interesting to explore the reason why models of the sequent rules are classical, while models for corresponding natural deduction rules need not be. When v(A→B)=f, it follows from the Read Values Theorem that Hv $\nVdash_v$ A→B, Gv. The fact that (→Right) preserves V-validity insures that there is a valuation v' in V with v'(Hv, A)=t and v'(Gv, B)=f. But this insures that v' is identical to v, hence v(A)=t and v(B)=f, with the result that the right to left portion of the classical truth condition holds.

$||\to||$r.t.l If v(A→B)=f then v(A)=t and v(B)=f.

This contrasts with the situation for natural deduction rules, where a set on the right-hand side is missing. For example, we find that the V-validity of (→ Introduction) only insures that when v(A→B)=f, there is some valuation v', such that v'(Hv, A)=t and v'(B)=f. (Review the proof of the S→ Expression Theorem, Section 6.1.)

(→ Introduction)
$$\frac{H, A \vdash B}{H \vdash A \to B}$$

Since we do not have v'(Gv)=f to identify v' with v, we obtain the weaker result that v'(A)=t and v'(B)=f *in some extension* v' of v. As a result, the truth condition enforced by (→ Introduction) only involves *extensions* of the point of evaluation v, rather than just v, and so what we have is the right to left portion of $||\to||$, the intuitionistic truth condition.

$||{\to}||$r.t.l If v(A→B)=f, then for some v′ in V, v≤v′ and v′(A)=t and v′(B)=f.

As we will argue more carefully below, the use of sequent rules simply amounts to a covert adoption of extensional truth clauses. On the other hand, natural semantics for natural deduction rules is essentially intensional because the missing set on the right-hand side means one loses the ability to enforce an extensional condition.

Given the last theorem, it follows immediately that the classical truth conditions (PL) form a natural semantics for GPL.

Theorem 11.1 (PL) is a natural semantics for GPL.

11.2 The meaning of the restriction on the right-hand side

These reflections throw light on what Hacking (1979, p. 293) calls the "magical fact" that intuitionistic logic can be formulated using standard sequent rules provided we restrict the negation and conditional rules so that their right-hand sides never contain more than a single wff. Note that this restriction on (→Right) is simply a way to obtain the spirit of natural deduction rule (→ Introduction) within the sequent framework, for the natural deduction rules can be expressed in sequent notation using single conclusions on the right-hand side. Results of this book help us see why intuitionistic semantics is the natural product of natural deduction rules for → and ~. The tight linkage between natural deduction format and intuitionistic semantics guarantees that any restriction on sequents that yields natural deduction rules will guarantee an intuitionistic reading of the connectives. So the difference between having a singular and multiple right-hand side corresponds to the difference between expressing intuitionistic and classical truth conditions.

These intuitions can be backed up with more careful reasoning. Note that when the requirement that there be no more than one formula on the right-hand side is imposed on (→Right), G must be empty and so this comes to (→ Introduction).

(→Right)	(→ Introduction) a.k.a. (→Right)r
H, A ⊢ B, G	H, A ⊢ B
H ⊢ A→B, G	H ⊢ A→B

So the restriction creates a rule ($\rightarrow$Right)r that expresses $||{\rightarrow}||$r.t.1

$||{\rightarrow}||$r.t.1 If $v(A{\rightarrow}B)$=f, then for some v' in V, $v{\leq}v'$ and $v'(A)$=t and $v'(B)$=f.

In the case of ($\sim$Right) the restricted rule ($\sim$Right)r forces the right-hand side to be the empty set {}.

($\sim$Right)	($\sim$Right)r
H, A $\vdash$ G	H, A $\vdash$ {}
H $\vdash$ $\sim$A, G	H, $\vdash$ $\sim$A

It is not difficult to verify that when $\leq$ is defined by $||{\leq}||$, $||{\rightarrow}||$ and $||{\neg}||$ are the natural semantics expressed by the systems G$\rightarrow$r and G$\sim$r that result from replacing ($\rightarrow$Right) and ($\sim$Right) with their restricted versions, ($\rightarrow$Right)r and ($\sim$Right)r.

Theorem 11.2.1* G$\rightarrow$r expresses $||{\rightarrow}||$.

Theorem 11.2.2* G$\sim$r expresses $||{\neg}||$.

The proofs of these theorems are easy given the strategies employed by the $\rightarrow$ and $\neg$ Expression Theorems (Sections 6.1 and 8.1). The details are found at the end of the chapter.

Now consider a language where $\leftrightarrow$ is missing, but defined from $\rightarrow$ and & in the usual way. Let GPLr be the system consisting of the rules of GPL for $\perp$, &, and $\vee$, and the result of replacing ($\rightarrow$Right) and ($\sim$Right) in GPL with their restricted versions ($\rightarrow$Right)r and ($\sim$Right)r. Since all the rules for connectives other than $\sim$ and $\rightarrow$ are not restricted, it follows immediately from the GPL Expression Theorem (Section 11.1) and the last two Theorems that GPLr is has a natural semantics $||KI||$ which consists of the conjunction of $||{\perp}||$, $||\&||$, $||{\rightarrow}||$, $||CV||$, and $||{\neg}||$, when $\leq$ is defined by $||{\leq}||$. But this is the intensional semantics that is isomorphic to Kripke's semantics given in Section 5.2. So we have an explanation for why the restriction on the right-hand side picks out intuitionistic logic. There is nothing magical about that fact.

Theorem 11.2.3 $||KI||$ is a natural semantics for GPLr.

11.3 Sequent systems are essentially extensional

There is another way to exploit the Read Values Theorem to quickly demonstrate that the natural semantics for GPL is classical. It is to show that that theorem entails that there is no distinction between global expression and local expression for sequent systems. Section 3.5 argued that local expression is incompatible with the inferentialist project, and that only global expression will do. Since sequents with multiple conclusions cannot tell the difference, they cannot be employed in the inferentialist project. Sequent rules have inputs and outputs of the shape H, H′ / G′, G, where the parameters for a rule occur in the sets H′ and G′. So the general form of a sequent rule is as follows.

> H, H1 / G1, G
> H, H2 / G2, G
>   ⋮
> ----------
> H, Hn / Gn, G

When V is a global model of such a rule, the rule preserves V-validity, and so we have the following.

> Hv, H1 $\vDash_V$ G1, Gv
> Hv, H2 $\vDash_V$ G2, Gv
>   ⋮
> ----------
> Hv, Hn $\vDash_V$ Gn, Gv

By the Read Values Theorem (Section 11.1), Hv, Hi $\vDash_V$ Gi, Gv comes to: Hi $\vDash$v Gi, for each i. Furthermore, the fact that v(Hv)=t and v(Gv)=f, entails that Hi $\vDash$v Gi holds iff Hv, Hi $\vDash$v Gi, Gv. So we may replace '$\vDash_V$' with '$\vDash$v' in the above schema to obtain:

> Hv, H1 $\vDash$v G1, Gv
> Hv, H2 $\vDash$v G2, Gv
>   ⋮
> ----------
> Hv, Hn $\vDash$v Gn, Gv

This amounts to the claim that when v satisfies the inputs of the rule, it satisfies the output. Since the rule guarantees this result for every choice of v in V, it follows that V is a local model of the rule. The upshot of this along with the fact that any local model of S is a global model of S is the following theorem.

Theorem 11.3.1 If S is a system of sequent rules (of the shape considered above), then V is a global model of S iff V is a local model of S.

It follows immediately that all results that can be derived for local expression apply to the case of global expression for sequent rules of GPL. Since the Local Expression Theorem of Section 3.3 shows that the ND rules express the classical truth conditions, and the ND rules are a special case of the sequent rules, it follows that GPL expresses the classical truth conditions as well.

It also follows that all sequent systems of the kind described above express extensional truth conditions, for Theorem 3.5 established that conditions locally expressed are always extensional. While some may be impressed by the expressive strength this offers, there is a cost. Sequent rules violate the standard etiquette one expects of rules that define the meaning of a connective. We would hope that a rule that defines one connective should leave unaffected the definitions previously given by other connectives. Therefore those rules should be a conservative extension of the system that regulates connectives previously defined. However, in a context where connectives have been given intensional interpretations using ND rules, the addition of a sequent rule for a new connective may disturb the interpretations previously given. For example, suppose that an intuitionistic system $S{\to}\neg$ is formulated in a language with an intuitionistic negation symbol $\neg$, and the sequent rules $G{\sim}$ for a new negation symbol $\sim$ are added to $S{\to}\neg$. Since the natural semantics for $G{\sim}$ is extensional, it will turn out that $\sim$ obeys the classical truth table for negation. This entails that the extension relation $\leq$ mentioned in the conditions for $\to$ and $\neg$ collapses to identity. (See Theorem 8.5.3.) The result is that both intuitionistic connectives $\to$ and $\neg$ now obey classical principles, with the result that adding $G{\sim}$ is non-conservative.

One might object that it was argued in Section 8.9 that failure of conservation in the case of the classical rules $S{\sim}$ for PL did not stand in the way of defining truth conditions for $\sim$. So why should anyone worry about the non-conservativity of G~? There is an important difference between the two cases. It was shown in Section 8.7 that S~ expresses the intuitionistic reading $\|\neg\|$ along with a structural condition $\|pLF\|$ on the behavior of propositional variables not related to the truth conditions for ~ nor to any complex wff. The loss of conservativity for S~ was entirely due to $\|pLF\|$. Therefore, the *truth condition* expressed by S~ was not responsible for the loss of conservation.

It is not possible to deploy this kind of defense in the case of G~. While one might say that G~ expresses the conjunction of $\|\neg\|$ with the condition ($\leq$=) that $\leq$ collapses to identity, ($\leq$=) cannot be expressed in terms of the truth behavior of propositional variables alone.

($\leq$=) $v \leq v'$ iff $v = v'$.

When $\leq$ is defined by $\|\leq\|$, which describes the behavior of complex wffs, ($\leq$=) says that a valuation has itself as its only extension. That happens when the valuations are all maximal, and negation behaves classically. However, the version of ($\leq$=) where $\leq$ is defined by $\|p\leq\|$, says something very different.

$\|p\leq\|$ $v \leq v'$ iff for each propositional variable p, if $v(p)=t$, then $v'(p)=t$.

In that case, ($\leq$=) would demand that all valuations agree on the values of all the propositional variables, something that G~ certainly does not express. Therefore the failure of conservativity in the case of G~ may not be written off as the product of a structural condition unrelated to the meaning it assigns to ~. Instead, it must be charged to an unacceptable feature of the (classical) *truth condition* it expresses.

11.4 What counts as a logic?

Questions about how to distinguish the logical from the non-logical constants have traditionally been associated with the controversy over which formal system counts as the real logic. For example, Hacking (1979, p. 298) tries to argue that non-standard connectives are less deserving of the title "logical" because their logics lack important formal features, such as the subformula property, conservativeness, cut-elimination, or absence of side conditions in their sequent formulations. This strategy assumes one's taste in the formal requirements for a true logic enforces corresponding decisions about which vocabulary counts as logical. But if formal features of sets of rules are to carry this weight, then the rules must identify the meanings of connectives that are to receive certification as truly logical. There is no interesting sense to make of the claim that an uninterpreted symbol is logical or non-logical. If a distinction between logical and non-logical connectives is to be generated from syntactic features of sets of rules, then those rules must insure that the symbols they regulate fix their intended interpretations; i.e. they must identify those connectives semantically. Given model-theoretic inferentialism, it would follow that formal systems that carry the weight of this kind of argument must have a natural semantics that gives the connectives their correct interpretations.

The requirement that rules be natural provides an independent way to identify (and justify) formal requirements on systems that certify connectives as logical. In Section 13.1 we will show that functional natural systems obey conservativity. Furthermore, compactness follows from completeness of natural systems, which is shown in Section 12.1. According to Hacking (1979, p. 298) cut elimination and absence of side conditions follow from conservativeness in sequent systems. So natural semantics can provide an independent framework for determining which of Hacking's formal features are legitimate requirements for defining logical constants. (However, see Sundholm (1981) for a convincing refutation of Hacking's project.)

Our results show that any argument to the effect that the classical connectives are the only logical constants must be framed using sequent calculi, rather than natural deduction rules, for the natural deduction rules express intuitionistic readings of the connectives. This may explain the (perhaps covert) pressure on Hacking to focus attention on sequent calculi. He simply dismisses natural deduction rules, despite citing (Hacking, 1979, p. 291) Gentzen's (1969) opinion that natural deduction "gets at the heart of logical reasoning" and that sequent calculi serve merely as a technical device.

Hacking (and others) may have assumed that sequent calculi are the only exceptions to the conventional wisdom that "syntax all by itself doesn't determine semantics" (Dennett, 1984, p. 28). If this were true, it would support the idea that sequent calculi are the only measures of the logical (and the only hope for MT inferentialism). But the results of this book show that the ND formulation of intuitionistic logic (or the restricted sequent system GPLr) is quite capable of enforcing intensional interpretations of the connectives. Furthermore, were Hacking to attempt to strengthen intuitionistic natural deduction rules by adding (say) Double Negation (Section 8.6) or Peirce's Rule (Section 6.2), he would lose conservation, one of his own desiderata. From the viewpoint of natural deduction, where many of the logical connectives are essentially intensional, the sequent rules, which require extensional truth conditions, are simply inappropriate.

Taken together, the results on sequent calculi and natural deduction suggest that the contest between the champions of classical and intensional logics ends in a draw. Therefore the best position to take is a brand of logical pluralism (Beall and Restall, 2006). There are natural systems for both intensional and classical connectives. It would appear that whether the logical connectives must be classical or not depends on one's taste in rules, i.e. on whether one prefers to frame one's logic in ND or sequent format. Problems we encountered in outfitting Sv with a natural semantics (Section 7.6) might tip the balance in favor of the classical side, for the sequent rules for disjunction, at least, clearly count as a natural semantics.

On the other hand, I believe (with Gentzen) that the choice between ND and sequent formats is not a mere matter of taste. There are good reasons for thinking that natural deduction format is more basic. Logic is, after all, the study of the correctness or incorrectness of *reasoning*, and reasoning is a process of drawing a conclusion C from a set of premises H. Therefore logic should focus on properties of *arguments*: H / C. ND rules codify correct reasoning by directly providing principles that generate correct *argument* patterns. Sequent calculi, on the other hand, are an artificial by-product of research dominated by interest in classical logic. As we argued in Section 1.8, sequent structure: H / G has no direct bearing on presentation of the notion of logical consequence found in the wild. A set G of formulas on the right-hand side interpreted as a multiple *disjunction* is not part of our intuitive understanding of the task or reasoning.

Perhaps there is some other way to argue that multiple conclusions are more basic. Shoesmith and Smiley defend themselves from evidence that multiple conclusions are foreign to normal human reasoning. However, the only positive argument they present for the idea that multiple conclusions are the starting point for logic begs the question. They note that S→ does not determine the standard reading for →, and that the only rules we know that would do so have multiple conclusions. Since we just *do* give → the standard reading, "one would have to conclude that standard logicians … have been speaking multiple conclusions all their lives without knowing it" (1978, p. 4).

In a context where one is not aware that S→ determines a legitimate (but non standard) reading for →, it seems plausible to conclude that one must assign to → the only reading known to be fixed by a set of rules: the standard one fixed by sequent calculi. One then argues backwards from this to the conclusion that we have been speaking multiple conclusions all along. This is a mistake. A penchant for extensional semantics has blinded us (so far) to the fact that S→ fixes an intentional reading of the connective →. Given this realization, there is no longer any pressure on one to find an extensional reading for →, and to claim that multiple conclusions underlie our intuitions. Natural deduction format is clearly the more natural vehicle for codifying logic. I conclude that if formal features carry any weight at all concerning what counts as a logical connective, the intuitionistic connectives defined by those ND rules that have a natural semantics are more truly logical.

There is a final worry to be faced for those who claim that the only logic is one with an extensional semantics. The issue concerns the quantifiers, so discussion of it will be delayed to Section 14.10. The gist, however, is this. Requiring extensional truth conditions means giving up the validity of the rule Universal Generalization and replacing it with the omega rule (Hacking, 1979, pp. 313ff.). However, the omega rule is non-constructive, and furthermore, accepting its validity entails adoption of the substitution interpretation, which is open to the criticism that it does not allow for quantification over real numbers or other superdenumerable domains. The upshot is that excessively extensional systems of logic eliminate the objectual interpretation of the quantifier, the standard adopted by almost everyone who prefers extensional logic.

11.5 Proofs of theorems in Section 11.2

Theorem 11.2.1 G→r expresses $||\to||$.

Proof. We must show that V is a model of G→r iff V obeys $||\to||$.

For the proof from left to right, assume V is a model of G→r, and show $||\to||$ left to right by assuming $v(A \to B) = t$ and $v \leq v'$ and showing that $v'(A) = f$ or $v'(B) = t$

as follows. Use the Read Values Theorem (Section 11.1) with ($\rightarrow$ Elimination) to obtain that if v'(A)=t and v'(B)=f, then v'(A$\rightarrow$B)=f, and so if v'(A$\rightarrow$B)=t, then either v'(A)=f or v'(B)=t. But in light of v$\leq$v' and v(A$\rightarrow$B)=t, v'(A$\rightarrow$B)=t, and so v'(A)=f or v'(B)=t as desired.

To show $||\rightarrow||$ right to left, assume v(A$\rightarrow$B)=f and demonstrate that there is a member v' of V such that v$\leq$v', v'(A)=t and v'(B)=f following the strategy of the S$\rightarrow$ Expression Theorem of Section 6.1.

For the proof from right to left, assume V obeys $||\rightarrow||$. That ($\rightarrow$Right)r, (that is ($\rightarrow$ Introduction)) preserves V-validity has been shown in the proof of the S$\rightarrow$ Expression Theorem of Section 6.1.

To show that ($\rightarrow$Left) preserves V-validity, assume H $\vDash_V$ A, G and H, B $\vDash_V$ G and H, A$\rightarrow$B $\nvDash_V$ G for reductio. From the last assumption there is a member v of V such that v(H, A$\rightarrow$B)=t and v(G)=f. This means that v(H)=t and v(A$\rightarrow$B)=t, and so by $||\rightarrow||$ and v$\leq$v, v(A)=f or v(B)=t. Suppose v(A)=f. Then since v(G)=f, we have v(A, G)=f. This with v(H)=t yields H $\nvDash_V$ A, G, which contradicts H $\vDash_V$ A, G. Suppose v(B)=t. Then v(H)=t and H, B $\vDash_V$ G, entail v(G)$\neq$f, which contradicts v(G)=f. Either way, we have the desired contradiction. $\square$

Theorem 11.2.2 G~r expresses $||\neg||$.

Proof. We must show that V is a model of G~r iff V obeys $||\neg||$.

For the proof from left to right, assume V is a model of G~r.

To show $||\neg||$ left to right, assume v(~A)=t and v$\leq$v' and show that v'(A)=f as follows. Since V is a model of G~r, (~Left) preserves V-validity, with the result that if Hv' $\vDash_V$ A, Gv', then Hv', ~A $\vDash_V$ Gv'. From the Read Values Theorem (Section 11.1), it follows that if v'(A)=t then v'(~A)=f. But in light of v$\leq$v' and v(~A)=t, v'(~A)=t, and so v'(A)=f as desired.

To show $||\neg||$ right to left, assume v(~A)=f and demonstrate that there is a member v' of V such that v$\leq$v', and v'(A)=t. Note that v(Hv)=t. So Hv $\nvDash_V$ ~A, and hence Hv, A $\nvDash_V$ {} because (~Right)r preserves V-validity. So for some v' in V, we have v'(Hv, A)=t and v'({})=f. But this means v'(A)=t and v'(Hv)=t. From the latter it follows that v$\leq$v', so v' is the desired member of v' such that v$\leq$v', and v'(A)=t.

For the proof from right to left, the soundness of G~r must be shown with respect to $||S\sim||$. Assume V obeys $||S\sim||$.

To show that (~Right)r preserves V-validity, assume H, A $\vDash_V$ {} and H $\nvDash_V$ ~A for reductio. Then for some v in V, v(H)=t and v(~A)=f. By $||\neg||$, there is a member v' of V such that v$\leq$v' and v'(A)=t. By v$\leq$v' and v(H)=t, v'(H)=t. From H, A $\vDash_V$ {}, it follows that v({})$\neq$f, which is impossible.

To show that (~Left) preserves V-validity, assume $H \vDash_V A, G$ and $H, \sim A \nvDash_V G$ for reductio. From the last assumption, there is a member v of V such that $v(H, \sim A)=t$ and $v(G)=f$. This means that $v(H)=t$ and $v(\sim A)=t$, and so by $\|\neg\|$ and $v \leq v$, $v(A)=f$. Since $v(G)=f$, we have $v(A, G)=f$. This with $v(H)=t$ yields $H \nvDash_V A, G$, which contradicts our first assumption.   □

12 Soundness and completeness for natural semantics

My initial interest in natural semantics was purely formal. I hoped to use it to obtain new results in quantified modal logic, since I realized its power in showing adequacy and, especially, completeness. In this chapter, a simple strategy for converting results about what rules express to corresponding adequacy theorems will be explained (Section 12.1). In Section 12.2, this tool will be applied to show adequacy of intuitionistic logic for path semantics, and in Section 12.4, the adequacy of sequent systems. Section 12.3 proves that completeness results using natural semantics are modular, that is, they may be used to show the completeness for any combination of two systems with a natural semantics. This result will be useful in Chapter 13, where relationships between natural semantics and conservativity are explored in detail.

12.1 A general completeness theorem for natural semantics

Throughout this section we will suppose that S is a system that expresses $\|S\|$. We first verify that S is always sound for $\|S\|$. (Remember that $H \vDash_{\|S\|} C$ means that $H \vDash_V C$ for every model V that obeys $\|S\|$.)

$\|S\|$ **Soundness Theorem.** If $H \vdash_S C$ then $H \vDash_{\|S\|} C$.

Proof. Simply note that since S expresses $\|S\|$, it follows that any model V that obeys $\|S\|$ must preserve the V-validity of the rules. □

The proof of the completeness of S for $\|S\|$ takes a route through results concerning the canonical model. A valuation v (for a given language L) *satisfies* system S iff if $H \vdash_S C$ and v(H)=t, then v(C)=t. The *canonical model* [S] for system S (and language L) is the set of all valuations that satisfy S. An important property of the canonical model was reported in the [S] Adequacy Theorem of Section 4.3.

[S] Adequacy Theorem. $H \vdash_S C$ iff $H \vDash_{[S]} C$.

A second important feature of the canonical model for S, proven in Theorem 4.3, is that it is always a model of S.

[S] Model Theorem. [S] is a model of S.

A central idea in the completeness proof is to show that the canonical model for S always obeys $\|S\|$. When S expresses $\|S\|$, this follows immediately, since every model of S obeys $\|S\|$, and by the [S] Model Theorem, [S] is a model of S.

Canonical Model Theorem. [S] obeys $\|S\|$.

The completeness result is now just around the corner.

$\|S\|$ Completeness Theorem. If $H \vDash_{\|S\|} C$, then $H \vdash_S C$.

Proof. Assume $H \nvdash_S C$ and show $H \nvDash_{\|S\|} C$ as follows. Consider the canonical model [S] for L. By the [S] Adequacy Theorem, $H \nvDash_{[S]} C$. By the Canonical Model Theorem, [S] obeys $\|S\|$, so it follows that $H \nvDash_{\|S\|} C$.   □

It follows immediately from the $\|S\|$ Completeness and Soundness Theorems that S is adequate for $\|S\|$.

$\|S\|$ Adequacy Theorem. $H \vdash_S C$ iff $H \vDash_{\|S\|} C$.

Furthermore, in light of the [S] Adequacy Theorem, we know that [S] obeys a characteristic property of a canonical model, namely that whether an argument is $\|S\|$-valid is determined exactly by whether it is valid on the canonical model.

$\|S\|=[S]$ Theorem. $H \vDash_{\|S\|} C$ iff $H \vDash_{[S]} C$.

Not only that, but [S] is the *maximal* model of S, in the sense that any other model of S is a subset of [S].

[S] Maximality Theorem. If V is a model of S, then $V \subseteq [S]$.

Proof. Suppose that V is a model of S. Then the rules of S preserve V-validity, and so each argument provable in S is V-valid. However, this means that every valuation v in V must satisfy S. Therefore, every member of V is a member of [S], so V⊆[S] as desired.   □

12.2 Sample adequacy proofs using natural semantics

The expression results developed in previous chapters, along with those of the last section, may be applied to show the adequacy of both classical and intuitionist systems with respect to several different semantics. We will first prove the adequacy of the intuitionistic logic I∨ for its natural semantics ‖I∨‖ and for path models, and then for ‖KI‖ and Kripke semantics. As an added bonus, we will obtain a very quick proof of the completeness of classical propositional logic for its classical semantics,

Let I∨ be the system for intuitionist logic that includes the symbols ⊥, &, →, ↔, ∨, and ~, and the rules S⊥, S&, S→, S↔, S∨, and S¬. Remember that ‖I∨‖ is the corresponding natural semantics for I∨, consisting of ‖⊥‖, ‖&‖, ‖→‖, ‖↔‖, ‖∨‖, and ‖¬‖. It was shown to be isomorphic to path semantics in Section 7.5.

Theorem 12.2.1 I∨ is complete for both ‖I∨‖ and path semantics.

Proof. Assume that H ⊬$_{I∨}$ C. By the ‖S‖ Completeness Theorem (Section 12.1), H ⊭$_{‖I∨‖}$ C. So I∨ is complete for ‖I∨‖. By the Path Isomorphism Theorem of Section 7.5, any model obeying ‖I∨‖ is isomorphic to a path model, so there is path model that serves as a counterexample to H / C as desired.   □

The soundness of I∨ for ‖I∨‖ follows from the ‖S‖ Soundness Theorem of the previous section. For the proof that I∨ is also sound for path semantics one could take a route though the Path Isomorphism Theorem of Section 7.5, which says that models that obey ‖I∨‖ are isomorphic to path models. However, there are complications, because we do not know that every path model is isomorphic to an ‖I∨‖-model. So it is easier to prove the result directly. We write: 'H ⊨$_p$ C' when the argument H / C is path-valid, which means in turn that for every path model U=<W, ⊆, N, υ>, and every w in W, if

$\vDash^U$ H, then $\vDash^U$ C, where $\vDash^U$ is the truth relation induced by U. (See Section 7.4 for the details on path models.)

Theorem 12.2.2 I∨ is sound for path-validity.

Proof. The proof is a straightforward exercise. The rules for connectives other than ∨ may be shown to preserve path-validity in the same way this is done for Kripke semantics, so that is left to the reader. What remains is to show that the rules of S∨ preserve path-validity.

(∨ Introduction). Assume $H \vDash_p A$ and show that $H \vDash_p A \lor B$ by assuming that w is any member of the set W of worlds of a path model such that w(H)=t, and proving that w(A∨B)=t as follows. In light of (P∨), w(A∨B)=t will follow if we demonstrate that for any set P if wNP, there is a member w′ of P such that either w′ $\vDash$ A or w′ $\vDash$ B. So assume wNP. Then by (N), there is a wff C such that w(C)=f and the members w′ of P are exactly those such that w⊆w′ and w′(C)=f. But in light of w⊆w and w $\nvDash$ C, w must be a member of P. From $H \vDash_p A$ and w $\vDash$ H, it follows that w $\vDash$ A. So w is a member of P such that w $\vDash$ A or w $\vDash$ B as desired. The proof that if $H \vDash_p A$ then $H \vDash_p A \lor B$ is similar.

(∨ Elimination). Assume (1) $H \vDash_p A \lor B$, (2) $H, A \vDash_p C$, and (3) $H, B \vDash_p C$; and show that $H \vDash_p C$, by reductio. From $H \nvDash_p C$, it follows that for some path model U=<W, ⊆, N, u> and some w ∈ W, w $\vDash$ H and w $\nvDash$ C. Given $H \vDash_p A \lor B$, it follows that w $\vDash$ A∨B. By (P∨), it follows that for every set P such that wNP, there is a member w′ of P such that w′ $\vDash$ A or w′ $\vDash$ B. Define set P′ so that w″ is in P′ iff w⊆w″ and w″ $\nvDash$ C. Since w $\nvDash$ C, (N) guarantees that wNP′. So there must be a member w′ of P such that w′ $\vDash$ A or w′ $\vDash$ B. Suppose w′ $\vDash$ A. Since w′ is in P, it follows that w⊆w′, and since ⊆ obeys (⊆), it follows that w′ $\vDash$ H. Given H, $A \vDash_p C$, it follows that w′ $\vDash$ C which contradicts w′ $\nvDash$ C. The case for w′ $\vDash$ B is similar.   □

Putting the last two theorems together it follows that I∨ is adequate for both ||I∨|| and path semantics.

Theorem 12.2.3 I is adequate for ||I∨|| and path semantics.

Our next project will be to demonstrate that I∨ is also adequate for ||KI|| where ||KI|| is like ||I∨|| except that the classical truth condition ||C∨|| is used in place of ||∨||. This follows immediately from Theorem 7.7.2, which tells us that when ||KS|| results from replacing ||∨|| with the classical condition ||C∨||

in a natural semantics $\|S\|$ for a system containing the disjunction rules $S\vee$, we have $H \vDash_{\|S\|} C$ iff $H \vDash_{\|KS\|} C$.

Theorem 12.2.4 $I\vee$ is adequate for $\|KI\|$.

The adequacy of $I\vee$ for Kripke semantics follows easily using the Isomorphism Theorem of Section 5.4.

Theorem 12.2.5 $I\vee$ is adequate for Kripke semantics.

Using exactly the same strategy, it is easy to see that PL is adequate for its intuitionistic semantics $\|PL\| = \|qPL\|$ (Section 8.7), and complete for the KR-semantics reported in Section 8.8 which is isomorphic to it. Since it is easily shown that PL is sound for the KR-semantics, we have the following.

Theorem 12.2.6 PL is adequate for both $\|qPL\|$, $\|PL\|$ and KR-semantics.

The method just used also provides a quick completeness proof for classical propositional logic PL on its classical semantics (PL). All that is needed is to use Theorem 7.7.2, which tells us that the result (PL$\vee$) of replacing $\|q\vee\|$ with $\|C\vee\|$ in the intuitionistic natural semantics $\|PL\|$ for PL leaves validity unaffected. The resulting semantics (PL$\vee$) obeys the classical truth tables by the Holism Theorem of Section 2.3.

12.3 Natural systems and modular completeness

Systems with a natural semantics exhibit an especially desirable form of completeness. When a set of rules is so strong that it allows no alternative interpretations for its connectives, the canonical model for that system will agree with the single interpretation allowed. As a result, any argument not provable in the system will have a counterexample in the canonical model and completeness follows immediately. But naturalness has a stronger consequence: the completeness for a natural semantics is modular, i.e. the completeness of any pair of systems entails the completeness of their sum for the combined semantics, so that one may confidently construct larger systems by adding together logics that have natural semantics.

Unfortunately, there are logics that are incomplete even though they are constructed from two (or more) complete subsystems. Past tense logic (with operator P) and future tense logic (with operator F) are complete, but their sum requires additional axioms to fix the relationships between P and F. The quantified modal logic QS4 is composed of two complete systems: S4 and classical quantification theory, but it is incomplete (at least on one standard account of its semantics) because the Barcan Formula is valid there but independent from QS4. This behavior can occur even though each of the two systems is a conservative extension of the other, because the new theorems are ones that include principles concerning the interaction between two connectives (say F and P, or $\forall$ and $\square$).

Such behavior is a frustration in intensional logics. One satisfying feature of natural systems is that they insure modularity. When two systems have a natural semantics, their sum is always complete with respect to the conjunction of their natural conditions. In cases where modularity fails, the blame lies with the fact that the intended semantics for the sum of the two systems is stronger than the conjunction of the natural conditions for each. So non-modularity emerges from a mismatch between the intended interpretation for some logical constants and their natural interpretation, i.e. the semantical conditions expressed by their rules. In the case of tense logic, the natural semantics says nothing about the connections between the relation < introduced in the truth condition for F (read: earlier than) and the relation > introduced for P (read: later than). Therefore, the sum of these two logics is complete for the natural semantics that combines their truth conditions and says nothing more about < and >. Similarly, the combination of objectual quantification (over a single domain) and S4 is incomplete for the combined semantics, but that is because the natural semantics for quantification is weaker that the objectual interpretation. (See Chapter 14.) The combination of the semantical conditions for S4 and the natural semantics for quantification therefore is complete and fails to validate the Barcan formula. So models of this kind can be used to show its independence.

Let us turn to the formal details needed to prove the modularity of that natural semantics. The reader might imagine that two systems S' and S" may be written in two entirely different languages L' and L" with no connective in common, in which case the language for the sum system S'+S" differs from the language of S' and S". To avoid complications, however, let us assume that a valuation assigns values to wffs of a single given language L which you may take to be the result of combining L' and L". As a result, systems S', S" and S=S'+S" will all be taken to be written in the same language L=L'+L'''. So the language of S'' may contain a connective c' that is regulated by the rules of S' and is absent from any rule of S'' or any clause of its semantics. Models of S'' assign arbitrary values to wffs Ac'B when c' is a connective of this kind.

Now consider two systems S' and S'' with natural semantics ||S'|| and ||S''|| respectively, let S = S'+S'' be the system that includes (exactly) the rules of both S' and S'', and let the semantics ||S|| = ||S'+S''|| for S'+S'' be conjunction of ||S'|| with ||S''||. The next theorem shows that the sum of the two natural systems S' and S'' has the sum semantics as its natural semantics.

Theorem 12.3.1 ||S'+S''|| is a natural semantics for S'+S''.

Proof. Let S' and S'' be natural systems with semantics ||S'|| and ||S''|| respectively. To show that ||S+S'|| is a natural semantics for S+S' it must be shown that V is a model of S = S'+S'' iff V obeys ||S||, the conjunction of ||S'|| with ||S''||. Suppose V is a model of S. Therefore S preserves V-validity. Then the rules of S' preserve V-validity, and V obeys ||S'||. Similarly, V also obeys ||S''||, hence V obeys their conjunction ||S'+S''||. Now suppose that V obeys ||S||. Then V obeys ||S'|| and ||S''||, and so both S' and S'' preserve V-validity, hence so does S.   □

It follows from this that natural systems have modular completeness results.

Theorem 12.3.2 The sum of any two natural systems S and S' is complete for its natural semantics ||S+S'||.

Proof. By the last theorem S+S' has ||S+S'|| as a natural semantics; so by the ||S|| Adequacy Theorem (Section 12.1), S+S' is complete for ||S+S'||.   □

12.4 Completeness of sequent calculi using natural semantics

It this section it will be shown in general that sequent systems GS with rules G∨ for disjunction are always adequate for their natural semantics.

||GS|| Adequacy Theorem. H ⊢$_{GS}$ G iff H ⊨$_{||GS||}$ G, provided that GS contains the rules of G∨ and ||GS|| is a natural semantics for GS.

In light of the fact that classical truth conditions (PL) are a natural semantics for GPL (Theorem 11.1) and ||KI|| is a natural semantics for GPLr (Theorem

11.2.3), the adequacy of GPL for ‖PL‖ and GPLr for ‖KI‖ will follow immediately.

GPL Adequacy Theorem. GPL is adequate for (PL).

GPLr Adequacy Theorem. GPLr is adequate for ‖KI‖.

The ‖GS‖ Adequacy Theorem supports a general methodology for solving the adequacy problem for sequent systems. Given any set of rules for connectives of any arity, use the Read Values Theorem to determine what is expressed. If that qualifies as a semantics, it is a natural one, and adequacy follows immediately.

The rest of this section is devoted to the proof of the ‖GS‖ Adequacy Theorem. The proof follows the strategy of adequacy proofs for ND systems, but modifications are needed to handle multiple conclusions. The canonical model for GS is not strong enough to guarantee the disjunctive property characteristic of valuations that satisfy sequents H / G, namely that one of the members of G be t. So it will be necessary to take a route through GS-prime models and to know that GS contains the rules G∨.

Remember that valuation v *satisfies* sequent H / G iff if v(H)=t then v(G)≠f, that is, one of the members of G is t. Let us say that valuation v satisfies GS iff v satisfies every sequent such that H ⊢GS G. Valuation v is said to be *GS-prime* iff v satisfies GS and if v(A∨B)=t then either v(A)=t or v(B)=t. The proof of the next theorem follows the strategy of the proof of Theorem 7.7.1. However, to begin we need a quick lemma.

Finitary Sequent Lemma. GPL is finitary, that is, for each sequent H / G, if H ⊢PL G, there are finite sets G' and H' such that H' ⊢PL G'.

Proof. By inspection of the rules.   □

GS Prime Theorem. If GS is any finitary sequent system that includes G∨ and the structural rules, and H ⊬GS G, then there is a GS-prime valuation v such that v(H)=t and v(G)=f.

Proof. Suppose GS includes (S∨), and assume H ⊬ G. We construct a GS-prime valuation v* such that v*(H)=t and v*(G)=f by the following recipe.

Construct an ordered list of all the wffs of the language. Then construct a series of sets $H_0, H_1, H_2, \ldots H_i, \ldots$, such that $H = H_0$, $H_i \subset H_{i+1}$, and a new list of wffs for each of the H_i as follows. For each index i, H_{i+1} is defined from H_i as follows. Consider the first disjunction $A \vee B$ in the list for H_i such that $H_i, A \vee B \nvdash G$. By the presence of $(\vee$ Left$)$ in GS, either $H_i, A \nvdash G$ or $H_i, B \nvdash G$, so let H_{i+1} be H_i, A if $H_i, A \nvdash G$, and H_i, B otherwise, and remove $A \vee B$ from the ordered list of wffs for H_i to obtain the list for H_{i+1}. Note that for each i, $H_i, \nvdash G$.

Now define v^* by $v^*(A) = t$ iff $H_i \vdash A$ for some H_i the series. Since $H \subseteq H_i$ for each i, $v^*(H) = t$. Note also that $v^*(G) = f$, for otherwise there would be a member B of G such that $H_i \vdash B$. So by (Right Weakening), $H_i \vdash G$, which contradicts $H \nvdash G$. (The fact that $v^*(G) = f$ guarantees that v^* counts as a (consistent) valuation.)

To show that v^* is prime, let $A \vee B$ be any disjunction such that $v^*(A \vee B) = t$ and show that $v^*(A) = t$ or $v^*(B) = t$ as follows. Since $v^*(A \vee B) = t$, it follows that $A \vee B \in H_i$ for some i. Let k be the first index where $A \vee B \in H_k$. In the construction of the series of sets, $A \vee B \in H_j$ for each $j \geq k$, and so there must be a point n such that $k \leq n$ in the series where $A \vee B$ was considered and one of its disjuncts was added to form H_{n+1}. Therefore either $H_{n+1} \vdash A$ or $H_{n+1} \vdash B$, and hence $v^*(A) = t$ or $v^*(B) = t$.

The valuation v^* must satisfy GS because presuming that $H' \vdash G'$ and $v^*(H') = t$, we may argue that $v^*(G') \neq f$ as follows. Given $H' \vdash G'$, there must be by the Finitary Sequent Lemma, finite subsets H'' and G'' of H' and G' such that $H'' \vdash G''$. By repeated applications of $(\vee$Right$)$, $H'' \vdash D_1 \vee \ldots \vee D_n$, where the disjuncts $D_1, \ldots, D_n$ are the members of G'', and hence members of G'. Since $v^*(H') = t$ and $H'' \subseteq H'$ it follows that $v^*(H'') = t$. Therefore for each wff A in H'', there is an index i such that $H_i \vdash A$. Since there are only finitely many members of H'', there must be a largest i such that $H_i \vdash A$ for any of the A in H''. Call this largest index h. Since each v_i is an extension of its predecessor, $H_h \vdash A$ for each member A of G''. By repeated applications of (Restricted Cut) and $H'' \vdash D_1 \vee \ldots \vee D_n$, it follows that $H_h \vdash D_1 \vee \ldots \vee D_n$, and so $v^*(D_1 \vee \ldots \vee D_n) = t$. But v^* is prime, and so $v^*(D) = t$ for one of the disjuncts of $D_1 \vee \ldots \vee D_n$. Remember all these disjuncts were members of G', so $v^*(G') \neq f$ as desired.   □

Let GS be any system that contains GV. Let Vp be the set that contains all the GS-prime extensions of the members of V. By the previous theorem, there is at least one such extension v^* for each member v of V. The next theorem demonstrates the adequacy of GS with respect to [GS]p, the result of "priming" the canonical model for GS. (For more on priming the canonical model, see Section 7.7.)

[GS]p Adequacy Theorem. $H \vdash_{GS} G$ iff $H \vDash_{[GS]p} G$, provided S contains GV. Furthermore, [GS]p is a model of GS.

Proof. Assume GS contains GV. For the proof of soundness (the proof from left to right), assume $H \vdash_{GS} G$, and show $H \vDash_{[GS]p} G$ by assuming that v is any member of [GS]p such that $v(H)=t$, and prove $v(G) \neq f$ as follows. The members of [GS]p are GS-prime. Hence the members of [GS]p satisfy GS, and so it follows that $v(G) \neq f$, as desired.

For the proof of completeness (the proof from right to left), it is sufficient to prove the contrapositive: if $H \nvdash_{GS} G$, then $H \nvDash_{[GS]p} G$, so suppose that $H \nvdash_{GS} G$. By the GS Prime Theorem, there is a GS-prime valuation v such that $v(G)=t$ and $v(H)=f$. Since v is a member of [GS]p, $H \nvDash_{[GS]p} G$ as desired.

To show that [GS]p is a model of S, simply use $H \vdash_{GS} C$ iff $H \vDash_{[GS]p} C$, to replace '$\vDash_{[GS]p}$' for '$\vdash_{GS}$' in the statement of the rules to show each rule preserves [GS]p-validity. □

With the last theorem in hand, we are ready to prove the ‖GS‖ Adequacy Theorem.

‖GS‖ Adequacy Theorem. $H \vdash_{GS} G$ iff $H \vDash_{\|GS\|} G$, provided that GS contains (SV) and ‖GS‖ is a natural semantics for GS.

Proof. Assume GS contains the rules of SV and ‖GS‖ is a natural semantics for GS. For soundness assume $G \vdash_{GS} H$. Since ‖GS‖ is a natural semantics, V is a model of GS, which means that the rules of GS preserve V-validity. So for any V obeying ‖GS‖, $H \vDash_V G$, and $H \vDash_{\|GS\|} G$ as desired.

For completeness, assume $H \nvdash_{GS} G$ and show $H \nvDash_{\|GS\|} G$ as follows. By the [GS]p Adequacy Theorem, $H \nvDash_{[GS]p} G$, and [GS]p is a model of GS. By the fact that ‖GS‖ is a natural semantics for GS, it follows that [GS]p obeys ‖GS‖. So $G \nvDash_{\|GS\|} H$ as desired. □

13 Connections with proof-theoretic semantics

In the introduction of this book, it was claimed that model-theoretic inferentialism and proof-theoretic inferentialism need not be enemies, and that results of this book can actually be of service to the proof-theoretic tradition. This chapter provides details to support that claim. The fundamental problem to be solved in the proof-theoretic paradigm is to find an answer to the problem of *tonk*. The rules for *tonk* show that not every collection of rules can define a connective, and so proof-theoretic conditions must be found that are independently motivated, and distinguish those rules that successfully define connective meaning from those that do not. Sections 13.1 through 13.3 discuss conservativity, one of the most widely discussed constraints of this kind. Here it is shown that natural semantics may be used to help motivate that condition. Section 13.4 discusses uniqueness. In Section 13.5, notions of harmony based on the inversion principle and normalization of proofs are briefly reviewed. In the following section, a model-theoretic notion called unity is introduced, and compared with harmony notions in the proof-theoretic tradition (Section 13.7). In the final section (13.8), it is shown that natural semantics can be revised in a near-trivial way to provide proof-theoretic accounts of logical consequence and harmony. Brief comparisons are drawn between proof-theoretic ideas in the literature and these new proposals.

13.1 Conservation and connective definition

Our investigation into the prospects for model-theoretic inferentialism has been inspired by the idea that natural deduction rules provide a syntactic method for defining the meanings of the connectives. However, not every set of ND rules will do. Prior (1960) showed that there is a pair of introduction and elimination rules for a connective c that determines no coherent interpretation of c. (See also Wagner (1981) and Hart (1982).) For example, if we try to define the connective *tonk* by the rules $A \vdash A\ tonk\ B$ and $A\ tonk\ B \vdash B$, we have the unwelcome result that $A \vdash B$ holds for any choice of A and B. The *tonk* rules don't fix a meaning for *tonk*; they disastrously alter the nature of deduction in the system.

Belnap (1962) defended inferentialism from this kind of pathology by laying down a proof-theoretic criterion for successful connective definition. The rules for a connective must form a conservative extension of the antecedently given rules, and in particular, the structural rules $S\vdash$ for natural deduction.

$S\vdash$:

(Hypothesis) $H \vdash C$, provided C is in H.

(Weakening) $$\frac{H \vdash C}{H, H' \vdash C}$$

(Restricted Cut) $$\frac{H \vdash A \qquad H', A \vdash C}{H, H' \vdash C}$$

(System S is a *conservative extension* of another system S' when S generates no new principles written in the language of S' beyond those already provable in S'.)

Belnap's requirement disqualifies *tonk* rules from defining a connective since they are not conservative. Adding them to the structural rules $S\vdash$ allows us to prove the argument A / B which increases the stock of structural principles. Since the familiar natural deduction rules for propositional logic can be shown to be a conservative extension of $S\vdash$, the misbehavior of *tonk* does not discredit the notion that those rules provide a satisfactory account of connective meaning.

Belnap's defense leaves us with nagging questions. An inferentialist presumes that rules define connective meanings, but it now appears that the doctrine must be revised to say that only *conservative* rules define connective meaning. Is there any reason to think that this additional stipulation is not *ad hoc*? Do we have any independent motivation for thinking that conservativity should be demanded for success at connective definition, apart from vague intuitions that one connective should not disturb the behavior of another? Furthermore, do we have any guarantee that some future example like that of *tonk* might cause us to be forced to deploy further restrictions on rules? Does conservation provide a necessary and sufficient condition fixing connective meaning? If it does, why does it do so?

Natural semantics provides a way to explore these questions. It provides an independent way to formulate a criterion for successful connective definition – one that vindicates Belnap's requirement that the rules for a connective qualify as a conservative extension of S⊢. We have argued in Section 5.5 that a set of rules Sc for a connective c defines the meaning for c when Sc has a functional natural semantics ‖Sc‖. It is not difficult to show that when Sc meets this condition, the system Sc+S⊢ forms a conservative extension of S⊢ just as Belnap required.

Theorem 13.1 If system Sc has a functional natural semantics for the language Lc containing c as the only connective, then Sc+S⊢ is a conservative extension of S⊢.

Proof. Assume that Sc has a functional natural semantics ‖Sc‖. It must be shown that if H / C is an argument that contains no occurrence of the connective c, and H ⊢$_{Sc}$ C, then H ⊢$_{S⊢}$ C. It will suffice to prove the contrapositive, so assume H ⊬$_{S⊢}$ C, and prove H ⊬$_{Sc}$ C as follows. Since H / C contains no occurrence of c, H / C contains propositional variables only and C is a propositional variable q. Define the atomic model W so that W={w*}, where w* is the atomic valuation defined by w*(p)=t iff H ⊢$_{S⊢}$ p, for each propositional variable p. By H ⊬$_{Sc}$ C, it follows that w*(C)=f, so w* is consistent and qualifies as a valuation. Given (Hypothesis) and (Weakening) it follows that H ⊢$_{S⊢}$ A whenever A is a member of H, hence w*(H)=t. Since ‖Sc‖ is functional, it follows that there is a unique extension V={v} of W that obeys ‖Sc‖, where v(p) =w*(p) for all the propositional variables p. Hence v(H)=t and v(q)=v(C)=f. It follows that H ⊬$_v$ C and V obeys ‖Sc‖, hence H ⊬$_{‖Sc‖}$ C. But ‖Sc‖ is a natural semantics for Sc, and by the ‖S‖ Adequacy Theorem of Section 12.1, it follows that H ⊬$_{Sc}$ C as desired.   ☐

This result may be extended to a wide range of alternative accounts S? of the structural rules. All we need for the proof of the theorem for system S? is that H ⊢$_{S?}$ A holds provided A is a member of H. However, the theorem does not necessarily work for the structural rules of a relevance logic where structural rules lack (Weakening).

13.2 Strong conservation

An intuitively desirable property of a standard formal semantics is that the truth definitions for the logical constants be independent. A model interprets the atomic wffs of the language, and the truth conditions extend the account of the truth-values for complex wffs in a unique way. Since each connective is given its truth conditions separately, adding truth conditions for one connective should not disturb the truth definition of the others. This independence entails a corresponding independence in the definition of validity, presuming that the definition of validity depends on the truth conditions for the connectives alone. Consider an argument H / C that contains only the connective c. Then only the truth conditions for c play a role in determining whether H / C is valid, since the truth-value induced on a model depends only on the truth behavior of connectives in H and C. So when ||S|| is a semantics for some system S, and ||Sc|| is the truth conditions in ||S|| for connective c, then H / C is ||S||-valid iff H / C is ||Sc||-valid.

More generally, *independence of a semantics* ||S|| means that an argument H / C written in a sublanguage L′ of the language of system S is ||S||-valid iff it is ||S′||-valid, where ||S′|| is the portion of ||S|| that mentions connectives of L′ only. To put it another way, independence means that validity defined for the whole language is always a "conservative extension" of validity defined for any sublanguage.

> (Independence)   Let ||S|| be a semantics for language L. Then ||S|| is *independent* iff for any sublanguage L′ of L, if ||S′|| consists of only the truth clauses of ||S|| that govern connectives of L′, then when H / C contains only the connectives of L′, H $\vDash_{\|S\|}$ C iff H $\vDash_{\|S'\|}$ C.

Suppose we have a system S that is adequate with respect to an independent semantics ||S||. Suppose further that the rules of S consist of the structural rules S⊢ and rules Sc for each connective c of the language. If ||S|| consists of the conjunction of a functional natural semantics ||Sc|| for each of the connectives, then a form of conservation will follow that is significantly stronger than conservation with respect to S⊢. If an argument written using only connectives in a sublanguage L′ has a proof at all in S, it can be proven using only the rules S′ that govern those connectives. To put it another way, the presence in S of rules for connectives not in L′ do not increase the stock of provable arguments written in L′. Such systems S are *strongly conservative*, which means that the rules of S are a conservative extension of the rules written in each sublanguage of S (including the special case of a language with / as the only sign).

The idea that a semantics that defines connective meaning should be independent helps motivate the strong conservation requirement. Given adequacy results for each of the subsystems S′ of S, one would expect that the independence of the semantics would transfer to the proof theory, thus insuring strong conservativity. Strong conservation insures that the rules be a conservative extension of the rules for *each of the connectives* as well. For example, although the system S~ for classical negation is a conservative extension of S⊢, it is not a conservative extension of S→ and so not strongly conservative.

Strong conservativity has strong attractions. The whole idea behind proof-theoretic definition with the natural deduction rules was that the roles of the connectives be independently defined. A rule that defines a connective c should affect only the deductive role of c. The *tonk* rules overstepped their bounds in changing the logical role of the consequence symbol '/'. They force us to reinterpret '/'. But what goes for '/' should go for all the connectives. For example, any rule for negation that affects the deducibility behavior of the conditional also says more than it should. In changing the conditional's role, it determines two meanings rather than one.

In Section 6.2, we discussed the fact that the rules for classical negation do not form a conservative extension of those for the conditional. Peirce's Law is not provable from S→, but it is in S→~, the result of adding the rules of S~ to those of S→. The fact that S→~ is not a conservative extension of S→, has been cited before as an argument that S~ does not define a connective (Hand, 1993, p. 125).

Natural semantics provides deeper insight into the situation. In Section 8.5, it was shown that the failure of conservation is related to the fact that the classical conditions ∥LL′∥ (or equivalently ∥pLF∥) and ∥C~∥ disrupt assignments of truth-values to complex wffs.

∥pLF∥ If $v(p)=f$, then for some $v'∈V$, $v≤v'$ and $v'(p)=F$.

∥C~∥ $v(∼A)=t$ iff $v(A)=f$.

These conditions affect ≤, and hence the truth behavior of other connectives that contain mention of ≤ in their natural truth conditions. For example, when the language contains two separate symbols for negation ¬ and ∼, with ¬ governed by intuitionistic rules S¬, the mere presence of classical truth conditions for ~ forces a classical reading of ¬ (see Hand, 1993).

This interference argues against the idea that S~ determines a properly independent account of the meaning of the negation symbol. The failure of conservation is a sign of a deeper malady, namely that the putative truth condition ‖S~‖ is non-functional – it is not always possible to extend sets of atomic valuations to models over the complex wffs, as Theorem 8.6 reports. For this reason, it is reasonable to worry that the "classical" condition ‖S~‖ does not really qualify as a semantics for negation. After all, truth conditions should not be incompatible with interpretations of the non-logical vocabulary that they are supposed to extend. In the context of the natural conditions expressed by the other connectives, imposing ‖S~‖ makes it impossible to extend certain atomic models to complex formulas. It is not just that the natural deduction rules for ~ violate conservation. The (so-called) truth condition ‖S~‖ for negation simply does not qualify as a func-tional semantics, at least not in a context where natural semantical con-ditions are used for the other connectives.

In Section 8.9, the definition of semantics was liberalized so that ‖S~‖ qualified. This lead to the surprising claim that conservativity is not always necessary for successfully defining a meaning for a connective. How is that stand consistent with the present concern that truth conditions should be independent? The answer is that it is crucial to distinguish between what S~ expresses, and *the truth condition* it expresses. S~ expresses ‖S~‖, the con-junction of the intuitionistic truth condition ‖¬‖ and a side condition ‖pLF‖, which, it was argued, has nothing to do with the interpretation of ~ (though it does affect the definition of validity). As the ‖KI‖ Theorem of Section 5.5 attests, the truth condition ‖¬‖ expressed by S~ is a functional natural semantics, and so counts as perfectly legitimate. This together with the fact that ‖pLF‖ is a requirement on the values assigned to propositional variables motivated the idea that ‖S~‖ ought to count as natural semantics, even though ‖S~‖ is not purely a truth condition.

The reason that strong conservation fails for S~ is that it expresses more than a truth condition by requiring ‖pLF‖ as well. As a result, classical systems that include S~ express conditions affecting the definition of val-idity that do not depend solely on the truth conditions for their connectives. While those truth conditions may be properly independent alone, what the system expresses says more. Therefore, whether a system qualifies as strongly conservative depends not just on success of its truth conditions, but on the presence of side conditions like ‖pLF‖ that may occur in its natural semantics. As a result, an attempt to prove strong conservation for a system S requires an examination of more than the *truth* conditions S expresses. It depends also on the presence of side conditions in the natural semantics for S. Although independence of *truth conditions* is strongly motivated by our intuitions, this book takes the position that independence of *what is expressed* by the rules for each connective, while desirable, is not a precondition for the legitimacy of a semantics.

The next project will be to demonstrate the connections between independence of a natural semantics and strong conservation. Let us say that a *system S is naturally independent* when S consists of rules Sc for each of the connectives of the language L of S, each of which has natural semantics ‖Sc‖, and the conjunction ‖S‖ of the ‖Sc‖ is independent. Then it follows that S is strongly conservative. (Note that it is independence of the natural semantics expressed by each connective that is required, not independence of its truth conditions.)

Theorem 13.2 Every naturally independent system is strongly conservative.

Proof. Let S be a naturally independent system, and let ‖S‖ be the conjunction of the natural semantics ‖Sc‖ for each connective c of the language L of S. Then by Theorem 12.3.1 applied repeatedly for each connective of the language of S, ‖S‖ is a natural semantics for S. Let S′ be the rules of S involving only the connectives in some sublanguage L′ of L. We must show that S is a conservative extension of S′, i.e. that S does not increase the stock of arguments proven by S′. It will suffice to show H ⊢$_S$ C iff H ⊢$_{S'}$ C. Let ‖S′‖ be conjunction of the ‖Sc‖ for connectives of L′, It follows from Theorem 12.3.1 applied repeatedly for each connective c, that ‖S′‖ is a natural semantics for S′. By the independence of ‖S‖, it follows that H ⊨$_{‖S‖}$ C iff H ⊨$_{‖S′‖}$ C. By the ‖S‖ Adequacy Theorem of Section 12.1, it follows that H ⊢$_S$ C iff H ⊢$_{S'}$ C as desired.   □

13.3 Semantical independence

The last theorem will help us understand better the circumstances under which strong conservation and semantical independence hold or fail. A revealing example of failure is the hybrid system S→+G~, which consists of the standard natural deduction rules S→ for the conditional and the sequent rules G~ for negation. S→ has ||→||, the intuitionistic truth condition, as its natural semantics, while the natural semantics for G~ is ||C~|| the classical account of negation. So the conjunction ||→~|| of ||→|| with ||C~|| is a natural semantics for system S→+G~. We know that ||C~|| entails that ||→|| collapses to the classical truth condition for →. (See Theorem 8.5.3 and the following discussion.) Therefore ||→~|| is classical for → as well as ~. It follows immediately that ||→~|| is a functional natural semantics for S→+G~, since every set of atomic models has a classical extension.

However S→+G~ is not strongly conservative, since adding G~ to S→ allows the derivation of Peirce's Law, which cannot be proven in S→ alone (see Section 6.2). So while every system with a functional natural semantics is a conservative extension of the structural rules S⊢, there are systems such as S→+G~ with a functional natural semantics for each of their connectives that fail to be strongly conservative. The requirement that a system have an *independent* natural semantics is therefore important for demonstrating strong conservation. By Theorem 13.2, we know, for example, that S→+G~ is not naturally independent. Its natural semantics ||→~|| is not independent, because the two conditions ||→|| and ||C~|| interact. Given the definition of ≤ embodied in ||≤||, the presence of ||C~|| affects which valuations bear the relation ≤, and this affects in turn the truth-value of conditionals on a given model V.

||≤|| v≤v′ iff for wff A, if v(A)=t, then v′(A)=t.

We could repair this lack of independence by replacing ||≤|| with ||p≤||.

||p≤|| v≤v′ iff for every propositional variable p, if v(p)=t, then v′(p)=t.

Since ||p≤|| defines ≤ in terms of the behavior of propositional variables only, it will follow that the semantics ||p→~|| consisting of the conjunction of ||p≤||, ||→||, and ||C~|| is independent. This follows immediately from the next theorem, which provides a sufficient condition for independence. Let us say that a semantics ||S|| is *well formed* when ||S|| is a conjunction of truth conditions for each connective c with the form:

$$v(AcB)=t \text{ iff } \mathbb{P},$$

and $\mathbb{P}$ mentions only V, the behavior of the valuations in V with respect to the propositional variables, and the subformulas A and B of AcB.

Theorem 13.3 If $\|S\|$ is well-formed, then $\|S\|$ is independent.

Proof. Assume that $\|S\|$ is well-formed. Then it follows by induction on the form of A that the value of A on valuation v in V depends on only V, the values of the propositional variables, and the values of subformulas of A. Therefore the value of A at valuation v depends only on the truth conditions for connectives that appear in A. To show that $\|S\|$ is independent, let L' be a sublanguage of L and let $\|S'\|$ be the conjunction of the truth clauses for connectives of L'. Then the values at v of wffs of L' depend only on the truth conditions that belong to $\|S'\|$. It follows immediately that $H \models_{\|S\|} C$ iff $H \models_{\|S'\|} C$ as desired.   □

The last theorem entails that $\|p \rightarrow \sim\|$ is independent, for it meets the require-ments for being a well-formed semantics, since $\leq$ is now defined by the behavior of propositional variables only. It follows immediately that $\|p \rightarrow \sim\|$ cannot be a natural semantics for $S \rightarrow + G\sim$, for if it were, Theorem 13.2 would entail the strong conservativity of $S \rightarrow + G\sim$, which, of course, is false. This raises a puzzle, since the $\leq$ Lemma of Section 5.4 says that it makes no difference whether one chooses $\|\rightarrow\|$ or $\|p \rightarrow\|$ in defining the natural seman-tics for $S \rightarrow$. However, that theorem was proven for an intuitionistic seman-tics that did not include $\|C\sim\|$. When $\|C\sim\|$ is present, it is a straightforward matter to show that the $\leq$ Lemma fails. This helps underscore the impor-tance of the $\leq$ Lemma in an attempt to define a natural and independent semantics. Without that lemma, it need not follow that the semantics is natural. This in turn underscores the worry (expressed in Section 5.3) that the use of $\|\leq\|$ rather than $\|p \leq\|$ in a semantical condition counts as improperly circular. The $\leq$ Lemma guarantees that that circularity can be eliminated. In cases, however, where the $\leq$ Lemma fails, it is not clear that $\|\rightarrow\|$, and other conditions that mention $\leq$, qualify as legitimate truth conditions.

13.4 Uniqueness

When Belnap (1962) defended the syntactic method of connective defini-tion from the problems created by *tonk*, he suggested two conditions on rules for a connective that would be necessary for successful connective definition. The first has been discussed; it is that the rules are a conservative extension of the structural rules for $/$, or all other rules of a given system. Belnap calls this condition (Existence). Theorems 13.1 and 13.2 identified sufficient conditions for these two brands of conservation. Belnap also required a second condition called (Uniqueness): that the rules define a unique role of inference for the connective. Here it will be shown that any system Sc governing a single connective with a functional natural semantics also obeys (Uniqueness).

First, we need to state the (Uniqueness) condition. Suppose we have two connectives c and c* with formally identical systems of rules (c) and (c*). Rules of (c) and (c*) are *formally identical* when they are identical save that connective c* appears in (c*) exactly where connective c appears in (c). Now let Sc result from adding (c) to the structural rules S⊢ and similarly Sc* = (c*) plus S⊢. The *roles of inference defined by Sc and Sc* are identical* iff $A \vdash_S A^*$ and $A^* \vdash_S A$, for any A which fails to contain c*, where S is the result of combining Sc with Sc*, and A* is the result of replacing c* for c in A. System Sc *defines a unique role of inference* for c iff any system Sc* formally identical to Sc has the same role of inference for c as does Sc.

Let us suppose that system Sc is outfitted with a functional natural semantics ‖Sc‖. Imagine that Sc* is formally identical to S in the sense that there is a 1–1 mapping * from the connective of Sc to the connective c* of Sc* which yields the rules of Sc* when applied to the rules of Sc. Now let S+ be Sc +Sc*, and let ‖S+‖ be the conjunction of ‖Sc‖ with ‖Sc*‖, where ‖Sc*‖ is identical to ‖Sc‖ save that occurrences of c in Sc are replaced with c* in Sc*. We will show that when ‖Sc‖ is a functional natural semantics for Sc, A and A* are semantically equivalent in ‖S+‖.

Theorem 13.4.1 If ‖Sc‖ is a functional natural semantics, then $A \vDash_{‖S+‖} A^*$ and $A^* \vDash_{‖S+‖} A$.

Proof. Assume that ‖Sc‖ is a functional natural semantics, that ‖Sc*‖ is ‖Sc‖ save that occurrences of c in ‖Sc‖ are replaced by c* in ‖Sc*‖, and ‖S+‖ is the conjunction of ‖Sc‖ with ‖Sc*‖. Show $A \vDash_{‖S+‖} A^*$ and $A^* \vDash_{‖S+‖} A$ by demonstrating that v+(A)=v+(A*), provided v+ belongs to a set of valuations V+ obeying ‖S+‖. Let v be v+ restricted to the language of Sc, and let v* be v+ restricted to the language of Sc*. Let V be the set of all valuations of V+ so restricted to Sc, and similarly for V*. V obeys the functional natural semantics ‖Sc‖. So ‖Sc*‖ is a natural semantics for system Sc*. This means that the value of every wff A of Sc is uniquely fixed by ‖Sc‖ and the values given to the atoms. Similarly, the value of a given wff A* of Sc* is uniquely fixed in the same way. So for each v in V, $v(A)=v^*(A^*)$. The valuation v was v+ restricted to the wffs of Sc and v* was v+ restricted to the wffs of Sc*. So we have for all A in the language of S, v+(A)= v(A) and for all A* in the language of S*, v+(A*)=v*(A*). Since $v(A)=v^*(A^*)$, v+(A)= v+(A*) as desired.   □

Theorem 13.4.2 If S has a functional natural semantics, then S defines a unique role of inference for its connectives.

Proof. Suppose S has a functional natural semantics ‖S‖. Let S* be formally identical to S, let S+=S+S*, and ‖S+‖=‖S‖&‖S*‖ as described above. To show that S defines a unique role of inference for the connectives, we must show that A ⊢$_{S+}$ A* and A* ⊢$_{S+}$ A. By the previous theorem applied to each of the connectives of S, A ⊨$_{‖S+‖}$ A* and A* ⊨$_{‖S+‖}$ A. It will follow that A ⊢ $_{S+}$ A* and A* ⊢ $_{S+}$ A if we can show that S+ is complete. Note that ‖S*‖ is a natural semantics for S, since the rules of S* are structurally identical to those for S. Since S+ is the sum of two systems S and S* that have natural semantics ‖S‖ and ‖S*‖ respectively, it follows from Theorem 12.3.2 that S+ is complete as desired.   □

13.5 Harmony in the proof-theoretic tradition

Demanding conservation and uniqueness is one tactic for meeting the challenge to the proof-theoretic tradition that is posed by *tonk*. We may think of these as demands that the introduction and elimination rules are in harmony with each other. (In fact, Dummett (1991, p. 250) calls strong conservation 'total harmony'.) However, there are several other proof-theoretic concepts that are more paradigmatic members of the harmony family. Inversion and normalization are two well-known examples. (See Prawitz, 1965, p. 33; Dummett, 1978, pp. 220–222; Weir, 1986; Tennant, 1997, pp. 308ff., and forthcoming.) A fundamental idea about connective definition that emerges in intuitionism is that a connective's introduction rule stipulates the meaning of the symbol introduced. However, the elimination rule for the same connective must be justified by being in harmony with the introduction rule if the pair of rules are to provide a meaning for the connective. (Some reverse the idea so that the elimination rule stipulates the meaning. Dummett (1991) discusses both sides of the issue, and explores the merits of giving the honor to elimination rules in Chapter 13.)

A fundamental intuition that captures the idea of harmony is the inversion principle, which says that the elimination rule should say no more and no less about the deductive role of the connective than what is justified by the introduction rule. If the introduction rule specifies a proof-theoretic requirement for obtaining the connective, then the elimination rule that says what may be derived from that connective must have an output with the same proof-theoretic "strength." For example, the ($\to$ Introduction) rule says that H / A$\to$B may be derived when one is able to prove the argument H, A/B that concludes B from H with the additional assumption of A. Therefore the elimination rule for $\to$ must say that from H / A$\to$B, one may derive the argument H, A / B that concludes B from H with the additional assumption of A. Therefore, harmony considerations require that the following should be the elimination rule for $\to$.

(Harmonious $\to$ Elimination)

$$\frac{H \vdash A \to B}{H, A \vdash B}$$

While this is not strictly identical to the version of ($\to$ Elimination) in our official definition of the system S$\to$, it is an easy matter to show that the two rules are deductively equivalent. Therefore, S$\to$ is a harmonious pair, and defines a meaning for $\to$.

A related requirement on rule pairs makes more explicit the idea that the elimination rule should exactly capture the deductive role inherent in the introduction rule. It is that the pair should satisfy a normalization principle, which we illustrate with S$\to$. Normalization means that if we are able to deduce H / A$\to$B by ($\to$ Introduction), and then apply ($\to$ Elimination) to H / A$\to$B at a later stage of the proof, (to obtain H / B), then there must be a shorter (normalized) proof of the same result that made no appeal to ($\to$ Introduction). It is easy to see that normalization holds for S$\to$. When we applied ($\to$ Introduction) to obtain H / A$\to$B, it must have been because we had a proof of H, A / B on a previous line. When we applied ($\to$ Elimination) to H / A$\to$B to obtain H / B, it must have been because we already had a proof of H / A. Since we had a proof of H, A / B, the argument H / B follows directly from (Cut), and so there was no need to apply ($\to$ Introduction) in the first place.

Original Proof   Normalized Proof

$$\begin{array}{cc} \vdots & \\ \underline{H,\ A\ /\ B} & \vdots \\ \underline{H\ /\ A{\to}B \qquad H\ /\ A} & \\ H\ /\ B & \end{array} \qquad \Longrightarrow \qquad \begin{array}{cc} \vdots \qquad \vdots \\ \underline{H,A\ /\ B \qquad H\ /\ A} \\ H\ /\ B \end{array}$$

The ability to normalize this proof shows that a principle of inversion holds. When we use the introduction rule, a subsequent use of the elimination rule takes us right back to the situation we had before the introduction rule was applied. That means that the contribution of the elimination rule is no stronger and no weaker than what was contributed by the introduction rule. As a second example, here is one half of a demonstration that $S\vee$ satisfies the inversion principle.

Original Proof   Normalized Proof

$$\begin{array}{c} \vdots \qquad \vdots \qquad \vdots \\ \underline{H\ /\ A} \qquad \vdots \qquad \vdots \\ \underline{H\ /\ A{\vee}B \quad H,A\ /\ C \quad H,B\ /\ C} \\ H\ /\ C \end{array} \quad \Longrightarrow \quad \begin{array}{c} \vdots \qquad \vdots \\ \underline{H\ /\ A \qquad H,A\ /\ C} \\ H\ /\ C \end{array}$$

The reader can supply the second half where $A{\vee}B$ is obtained from B using ($\vee$ Introduction).

It is interesting to note that while the rules for intuitionistic negation are harmonious in this sense, the rules for classical negation are not (Schroeder Heister, forthcoming, Section 4.5). Although a revision of the notion of harmony can be created for the classical rules (Weir, 1986), the revised version of harmony does not work with $S\vee$, but only with alternative rules involving $\vee$ and $\sim$ together. This does not, by our lights, count as a legitimate way to define $\vee$, since the rules govern two connectives rather than $\vee$ alone.

Another point worth noting is that the concepts in the harmony family can come apart. For example, Read (2010, p. 571) gives an example of a pair of rules that define a connective where normalization and conservativity fail, but where what he calls general-elimination (ge) harmony holds. This version of harmony occurs when the elimination rule for c is constructed from the introduction rule by a recipe (p. 563) that guarantees that the elimination rule discharges exactly what the introduction rules require to prove AcB.

13.6 Unity: a model-theoretic version of harmony

The literature on harmony reveals a rich variety of ideas about how to find the right proof-theoretic constraint for the successful definition of connective meaning by rule pairs. The brief summary in the previous section provides only a glimpse at what has been done. In this section, a model-theoretic notion called unity will be introduced in hopes that exploring it will help clarify the state of play for harmony on the proof-theoretic side.

From the natural semantics standpoint, it is easy to see how two rules Sc must interact if they are to define a truth condition for connective c. Sc must express a property of models that takes the form of a biconditional:

v(AcB)=t iff $\mathbb{P}$,

where v ranges over arbitrary members of V and $\mathbb{P}$ mentions the truth behavior of A and B on valuations in V. (Here we have assumed that c is a binary connective, but the reader can easily make the appropriate adjustments for unary and n-ary cases.) Presuming that Sc is a pair of natural deduction rules, we know something about the form of its introduction rule. Its output has the shape: H / AcB, and its input(s) is (are) arguments involving mention of H, A, and B. As we will soon illustrate, the V-validity preservation of such a rule expresses a claim of the form $\|\mathbb{P}$ Left$\|$.

$\|\mathbb{P}$ Left$\|$ If $\mathbb{P}$, then v(AcB)=t.

A "harmonious" (c Elimination) rule will have to express the balancing conditional $\|\mathbb{P}$ Right$\|$ so that the two together express a truth condition of the form v(AcB)=t iff $\mathbb{P}$, for all v in V.

$\|\mathbb{P}$ Right$\|$ If v(AcB)=t, then $\mathbb{P}$.

Therefore, a successful pair of rules Sc must be unified in the following sense.

(Unified) Sc is *unified* iff (c Introduction) expresses a condition of the form: If $\mathbb{P}$, then v(AcB)=t, while (c Elimination) expresses a condition of the form: If v(AcB)=t, then $\mathbb{P}$.

To illustrate this definition, consider S→. The (→ Introduction) rule expresses the condition $\|$Left →$\|$, where the part $\mathbb{P}$ is underlined.

($\rightarrow$Introduction) $\qquad \dfrac{\text{H, A} \vdash \text{B}}{\text{H} \vdash \text{A} \rightarrow \text{B}}$

$\|$Left $\rightarrow\|$ $\qquad$ If for every v′ in V, if v≤v′ then v′ (A)=f or v′ (B)=t, then v(A→B)=t.

We can see this is so by taking any v in V, and defining Hv to be the set of all wffs B such that v(B)=t. Then validity preservation for all these choices Hv comes to the following, since v′(Hv)=t iff v≤v′.

$\qquad$ If for every v′ in V, if v≤v′, then v′(A)=f or v′(B)=t, $\qquad$ then for every v′ in V, if v≤v′, then v′(A→B)=t.

However the consequent of this conditional with v≤v entails v(A→B)=t, and so we have $\|$Left $\rightarrow\|$.

$\qquad$ If for every v′ in V, if v≤v′ , then v′ (A)=f or v′ (B)=t, $\qquad$ then v(A→B)=t.

The same strategy may be used with any natural deduction introduction rule to show that it expresses a condition of the form $\|\mathbb{P}$ Left$\|$.

Now is S→ unified? It is, because inspection of the proof of the S→ Expression Theorem of Section 6.1 shows that (→ Elimination) expresses $\|$Right $\rightarrow\|$.

$\|$Right $\rightarrow\|$ $\qquad$ If v(A→B)=t, then $\qquad$ if for every v′ in V, if v≤v′ then v′(A)=f or v′ (B)=t.

A unified pair of rules has the feature that the introduction rule expresses the exact inversion of the elimination rule. What $\|\mathbb{P}$ Left$\|$ requires to establish AcB's truth (namely $\mathbb{P}$) is exactly what follows from knowing that AcB is true. Unity also entails a trivial brand of "normalization" in the metalanguage, for if one uses $\|\mathbb{P}$ Left$\|$ to introduce the claim that AcB is true, and then eliminates that claim using $\|\mathbb{P}$ Right$\|$, the result can be obtained without the use of $\|\mathbb{P}$ Left$\|$.

$\qquad\qquad$ Original proof $\qquad$ Normalized proof

$\qquad\qquad\qquad$: $\qquad\qquad\qquad\qquad$:

$\qquad\qquad\qquad$ $\mathbb{P}$ $\qquad\qquad\qquad\qquad$ $\mathbb{P}$

$\qquad\qquad \dfrac{}{\text{v(AcB)=t}}$

$\qquad\qquad\qquad$ $\mathbb{P}$

It is instructive to examine a case where unification fails. Consider *tonk*. The rules S* for (*tonk*) are listed below with what is expressed beneath each. (In determining what is expressed, we have taken advantage of the structural rules to show that $A \vdash_{S^*} A^*B$ and $A^*B \vdash_{S^*} B$.)

S*:   (* Introduction)   (* Elimination)

$$\frac{H / A}{H / A^*B}$$ $$\frac{H / A^*B}{H / B}$$

If $\underline{v(A)=t}$, then $v(A^*B)=t$.   If $v(A^*B)=t$, then $\underline{v(B)=t}$.

S* cannot be unified because the introduction rule expresses a condition $v(A)=t$ for introducing $v(A^*B)=t$ that differs from the condition $v(B)=t$ obtained from eliminating $v(A^*B)=t$. Putting these two conditionals end to end, we obtain an unacceptable structural semantical condition on valuations, showing that *tonk* does not define a connective.

If $v(A)=t$ then $v(B)=t$.

One might worry that unification is too strong a requirement for successful connective definition. The $S\bot$ Theorem of Section 4.2 shows that $\|\bot\|$ is a natural semantics for $S\bot$, the system consisting of a single rule ($\bot$ Elimination).

($\bot$ Elimination) $$\frac{H \vdash \bot}{H \vdash B}$$ $\|\bot\|$ $v(\bot)=f$.

Intuitively, $S\bot$ defines the meaning of $\bot$, but $S\bot$ does not include an introduction rule for which the notion of unification can be defined. Actually, we can prove that $S\bot$ is unified nonetheless. Simply declare that ($\bot$ Introduction) is the null rule (the rule that does nothing). This expresses any empty requirement on $\bot$, including $\|$Left $\bot\|$.

$\|$Left $\bot\|$ If $\underline{v(B)=t \text{ for each wff } B}$, then $v(\bot)=t$.

The matching condition, $\|$Right $\bot\|$, follows from $\|\bot\|$, and so $S\bot$ is unified after all.

$\|$Right $\bot\|$ If $v(\bot)=t$, then $\underline{v(B)=t \text{ for each wff } B}$.

The system S~E for classical negation consisting of (~ Elimination) alone serves as another example of a single rule system, but here, despite all attempts at being accommodating, unification fails.

S~E: (~ Elimination) $$\frac{H, {\sim}A \vdash B \qquad H, {\sim}A \vdash {\sim}B}{H \vdash A}$$

S~E is a sufficient system for classical negation because from (~ Elimination) both (Double Negation) and (~ Introduction) may be derived, which the reader can check as an exercise.

(~ Introduction) $\dfrac{\text{H, A} \vdash \text{B} \qquad \text{H, A} \vdash \text{~B}}{\text{H} \vdash \text{~A}}$ (Double Negation) $\dfrac{\text{H} \vdash \text{~~A}}{\text{H} \vdash \text{A}}$

Therefore, it is a simple matter to extract from the S~ Expression Theorem of Section 8.2 that S~E expresses the conjunction of three conditions.

‖Left ~‖	If for all v' in V, if $v \leq v'$, then $v'(A){=}f$, then $v(\sim A){=}t$.
‖Right ~‖	If $v(\sim A){=}t$, then for all v' in V, if $v \leq v'$, then $v'(A){=}f$.
‖LF‖	If $v(A){=}f$, then for some v' in V, $v \leq v'$ and $v'(A){=}F$.

One might hope to show that S~E is unified by declaring that (~ Introduction), being derivable, is the introduction rule implicit in S~E. While it is true that (~ Introduction) expresses ‖Left ~‖, (~ Elimination) is not sound for ‖Right ~‖, and so does not express it. The reason is that to show (~Elimination) is sound we also need ‖LF‖. Furthermore (as was shown in Section 8.9), there is no repair by way of modifying the under-lined portions of ‖Left ~‖ and ‖Right ~‖ so as to somehow smuggle in ‖LF‖. For example, if we let $\mathbb{P}$ = for all v' in V, if $v \leq v'$, then $v'(A){=}f$, and let $\mathbb{P}'$ be the conjunction of $\mathbb{P}$ with ‖LF‖, the revised versions of ‖'Left ~‖ and ‖'Right ~‖, with $\mathbb{P}'$ in place of $\mathbb{P}$, cannot be used to unify S~E. The reason is that ‖Left ~‖ and ‖Right ~‖ already establish $v(\sim A)$ iff $\mathbb{P}$. Therefore if $\mathbb{P}'$ were a unifier, we would have $v(\sim A){=}t$ iff $\mathbb{P}'$, with the result that $\mathbb{P}$ iff $\mathbb{P}'$. But that means $\mathbb{P}$ would have to entail ‖LF‖, which it does not. In general, any attempt to find a unifier for S~E by making a non-trivial modification of $\mathbb{P}$ will meet the same fate. It follows that the fact that ‖LF‖ is part of what S~E expresses is an insurmount-able obstacle to its unification. This example raises an interesting question for future research. Is it always possible to show that if a system is not unified, then it expresses an ineliminable structural condition on the set of valua-tions, such as ‖LF‖?

13.7 Unity and harmony compared

Harmony is a focal point in proof-theoretic semantics. One wonders what the relationships are between the idea of unification presented here and ideas in that literature. Working this out is a massive endeavor, in part because there are some many variations in the notion of harmony to consider. (See Tennant (forthcoming) for a helpful discussion of the variety.) However, this is fruitful ground, because interesting questions are wide open, and answering them promises to bring the more viable proof-theoretic notions of harmony into better focus. That project lies well outside what can be adequately covered in this book; however, here are two examples worth notice.

A review of the S∨ Expression Theorem of Section 7.2, and the S¬ Expression Theorem of Section 8.1, reveals that S∨ and S¬ are both unified. (The reader may wonder at this since deep concerns were expressed in Section 7.3 about whether what S∨ expresses is a truth condition. Note, however, that unity is intended as a necessary but not sufficient condition for providing a successful truth condition.) A question arises about the unity of S∨, for (∨ Introduction) clearly expresses (∨ Left), and so were S∨ to be unified, the condition expressed would have to be the classical one.

(∨ Introduction)
$$\frac{H \vdash A}{H \vdash A \vee B} \qquad \frac{H \vdash B}{H \vdash A \vee B}$$

(∨ Left) If <u>$v(A)$=t or $v(B)$=t</u>, then $v(A \vee B)$=t.

The puzzle is resolved by noting that the same rule may express several different conditions with different choices of $\mathbb{P}$. Since (∨ Introduction) *also* expresses ‖∨ Left‖, unification is possible by setting $\mathbb{P}$ equal to its weaker underlined portion.

‖∨ Left‖ If <u>for every wff C, if $v(C)$=f, then there is a v' in V such that $v \leq v'$, $v'(C)$=f, and either $v'(A)$=t or $v'(B)$=t</u>,

then $v(A \vee B)$=t.

The fact that unification typically requires finding common ground among a range of stronger and weaker conditions expressed by the introduction and elimination rules conflicts with the spirit of one approach to harmony championed by Tennant (1979, p. 74):

> a sentence with c dominant expresses the strongest proposition which can be inferred from the stated premises when the conditions for c-introduction are satisfied, while it expresses the weakest proposition possible under the conditions described by c-elimination.

If A∨B were to express the strongest proposition that can be inferred from what is expressed by (∨ Introduction), then it would express: v(A)=t or v(B)=t. However, to achieve unification, the weaker condition underlined in ‖∨ Left‖ must be chosen for what A∨B asserts. There is nothing wrong with Tennant's way of defining harmony within the proof-theoretic tradition. However, it might have helped his case were there some independent evidence for his idea provided by natural semantics.

Given the model-theoretic notion of unity presented here, neither introduction nor elimination rules should take pride of place in defining connective meaning. Each rule is responsible for one side of a truth condition. Determining which truth condition the rules for a connective express *together* (if they express any at all) involves a negotiation between a range of things the introduction rule and the elimination rule express.

A related point arises concerning the position taken by Read (2010, p. 570) who considers the following formulation S¬* for intuitionistic negation.

$$S\neg^*: \quad (\neg \text{ Introduction}^*) \qquad (\text{Contradiction})$$

$$\frac{H, A \vdash \neg A}{H \vdash \neg A} \qquad \frac{H \vdash A \quad H \vdash \neg A}{H \vdash B}$$

He follows the standard line in the proof-theoretic literature that the introduction rule defines the meaning of the connective introduced, and that the elimination rule must be justified by showing that it is in harmony. Read's notion of ge-harmony provides an algorithm for constructing the elimination rule from the introduction rule. He argues that (¬ Introduction*) does not give the full meaning of ¬, while the more common formulation S¬ succeeds.

$$S\neg: \quad (\neg \text{ Introduction}) \qquad (\text{Contradiction})$$

$$\frac{H, A \vdash B \quad H, A \vdash \neg B}{H \vdash \neg A} \qquad \frac{H \vdash A \quad H \vdash \neg A}{H \vdash B}$$

The reason is that his algorithm for creating an elimination rule from (¬ Introduction*) produces one weaker than (Contradiction). So, ge-harmony rates S¬* an odd duck – since (Contradiction), the elimination rule, has to take up the slack left by an introduction rule that is overly weak. On the other hand, the problem does not arise for S¬, which satisfies ge-harmony.

This outcome seems suspicious, since S¬* and S¬ are equivalent. They prove exactly the same arguments, as (¬ Introduction*) is derivable in S¬ and (¬ Introduction) in S¬*. How could the outcome concerning successful definition of meaning be so different for two systems that set up exactly the same deductive relationships? That makes one wonder about ge-harmony. What independent motive would an inferentialist have for making such fine discriminations?

However, considerations of unity appear at first to support Read's position. It is not difficult to show that (¬ Introduction*) alone expresses ‖Left ¬*‖, which differs from ‖Left ¬‖, the right-to-left portion of the intuitionistic condition ‖¬‖ expressed by S¬*, where the bold '**and v′(¬A)=f**' is missing.

‖Left ¬*‖   If for all v′ in V, if v≤v′ **and v′(¬A)=f**, then v′(A)=f,
             then v(¬A)=t.

‖Left ¬‖   If for all v′ in V, if v≤v′, then v′(A)=f,
            then v(¬A)=t.

Theorem 13.7 (¬ Introduction*) expresses ‖Left ¬*‖.

Proof. The proof of soundness is left to the reader. To show forcing, assume V is a model of (∼ Introduction*) and show the contrapositive of ‖Left ¬*‖, by assuming v(¬A)=f. Then for Hv = {B: v(B)=t}, we have Hv ⊬_V ¬A, hence by validity preservation, Hv, A ⊬_V ¬A. So there is a v′ in V such that v′(Hv)=t (that is v≤v′) **and** v(¬A)=f and v′(A)=t as desired.   □

Read seems vindicated because the condition ‖Left ¬*‖ expressed by (¬ Introduction*) is clearly defective. The inclusion of '**and v′(¬A)=f**' in the underlined portion renders any "truth condition" using this as the unifying ℙ wildly circular. Read's point about the role of (Contradiction) also appears to be made good when we note that the correct condition ‖Left ¬‖ is not alone sufficient to establish the soundness of (¬ Introduction*) but must be supplemented with ‖Contradiction‖, what (Contradiction) expresses.

‖Contradiction‖ If v(¬A)=t, then v(A)=f.

So it appears that Read is right to say that (¬ Introduction*) fails to properly define a connective.

All would be well for Read were we able to show that (¬ Introduction) does not suffer from the same failing, for S¬, which uses that rule, satisfies his criterion for ge-harmony, and so should successfully define a non-defective portion of the meaning of ¬. However, exactly the same problem arises for (¬ Introduction). The reader may show by reviewing the strategy of the proof of the previous theorem that (¬ Introduction) expresses the following defective condition. (Note the part in bold.)

If for all v′ in V, if v≤v′ **and either v′(¬B)=f or v′(B)=f**, then v′(A)=f, then v(¬A)=t.

Furthermore, the soundness of (¬ Introduction) cannot be shown without the help of ‖Contradiction‖. As a matter of fact, this same kind of interaction turns up in the case of disjunction. I submit that this shows that the notion of ge-harmony makes excessively fine and counterintuitive distinctions.

From the natural semantics viewpoint, it is pointless to try to isolate the contributions of the introduction and elimination rules as independent features of meaning fixation. It is also pointless to require that one of the rules gets pride of place. Instead, a pair of rules defines meaning as a corporate body. Whether this should persuade anyone in the proof-theoretic tradition, I leave to the reader. However, the decided failure of consensus in the literature on the technical details about how harmony should be defined speaks volumes for the need to bring new constraints to bear. Excessive interest in the technical problem of eliminating *tonk* and all of its possible cousins diverts attention from the fundamental problem for proof-theoretic semantics. It is to independently characterize sufficient conditions for successful definition of connective meaning in purely syntactic vocabulary. Given that broad intuitions about what it takes to define meaning are hard to flesh out in purely proof-theoretic terms, it is time to see what model-theoretic inferentialism has to offer.

What do Alpha Centaurian anthropologists have to say about this? They might very well remind us that attempts to come up with a purely proof-theoretic account of successful connective definition using a technical concept of harmony requires locating that concept in our inferential practices, in particular those related to the practice of defining meaning. They wonder whether the proof-theoretic tradition has convincing evidence that the technical notions of harmony they use are to be found in the wild.

13.8 A proof-theoretic natural semantics

At the end of Section 1.2, it was argued that there is room for the model-theoretic inferentialist to adopt a brand of ontological quietism about the concepts of model-theoretic semantics such as reference and truth. Here that point is brought home by showing how to transform natural semantics to a proof-theoretic version. The basic idea is very simple. The notation '$v(A)$ $=t$' suggests a correspondence between what A says and reality. However, it is an easy matter to find a corresponding proof-theoretic expression that eschews any explicit mention of truth. Instead of taking valuations v in V to be functions from the set of wffs to the truth-values, let a valuation v be a consistent and deductively closed set in the system S for which the proof-theoretic account is being constructed. Now for '$v(A)=t$' write '$v \vdash_S A$' in its place. On this new reading, $\|\leq\|$ together with the fact that sets v are deductively closed entail that $\leq$ amounts to the subset relation, and so the proof-theoretic reading for S→ will come to {S→}, for any v in V (where we abbreviate '$\vdash_{S\rightarrow}$' to '$\vdash$').

  {S→} $v \vdash$ A→B iff for all v' in V, if $v \subseteq v'$ and $v' \vdash$ A then $v' \vdash$ B.

The definition of proof-theoretic V-validity can be modified in the same way as follows.

  H $\vDash_V$ C iff for all v in V, if $v \vdash$ H, then $v \vdash$ C, where $v \vdash$ H iff $v \vdash$ B for
      each B in H.

The notion of what a system of rules S expresses needs hardly any modification at all. S proof-theoretically expresses condition {S} on models containing consistent and deductively closed sets rather than valuations exactly when V-validity of the rules of S is preserved iff V obeys {S}. Furthermore, the very notion of unity may be transformed as well.

  (Proof-Theoretic Unification) Sc is proof-theoretically unified iff
  (c Introduction) expresses a condition of the form: If $\mathbb{P}$ then $v \vdash$ AcB,
  while (c Elimination) expresses a condition of the form If $v \vdash$ AcB then $\mathbb{P}$.

I submit that the above notion is as worthy a candidate for a criterion of harmony as any other. We already know a lot about it because all of the results in this book are preserved under the transformation to proof-theoretic terminology. (We could, after all, have adopted the convention that the symbols 'v(A)=t' in the formal metalanguage be read: 'A has a proof in S from the set v'.) It is an interesting open question whether proof-theoretical unification classifies systems that define connectives in a way that is intuitively acceptable across the board. However, it resolves the problem with *tonk*, and generally agrees with main results sketched out by other forms of harmony, for example that systems for classical negation lack harmony while those for intuitionistic negation, conjunction, the conditional, and disjunction all have it. As we saw in the previous section, it does not agree with the verdicts of Read's ge-harmony in some cases, and it is not compatible in spirit with Tennant's talk of 'strong' and 'weak'. However, these may be taken to be features of the view rather than draw-backs. Finally, once one agrees to adopt the proof-theoretic definition of validity above and the corresponding notion of expression, it follows from the results on natural semantics in this book that the proof-theoretic ver-sion of natural semantics is the *preferred* proof-theoretic reading of the connectives. So Alpha-Centaurian anthropologists who somehow become convinced that we do adopt some version of a proof-theoretic semantics and can discern that we treat validity and expression in the natural semantics guise, will conclude that natural proof-theoretic semantics is to be preferred over all others.

It is worth reflecting on the relationships between natural proof-theoretic conditions like {S→} and the corresponding readings found in the intuitionistic proof interpretation (or BHK interpretation) (Troelstra and van Dalen, 1988, p. 9), which follow.

⊥. Contradiction ⊥ has no proof.
&. A proof of A&B is given by presenting a proof of A and a proof of B.
→. A proof of A→B is a construction that permits us to transform any proof of A into a proof of B.
∨. A proof of A∨B is given by presenting either a proof of A or a proof of B.

There is direct agreement on & and ⊥. As for →, {S→} says something in the same spirit: v proves A→B iff the existence of some other proof of A from resources v′ extending those of v entails the existence of a proof of B from the same resources v′. However, there is no mention (of course) of construc-tions. Furthermore, the treatment of disjunction is quite different, since the BHK-interpretation amounts to the classical requirement that proving A∨B (from v) requires a proof of A (from v) or a proof of B (from v).

As a final note, there is a passing resemblance between the definition of validity given above and Sandqvist's treatment of proof-theoretic validity in (2009). Sandqvist reports that S→ is incomplete for this notion of validity because it validates Peirce's Law. (See also the discussion in de Campos Sanz, et al. (forthcoming).) An idea worth exploring is that that incompleteness is the result of taking what is in essence the local model interpretation of S→, which forces a classical reading and hence verification of Peirce's Law.

14 Quantifiers

The natural semantics for standard ND rules for the quantifiers may come as something of a surprise, for it differs from both the objectual and the substitution interpretations (Section 14.3). The semantics that is expressed by the rules for the universal quantifier ∀, dubbed the sentential interpretation, is distinctly intensional and requires a side condition ensuring that the variables all denote in the same virtual domain (Section 14.4). Because of this, the sentential interpretation is not functional, and so it will be important to establish an isomorphism result to establish that it qualifies as a semantics (Section 14.5). One might hope that sequent systems that force a classical treatment of negation might be strong enough to eliminate the difference between the sentential interpretation and familiar readings of the quantifier, but Section 14.6 reveals that the difference persists. Section 14.7 shows how that difference may be exploited to establish that natural semantics (even for sequent systems with multiple conclusions) fails to be referential, that is, there is no guarantee that models of those systems can be treated as if their variables referred to objects in a virtual domain. Section 14.8 turns to the natural semantics for ∃, the existential quantifier. The surprise here is that ∃ lacks existential import. Section 14.9 points out that adoption of the omega rule is sufficient to force the substitution interpretation of the quantifiers. In Section 14.10, results of the chapter are marshaled for a criticism of Hacking's program to limn the logical.

14.1 Syntax and natural deduction rules for the quantifiers

The symbols of a quantifier language include a set *Var* of *variables* x, y, z, x′, y′, z′, ..., a set *Pred* of *predicate letters* P, Q, R, P′, Q′, R′, ..., connectives

$\perp$, &, $\rightarrow$, $\leftrightarrow$, $\vee$, and $\sim$ for propositional logic, the quantifier $\forall$, (and later $\exists$) and finally parentheses and the comma. For the moment, there will be no terms in the language other than the variables.

The *wffs* of the language are defined as follows. The *atomic wffs* have the forms $\perp$, and $P(x_1, x_2, \ldots, x_i)$, where P is any predicate letter and $(x_1, x_2, \ldots, x_i)$ is any list of variables. It is presumed that each predicate letter comes with an index i indicating the number of arguments in its variable list. When i=0, predicate letters serve as propositional variables. The official notation for a list requires parentheses and commas. However, we will write, for example, 'Lx,y', or even 'Lxy', in place of 'L(x, y)' when no ambiguity will arise. The set Wff of wffs of QL is defined to be the smallest set that includes the atomic wffs, and such that whenever A and B are in Wff, so are (A&B), (A$\rightarrow$B), (A$\leftrightarrow$B), (A$\vee$B), $\sim$A, and $\forall$xA. (According to this definition, open sentences count as wffs.)

A natural deduction system S$\forall$/ for quantificational logic consists of adding the following two natural deduction rules for $\forall$ to the structural rules S$\vdash$ of Section 3.1 (also found in Section 13.1). The notation 'A^y/x' is used to indicate the result of replacing variable y properly for every occurrence of free x in A. (By a proper replacement of y for x in A we mean that in case an occurrence of x lies in the scope of a quantifier $\forall$y, the quantifier and its variable occurrences y are all replaced with a quantifier $\forall$z, and variables z where z was chosen new to A. The purpose of this is to avoid placing y in a position where it would be bound by some quantifier already in A.) For each variable y, we call A^y/x an *instance* of the wff $\forall$xA.

S$\forall$/:   ($\forall$/ Elimination)
$$H \vdash \forall xA$$
$$H \vdash A^y/x$$

($\forall$/ Introduction)
$$H \vdash A^y/x$$
$$H \vdash \forall xA \qquad \text{provided y appears free in neither H nor } \forall xA.$$

Garson (1990, pp. 170ff.) introduced a different formulation of the quantifier rules that is equivalent to S$\forall$/. The idea was to separate the introduction and elimination of the quantifier $\forall$x from the process of substituting one free variable x for another variable y exemplified in (Sub) below. S$\forall$ results from adding the following three rules to the structural rules S$\vdash$.

S∀:   (∀ Elimination)

$$\frac{H \vdash \forall xA}{H \vdash A}$$

(∀ Introduction)

$$\frac{H \vdash A}{H \vdash \forall x\, A}$$ provided x does not appear free in H.

(Sub)

$$\frac{H \vdash A}{H \vdash A^y/x}$$ provided x does not appear free in H.

Since (Sub) is a rule that involves no logical symbol, we may take it to be one of the structural rules. (Dosen (1989, p. 365) presents a similar approach for sequent calculi with multiple conclusions, where a rule of term substitution appears as a separate structural rule.) We present S∀ because it provides a simple framework for developing a natural semantics for the quantifier rules – one that helps us find a natural semantics for S∀/ as well. Before we go further, let us verify that the two systems prove exactly the same arguments. (As usual, proofs of starred theorems are at the end of the chapter.)

Theorem 14.1* $H \vdash_{S\forall/} C$ iff $H \vdash_{S\forall} C$.

The last theorem guarantees that S∀ and S∀/ are equivalent. So being a model of S∀ and being a model of S∀/ amount to the same thing, hence S∀ expresses exactly what S∀/ expresses. Presenting predicate logic using the three-rule system S∀ will make it easier to prove results about what S∀/ expresses. The system PL∀ of classical predicate logic results from combining S∀ with the natural deduction rules of PL (the system for classical propositional logic) presented in Section 3.1. Similarly, I∨∀ is the result of adding S∀ to the system I∨ of intuitionistic propositional logic with disjunction. (See the end of Section 7.2.)

14.2 The objectual and substitution interpretations

This chapter compares the natural semantics for S∀ (or S∀/) with two well-known ways of reading the quantifiers, the substitution and objectual interpretations. For simplicity, we will adopt the convention that valuations assign truth-value to all the wffs, including those that contain free variables.

If you wish, you may think of valuations as including (implicitly) an assignment of values to the free variables.

Let us begin with the objectual interpretation. For smoothest connection with the treatment of valuations used in natural semantics, we adopt Smullyan's (1968, pp. 46–47) device of substituting objects of a domain for variables in the quantifier truth clause. An *objectual model* <D, V> consists of a domain D of objects, together with a set V of valuations that are defined over hybrid wffs. A *hybrid wff* is defined recursively so that any wff is a hybrid wff, and when A is a hybrid wff, so is any result A^d/x of replacing an object d from D for all occurrences of a free variable x in A. Truth conditions for connectives of propositional logic are given as before, but with the understanding that valuations range over hybrid wffs. The *objectual truth clause* for the quantifier is now given by condition $\|d\forall\|$ on <D, V> where v is any member of V.

$\|d\forall\|$ $v(\forall xA)=t$ iff for all d in D, $v(A^d/x)=t$.

One might have presented the objectual interpretation using the method of Church, where valuations over variables are introduced, or the method of Tarski where the satisfaction of open sentences by sequences of objects is defined, or the method of Mates. (See, for example, Boolos and Jeffrey (1974, p. 104).) However, definitions that introduce functions that assign values to the variables directly take us further afield. In a natural semantics, and in the model-theoretic inferentialist program in general, rules express constraints on how truth-values are assigned to wffs. Therefore, the best that can be done in a natural semantics is to express properties involving the truth-value of wffs. Natural semantics is consequently committed to some variety of a truth-value semantics (Leblanc, 1976). Hence, $\|d\forall\|$ will be the closest we can come to defining an objectual quantifier condition.

Unfortunately, $\|d\forall\|$ is not close enough. As we will see in the next section, $S\forall$ does not express $\|d\forall\|$, because the $S\forall$ rules allow objectual models where $v(A^d/x)=t$ for each d∈D, and yet $v(\forall xA)=f$.

Things fare no better for the substitution interpretation $\|s\forall\|$, and for roughly the same reasons.

$\|s\forall\|$ $v(\forall xA)=t$ iff for all variables y in Var, $v(A^y/x)=t$.

Here, the $\forall xA$ counts as true when each of its instances is true. The substitution interpretation is a close relative of the objectual interpretation, since it counts as a special case of $\|d\forall\|$ where D is simply the set Var of variables.

However, $\|s\forall\|$ is not equivalent to $\|d\forall\|$. Consider the *omega rule* $(\forall\infty)$, the argument with conclusion $\forall xA$, and whose premises consist of the set of all instances A^y/x for each of the variables y of the language.

$(\forall\infty)$ $\{A^y/x: y\in Var\} \vdash \forall xA$

Now consider the notion of s-validity generated by $\|s\forall\|$. It is presumed that we are given a fixed language L with its set Var of variables, and an argument is counted valid iff on every model V over L, a valuation v makes the conclusion true if v assigns t to all the premises. In light of $\|s\forall\|$, the omega rule is s-valid, but the result of taking any finite subset of its hypotheses would be s-invalid. This means that s-validity is not compact, where a notion of validity is *compact* iff whenever an argument H / C is valid, there is another valid argument H' / C, where H' is a finite subset of H. Since s-validity is not compact, (strong) completeness for quantifier systems PL$\forall$ and I$\vee\forall$ with respect to s-validity will automatically fail, since those systems are finitary. The failure of completeness has immediate implications for expressive power. Since it was shown in Section 12.1 that every system is complete on its natural semantics, $\|s\forall\|$ cannot qualify as a natural semantics for any finitary system, and so it is not a natural semantics for S$\forall$.

The difficulty that the substitution interpretation validates the omega rule is well known, and a number of repairs have been offered. (See Leblanc (1976) or Belnap and Dunn (1968) or Garson (1979).) A standard move is to modify the definition of validity so that the omega rule becomes invalid. The trick is to bring mention of the language into the definition. For example, a modified version for $\vDash_{\|P\|}$, validity with respect to a set of semantical conditions $\|P\|$ would go like this.

(Validity for the Substitution Interpretation)
H $\vDash_{\|P\|}$ C iff for every language L that includes the symbols occurring in H / C, and every set V of valuations over L, every member v of V satisfies H / C.

On such a revised definition, the omega rule is no longer $\|s\forall\|$-valid since given $\{A^y/x: y\in Var\} / \forall xA$ for Var of a language L, there are extensions of L that include variables not in Var that will provide a counterexample to it. As a result, strong completeness can be proven given the revised definition.

However, this modification entails a major complication for the project of natural semantics. Models must now include valuations over different languages, and the truth conditions expressed by $\rightarrow$, $\leftrightarrow$, $\lor$, and $\sim$ must include mention of valuations for extensions of the language at which a sentence is being evaluated. Since this complicates isomorphism results, the project is left to another day. In any case, it is clear that given (Validity for the Substitution Interpretation) the quantifier rules would still not express $\|s\forall\|$, for $\|s\forall\|$ does not mention alternative languages.

14.3 Negative results for what quantifier rules express

Good reasons have been given for thinking that the substitution interpretation could not be a natural semantics for $S\forall$. That result will be shown below with more care, and in such a way as to obtain a negative result for the objectual interpretation as a side effect. (The proof is found at the end of this chapter.)

Theorem 14.3* $S\forall$ does not express $\|s\forall\|$, nor does it express $\|d\forall\|$.

In the following section, the natural semantics for $S\forall$ will be introduced along with an explanation of how it differs from the objectual and substitution interpretations.

Given the negative result for $\|d\forall\|$, it will come as no surprise that the same holds for more traditional formulations of the objectual interpretation of the quantifier. It is a straightforward but tedious matter to show that the objectual models that use $\|d\forall\|$ are all isomorphic to models that are defined using Church's or Tarski's methods. So QL fails to express these formulations as well. (Furthermore, the same holds for Baldwin's (1979, pp. 224ff.) "substitutional" definition of quantification, which (as Williams (1980) shows) is really just the objectual interpretation in disguise.)

Perhaps it is not too surprising that $S\forall$ would fail to force the objectual interpretation of the quantifier; it would be a lot to ask of rules governing wffs that they require the presence of an objectual domain in their models related to the quantifier truth condition in the right way. The substitution interpretation truth condition adverts only to the truth behavior of wffs, so it might have a better chance of being forced by $S\forall$. But as we just have seen, that guess is incorrect.

14.4 The sentential interpretation

Here the interpretation for the universal quantifier expressed by S∀ will be presented. The following section will show that it qualifies as a semantics. For simplicity, let us first investigate the natural semantics for system S∀-, the system consisting of (∀ Elimination) and (∀ Introduction), but not (Sub). The first result is that S∀- expresses $\|\forall\|$.

$\|\forall\|$ $v(\forall xA)=t$ iff for every v' in V, if $v \leq_x v'$, then $v'(A)=t$.

Here, $v \leq_x v'$ holds exactly when v' is an extension of v save for formulas containing free x. More formally, $\leq_x$ is defined by $\|\leq_x\|$.

$\|\leq_x\|$ $v \leq_x v'$ iff for every wff A which fails to contain free x, if $v(A)=t$, then $v'(A)=t$.

So when we say that V obeys $\|\forall\|$, it is understood that $\|\leq_x\|$ holds.

Since $\|\forall\|$ involves values assigned to (open) sentences, we call this condition the *sentential interpretation* of the quantifier. $\|\forall\|$ has an intensional flavor, for when valuations are identified with possible worlds, $\|\forall\|$ takes on the general shape of a condition for a modal operator $\forall x$ with a corresponding accessibility relation $\leq_x$.

Note that $\|\forall\|$ differs from the substitution interpretation in that the omega rule is invalid. There are models V that obey $\|\forall\|$ where v is a member of V and $v(\{A^y/x: \in Var\})=t$ and $v(\forall xA)=f$. (See Theorem 14.4.4 below for details.) Therefore, there is no need to adjust the definition of validity as was necessary for the substitution interpretation. Furthermore, since the set V of valuations over the wffs is potentially superdenumerably infinite, $\|\forall\|$ is compatible with a covert intention to quantify over the real numbers. Therefore the well-known complaint that the substitution interpretation cannot handle quantification over superdenumerable domains does not apply to $\|\forall\|$. (The complaint is discussed, for example, in Haack, 1996, pp. 145–146.)

The sentential interpretation may have gone unnoticed because of a failure to perceive the taxonomy of quantifier interpretations in the right way. The objectual interpretation instructs us to check the value of $\forall xA$ at valuation v by looking at the value of A given new valuations of the variable x to members of the domain (valuations like v save at x). The substitution interpretation instructs us to check the values of new sentences A^y/x. This suggests that ontological commitment "goes with" the new valuations technique, while the new sentences method lacks it. Actually, Smullyan's interpretation already shows that it is possible to have ontological commitment with the new (hybrid) sentences method. The existence of the sentential interpretation shows that the choice between methods is completely orthogonal to the choice for or against ontological commitment. All four combinations are possible as is illustrated in the following chart.

Ontological commitment	New values method	New sentences method
Yes	Objectual interpretation	Smullyan's interpretation
No	Sentential interpretation	Substitution interpretation

The next theorem asserts that S$\forall$- expresses the sentential interpretation $\|\forall\|$.

Theorem 14.4.1* S$\forall$- expresses $\|\forall\|$.

However, $\|\forall\|$ is weaker than any classical semantics for the quantifier because it does not validate (Sub), which is provable there.

Theorem 14.4.2 (Sub) does not preserve $\|\forall\|$-validity.

Proof. It will suffice to show that $\forall xPx \nvDash_{\|M\|} Py$. Let V contain a single valuation v such that v(Px)=t, and v(Py)=f. Let values for the complex sentences be fixed by $\|PL\|$ and $\|\forall\|$. Since the only valuation $v' \in V$ such that $v \leq_x v'$ is v, and v(Px)=t, it follows that v($\forall$xPx)=t. So v($\forall$xPx)=t and v(Py)=f, and $\forall xPx \nvDash_{\|M\|}$ Py as desired.   □

The last theorem entails that $\|\forall\|$ fails to validate $\forall xA / A^y/x$. In calculating v($\forall$xA), one searches only valuations v' in V such that $v \leq_x v'$. If V does not contain a valuation v' such that $v \leq_x v'$ and $v'(A)=t$, then v($\forall$xA)=t even when while $v(A^y/x)=f$. Under these circumstances, it is as if y did not denote in the virtual domain generated by V. It follows that S$\forall$-, the logic of $\|\forall\|$, is not classical.

S∀- is best understood as a system that has separate virtual domains for each of the variables. In order to generate a natural semantics for classical logic, we must supplement ‖∀‖, with a condition that (Sub) expresses.

‖Sub‖ If $v(A^y/x)=f$, then for some v' in V, $v \leq_x v'$ and $v'(A)=f$.

The condition ‖Sub‖ insures the validity of $\forall xA \rightarrow A^y/x$, and so says that all variables y "denote" in the same virtual domain.

Theorem 14.4.3* (Sub) expresses ‖Sub‖.

It follows immediately from Theorems 14.4.1 and 14.4.3 that the system S∀ expresses ‖S∀‖, the conjunction of ‖∀‖ with ‖Sub‖.

S∀ **Expression Theorem.** S∀ expresses ‖S∀‖.

This together with the completeness result reported in Section 12.1 shows that the omega rule is invalid on the sentential interpretation.

Theorem 14.4.4 The omega rule is invalid for models V obeying ‖S∀‖.

Proof. Suppose for reductio that the omega rule is ‖S∀‖-valid. Then by the ‖S‖ Adequacy Theorem of Section 12.1, and the S∀ Expression Theorem, the finitary system S∀ would be complete for ‖S∀‖-validity. Therefore the omega rule would be provable in S∀. But we know that no finitary system can prove the omega rule.   □

The S∀ Expression Theorem may be combined with previous results to show what is expressed by I∨∀, the system formed by adding S∀ to intuitionistic logic I∨, and PL∀, the result of adding S∀ to classical logic PL. Let ‖I∨∀‖ be the conjunction of ‖S∀‖ with ‖I∨‖. Similarly ‖PL∀‖ is the conjunction of ‖S∀‖ with ‖qPL‖, the simplified semantics for PL that uses the quasi-truth interpretation of disjunction. Then the I∨ Expression Theorem of Section 7.2, and the qPL Expression Theorem of Section 8.7, may be used to establish the next results.

I∨∀ **Expression Theorem.** I∨∀ expresses ‖I∨∀‖.

PL∀ Expression Theorem. PL∀ expresses ‖PL∀‖.

14.5 Showing the sentential interpretation is a semantics

If we can certify ‖S∀‖ as a semantics, it will follow that ‖S∀‖ is the natural semantics for S∀. Unfortunately, it will not be possible to prove that ‖S∀‖ is a functional. However, functionality holds for neither the natural semantics ‖I∨‖ for intuitionistic logic I∨ (due to problems with disjunction) nor the natural semantics ‖PL‖ for classical logic (due to problems related to negation). So the best that can be done is to prove an isomorphism between models obeying ‖S∀‖ and models with more standard truth conditions that are clearly well-founded.

We will prove an isomorphism theorem for the intuitionistic semantics ‖I∨∀‖ and then explain how to use it to derive one for the classical ‖PL∀‖. For the intuitionistic case, let us amplify the neighborhood models <W, ⊆, N, u> of Section 7.4 so that the interpretation function u now assigns truth-values to all the atomic wffs of the language L. (Hereafter the metavariable 'p' will range over atomic wffs rather than just over propositional variables.) We will also need to introduce a relation $\subseteq_x$ for each variable x of the language to serve in the truth condition for ∀. Therefore, a *quantified neighborhood model* <W, ⊆, N, X, u> is such that <W, ⊆, N, u> is a neighborhood model, and X is a set containing for each variable x of L, a reflexive and transitive binary relation $\subseteq_x$ over W. The truth conditions (K⊥), (Kp), (K&), (K→), (K↔), (K¬), (P∨), for the propositional connectives are the same, and (K∀) is added for the universal quantifier.

(Kp) $w \vDash p$ iff u(w, p)=t, for atomic wffs p.

(K⊥) $w \nvDash \perp$.

(K&) $w \vDash A\&B$ iff $w \vDash A$ and $w \vDash B$.

(K→) $w \vDash A{\to}B$ iff for every w′ in W, if w⊆w′, then $w' \nvDash A$ or $w' \vDash B$.

(K↔) $w \vDash A{\leftrightarrow}B$ iff for every w′ in W, if w⊆w′, then $w' \vDash A$ iff $w' \vDash B$.

(K¬) $w \vDash {\sim}A$ iff for every w′ in W, if w⊆w′, then $w' \nvDash A$.

(P∨) $w \vDash A{\vee}B$ iff for every subset P of W such that wNP, there is a w′∈P such that $w' \vDash A$ or $w' \vDash B$.

(K∀) $w \vDash \forall xA$ iff for every w′ in W if w⊆ₓw′, then $w' \vDash A$.

The restrictions ($\subseteq$) and (N) on neighborhood models are given as before, and new conditions (Sub) and (X) are required. So a *quantified path model* is any quantified neighborhood model that meets the following four conditions, for all w and w' in W,

($\subseteq$) $w \subseteq w'$ iff for all wffs A, if $w \vDash A$, then $w' \vDash A$.

(N) wNP iff there is some wff D such that $w \nvDash D$, and P = {w': $w \subseteq w'$ and $w' \nvDash D$}.

(Sub) If $w \nvDash A^y/x$, then for some member w' in W, $w \subseteq_x w'$ and $w' \nvDash A$.

(X) For each variable x, $w \subseteq_x w'$ iff for all wffs A that do not contain free x, if
$$w \vDash A \text{ then } w' \vDash A.$$

Some readers may find (Sub) and (X) unacceptable because they mention complex wffs. However (Sub) is no worse than the conditions ($\subseteq$) and (N) on path models. So (X) and (Sub) contribute no problems which were not already endemic to path semantics.

A set of valuations V will be said to be *isomorphic* to U=<W, $\subseteq$, N, X, u> iff the structure <V, $\le$> is isomorphic to <W, $\subseteq$, N, X, u>, which means in turn that there is a 1–1 mapping * from V into W such that $v \le v'$ iff $v^* \subseteq v'^*$, $v \le_x v'$ iff $v^* \subseteq_x v'^*$ for each $\subseteq_x$ in X, and u fixes values of wffs so that v(A)=t iff $v^* \vDash^U A$.

Quantified Path Isomorphism Theorem*. V obeys $\|I \forall \forall\|$ iff <V, $\le$> is isomorphic to some quantified path model.

The next project is to demonstrate an isomorphism result for quantified logics based on classical propositional logic. The strategy will be similar to the one employed to show an isomorphism result for PL. There we used the Path Isomorphism Theorem to show an isomorphism with path models. In the case of PL, those models obeyed (KR), and so appeal to the KR Theorem showed that the path models in question allowed replacement of the path bundle truth condition (P$\lor$) for $\lor$ with the quasi-truth interpretation (Kq$\lor$), thus eliminating the need for the neighborhood relation N. The result is an isomorphism result for KR-models.

KR Theorem. If a path model obeys (KR) then the path bundle truth condition (P$\lor$) holds iff the quasi-truth condition (Kqv) holds.

(P∨)   w ⊨ A∨B iff for every subset P of W such that wNP, there is a w′∈P such that w′ ⊨ A or w′ ⊨ B.

(Kq∨) w ⊨ A∨B iff for every w′ in W, if w⊆w′, then there is a w″ in W such that w″ ⊨ A or w″ ⊨ B.

Here are the formal details. A quantified *PL-model* U = <W, ⊆, X, u> is such that <W, ⊆, u> is a Kripke model and X is a collection of reflexive and transitive relations ⊆$_x$, on W, one for each variable x of the language L. The truth relation ⊨ for quantified PL-models adds the quantifier clause (K∀) to those for KR-semantics, so ⊨ is defined as follows.

(Kp)   w ⊨ p   iff u(w, p)=t, for atomic wffs p.
(K⊥)   w ⊭ ⊥.
(K&)   w ⊨ A&B   iff w ⊨ A and w ⊨ B.
(K→)   w ⊨ A→B   iff for every w′ in W, if w⊆w′, then w′ ⊭ A or w′ ⊨ B.
(K↔)   w ⊨ A↔B   iff for every w′ in W, if w⊆w′, then w′ ⊨ A iff w′ ⊨ B.
(K¬)   w ⊨ ~A   iff for every w′ in W, if w⊆w′, then w′ ⊭ A.
(Kq∨) w ⊨ A∨B   iff for every w′ in W, if w⊆w′, then there is a w″ in W such that w′⊆w″ and w″ ⊨ A or w″ ⊨ B.
(K∀)   w ⊨ ∀xA   iff for every w′ in W if w⊆$_x$w′, then w′ ⊨ A.

You may remember that in the course of proving the PL Isomorphism Theorem that the KR Lemma was used to show that (Refinability) entails (KR), the analog of ‖LF‖ for complex wffs.

(KR) If w ⊭A, then for some w′∈W, w⊆w′ and w′(A)=F.
‖LF‖ If v(A)=f, then for some v′∈V, v≤v′ and v′(A)=F.

Unfortunately, the KR Lemma fails when the quantifier is in the language. Therefore in defining quantified KR-models, it will be necessary to adopt (⊆), (X), (Sub), and (KR) directly, as we did for quantified path semantics.

(⊆) w⊆w′ iff for all wffs A, if w ⊨ A, then w′ ⊨ A.

(X) For each variable x, w⊆$_x$w′ iff for all wffs A that does not contain free x, if w ⊨ A then w′ ⊨ A.

(Sub) If w ⊭ Ay/x, then for some member w′ in W, w⊆$_x$w′ and w′ ⊭ A.

So a quantified KR-model is any PL-model that meets the four conditions (KR), (⊆), (X), and (Sub). Quantified KR-validity is defined as expected.

The next project will be to show that any model V obeying ‖PL∀‖ is isomorphic to a quantified KR-model, where the notion of an isomorphism is defined by the following requirements: v≤v′ iff v*⊆v′*, v≤ₓv′ iff v*⊆ₓv′* for each ⊆ₓ in X, and v(A)=t iff v* ⊨ᵁ A. The proof appeals to the Quantified Path Isomorphism Theorem and recapitulates the strategy of the PL Isomorphism Theorem (Section 8.8).

Quantified KR Isomorphism Theorem. V obeys ‖PL∀‖ iff <V, <> is isomorphic to some quantified KR-model.

The last two isomorphism theorems guarantee that ‖I∨∀‖ and ‖PL∀‖ qualify as semantical conditions. So the I∨∀ Expression Theorem and the PL∀ Expression Theorem of the previous section assure us that these are their natural semantics.

14.6 Quantification in a classical setting

Theorem 14.3 and the S∀ Expression Theorem show the sentential interpretation is the reading of ∀ expressed by S∀, and that this reading differs from the substitution and objectual interpretations. One might wonder whether the difference would disappear when stronger requirements are placed on models, for example the requirement that V obey the classical truth tables. However, even when the classical truth condition ‖C~‖ for negation is adopted, the differences persist. Understanding those differences is important to the topic of the next section, where we show that the conjunction of ‖S∀‖ with ‖C~‖ is too weak to guarantee that models are referential, which means that terms of the language (in our case the variables) can be treated as if they referred to objects in a domain.

Sequent systems with multiple conclusions are used here, since they force the standard truth conditions for all the propositional connectives. It still turns out that the objectual and substitution interpretations of the quantifier are unsound for (∀ In) and so do not qualify as a natural semantics. The quantifier condition that is expressed is somewhat stronger than the sentential interpretation, but it has a similar intensional flavor.

Let GS$\forall$ consist of the sequent rules GPL for propositional logic (see Section 11.1) along with the following pair G$\forall$ for the universal quantifier, and the structural rule (GSub) borrowed from Dosen (1989).

G$\forall$: ($\forall$Left)   ($\forall$Right)

$$\frac{H, A \vdash G}{H, \forall xA \vdash G}$$ $$\frac{H \vdash A, G}{H \vdash \forall xA, G}$$ x does not appear free in

H or G.

(GSub) $$\frac{H \vdash G}{H^y/x \vdash G^y/x}$$

(Gsub) is motivated by the thought that logic ought to be permutation invariant, that is, whether an argument counts as correct should not depend on how objects are assigned values to the terms. (For a good source on permutation invariance as a mark of the logical, see MacFarlane (2009, Section 5).)

It is a straightforward matter to show that the system G$\forall$, composed of the structural rules and these three, expresses $\|G\forall\|$, which consists of the following truth condition $\|\forall=\|$ for $\forall$, along with the structural condition $\|Gsub\|$.

$\|\forall=\|$ $v(\forall xA)=t$ iff for all v' in V, if $v=_x v'$, then $v'(A)=t$.

$\|Gsub\|$ For each v in V, v^y/x is in V.

Definitions for: '$=_x$' and: 'v^y/x' follow.

(Def $=_x$) $v=_x v'$ iff for all wffs B that contain no free x, $v(B)=v'(B)$.

(Def v^y/x) $v^y/x(A)=v(A^y/x)$.

Theorem 14.6.1* G$\forall$ expresses $\|G\forall\|$.

Let GPL$\forall$ be the system formed by adding G$\forall$ to GPL, and let $\|GPL\forall\|$ be the conjunction of the classical conditions for the connectives with $\|G\forall\|$. Then clearly GPL$\forall$ expresses $\|GPL\forall\|$. Furthermore, an isomorphism result showing $\|GPL\forall\|$ is a properly defined semantics is straightforward, so $\|GPL\forall\|$ is the natural semantics for GPL$\forall$.

Theorem 14.6.2 GPL$\forall$ has $\|GPL\forall\|$ as its natural semantics.

The next project will be to demonstrate that even in $\|GPL\forall\|$ the objectual and sentential interpretations differ. Since GPL$\forall$ has $\|GPL\forall\|$ as a natural semantics, we know that (∀ Introduction) preserves V-validity for models V that obey ‖GPL∀‖. However, the next theorem shows that there are models V where ‖s∀‖ is used in place of ‖∀‖, where V-validity of (∀ Introduction) is not preserved.

Theorem 14.6.3 There is a model V obeying classical truth tables and ‖s∀‖ such that the V-validity of (∀ Introduction) is not preserved.

Proof. For simplicity, consider a language with a single predicate letter F, whose set Var of variables contains just three: x, y, and z. Define model V^* so that $V^* = \{v, v'\}$ with v(Fx)=t, v(Fy)=t, v(Fz)=f, v'(Fx)=t, v'(Fy)=f, v'(Fz)=f. Calculate the values of complex formulas using the classical truth tables and ‖s∀‖. Since every valuation in V that makes Fy true also makes Fx true, we have Fy ⊨$_V$ Fx. Furthermore, x does not appear in Fy. However, Fy ⊭$_V$ ∀xFx, given ‖s∀‖, because v(Fy)=t and v(Fz)=f.   □

The reader may be puzzled at the last result. Isn't it well known that the quantifier rules are sound for the substitution interpretation? However, soundness means something stronger in the case of natural semantics. To show that (∀ Introduction) is sound it must follow *for any model* V, when H / A is V-valid, so is H / ∀xA. The model V^* defined in the previous theorem validates Fy / Fx because every valuation in V^* that satisfies Fy just happens to satisfy Fx. So models V may exhibit patterns among the valuations that fix consequence relations between atoms, and this leads to the failure of the brand of soundness that is needed to prove an expression result. While it is true that were H / A to be satisfied on every conceivable model, then so would H / ∀xA, but that is not how validity preservation is defined in natural semantics.

This failure of soundness for the substitution interpretation can be explained by the fact that that truth condition is excessively extensional. Given ‖s∀‖, the value of ∀xA at v is calculated by looking only at the behavior of instances A^y/x *at v*. Therefore that calculation is insensitive to inferential patterns (such as the validity of Fy / Fx in V^* above) set up by valuations in V other than v. In the case of the sentential interpretation, however, any attempt to show (∀ Introduction) unsound fails. In the example given in the previous theorem, a valuation v where v(Fy)=t and v(∀xFx)=f requires (by ‖∀‖) that there be a v″ in V such that v<$_x$v″ and v″(Fx)=f. In this v″, v″(Fy)=t thus invalidating Fy / Fx.

The takeaway point is this. The natural semantics for S∀ is essentially intensional, and the failure of the substitution interpretation to qualify as natural is due to its being extensional. A similar point may be made for the objectual interpretation, since the substitution interpretation just is the objectual interpretation in the special case where D=Var. Alpha Centaurian anthropologists, who have understood this lesson, are very puzzled as to why Earthlings advocate unnatural extensional accounts of the quantifiers.

14.7 The prospects for referential semantics

Inferentialists propose that meaning is defined by inferential role. Since only wffs bear the relation of inference, it follows that the meanings of terms and predicate letters must be explained by the contribution they make to the truth behavior of wffs containing them. Therefore, natural semantics is by its very nature a truth-value semantics (Leblanc, 1976), where all truth conditions are explained by reference to truth behavior of wffs on various valuations. However, in standard model theory, terms and predicate letters are assigned objects and sets as their referents, and the values of atomic wffs are determined by those assignments. Since what logical rules express is at best a truth-value characterization, it is natural to ask whether the conditions enforced by natural semantics are strong enough to determine specific roles for the terms and predicate letters.

If the ground rules for what counts as a role are quite liberal, the answer is an easy 'Yes'. The role or *signature* of term x in V can be taken to be a function taking each atomic wff A containing free x and each valuation v in V to a truth-value, namely v(A). Signatures of the different terms (variables in our case) can then be taken as their meanings, for they explain the contribution a term makes to the truth behavior of wffs it contains. (We are imagining here that the signatures over atomic wffs are sufficient to determine variable roles in complex wffs.) A similar tactic could be used to isolate meanings of the predicate letters.

While this idea has some attractions, it also smacks of triviality. The interesting question is whether inferential roles connect with a *subatomic* model-theoretic semantics where the components of atoms such as the terms are assigned denotations in a domain. So let us consider a stronger requirement, namely that the meanings (or signatures) assigned to terms and predicate letters on a truth-value model map into the entities ordinarily used in a subatomic semantics. In a subatomic model, terms are assigned members of a domain, and predicate letters map into sets (of n-tuples) from that domain. Furthermore, the truth-values of the atomic wffs are fixed by what is assigned to the terms and predicate letters they contain. We want to know whether conditions expressed by quantifier systems are sufficient to enforce a kind of discipline on the valuations in a truth-value model. For example, is there any guarantee that the signatures assigned to the terms by a truth-value model are compatible with the idea that those terms are referential, that is, that they pick out objects in some domain of a subatomic model in a way that is compatible with values assigned to atoms?

One response to this question is to simply stipulate that a domain for the desired subatomic model consist of the signatures for each of the variables for a given model V. But this alone will not guarantee that the truth-value of the wffs across V coordinate with the referents of the variables so assigned. For example, suppose we consider the signatures for two variables x and y. Will the values v assigns to atoms containing x and y coordinate properly with the signatures referred to by x and y? Here is a reason to worry. Consider atomic wffs containing both variables such as Fxy, and imagine that v(Fxy)=t. Now consider a valuation v′ that reflects an assignment of values to variables which was just like the assignment of variables implicit in v save that the variable x is assigned a new object whose signature differs at v so that v′(Fxy)=f. One would hope that v′ would reflect only a change in the referent of x, and not the other variables. However v′ changes the signature of both x and y from what they were in v, for y's value for Fxy is also different at v′ from what it was at v. Truth-value semantics seems unable to protect variables' signatures from a kind of interaction as we move from one valuation to another. Where subatomic models allow variation in the referents of terms individually, signatures of a truth-value semantics exhibit an untoward sort of holism. Changing one variable's signature may affect the signature of many others.

One might attempt to escape from the problem by fiat. In the canonical model for predicate logic, one may let variables refer to themselves (and predicate letters as well). Then by stipulation, each variable picks out a value that cannot be affected by the value of any other variable. However, this flies in the face of the crucial idea in model-theoretic semantics, namely that terms may take on different referents in different valuations. That idea is crucial to the way in which the objectual interpretation of the quantifier is defined.

The natural semantics for the quantifier in a multiple conclusion (hence classical setting) has been explored to help calibrate how the natural semantics for the quantifier differs from familiar approaches such as the objectual and substitution interpretations. However, this also helps resolve present questions about whether it is always possible to outfit a model of S∀ with a semantics that is referential, that is, one where we may think of the valuations v in V as representing different ways the variables may be assigned objects in a domain.

We could provide a benchmark for what counts as referential model V using the idea of an isomorphism to a subatomic model; however for the present purposes, a weaker condition will suffice. Consider the hybrid wffs defined over a given domain of objects D, and imagine that two valuations v and v' in V are such that $v=_xv'$. Then if V is referential, the difference between v and v' ought to be explained by the fact that the referent of x in v differs from its referent in v'. It follows that when $v(Fx)=t$ and $v'(Fx)=f$, there must be a member d in D such that $v'(Fd)=f$, which explains the fact that v' (Fx)=f by what x refers to, namely an object d different from the one that was (implicitly) assigned to x in v. Let us define the notation 'v^d/x' so that $v^d/x(A)=v(A^d/x)$. Therefore, we expect a referential model V to obey the following minimal condition for v and v' in V.

> (Referential)   V is *referential* only if there is a domain D such that for all v and v' in V, if $v=_xv'$, then for some $d \in D$ $v'=v^d/x$.

Given the fact that G∀ expresses ‖GSub‖, one might hope that any model of G∀ is referential.

> ‖Gsub‖ for each v in V, v^y/x is in V.

However, the next theorem shows that is not so.

Theorem 14.7* There are models that obey ‖GPL∀‖ that are not referential.

This is interesting news for model-theoretic inferentialism. The rules of predicate logic, even in a classical setting created by using multiple conclusions, underdetermine the requirement needed to secure a referential semantics. Alpha Centaurian anthropologists looking at inferential roles alone have no reason to think that our models are referential.

14.8 The existential quantifier

In classical logic, the existential quantifier ∃ may be defined from ∀ by (Def ∃).

(Def∃) ∃xA =$_{df}$ ~∀x~A

However, in intuitionistic logic, ∃xA and ~∀x~A are not equivalent. Therefore in order not to prejudice matters, let us assume ∃ is primitive and ruled by the following pair of natural deduction rules.

S∃:   (∃ Elimination)

H ⊢ ∃xA

H, A ⊢ C

H ⊢ C   provided x does not appear free in H or C.

(∃ Introduction)

$$\frac{H \vdash A}{H \vdash \exists xA}$$

Let S∃ be the system that adds (∃In) and (∃Out) to the structural rules, which now, remember, include (Sub).

(Sub)

$$\frac{H \vdash A}{H \vdash A^y/x}$$ provided x does not appear free in H.

It is a straightforward matter to show that S∃ is equivalent to a more traditional system that adopts the following pair, presuming that the rules S∀ for ∀ are available (to guarantee the derivability of (Sub) in S∃/).

S∃/: (∃/ Elimination)

H ⊢ ∃xA

H, A^y/x ⊢ C

H ⊢ C   provided y does not appear free in H, A, or C.

(∃/ Introduction)

$$\frac{H \vdash A^y/x}{H \vdash \exists xA}$$

We are now ready to show that S∃ expresses ‖S∃‖ – the conjunction of ‖Sub‖ with the following truth condition ‖W∃‖ for ∃, which resembles the truth condition ‖W∨‖ for disjunction.

||W∃|| v(∃xA)=t iff for every wff C that contains no free x, if v(C)=f, then there is a v' in V such that v≤ₓv', v'(C)=f and v'(A)=t.

||W∨|| v(A∨B)=t iff for every wff C, if v(C)=f, then there is a v' in V such that v≤v', v'(C)=f, and either v'(A)=t or v'(B)=t.

Theorem 14.8.1* S∃ expresses ||S∃||.

By combining the last result with the I∨∀ Expression Theorem (Section 14.4), it follows that IQ (which is I∨∀ plus S∃) expresses ||IQ|| the conjunction of ||I∨∀|| with ||S∃||.

IQ Expression Theorem. IQ expresses ||IQ||.

In the case of classical logic, where the semantical condition ||LF|| for (Double Negation) is available, a new truth condition for ∃ is expressed which avoids mention of complex wffs C.

||LF|| If v(A)=f, then for some v', v≤v' and v'(A)=F.

It has some resemblance to ||q∨|| the quasi-truth interpretation for disjunction, and can be read off from the equivalence of ∃xA with ~∀x~A.

||q∃|| v(∃xA)=t iff for all v' in V, if v≤v', then
for some v" in V, v'≤ₓv" and v"(A)=qT.

||q∨|| v(A∨B)=t iff for all v' in V, if v≤v', then v'(A)=qT or v'(B)=qT.

(Def qT) v"(A)=qT iff v"(A)≠F, that is, for some u in V, v"≤u and u(A)=t.

Let QL (classical quantified logic) be the system PL∀, plus rules S∃ for the existential quantifier, and let ||QL|| be the conjunction of ||q∃|| with ||PL∀||. Then QL expresses ||QL||.

QL Expression Theorem*. QL expresses ||QL||.

Just as in the case of disjunction, the interpretation expressed by S∃, is both unfamiliar and complex, even in the classical context QL. ∃xA can be true in a valuation v where no instance Aʸ/x is true at v. All that is necessary is that for every extension v' of v, we can find some extension v", such that v'≤ₓv" where A is quasi-true. Alpha Centaurian anthropologists, who know this fact, are totally puzzled by Quine's doctrine (1953) that ∃ limns our ontology. The objectual interpretation, which he espouses, is simply not the way of understanding ∃ that is justified by the rules we use. On its natural reading, ∃ lacks existential import.

We can close this section with a brief explanation of how isomorphism results may be obtained for ‖QL‖, and ‖IQ‖, the semantics that results from adding ‖S∃‖ to the intuitionistic semantics ‖I∨∀‖. The first case can be simplified by assuming that ∃ is defined by $\exists xA =_{df} \sim\forall x\sim A$. Then an isomorphism from ‖QL‖ to quantified KR-models follows directly from the Quantified KR Isomorphism Theorem of Section 14.5.

In the intuitionistic case ‖IQ‖, the situation is more complicated. Because of the reference to complex wffs C in ‖W∃‖, quantified neighborhood models $<W, \subseteq, N, X, u>$ must be expanded to include new neighborhood structures N_x. So a ∃ *neighborhood model* $U=<W, \subseteq, N, X, NX, u>$ is a quantified neighborhood model that also includes a new set NX containing a neighborhood structure N_x for each variable x. The truth condition (P∃) for ∃ on such models is defined on analogy with the case of disjunction.

(P∃) $w \vDash \exists xA$ iff for every subset P of W such that wN_xP, there is a $w' \in P$ such that $w' \vDash A$.

(P∨) $w \vDash A \lor B$ iff for every subset P of W such that wNP, there is a $w' \in P$ such that $w' \vDash A$ or $w' \vDash B$.

Then the analogs (N_x) of the condition (N) must be added to obtain the definition of an ∃ *path model*.

(N_x) wN_xP iff there is some wff D containing no free occurrence of x, such that $w \nvDash D$, and $P = \{w': w\subseteq_x w'$ and $w' \nvDash D\}$.

The reader may obtain the isomorphism result for ∃ path models by following the strategies used for the Quantified Path Isomorphism Theorem of Section 14.5.

∃ Path Isomorphism Theorem. V obeys ‖IQ‖ iff $<V, <>$ is isomorphic to some ∃ path model.

It should be admitted that this appeal to yet further structure to rescue ∃ is ugly, and may do little to impress a reader who is deeply concerned about whether ‖W∃‖ is a legitimate truth condition. Of course, it will be of no help at all for someone who demands that truth conditions be functional. Therefore, it is not possible to convince those readers that the quantifier rules determine a meaning for ∃.

14.9 The omega rule and the substitution interpretation

In Section 14.3, we learned that the substitution interpretation is not a natural semantics for S∀. It appears we need a different rule for introducing the universal quantifier if we hope to find a system that has the substitution interpretation as its natural semantics. A straightforward suggestion is to replace (∀ Introduction) with the omega rule (∀∞).

(∀∞)   {A^y/x: y∈Var} ⊢ ∀xA

A convenient formulation S∀∞ of such a logic consists of (∀ Elimination) and (∀∞). (Sub) will no longer be needed as a structural rule, but see below, where the need to adopt an infinitary version of (Cut) is explained.

S∀∞:   (∀ Out)   (∀∞)

          ∀xA ⊢ Ay/x   {A^y/x: y∈Var} ⊢ ∀xA

Both these rules are "axiomatic," as they allow one to simply enter an argument to a derivation without establishing any input sequent or sequents. A common complaint against the omega rule is that its use requires that proofs are no longer finite, since its application to produce the conclusion ∀xA requires infinitely many premises. However natural deduction rules in this book are formulated over arguments, and we have treated the hypothesis H of an argument as a (potentially) infinite set. Within this formulation, the omega rule does not seem out of place. Entering the omega rule in a sequent proof occupies a single line, and so proofs involving this rule will be finite. Granted the hypothesis list {Ay/x: y∈Var} is more likely than not infinite (though it depends on the language). But (∀∞) is no different from the other ND rules in being defined over arguments with (potentially) infinite hypothesis sets.

However, there is still a problem with S∀∞ to be faced. The Finitary Lemma of Section 4.3 no longer can be proven, since in languages with infinitely many variables, (∀∞) is no longer finitary. We used the Finitary Lemma in one place to prove the Cut Lemma, which in turn was needed to show the [S] Adequacy Theorem (Section 4.3), that is, that a system is always adequate with respect to its canonical model. This in turn was used in many ways, for example, to show completeness and to show negative results on expressive power. In order to deploy this tool for S∀∞, there must be a way to establish the Cut Lemma without the help of the Finitary Lemma. The solution will be simply to adopt the relevant cut rule (Cut∞) directly by stipulating that it is one of the structural rules.

(Cut∞) If H ⊢ A for each A in G, and G ⊢ C, then H ⊢ C.

Therefore the structural rules of S∀∞ consist of those found in Section 3.1 plus (Cut∞). Since an application of (Cut∞) requires the derivation of a potential infinity of arguments, we have not avoided the problem that proofs in S∀∞ may fail to be finite. Note that we must pay this cost in order to obtain any result that appeals to the Cut Lemma; however, expression results in this section do not depend on it.

It is easy to show that the natural semantics for S∀∞ picks out exactly the substitution interpretation of the quantifier.

Theorem 14.9 S∀∞ expresses ‖s∀‖.

Proof. We must show that V is a model of S∀∞ iff V obeys ‖s∀‖. The proof from left to right (soundness) is straightforward, and for the proof from left to right (forcing) assume that V is a model of S∀∞ and prove ‖s∀‖ as follows. To show ‖s∀‖ from left to right assume $v(\forall xA)=t$. From (∀ Out) we have $\forall xA \vDash_V A^y/x$, for any variable y, and so we have $v(A^y/x)=t$ for any variable y as desired. Now suppose that $v(A^y/x)=t$ for each variable y. Then by (∀∞), and $v(\{A^y/x: y \in Var\})=t$, we have $v(\forall xA)$ as desired.   □

Even when the omega rule is present, thus forcing the substitution interpretation of the quantifier, it does not follow that ∃ takes on the substitution interpretation – at least not in natural deduction systems, where negation has the intuitionistic reading. It is not difficult to show that ‖s∀‖, together with ‖¬‖ and (Def ∃), yields the following truth condition for ∃.

‖∞∃‖ $v(\exists xA)=t$ iff for all v' in V, if $v \leq v'$, then for some y in Var, $v'(A^y/x)=qT$.

To obtain the substitution interpretation for ∃, a stronger set of rules is needed. A system that expresses ‖s∃‖ may be formulated using (∃ Introduction) and (∃∞), the mirror image of (∀∞).

$\|s\exists\|$ $v(\exists xA)=t$ iff for some y in Var, $v(A^y/x)=t$.

($\exists\infty$) $\exists xA \vdash \{A^y/x: y\in Var\}$

Notice, however, that the use of ($\exists\infty$) requires (possibly infinite) sets on the right-hand side, which if employed for ~ forces a classical reading of the propositional connectives.

While systems that use the omega rule face objections on the proof-theoretic side, there is a semantical compensation. Section 14.5 revealed that the sentential interpretation is isomorphic to a semantics where conditions are placed on complex wffs after the truth conditions were defined. This caused some concern about the viability of that semantics. However, in classical systems that adopt the omega rule, the problem is resolved, for both the $\leq$ Lemma and LF Lemma (Section 8.7) can be proven for the substitution interpretation. This means that the definition $\|\leq\|$ of $\leq$ and $\|LF\|$, the classical side condition, can both be recast in forms $\|p\leq\|$ and $\|pLF\|$ that mention the behavior of atomic wffs p only.

$\|p\leq\|$ $v\leq v'$ iff for all atomic wffs p, if $v(p)=t$ then $v'(p)=t$.

$\|pLF\|$ For all atomic wffs p, if $v(p)=f$, then for some $v'\in V$, $v\leq v'$ and $v'(p)=F$.

Let $\|\infty QK\|$ be the classical semantics $\|QL\|$ save that $\|s\forall\|$ is the quantifier truth condition. Then the next lemma ensures that the conditions on complex wffs above are equivalent to their atomic versions. Therefore an isomorphism result is available for $\|\infty QK\|$ with respect to a standard semantics where models are defined by conditions on the behavior of atomic wffs. The next lemma provides the crucial steps in that reasoning.

∞QK Lemma. If $<V, <>$ obeys $\|\infty QK\|$, then V obeys $\|p\leq\|$ iff it obeys $\|\leq\|$, and presuming that $\|\leq\|$ holds, it obeys $\|LF\|$ iff it obeys $\|pLF\|$.

Proof. It is sufficient to show that if V obeys $\|p\leq\|$ then it obeys $\|\leq\|$, and if it obeys $\|\leq\|$ and $\|pLF\|$, then it obeys $\|LF\|$. The proof is by induction on the form of A. The cases other than the one for the universal quantifier are given in the $\leq$ Lemma (Section 5.4) and the LF Lemma (Section 8.7). For wffs of the form $\forall xAx$, the reasoning goes as follows:

$\|\leq\|$. Suppose $v(\forall xAx)=t$ and $v\leq v'$ (where $\leq$ is defined by $\|p\leq\|$), and show v' $(\forall xAx)=t$ as follows. By $\|s\forall\|$, $v(A^y/x)=t$ for each $y\in Var$. By the hypothesis of the induction, $v'(A^y/x)=t$, for each $y\in Var$. So $v'(\forall xAx)=t$ follows by $\|s\forall\|$.

$\|LF\|$. Suppose $v(\forall xAx)=f$, and show that for some $v' \in V$, if $v \leq v'$ $v'(\forall xAx)=F$ as follows. By $\|s\forall\|$ and $v(\forall xAx)=f$, there is a $y \in Var$, such that $v(A^y/x)=f$. By the hypothesis of the induction, there is a $v' \in V$ such that $v \leq v'$ and $v'(A^y/x)=F$. It follows from $\|s\forall\|$ that $v'(\forall xAx)=F$.   □

14.10 Hacking's program and the omega rule

In his famous paper "What is Logic?" Hacking (1979) begins with classical presuppositions, and then asks where one should draw the line between logical and extra-logical formal systems. Multiple conclusion sequent systems are central to his discussion. This makes sense, since those systems are the ones that express the classical readings of the connectives. (See the GPL Expression Theorem of Section 11.1.) However, when he turns to the rules for the quantifiers, Hacking is faced with a problem. The rule ($\forall$Right), for example, includes a side condition stating that the variable from which $\forall xA$ is to be generalized may not appear free in the conclusion.

($\forall$Right)

$$\frac{H \vdash A, G}{H \vdash \forall xA, G}$$ provided x appears free in neither H nor G.

Given his preference for extensional systems, Hacking felt he must reject generalization rules for $\forall$ that involve side conditions. The results of Section 14.6 show that he was right about this, for the natural semantics for the multiple conclusion formulation of classical predicate logic is inescapably intensional. The only generalization rule that is free of side conditions is the omega rule, which expresses an extensional truth condition $\|s\forall\|$. So Hacking is forced to adopt the omega rule and must count as logical a system stronger than the standard first-order finitary formulation.

This choice is costly in at least two respects. The idea that logical consequence is no longer compact, and that the notion of proof transcends what can be understood by finite minds, will go down hard for almost anyone who takes seriously the idea that what counts as a proof should be epistemologically accessible. Second, Hacking's adoption of the omega rule means he is saddled with the substitution interpretation of the quantifier. In this he differs from the opinion of almost everyone else who hopes to vindicate classical predicate logic. The standard line is to adopt the objectual interpretation of the quantifiers. Here the omega rule is invalid in models where the objects referred to by the terms do not exhaust the domain. The choice of the objectual interpretation is crucial for anyone with an intention to employ predicate logic to generate theories that quantify over superdenumerable infinites such as a continuum of points in space-time. By requiring the substitution interpretation, Hacking threatens the project of formalizing scientific theories in an extensional logic, especially if one thinks that quantification determines one's ontology. Oddly, Hacking's program requires a reading of the quantifier that is incompatible with standard doctrine adopted by almost everyone with extensionalist sympathies.

One might try to exit the dilemma by appealing to the Lowenheim–Skolem Theorem. Since any theory of predicate logic always has a denumerable model, one might claim that there is no need to worry about the divide between the substitution interpretation and the objectual interpretation. It could even be argued that the Lowenheim–Skolem theorem shows that first-order logic underdetermines the very concepts needed to draw a distinction between denumerable and superdenumerable domains.

However, an appeal to the Lowenheim–Skolem theorem will not help in the present context. Remember that the normal practice when one adopts the substitution interpretation is to modify the definition of validity so that the omega rule is rejected. (See Section 14.2.) It is only under these circumstances that a difference between the objectual and substitution interpretations is eliminated. (See Garson (1979) where it is shown that the Lowenheim–Skolem theorem holds iff replacement of the substitution interpretation with the objectual interpretation fails to affect the class of valid arguments, assuming modified notion of validity that invalidates the omega rule.) However, Hacking accepts the omega rule. Since the objectual interpretation rejects that rule, Hacking's logic rejects the objectual interpretation flat out. No appeal to the Lowenheim–Skolem theorem can block that disturbing outcome.

The moral of the story is that an extensionalist account of quantification is in serious trouble. That dovetails nicely with lessons learned from the natural semantics for quantification. This chapter shows that the standard quantifier rules S$\forall$ express truth conditions for $\forall$ that are essentially intensional. Once that is clear, one has good reason to abandon Hacking's losing game of trying to find the right extensional logic of quantification.

14.11 Proofs of theorems in Chapter 14

Theorem 14.1 $H \vdash_{S\forall/} C$ iff $H \vdash_{S\forall} C$.

Proof. It is easy to see that any argument provable in $S\forall$ is provable in $S\forall/$, for ($\forall$ Elimination) and ($\forall$ Introduction) are special cases of their counterparts in $S\forall/$, and (y/x Introduction) is derived by applying ($\forall/$ Introduction) to $H \vdash A$, followed by ($\forall/$ Elimination). To show that any argument provable in $S\forall/$ is also provable in $S\forall$, first show $\forall x A \vdash A^y/x$, by applying ($\forall$ Elimination) and then (Sub) to $\forall x A \vdash \forall x A$. (Here, the subscript '$S\forall$' for '$\vdash$' is understood.) Then ($\forall/$ Elimination) follows from $H \vdash \forall x A$ by (Restricted Cut). To show the derivability of ($\forall/$ Introduction) in $S\forall$, prove the following argument allowing change of bound variables when y is not free in A: $\forall y A^y/x \vdash \forall x A$.

$\forall y A^y/x \vdash \forall y A^y/x$

$\forall y A^y/x \vdash A^y/x$ ($\forall$Elimination)

$\forall y A^y/x \vdash A^y/x^x/y$ (Sub), y is not free in $\forall y A^y/x$

$\forall y A^y/_x \vdash A$ since y is not free in A, $A = A^y/x^x/y$

$\forall y A^y/x \vdash \forall x A$ ($\forall$ Introduction)

($\forall/$ Introduction) is then shown derivable in $S\forall x$ as follows. Presuming $H \vdash A^y/x$ and y is free in neither H nor $\forall x A$, first apply ($\forall$ Introduction) to obtain $H \vdash \forall y A^y/x$. Since y is not free in $\forall x A$ it is not free in A, hence from (Restricted Cut) and $\forall y A^y/x \vdash \forall x A$, it follows that $H \vdash \forall x A$ as desired.   □

Theorem 14.3 $S\forall$ does not express $\|s\forall\|$, nor does it express $\|d\forall\|$.

Proof. We show that $S\forall$ forces neither $\|s\forall\|$ nor $\|d\forall\|$ by constructing a model of $S\forall$ that violates $\|s\forall\|$ and an objectual model $<D, V>$ of $S\forall$ that violates $\|d\forall\|$. Consider $[S\forall]$ the canonical model for $S\forall$, that is, the set consisting of all valuations over wffs of a given language L that satisfy $S\forall$. By the [S] Adequacy Theorem of Section 4.3, $[S\forall]$ is a model of $S\forall$. Note that there is a member v^* of $[S\forall]$ which disobeys $\|s\forall\|$. The set $\{A^y/x:$ y is a variable of L$\} \cup \{\sim\forall x A\}$ is consistent in $S\forall$, and the set e of all wffs B such that $\{A^y/x:$ y is a variable of L$\} \cup \{\sim\forall x A\} \vdash B$ is deductively closed and so a member of $[S\forall]$. The set e contains A^y/x for each variable y, but does not contain $\forall x A$ on pain of inconsistency. The representing function for set e is a classical valuation v^* which disobeys $\|s\forall\|$. So v^* is the desired member of $[S\forall]$ that violates $\|s\forall\|$. To construct an objectual model <D, V> that violates $\|d\forall\|$ simply let D be the set of all variables of L, and use v^* again. ☐

Theorem 14.4.1 S∀- expresses $\|\forall\|$.

Proof. To show that S∀- is sound for $\|\forall\|$, assume that V obeys $\|\forall\|$ and show that (∀ Elimination) and (∀ Introduction) preserve V-validity as follows.

(∀ Elimination). Assume $H \vDash_V \forall xA$, and show $H \vDash_V A$ by assuming v is any member of V such that v(H)=t and proving v(A)=t as follows. From v(H)=t and $H \vDash_V \forall xA$, we have that v(∀xA)=t. By $v \leq_x v$ and $\|\forall\|$, we have v(A)=t as desired.

(∀ Introduction). Assume $H \vDash_V A$, and that x is not free in H, and suppose that $H \nvDash_V \forall xA$ for reductio. Then v(H)=t and v(∀xA)=f. By $\|\forall\|$, for some v' in V such that $v \leq_x v'$, v'(A)=f. But v(H)=t and no free x occurs in H, so v'(H)=t and in light of $H \vDash_V A$, v'(A)=t, which conflicts with v'(A)=f.

To show that S∀- forces $\|\forall\|$, assume V is a model of S∀-, and show $\|\forall\|$ as follows. To show $\|\forall\|$ left to right, assume v(∀xA)=t and $v \leq_x v'$ and show v'(A)=t as follows. Since $v \leq_x v'$ and x is not free in ∀xA it follows that v'(∀xA)=t. By (∀ Elimination) we have $\forall xA \vdash_{S\forall-} A$, and since S∀- preserves V validity, $\forall xA \vDash_V A$. Since v'(∀xA)=t, we have v'(A)=t as desired.

To show $\|\forall\|$ right to left, assume v(∀xA)=f and demonstrate that there is a member v' of V such that $v \leq_x v'$ and v'(A)=f as follows. Let Hv be the set {B: v(B)=t and B does not contain free x}. Since V is a model of S∀-, (∀ Introduction) preserves V-validity. The contrapositive of this, together with the fact that x is not free in Hv, yields the following.

$$\text{If } Hv \nvDash_V \forall xA, \text{ then } Hv \nvDash_V A.$$

Since v(Hv)=t and v(∀xA)=f, the antecedent of this holds, and so Hv $\nvDash_V$ A. So there is a valuation v' in V such that v'(Hv)=t and v'(A)=f. But when v'(Hv)=t, it follows that for every wff B such that v(B)=t and B contains no free x, v'(B)=t. This means that $v \leq_x v'$, so v' is the desired valuation such that $v \leq_x v'$ and v'(A)=f. ☐

Theorem 14.4.3 (Sub) expresses $\|Sub\|$.

Proof. To show that (Sub) is sound for $\|Sub\|$, assume V obeys $\|Sub\|$ and show V is a model of (Sub) as follows. Assume $H \vDash_V A$ and that x does not appear in H. Show $H \vDash_V A^y/x$, by deriving a contradiction from $H \nvDash_V A^y/x$. From $H \nvDash A^y/x$, it follows that for some v in V, $v(H){=}t$ and $v(A^y/x){=}f$. From $\|Sub\|$ it follows that for some v' in V, $v{\leq}_x v'$ and $v'(A){=}f$. Since x does not appear in H, $v'(H){=}t$, and $v'(A){=}t$ follows from $H \vDash_V A$. But $v'(A){=}t$ contradicts $v'(A){=}f$.

To show that (Sub) forces $\|Sub\|$, assume $v(A^y/x){=}f$, and let Hv be the set {B: $v(B){=}t$ and B does not contain free x}. V is a model of (Sub), and since Hv does not contain free x, we have the following.

$$\text{If } Hv \nvDash_V A^y/x, \text{ then } Hv \nvDash_V A.$$

Since $v(Hv){=}t$ and $v(A^y/x){=}f$, the antecedent of this holds, and so $Hv \nvDash_V A$. So there is a valuation v' in V such that $v'(Hv){=}t$ and $v'(A){=}f$. But when $v'(Hv){=}t$, it follows that $v{\leq}_x v'$, so v' is the desired valuation such that $v{\leq}_x v'$ and $v'(A){=}f$. □

Quantified Path Isomorphism Theorem. V obeys $\|I\lor\forall\|$ iff $<V, \leq>$ is isomorphic to some quantified path model.

Proof. The proof follows the strategy of the Path Isomorphism Theorem of Section 7.5.

For the proof from left to right, assume V obeys $\|I\lor\forall\|$, and construct a quantified path model $U = <W, \subseteq, N, X, u>$ by setting W to V, $\subseteq$ to $\leq$, and each member $\subseteq_x$ of X to $\leq_x$, and defining N so that vNP holds iff P is a path bundle through v, and u so that $u(v, p){=}v(p)$ for atoms p. Clearly $U{=}<V, \leq, N, X, u>$ is a neighborhood model. Once the isomorphism between U and V is proven, it will follow that U is the desired quantified path model isomorphic to V. To show that $<V, \leq>$ is isomorphic to the model $U{=}<V, \leq, N, X, u>$, all that remains is to show that $v(A){=}t$ iff $v \vDash^U A$. This is shown by induction on the length of A. Cases for connectives other than $\forall$ proceed as in the Path Isomorphism Theorem, and the case for $\forall$ is easy in light of the fact that $\subseteq_x$ is $\leq_x$ for each variable x.

It remains to show that $U{=}<V, \leq, N, u>$ is a quantified path model. The demonstration that U obeys $(\subseteq)$ and (N) is given in the Path Isomorphism Theorem, so all that remains is to show (Sub) and (X).

(Sub) If $w \nvDash Ay/x$, then for some w' in W, $w \subseteq_x w'$ and $w' \nvDash A$.

But (Sub) follows immediately in light of $\|Sub\|$, $v(A){=}t$ iff $v \vDash^U A$, and the identification of $\subseteq_x$ with $\leq_x$. (X) follows in the same way.

For the proof of the theorem from right to left, what is needed is to show that when V is isomorphic to a quantified path model, then V obeys $\|I\lor\forall\|$. So assume that V is isomorphic to a quantified path model $<W, \subseteq, N, X, u>$. That means there is a 1–1 mapping $*$ from V into W such that $*$ is *faithful*, which means that $v \leq v'$ iff $v^* \subseteq v'^*$, $v \leq_x v'$ iff $v^* \subseteq_x v'^*$, and $v(A) = t$ iff $v^* \vDash A$, for any wff A. Each of the truth conditions $\|\perp\|$, $\|\&\|$, $\|\leftrightarrow\|$, $\|\neg\|$, $\|\vee\|$ of $\|\mathbf{I}v\|$ is shown as in the Path Isomorphism Theorem of Section 7.5. What remains is the case for $\|\forall\|$. By (K∀), we have for all w in W:

$w \vDash \forall xA$ iff for every w' in W, if $w \subseteq_x w'$, then $w' \vDash A$.

Since $*$ is 1–1, it follows that $W = \{v^*: v \in V\}$, and so we may write:

$v^* \vDash \forall xA$ iff for all v' in V, if $v^* \subseteq_x v'^*$, then $v'^* \vDash A$.

But $*$ is faithful, so we have $\|\forall\|$ as desired.

$\|\forall\|$ $v(\forall xA) = t$ iff for all v' in V, if $v \leq_x v'$ then $v'(A) = t$.

To complete the theorem, we must show $\|\leq\|$, $\|\leq_x\|$, and $\|Sub\|$ all hold. This follows in light of the faithfulness of $*$ together with ($\subseteq$), (X), and (Sub). We illustrate in the case of (Sub).

(Sub)   If $w \nvDash A^y/x$, then for some w' in W, $w \subseteq_x w'$ and $w' \nvDash A$.

Since $*$ is 1–1 we may rewrite (Sub) as follows.

If $v^* \nvDash A^y/x$, then for some v' in V, $v^* \subseteq_x v'^*$ and $v'^* \nvDash A$.

Since $*$ is faithful, we obtain $\|Sub\|$ as desired.

$\|Sub\|$ If $v(A^y/x) = f$, then for some v' in V, $v \leq_x v'$ and $v'(A) = f$.   □

Theorem 14.6.1 G∀ expresses $\|G\forall\|$.

Proof. We must show that V is a model of G∀ iff V obeys $\|G\forall\|$. The reader can easily check soundness (the proof from right to left).

For the proof from left to right (forcing), assume V is a model of G∀, and show $\|\forall=\|$ and $\|GSub\|$ as follows. For $\|\forall=\|$ left to right, assume $v(\forall xA) = t$ and $v =_x v'$, and demonstrate $v'(A) = t$ as follows. $\forall xA$ contains no free x, so $v'(\forall xA) = t$. We have $\forall xA \vDash_V A$ and so $v'(A) = t$ as desired. For $\|\forall=\|$ right to left, assume v $(\forall xA) = f$. Let $Hv = \{B: x$ is not free in B and $v(B) = t\}$. Similarly $Gv = \{B: x$ is not free in B and $v(B) = f\}$. We have $Hv, \nvDash_V \forall xA, Gv$, and since x is not free in Hv or Gv, it follows from the fact that (∀Right) preserves V-validity that $Hv \nvDash_V A, Gv$. So there is a member v' of V such that $v'(Hv)$=t, $v'(Gv)$=f and $v'(A)$=f. Since $v'(Hv)$ =t and $v'(Gv)$=f, v' agrees with v on all values of wffs B that fail to contain free x, so $v=_x v'$, and v' is the desired valuation such that $v=_x v'$ and $v'(A)$=t.

To show that (GSub) forces ||GSub||, let v be any member of V and let x and y be any two variables, and define Hv, and Gv as follows: Hv={B: $v(B^y/x)$=t} and Gv={B: $v(B^y/x)$=f}. Then $v(Hv^y/x)$=t and $v(B)$=f for every B in Gv^y/x. (The reason for $v(Hv^y/x)$=t is this. Let C be any member of Hv^y/x and prove $v(C)$=t as follows. C must be D^y/x for some $D \in Hv$. But by the definition of Hv, $v(D^y/x)$=t=$v(C)$. Similar reasoning establishes $v(Gv^y/x)$=f.) So we have $Hv^y/x \not\vDash_V Gv^y/x$, and since (GSub) preserves V-validity, Hv $\not\vDash_V$ Gv. Therefore, for some v' in V, $v'(Hv)$=t and $v'(B)$=f, for every member B of Gv. This means that $v'=v^y/x$, for when $v(B^y/x)$=t, B $\in$ Hv and $v'(B)$=t. Similarly, when $v(B^y/x)$=f, B $\in$ Gv and $v'(B)$=f. So $v'(B) = v(B^y/x)$ for each wff B. Hence $v'=v^y/x$ is a member of V as desired. □

Theorem 14.7 There are models that obey ||GPL∀|| that are not referential.

Proof. Assume for reductio that every model V that obeys ||GPL∀|| is refer-ential. Consider the objectual model <D, V> where D=Var. It will follow that whenever ||GPL∀|| holds for V that ||d∀|| holds as well.

||d∀|| $v(\forall xA)$=t iff for every d in D, $v(A^d/x)$=t.

Here is why. Given V obeys ||GPL∀||, we know ||∀=|| and ||GSub|| hold of V. We then demonstrate that the right-hand sides of ||∀=|| and ||d∀|| are equivalent as follows.

||∀=|| $v(\forall xA)$=t iff for all v' in V, if $v=_x v'$, then $v'(A)$=t.

Assume the right-hand side of ||∀=||, and let d be any member of D. Then since D=Var, d is some variable y. We know from ||GSub|| that v^y/x is in V. Valuations v and v^y/x agree on all wffs that contain no free x, so $v=_x v^y/x$. From the right-hand side of ||∀=||, $v^y/x(A)$=t, hence $v(A^y/x)=v(A^d/x)$=t. Now assume the right-hand side of ||d∀|| and let v' be any member of V such that $v=_x v'$. Then since ||GPL∀|| is referential, for some d∈D $v'=v^d/x$, which means $v'=v^y/x$ for some variable y. By the right-hand side of ||d∀|| $v(A^y/x)$=t. This means that $v^y/x(A)$=t and since $v'=v^y/x$ we have $v'(A)$=t as desired.

Therefore ∀ takes on the objectual interpretation in any model <D, V> such that D=Var and V obeys ||GPL∀||. But that means V obeys ||s∀||, the substitution interpretation and the sentential interpretation ||∀=|| simultaneously. We also know from Theorem 14.6.2 that the V-validity of (∀ Introduction) is preserved for any V obeying ‖∀=‖. However, by Theorem 14.6.3, there is a model V obeying ‖s∀‖ (which, as we just said, just amounts to ‖∀=‖) such that that V-validity of (∀ Introduction) is not preserved. This completes the reductio, so we conclude that not all models of ‖GPL∀‖ are referential.   □

Theorem 14.8.1 S∃ expresses ‖S∃‖.

Proof. We leave the proof of soundness to the reader. To show that S∃ forces ‖S∃‖, assume that the rules of S∃ preserve V-validity and show ‖W∃‖ as follows. For the proof from left to right, assume $v(\exists xA)=t$, $v(C)=f$, and x is not free in C, and show for some v' in V, $v \leq_x v'$ and $v'(C)=f$ and $v'(A)=t$ as follows. Let Hv = {B: x is not free in B and $v(B)=t$}. Establish Hv ⊨$_v$ ∃xA using $v(\exists xA)=t$ and the fact that x is not free in Hv. Note that Hv ⊭$_v$ C. So by the fact that (∃ Elimination) preserves V-validity, we have Hv, A ⊭$_v$ C. Hence there is a member v' of V such that $v'(Hv)=t$ (hence $v \leq_x v'$), $v'(A)=t$ and $v'(C)=f$, and v' is the desired valuation. For the proof from right to left, assume $v(\exists xA)=f$, and show that for some C containing no free x, $v(C)=f$, and for every v' such that $v \leq_x v'$ and $v'(C)=f$, then $v'(A)=f$, as follows. Let C be ∃xA. Assume $v \leq_x v'$ and v' (∃xA)=f. Use A ⊨$_v$ ∃xA to establish $v'(A)=f$, so that v' is the desired valuation. □

QL Expression Theorem. QL expresses ‖QL‖.

Proof. We must show V is a model of QL iff V obeys ‖QL‖.
Proof of Soundness. Assume V obeys ‖QL‖ and show that the rules of QL preserve V-validity as follows. The demonstration for rules other than those of S∃ follows from the **I** Theorem of Section 8.1, and the S∀ Expression Theorem of Section 14.4. What remains to show is that (∃ Elimination) and (∃ Introduction) preserve V-validity.

(∃ **Elimination**). Assume H ⊨$_v$ ∃xA, and H, A ⊨$_v$ C, and that x is free in neither H nor C. Now show that H ⊨$_v$ C by reductio. From H ⊭$_v$ C it follows that for some v in V, $v(H)=t$ and $v(C)=f$. Given H ⊨$_v$ ∃xA, it follows that $v(\exists xA)=t$. By ‖LF‖ (See Section 8.7) and $v(C)=f$, it follows that for some v' such that $v \leq v'$, $v'(C)=F$. By ‖q∃‖, and $v \leq v'$, it follows that for some v'' in V such that $v' \leq_x v''$, $v''(A)=qT$. By the qT Lemma of Section 8.7, there must be some u∈V such that $v'' \leq u$ and $u(A)=t$. By $v(H)=t$, $v \leq v'$, $v' \leq_x v''$, $v'' \leq u$ and the fact that x is not free in H, it follows that $u(H)=t$. From $u(A)=t$ and H,

A $\vDash_V$ C, we have u(C)=t. By $v'\leq_x v''$, $v''\leq u$, the fact that x is not free in C and $v'(C)$=F it follows that u(C)=f, a contradiction.

($\exists$ **Introduction**). Assume H $\vDash_V$ A and show that H $\vDash_V$ $\exists$xA by assuming that v is any member of V such that v(H)=t, and proving that v($\exists$xA)=t as follows. In light of $\|q\exists\|$, v($\exists$xA)=t will follow if we demonstrate that whenever $v\leq v'$, for some v'' in V, $v'=_x v''$ and $v''(A)$=qT. So let v' be any member of V such that $v\leq v'$. From H $\vDash_V$ A and v(H)=t, it follows that v(A)=t. Hence by $v\leq v'$, $v'(A)$ =t. So there is a v'' such that $v'\leq_x v''$ (namely v' itself) where $v'(A)$=t. Since $v'(A)$ =t, $v'(A)$=qT as desired.

Proof that QL forces $\|QL\|$. Show that when the rules of QL preserve V-validity, V obeys $\|QL\|$. The proof that V obeys conditions of $\|QL\|$ other than $\|q\exists\|$ follows from the qPL Expression Theorem of Section 8.7 and the S$\forall$ Theorem, so all that remains is to show that when the rules of QL preserves V-validity, $\|q\exists\|$ holds.

Proof of $\|q\exists\|$ from left to right. Assume that v($\exists$xA)=t, and $v\leq v'$ for an arbitrary member v' of V, and show that there is a member v'' of V such that $v'\leq_x v''$ and $v''(A)$=qT as follows. Since v' is a valuation, there is a wff C such that $v'(C)$=f. Let $H_{v'}$ = {B: B contains no free x and $v'(B)$=t}. Given x is not free in $\exists$xA, it follows that $H_{v'}$ $\vDash_V$ $\exists$xA. But we also have $v'(H_{v'})$=t and $v'(C)$=f, so $H_{v'}$ $\nvDash_V$ C. It follows from the fact that ($\exists$ Elimination) preserves V-validity that $H_{v'}$, A $\nvDash_V$ C. So there must be a valuation v'' such that $v''(H_{v'}, A)$=t and $v''(C)$=f. Because $v''(H_{v'})$=t, it follows that $v'\leq_x v''$. Since $v''(A)$=t, $v''(A)$=qT. So v'' is the desired member of V such that $v'\leq_x v''$ and $v''(A)$=qT.

Proof of $\|q\exists\|$ from right to left. Assume that if $v\leq v'$ then for some v'' in V, $v'\leq_x v''$ and $v''(A)$=qT, and show that v($\exists$xA)=t as follows. By the contra-positive (CLF) of $\|LF\|$, it will be sufficient for proving v($\exists$xA)=t to show that for any $v'\in V$ if $v\leq v'$, then $v'(\exists xA)\neq$F.

(CLF) If for all $v'\in V$, if $v\leq v'$ then $v'(A)\neq$F, then v(A)=t.

So let v' be any member of V such that $v\leq v'$ and show $v'(\exists xA)\neq$F as follows. By our initial assumption and $v\leq v'$, we have for some v'' in V, $v'\leq_x v''$ and $v''(A)$=qT. By the qT Lemma, for some u in V, $v''\leq u$ and u(A)=t. Since the V-validity of the rules of PL is preserved, all provable arguments of QL are V-valid including A $\vdash_{QL}$ $\exists$xA. Hence A $\vDash_V$ $\exists$xA, and so by u(A)=t, it follows that u($\exists$xA)=t. By transitivity of $\leq$, $v'\leq u$. Therefore $v'(\exists xA)\neq$F as desired. $\square$

15 The natural semantics of vagueness (with Joshua D. K. Brown)

(This chapter draws heavily from Brown and Garson (in preparation).)

Timothy Williamson (1994, p. 142 and elsewhere) presents a number of powerful arguments against supervaluationist treatments of vagueness. In light of the failure of those and other accounts that do not preserve classical logic, Williamson concludes that the only tenable theory of vagueness is epistemic. His view adopts the counterintuitive thesis that there are facts of the matter as to whether a borderline case counts as (for example) being bald, and that our inability to decide such a case is simply the reflection of limitations in our knowledge of that reality.

This chapter shows that ‖QL‖, the natural semantics for classical predicate logic, provides a semantics for vagueness that preserves the core intuition behind supervaluationism, namely that some sentences are undecided in truth value (Section 15.2). However, ‖QL‖ faces none of the problems put forward by Williamson (Section 15.3). Once this alternative to supervaluations is in place, pressures for accepting an epistemological account of vagueness can be resisted (Section 15.4).

Four major objections to supervaluations given by Williamson are these. (1) Although supervaluations preserve the theorems of classical propositional logic, natural deduction rules such as ($\rightarrow$ Introduction), ($\sim$ Introduction), and ($\vee$ Elimination) must be rejected, and this flies in the face of the widespread applicability of these rules in mathematics and science. (2) Despite machinery allowing sentences to be undecided, supervaluationists are still forced to accept some claims of excessive precision. For example, they must accept the existential claim that for some number i, having i hairs qualifies one as bald, while having i+1 qualifies one as not bald. (3) Supervaluations cannot give a coherent account of second-order vagueness, for any coherent logic of determination undermines it. (4) Acceptance of the classical principle of Excluded Middle entails that there is no room for undecided

truth-values, unless supervaluations abandon the disquotational principle –
Tarski's Convention T.

While Williamson is right that supervaluations suffer from most of these
problems, they are all solved using the natural semantics $\|QL\|$ (or natural
semantics for short). Natural semantics provides just what we need for a
good account of vagueness – one that takes vagueness to be more than a
reflection of our epistemological limitations, but an essential feature of the
interpretation for the connectives expressed by classical logic.

15.1 Formal preliminaries

In this chapter, we show how to deploy $\|QL\|$ to provide an acceptable logic
of vagueness. In order to formalize arguments about the number of hairs on
a bald man's head, let us introduce to the language L the constant 0 (for zero)
and the functional symbol s (for successor of) and the predicate letter B (to
abbreviate: 'a person with ___ hairs on his/her head is bald'). We will call 0,
s(0), s(s(0)), ... the *numerals* of L. The *terms* of L are the variables or numerals
of L. For ease of exposition, we will make use of standard notation for
numbers 'B1', 'B2', 'Bx+1', etc. in place of the corresponding notation
using s. We write 'i<j' when numeral i is shorter than j, that is, when i
indicates a number smaller than the one j does. It is helpful to collect
together the conditions that make up $\|QL\|$ in one place. When a set of
valuations V obeys $\|QL\|$, V obeys the following, for any valuation v in V,
for all wffs A and B, where $\leq$ is defined by $\|<\|$.

$\|\leq\|$	$v \leq v'$ iff for all wffs A of L, if $v(A)=t$, then $v'(A)=t$.
$\|LF\|$	If $v(A)=f$, then for some v' in V, $v \leq v'$ and $v'(A)=F$.
$\|\&\|$	$v(A\&B)=t$ iff $w(A)=t$ and $w(B)=t$.
$\|\rightarrow\|$	$v(A \rightarrow B)=t$ iff for all v' in V, if $v \leq v'$, then $v'(A)=f$ or $v'(B)=t$.
$\|\neg\|$	$v(\sim A)=t$ iff for all v' in V, if $v \leq v'$, then $v'(A)=f$.
$\|\leftrightarrow\|$	$v(A \leftrightarrow B)=t$ iff for all v' in V, if $v \leq v'$, then $v'(A)=v'(B)$.
$\|q\vee\|$	$v(A \vee B)=t$ iff for all v' in V, if $v \leq v'$, then $v'(A)=qT$ or $v'(B)=qT$.
$\|\forall\|$	$v(\forall xA)=t$ iff for every v' in V, if $v \leq_x v'$, then $v'(A)=t$.
$\|q\exists\|$	$v(\exists xA)=t$ iff for all v' in V, if $v \leq v'$, then for some v'' in V, $v' \leq_x v''$ and $v''(A)=qT$.
$\|Sub\|$	If $v(A^n/x)=f$, then for some v' in V, $v \leq_x v'$ and $v'(A)=f$, for any term n of L.

As a reminder, here are the definitions for determined values T, F, U, and qT, as these ideas are also central to the discussion. (Here, 'v' ranges over a given model V.)

(DefT) $v(A)=T$ iff for all $v'\in V$, if $v\leq v'$, then $v'(A)=t$.

(DefF) $v(A)=F$ iff for all $v'\in V$, if $v\leq v'$, then $v'(A)=f$.

(DefU) $v(A)=U$ iff neither $v(A)=T$ nor $v(A)=F$.

(DefqT) $v(A)=qT$ iff $v(A)\neq F$, that is, for some v' in V, $v\leq v'$ and $v'(A)=t$.

The following results, most of which were developed in Section 10.2, will help with what is to come.

(t=T) $v(A)=T$ iff $v(A)=t$.

(t=T) tells us that truth and determined truth are the same thing in $\|QL\|$. This is a point of difference between $\|QL\|$ and supervaluation semantics, where truth and supertruth are distinguished. (Note that the proof of (t=T) follows directly from the definition $\|\leq\|$ of $\leq$, and the fact that $\leq$ is therefore reflexive.)

$\|\sim F\|$ $v(\sim A)=t$ iff $v(A)=F$.

$\|\sim F\|$ is just the truth condition for $\sim$ simplified using the notation '$v(A)=F$'. It will be important for what follows to decide whether '$v(A)=F$' or '$v(A)=f$' corresponds to the English 'A is false at v'. $\|\sim F\|$ shows that negation is tied to being determined false, not to having the value f. Therefore we must associate '$v(A)=F$' with the claim that A is false. Saying A is f says something else, for it amounts to the claim that A is either (determined) false or undetermined.

U Lemma. $v(A)=U$ iff both $v(A)=f$ and $v(\sim A)=f$.

The U Lemma says that an undetermined sentence is simply one for which neither it nor its negation is true. As a result, any valuation where A is U is one where $\sim A$ is also U.

Excluded Middle Lemma. $v(A\lor\sim A)=T$.

This lemma entails a key feature of supervaluation semantics, that Excluded Middle is true even when its disjuncts are undetermined. This follows directly from the truth conditions for $\lor$ and $\sim$.

15.2 How vagueness is handled in natural semantics

We may think of the relation $\leq$ as representing the process of being more precise about the extensions of vague predicates. Remember Bi abbreviates the sentence 'a person with i hairs on his/her head is bald'. Since 'is bald' is vague, there is a subrange of atoms Bi, ..., Bk in the series B0, B1, B2, ... that are undetermined because there is no clear answer about baldness in these cases. We may reflect this situation with the following assignments: v(Bj)=T when j < i, and v(Bj)=F when j > k and v(Bj)=U otherwise. Think of $\leq$ as representing the process of coming to greater precision about baldness. When v$\leq$u, u may add some true claims to those of v, so that, for example, where before v(Bi)=U and v($\sim$Bk)=U, it might be that u(Bi)=T and u($\sim$Bk)=T. This narrows the range of undetermined sentences concerning baldness, but does not eliminate it. So the precisification expressed by the $\leq$ relation is only partial.

Natural semantics $\|QL\|$ handles the *sorites* paradoxes along the lines of the supervaluation strategy. Faced with the argument from B0 and $\forall$x(Bx$\rightarrow$Bx+1) to Bk, where k indicates more than enough hairs to count one as not bald, the advocate of natural semantics claims the argument is valid, but demonstrates that $\forall$x(Bx$\rightarrow$Bx+1) is not true. Presuming that valuation v admits vagueness, then for some choice of numeral i, v(Bi)=T and v(Bi+1)=U. Therefore v(Bi)=t and v(Bi+1)=f, which by $\|\rightarrow\|$, and the reflexivity of $\leq$, entails v(Bi$\rightarrow$Bi+1)=f. By $\|Sub\|$, it follows that there is a valuation v' such that v$\leq_x$v' and v'(Bx$\rightarrow$Bx+1)=f, and so v($\forall$x(Bx$\rightarrow$Bx+1))=f, by $\|\forall\|$.

That is how natural semantics provides resources for solving the *sorites* puzzle. So it displays the main virtue of the strategy of supervaluationists. On the other hand, it can also resolve the four problems Williamson lodges against them.

15.3 How Williamson's objections are resolved

Although Williamson (1994) has many different objections to supervaluations, it is fair to classify them into four main complaints. Here is a description of each along with its natural semantics solution.

Problem 1

The first problem for supervaluations is that they fail to preserve the validity of the natural deduction rules of PL. As we proved in Section 9.4, Contraposition (CN), Conditional Proof ($\rightarrow$ Introduction), Argument by Cases ($\vee$ Elimination), and Reductio ad Absurdum ($\sim$ Introduction) are all invalid according to supervaluationism. Williamson (2004, p. 120) argues, "if we think of classical logic as comprising those forms of logical inference tried and tested in mainstream mathematics and other branches of science ... the methodological cost of rejecting them is similar (perhaps not identical) to the cost of rejecting [the classical theorems]." Further support for this worry was developed in Section 9.5, where we argued that failure of validity preservation is a symptom of a deeper problem, namely that supervaluations do not provide a coherent interpretation for the connectives.

Of course Williamson's first objection is easy to dispose of in natural semantics. Natural semantics is *defined* by the requirement that the rules preserve validity, so every model that obeys ‖QL‖ preserves the validity of all the classical rules.

Problem 2

The second problem is that supervaluation semantics is forced to count as true existential claims of excessive precision concerning vague predicates. For example, since every precisification in supervaluation semantics completely closes the gap between what is bald and what is not bald, it follows that Bi&~Bi+1 counts as true for some choice of the numeral i in every admissible supervaluation, and so $\exists$x(Bx&~Bx+1) is supertrue, that is, it has the analog of determinate truth. As Williamson rightly argues, our strong intuition that there is no precise boundary between bald and not bald was the motivation for deploying supervaluations in the first place. Although supervaluation semantics may assign Bi undetermined values for various choices of i so as to meet those intuitions in the case of atomic sentences, the fact that it cannot reject the counterintuitive existential claim $\exists$x(Bx&~Bx+1) is troubling.

Natural semantics solves the problem because its version of precisification is partial. (See Shapiro (2008, p. 333) who also recommends partial precisifications, and adopts a truth condition similar to $\|{\to}\|$.) The wff Bi&~Bi+1 need not hold for any numeral i in a given valuation v. For example, Bi+~Bi+1 fails to hold in any valuation that assigns one or more U values in the series B0, B1, ... Assume, for example, that v(Bi)=t for i<k, v(Bk)=U and v(~Bm)=t for m>k. Then for no numeral j does it hold that v(Bj&~Bj+1)=t. The reason is that v(Bj&~Bj+1)=t entails v(Bj)=T and v(Bj+1)=F, and at no point j in the series do the values T and F occur in sequence. Therefore we have an explanation for the intuition that it is wrong to claim that in every valuation there must always be a numeral j such that (Bj&~Bj+1)=t.

We must grant, however, that this does not mean that v rejects ∃x(Bx&~Bx+1) in the example just given. (This point was made clear to us by B. Jacinto.) There we had v(~Bk+1)=t, reflecting the intuition that for some number of hairs k+1 one is definitely not bald. Since the argument B0, ~Bk+1 / ∃x(Bx&~Bx+1) is provable in classical logic, and $\|QL\|$ is sound there, it follows that v(∃x(Bx&Bx+1))=t.

The truth of ∃x(Bx&Bx+1) is problematic for supervaluationists, who presumably accept the objectual or substitution interpretations of the quantifier. On that reading, ∃x(Bx&~Bx+1) asserts the existence of a sharp cutoff between non-baldness and baldness. However, in natural semantics, the truth of ∃x(Bx&Bx+1) does not challenge our intuitions, because here ∃ takes on the quasi-truth reading $\|q\exists\|$. Given $\|q\exists\|$, ∃x(Bx&Bx+1) can be true on v even when there is no number of hairs i such that v(Bi&~Bi+1)=t. So on this reading, v(∃x(Bx&Bx+1))=t does not fly in the face of our intuitions.

What would happen if we were to simply demand that ∃ take the objectual reading so as to match expectations about what we think ∃x(Bx&Bx+1) says? That would amount to adopting a semantics $\|QLd\|$ where the objectual readings $\|d\forall\|$ and $\|d\exists\|$ are chosen. Then in the above example, ∃x(Bx&Bx+1) is false at v, and our intuitions about the lack of a sharp cutoff are vindicated. Note, however, that this means that the argument B0, ~Bk+1 / ∃x(Bx&~Bx+1) comes out $\|QLd\|$-invalid. An adequate logic for $\|QLd\|$ is therefore non-classical. Given Williamson chooses classical logic as the starting point, ∃x(Bx&~Bx+1) (globally) expresses a claim that is too weak to challenge our intuitions about precision. If you insist that ∃x(Bx&Bx+1) takes an objectual reading, however, then you adopt a non-classical logic where ∃x(Bx&Bx+1) can be false. Either way, the problem is resolved. (Notice that even if the omega rule is adopted for ∀, to force the substitution interpretation, the reading of the existential quantifier $\|\infty\exists\|$ is still weaker than the substitution interpretation of $\exists$ (Section 14.9), so the same defense may be employed.)

Problem 3

The third problem for supervaluations is to give a coherent account of second-order vagueness. A problem natural semantics faces is to pacify the intuition that a valuation v that chooses $v(Bj)=T$ and $w(Bj+1)=U$ makes an unacceptably precise decision in the metalanguage about where the boundary between determinate truth and indeterminacy should lie. Given the QL Expression Theorem of Section 14.8, we know that the classical system QL of natural deduction rules provably selects natural semantics $\|QL\|$ as its interpretation. Presuming that we accept QL in our metareasoning as Williamson claims we should, it follows that we have strong and independent evidence that natural semantics gives the correct account of the semantics of connectives of our metalanguage. Therefore it is legitimate to deploy the natural semantics strategy in evaluating such claims as whether $v(A)=t$. Such claims could be determined true, determined false and undetermined in cases where it is not clear exactly where a boundary lies.

One might worry that the distinction between the determined and undetermined is illegitimate. Can we introduce an operator D for determination with a coherent logic? Were we to introduce D in the object language with the truth condition $v(DA)=t$ iff $v(A)=T$, it would follow by (t=T) that DA $\leftrightarrow$ A is $\|QL\|$-valid. Therefore, the modal logic of D for the object language is trivial.

However, the inability to express determination and non-determination in the object language is not a defect, for it does not follow from this that the logic of D is a problem in the metalanguage. The lesson of the truth paradoxes is that definition of truth requires semantic ascent. Why shouldn't the same be true for determinate truth (which, according to (t=T), is the same thing as truth)? If that is cogent, then an operator D characterizing determined truth for the object language sentences is properly located in the metalanguage. Therefore D is a two-place metalinguistic predicate such that $D(v, A)$ holds exactly when $v(A)=T$. Then determined true: $D(v, A)$, determined false: $D(v, \sim A)$, and undetermined: neither $D(v, A)$ nor

D(v, ~A), are all expressed in the metalanguage using D. To secure the idea that a sentence of the form D(v, A) is itself undetermined, we may ascend to the metametalanguage. Iteration of D is not possible in any language, and so questions as to whether the logic of D is or is not S5 are beside the point. This is important because Williamson (1994, pp. 156ff.) uses considerations concerning the iteration principles for the modal operator D to try to establish that supervaluations cannot give a coherent account of second-order vagueness. Given our thesis that determination requires semantic ascent, his worries cannot get off the ground. If complaints about excess precision are lodged at any level, semantic ascent and the use of natural semantics secures an answer at the next level. There is no infinite regress, since a complaint must be lodged in a language at some level, and the response is available in a metalanguage for that language. Therefore, simultaneous deployment of natural semantics at all levels resolves all complaints.

This deployment is more than just an option we choose. It is *required* for anyone (like Williamson) who is committed to classical rules in the metalanguage, and who determines what the semantics for that language should be based on the demand that the rules preserve validity (something on which Williamson insists). As we explained, the semantics generated by this requirement is not classical. It is natural semantics instead. Therefore, there is strong independent evidence to motivate the solution proposed here.

Problem 4

The fourth problem for supervaluation semantics presented by Williamson is an argument that purportedly shows that supertruth is not disquotational, and so fails to satisfy the defining feature of any notion of truth. Choosing truth over supertruth in response undermines the whole point of introducing supervaluations. In natural semantics, this problem can be disposed of instantly. It is guaranteed by (t=T) that truth and determined truth are equivalent. Therefore a disquotational theory of truth entails a corresponding disquotational theory of determined truth.

While this shows that the natural semantics notion of determined truth must be disquotational (presuming truth is), it is still worth reviewing the argument Williamson gives in the case of supervaluations to see why it fails for natural semantics. As will be evident, the similarities between his reasoning and arguments for fatalism reviewed in Section 10.5 is striking. The strategies deployed there to protect ‖PL‖ from fatalist conclusions may be used here to protect ‖QL‖ from Williamson's complaint. (See also Mares (2004, pp. 84–85) for a related refutation of Williamson.)

Let us replace 'T' for 'supertrue' in the presentation of Williamson's argument (1994, pp. 187ff. and pp. 300ff.), which we modify (without changing the core idea) to bring out the similarities with the Ur Argument of Section 10.5. Let m be a function that takes each object language sentence A into its translation m(A) in the metalanguage. Then presuming that v is the relevant point of evaluation for truth, we may express the disquotational principle for determined truth as follows.

(T) m(A) iff v(A)=T.

As a special case of (T), it would seem that we would have (F).

(F) not-m(A) iff v(A)=F.

Since the metalogic is classical, we must accept:

(EM) m(A) or not-m(A).

Furthermore by the classically valid argument ($\vee$ Elimination), (T), (F), and (EM) together yield (No U).

(No U) v(A)=T or v(A)=F.

But this is fatal, since (No U) eliminates the possibility that any sentence is undetermined. Since we cannot reject (EM), and the whole strategy for a logic of vagueness denies (No U), it seems that disquotation has got to go. Summarizing, the argument has the following form.

Williamson Argument

(EM)	m(A) or not-m(A).	Excluded Middle
(T)	m(A) iff v(A)=T.	Disquotation
(F)	not-m(A) iff v(A)=F.	Disquotation
(No U)	Therefore v(A)=T or v(A)=F.	

The mistake in this reasoning may be located by following the strategy presented in Section 10.5. Diagnosis of the argument depends on how we understand: not-m(A). Presuming first that 'not' in 'not-m(A)' is read in the object language, 'not-m(A)' means m(~A). So the argument has the form.

Williamson Or Argument

(~EM)	m(A) or m(~A).	?????
(T)	m(A) iff v(A)=T.	Disquotation
‖~F‖	m(~A) iff v(A)=F.	Disquotation
(No U)	Therefore v(A)=T or v(A)=F.	

However, as we argued in the case of the Or Argument for Fatalism, there is no reason to accept the first premise, as it does not have the form of Excluded Middle. Furthermore, it begs the question in claiming that either the meaning of A or the meaning of ~A is true (hence determined true).

An attempt to solve the problem by bringing negation into the meta-language and adjusting the third premise to ensure that the argument has the form of (∨ Elimination), yields the following.

Williamson Or Not Argument

(EM)	m(A) or not m(A).	Excluded Middle
(T)	m(A) iff v(A)=T.	Disquotation
(notF)	not m(A) iff v(A)=F.	?????
(No U)	Therefore v(A)=T or v(A)=F.	

But now the third premise (notF) is unacceptable. It does not follow from disquotation because disquotation yields m(~A) iff v(~A)=T, which by ‖~F‖ amounts to:

> m(~A) iff v(A)=F.

But to get (notF) from this you need (~ not), which is false.

> (~ not)   m(~A) iff not m(A).

Here is why (~ not) is wrong. According to disquotation,

> not m(A) iff not v(A)=T.

By (t=T), and the fact that not v(A)=t iff v(A)=f, this yields

> not m(A) iff v(A)=f.

In comparison, we had

> m(~A) iff v(A)=F.

The difference on the right-hand sides could not be more apparent. Saying that v(A)=f entails that *either* v(A)=U or v(A)=F, and in natural semantics this is not the same thing as saying v(A)=F, on pain of eliminating the possibility that v(A)=U.

The explanation of Williamson's error is that he either failed to discriminate between the object language '~' and the metalanguage 'not' and/or that he did not credit the possibility that there is a difference between being determined false and merely non-true. Identifying 'not m(A)' with 'm(~A)' amounts to identifying U with F, and this begs the question against natural semantics, and other strategies which propose vagueness in the metalanguage. In one respect, this underscores a point where we agree with Williamson, for it vindicates his suspicion (recorded, for example, in (1994, p. 192)) that any successful treatment of vagueness must be carried out in a vague metalanguage.

15.4 Why vagueness runs deep

One might object that semantics for a language is illegitimate unless its conceptions are determinate. However, this begs the question against those who presume that vagueness is to be found at every level. That view is independently vindicated by the fact that the natural semantics expressed by QL rules has models that provide ample room for indeterminacy. Our research on natural semantics shows that indeterminacy is built into the very core of our traditional forms of reasoning. If we accept classical rules, as Williamson surely does, the conclusion should be that vagueness is both pervasive and very deep. It is not just that ‖QL‖ is helpful in solving the problems that Williamson identifies. That natural semantics is mandatory, since it is exactly what the classical rules express. Deployment of natural semantics in the metalanguage at every level is therefore required by anyone who, like Williamson, endorses the classical rules. Classical logic is not just compatible with an account of indeterminacy, it demands it.

16 Modal logic

This chapter is an introduction to the natural semantics for modal logics. A pleasing result is that the basic modal logic K expresses the standard truth condition for □, where the accessibility relation R is defined as this is done in canonical models for modal logic (Section 16.1). Extensions of K such as the logics (M=T, S4, and S5) are treated in Section 16.2. Here we learn that some modal axioms involving □ (such as (M) and (4)) express their corresponding frame conditions, but others involving ◇ such as (B) and (5) do not. A more detailed treatment of the natural semantics for ◇ rules follows (Section 16.3). It shows that the interpretation of ◇ is novel and doubly intensional. Section 16.4 reveals how complications that arise for the completeness of quantified modal logic may be explained by the fact that the natural semantics for the quantifiers differs from the substitutional and objectual readings. The chapter closes (Section 16.5) with the description of an interesting but failed project. It is to modify the definition of validity to more faithfully capture what is expressed by natural deduction rules that involve the use of modal (or boxed) subproofs. Though clean results on the natural semantics of those systems are not available, we hope the reader will find the discussion an inspiration for further research using variations on the definition of validity.

16.1 Natural semantics for the modal logic K

Let us introduce the (unary) operator □ (for necessity) to the syntax with the standard formation rules. For starters, imagine that □ is the only connective in the language, and that the basic model logic SK is defined by adding (K) to the structural rules S⊢ of Section 3.1.

(K) $\dfrac{H \vdash C}{\Box H \vdash \Box C}$

Here □H is understood to be {□A: A∈H}, that is, the set that results from prefixing each member of H with □.

The standard semantics for modal logic introduces a *frame* <W, R> containing a set W of possible worlds, and a binary relation R on W called the *accessibility relation*. Modal logic frames <W, R> are of course close cousins of the Kripke frames <W, ⊆> introduced in Kripke semantics for intuitionistic logic. The natural semantics for → and ~ (discussed in Chapters 6 and 8) simulated Kripke models by allowing sets of valuations to play the role of W and by defining the relation ≤ to play the role of ⊆. In natural semantics for modal logic, a similar strategy is employed. The accessibility relation R_V will be defined for members v and v′ of a set V of valuations by $\|R_V\|$, a definition reminiscent of what is used in the canonical model for modal logic.

$\|R_V\|$ $vR_Vv′$ iff for all wffs A, if v(□A)=t then v′(A)=t.

Given $\|R_V\|$, one may generate for each set of valuations V, a structure <V, R_V> that simulates a modal logic frame. With $\|R_V\|$ in place, the truth condition $\|□\|$ for the modal operator □ may be given as follows, where 'v' ranges over members of V.

$\|□\|$ v(□A)=t iff for every v′ in V, if $vR_Vv′$, then v′(A)=t.

The basic modal logic SK is formed by adding rule (K) to the structural rules S⊢.

(K) $\dfrac{H ⊢ C}{□H ⊢ □C}$

When the language contains only the connective □, it is a simple matter to show that SK expresses $\|□\|$.

SK Expression Theorem. SK expresses $\|□\|$.

Proof. We must prove that V is a model of SK iff V obeys $\|□\|$. The reader can easily check soundness, that is, that (K) preserves V-validity when V obeys $\|□\|$.

To show (K) forces $\|□\|$, assume that V is a model of (K) and show V obeys $\|□\|$ as follows. It is easy to see that $\|R_V\|$ guarantees $\|□\|$ from left to right. For the other direction, we must show $\|□f\|$.

$\|□f\|$ If v(A)=f, then for some v′∈V, $vR_Vv′$ and v′(A)=f.

Assume then that v(□A)=f and show that there is a valuation u in V such that vR_Vu and u(A)=f as follows. Let H_v be {B: v(□B)=t}. It follows that $□H_v$ is {□B:

v($\Box$B)=t}. So v($\Box$H$_v$)=t and v($\Box$A)=f. By contraposing the statement that (K) preserves V-validity, we obtain (CK).

(CK) If for some v″∈V, v″($\Box$H$_v$)=t and v″($\Box$A)=f, then for some u′∈V, u′(H$_v$)=t and u′(A)=f.

The antecedent of (CK) holds (let v″ be v), so there is an valuation u′∈V with u′(H$_v$)=t and u′(A)=f. Since u′(H$_v$)=t, vR$_v$u′ holds, and so u′ is the desired valuation. □

Since the above theorem depends only on the presence of (K) and the structural rules, it will continue to hold in modal logics that include rules for other connectives, such as the result IQ+K of adding (K) to system IQ (intuitionistic predicate logic) and the result QL+K of adding (K) to QL (classical predicate logic). Given the IQ Expression Theorem, and the QL Expression Theorem of Section 14.8, it is easy to see that expression results for IQ+K and QL+K follow from "pasting together" these results with the last theorem.

Theorem 16.1.2 IQ+K expresses ‖IQ+K‖ the conjunction of ‖IQ‖ with ‖$\Box$‖, and QL+K expresses ‖QL+K‖, the conjunction of ‖QL‖ with ‖$\Box$‖.

However, before we can declare that ‖QL+K‖ and ‖IQ+K‖ qualify as the natural semantics for QL+K and IQ+K, we need to resolve the apparent circularity introduced by the mention of R$_V$ in ‖$\Box$‖. One tactic for certifying ‖$\Box$‖ is, unfortunately, not available. It would be to rewrite the definition of R$_V$ so that it only mentions the behavior of propositional variables. This would head off the circularity, since the new definition of R$_V$ would not mention the behavior of any complex wffs. Then we could hope to prove the analog of the ≤ Lemma, to show that it does not matter which of the two definitions we chose.

However, as soon as we consider ‖R$_V$‖, the definition as things stand, the problem is apparent.

‖R$_V$‖ vR$_V$v′ iff for all wffs A, if v($\Box$A)=t then v′(A)=t.

‖R$_V$‖ explicitly mentions the behavior of complex wffs prefixed by $\Box$, so substituting 'p' for 'A's in ‖R$_V$‖ will do no good. Furthermore, an attempt to eliminate the mention of $\Box$ in ‖R$_V$‖ using ‖$\Box$‖ introduces R$_V$ all over again.

So circularity in the modal case is especially recalcitrant. This is under-scored by the fact that an attempt to prove the ≤ Lemma is blocked when □ is in the language. (The reader may inspect the □ case for the induction to see the problem.) Therefore, there is no hope for proving that the conditions expressed by the modal logics are functional. (See the end of Section 5.5 for a discussion of the role of the ≤ Lemma in proving that a semantics is functional.) Though we already faced the same problem for the quantifiers, hopes for propositional modal logics must be given up as well. Humberstone (1981), faced with essentially the same difficulty, stip-ulates conditions on the interaction between R and ≤ that ensures that the analog of the ≤ Lemma can be recovered. However, these conditions are artificial from our point of view, since they are not expressed by the rules of the modal logic QL+K.

However, there is still the possibility that we might rescue ‖IQ+K‖ and/or ‖QL+K‖ with an isomorphism result. So the first project will be to modify the Quantified Path Isomorphism Theorem (of Section 14.5) to handle ‖IQ+K‖. With that theorem in place, modifications embodied in the Quantified KR Isomorphism Theorem will deal with ‖QL+K‖.

Let a *modal quantified neighborhood model* U=<W, ⊆, N, X, NX, R, u> be defined so that <W, ⊆, N, X, NX, u> is a neighborhood model (see Section 14.8), and <W, R> is a *modal frame*, that is, R is a binary relation over W. The truth relation ⊨ is then defined using conditions (Kp), (K⊥), (K&), (K→), (K↔), (P∨), (K∀), (K∃), and the following standard truth condition (K□) for the modal operator □.

(K□) w ⊨ □A iff for every w' in W, if wRw', then w' ⊨ A.

A *modal quantified path model* will be a modal quantified neighborhood model that obeys the conditions for a quantified path model below, along with (RN) which guarantees that R meets the analog of ‖R∨‖. (Again it is under-stood that w and w' are arbitrary members of W.)

(⊆) w⊆w' iff for all wffs A, if w ⊨ A then w' ⊨ A.

(N) wNP iff there is some wff D such that w ⊭ D, and P = {w': w⊆w' and w' ⊭ D}.

(Sub) If w ⊭ Ay/x, then for some member w' in W, w⊆ₓw' and w' ⊭ A.

(X) For each variable x, w⊆ₓw' iff for all wffs A that do not contain free x, if w ⊨ A, then w' ⊨ A.

(N_x) wN_xP iff there is some wff D containing no free occurrence of x, such that $w \nvDash D$, and $P = \{w': w \subset_x w'$ and $w' \nvDash D\}$.

(RN) wRw' iff for all wffs A, if $w \vDash \Box A$, then $w' \vDash A$.

<V, $\leq$> will be said to be isomorphic to a modal quantified path model <W, $\subseteq$, N, X, R, u> iff there is a 1–1 mapping * from V into W such that $v \leq v'$ iff $v^* \subseteq v'^*$, vR_Vv' iff $v^*Rv'^*$, and u fixes the values of the propositional variables so that $v(A)=t$ iff $v^* \vDash A$. Let $\|IQ+K\|$ the conjunction of $\|IQ\|$ with $\|\Box\|$. Again, it is understood that when we say that V obeys $\|IQ+K\|$ we mean that $\leq$ is defined by $\|\leq\|$.

$\|\leq\|$ $v \leq v'$ iff for all wffs A of L, if $v(A)=t$, then $v'(A)=t$.

Theorem 16.1.3 V obeys $\|I \lor \lor +K\|$ iff <V, $\leq$> is isomorphic to some modal quantified path model.

Proof. For the proof from left to right, assume that V obeys $\|IQ+K\|$ and show that <V, $\leq$> is isomorphic to a modal quantified path model U=<V, $\leq$, N, X, NX, R_V, u>. To establish the isomorphism, it is shown that $v(A)=t$ iff $v^* \vDash A$ by induction on the length of A exactly as in the $\exists$ Path Isomorphism Theorem of Section 14.8. Only the case where A has the form $\Box B$ needs to be checked, but in light of the identification of W in U with V, and R with R_V respectively, the right-hand side of condition (K$\Box$) comes to the following.

For every v' in V, if vRv', then $w' \vDash A$.

By the hypothesis of the induction, this is equivalent to the right-hand side of $\|\Box\|$. Therefore $v(\Box B)=t$ iff $v \vDash \Box B$ as desired.

For the proof from right to left, assume V is isomorphic to some modal quantified path model U, and show that V obeys $\|IQ+K\|$ as follows. The proof that $\|IQ\|$ holds (and that $\leq$ is defined by $\|\leq\|$) follows the reasoning of the $\exists$ Path Isomorphism Theorem, so all that remains is to show that $\|\Box\|$ and $\|R_V\|$ hold. From (K$\Box$) and the fact that the isomorphism * is 1–1, we have the following.

$v^* \vDash \Box A$ iff for all v'^* in V, if $v^*Rv'^*$ then $v'^* \vDash A$.

Since V and U are isomorphic we have vR_Vv' iff $v^*Rv'^*$, $v^* \vDash \Box A$ iff $v(\Box A)=t$, and $v'^* \vDash A$ iff $v'(A)=t$. So $\|\Box\|$ follows as desired. Furthermore, from (RN) it is easy to prove $\|R_V\|$ in similar fashion. $\Box$

Now let us turn to modal logics based on classical predicate logic QL. Let a *modal quantified KR-model* U = <W, ⊆, R, X, u> be such that <W, ⊆, X, u> is a quantified KR-model, and <W, R> is a Kripke frame. The truth relation ⊨ is defined the way it was for quantified KR-models, and (K□) is added to govern the truth evaluation of wffs with the shape □A.

(K□) w ⊨ □A iff for every w′ in W, if wRw′, then w′ ⊨ A.

An isomorphism result for ∥QL+K∥ with respect to modal quantified KR-models may be obtained by piggybacking it on the last theorem. Simply use the KR theorem and the strategy of the Quantified Path Isomorphism Theorem of Section 14.5.

Theorem 16.1.4 V obeys ∥QL+K∥ iff V is isomorphic to some modal quantified KR-model.

16.2 Natural semantics for extensions of K

The idea of correspondence of a modal logic axiom to a condition on the Kripke relation has been a focal point of interest in modal logic. (See van Bentham (1984) and Sahlqvist (1975).) In fact it was this very concept that inspired my research into natural semantics. The idea that modal axioms or rules could express properties of frames is just a special case of the topic of this book: where rules in general express properties of models. In modal logic, the axiom □A→A (for example) corresponds to reflexivity because (roughly) □A→A is valid on a frame just in case that frame is reflexive. To say that a formula is valid on a frame <W, R> means that it is true on every (modal) Kripke model <W, R, u> with frame <W, R>. More generally, a set of wffs S *corresponds for frames* to property P iff for every frame <W, R>, all members of S are valid on <W, R> iff property P holds of <W, R>. The interesting part of the notion of correspondence for frames is what Sahlqvist (1975, p. 116) calls reflection: if formulas are valid for a frame, then the frame must obey the corresponding property. (This is just the analog of 'forces' in our definition of expression.) Reflection is pleasing because when it holds, we know that the validity of our set of formulas forces the frame to behave as we expect, according to the semantics for that system. Acceptance of the axioms forces a corresponding "interpretation" on the frame.

In the present context, where sets of valuations V generate frames <V, R_V>, the analog notion of correspondence to axioms or rules governing the modal operator □ would be the following. Rule ℝ would correspond to condition ‖ℝ‖ on frames iff V is a model of ℝ iff <V, R_V> obeys ‖ℝ‖. But of course this just amounts to the claim that ℝ expresses that <V, R_V> obeys ‖ℝ‖. So the notion of correspondence in modal logic amounts to the notion of what rules express.

Despite the similarities between the notions of correspondence in the modal setting and expression in our setting, results on correspondence diverge. Part of the explanation for this is that in the standard modal setting, the classical treatment of the propositional connectives is simply presumed, while natural semantics selects weaker interpretations, at least when ND rules are used. In particular, the non-classical treatment of negation stands in the way of obtaining expression results that mirror those that are found in Kripke semantics for modal logic. True, there are some positive results for rules that do not involve negation. For example, the rules (M): □A ⊢ A and (4): □A ⊢ □□A, express the condition that <V, R_V> is reflexive and transitive respectively.

(M): □A ⊢ A

(4): □A ⊢ □□A

Theorem 16.2.1 If V obeys ‖□‖, then (M) expresses reflexivity of <V, R_V>, and (4) expresses the transitivity of <V, R_V>.

Proof. Assume V obeys ‖□‖. To show that (4) expresses the transitivity of <V, R_V>, let V be any set of valuations, and show that V is a model of (4) iff <V, R_V> is transitive. For the proof from left to right, suppose V is a model of (4), that is, □A ⊨$_V$ □□A. To show <V, R_V> is transitive, let u, u', and u" be any members of V and assume $uR_V u'$ and $u'R_V u"$ and show $uR_V u"$ as follows. Given ‖R_V‖, $uR_□ u"$ will follow if we can show that for all wffs B if u(□B)=t then u"(B)=t. Assuming u(□B)=t we have u(□□B)=t by □B ⊨$_V$ □□B, and by ‖R_V‖, it follows that u'(□B)=t and u"(B)=t as desired. For the other direction, assume that <V, R_V> is transitive, and assume for any member v of V, that v(□A)=t and show v(□□A)=t as follows. By ‖□‖, v(□□A)=t follows if we can show that for all u, and u' in V if $vR_V u$ and $uR_V u'$, then u'(A)=t. So suppose $vR_V u$ and $uR_V u'$. By the transitivity of <V, R_V>, $vR_V u'$, and so by (Def R_V) and v(□A)=t, we have u'(A)=t as desired. The proof for (M) reflexivity is similar and easier.   □

The last theorem is a simple variant of the well-known argument to show the completeness of classical systems including (M) and (4) for their corresponding conditions on frames in the so-called canonical model. (See, for example, Garson (2006, pp. 202–203).) Given the adequacy results for natural semantics found in Section 12.1, the last theorem provides a quick proof of the adequacy of all modal logics that extend either the intuitionistic logic IQ+K or the classical QL+K by adding one or more of (M) and (4) with respect to models whose frames obey the corresponding conditions.

However these results do not apply to other rules commonly used to extend K. Assume for the moment that the operator $\Diamond$ (for possibility) is defined by $\|\Diamond\|$.

$\|\mathrm{Def}\ \Diamond\|\ \Diamond A =_{\mathrm{df}} {\sim}\Box{\sim}A.$

Consider two famous rules (B) and (5) that involve $\Diamond$ (and therefore negation).

(B) $A \vdash \Box\Diamond A$

(5) $\Diamond A \vdash \Box\Diamond A$

Neither of these rules expresses its corresponding condition on frames.

$\|B\|$ $<V, R_V>$ is *symmetric*, i.e. for all v and v′ in V, if vR_Vv' then $v'R_Vv$.

$\|5\|$ $<V, R_V>$ is *euclidean*, i.e. for all v, v′ and v″ in V, if vR_Vv' and vR_Vv'', then $v'R_Vv''$.

The next theorem shows this failure is deep-rooted. Not only does (B) not express the symmetry of $<V, R_V>$, nothing else can. (A similar result can be obtained for the euclidean property.)

Theorem 16.2.2 If S is any extension of IQ+K plus (M) or QL+K plus (M) such that $\nvdash_S p$ for some atom p, then S does not express the symmetry of $<V, R_V>$.

Proof. Assume the antecedent of the theorem. Consider the canonical model [S] for S. We know by the [S] Adequacy Theorem of Section 4.3 that [S] is a model of S. However, the R_V generated from [S] using $\|R_V\|$ is not symmetric by the following reasoning. Let v and v′ be defined so that v(A)=t iff $\vdash_S A$ and v′(A)=t iff $\Box p \vdash_S A$, where p is an atom such that $\nvdash_S p$. Clearly v and v′ are members of [S]. If v($\Box$A)=t, then $\vdash_S \Box$A, $\vdash_S$ A, $\Box p \vdash_S$ A, and v′(A)=t, so vR_Vv'. However since $\nvdash_S p$, v(p)=f, and since $\Box p \vdash_S \Box p$, v′($\Box$p)=t. It follows that not $v'R_Vv$. Therefore [S] qualifies as a model of S where R is not symmetric. $\Box$

It was crucial to the last theorem that the valuations used not be classical. If attention is restricted to sets of valuations obeying the classical readings of the connectives, it is possible to show that (B) does express the symmetry of $<V, R_V>$. However obtaining the classical interpretation of the propositional connectives would require the adoption of systems of modal logic with multiple conclusions, a topic we will leave to another occasion.

16.3 The possibility operator

The previous section pointed out that the axiom (B) does not express the symmetry of frames. One explanation for this is that $\Diamond$ does not receive its ordinary reading on natural semantics. The easiest way to see why is to consider a system based on classical logic where $\Diamond$ is defined by ||Def $\Diamond$||.

||Def $\Diamond$|| $\Diamond A =_{df} \sim\Box\sim A$.

Now construct the truth condition for $\Diamond$ using ||$\Box$|| and ||$\neg$||, the intuitionistic account of negation. It comes as no surprise that the result ||q$\Diamond$|| is similar to the quasi-truth interpretation ||q∃|| of ∃ obtained from ∀ in the analogous way.

||q$\Diamond$|| $v(\Diamond A)$=t iff for all v' in V, if $v\leq v'$, then
             for some v'' in V, $v'R_V v''$ and $v''(A)$=qT.
||q∃|| $v(\exists xA)$=t iff for all v' in V, if $v\leq v'$, then
             for some v'' in V, $v'\leq_x v''$ and $v''(A)$=qT.

(Humberstone (1981, p. 327) presents what is essentially the same interpretation for $\Diamond$.) The reader can verify that ||Def $\Diamond$|| and ||$\Box$|| entails ||q$\Diamond$||. This "non-standard" reading of $\Diamond$ differs from the truth condition ||K$\Diamond$|| normally used in Kripke semantics for modal logic,

||K$\Diamond$|| $v(\Diamond A)$=t iff for some v' in V, $vR_V v'$ and $v'(A)$=t.

The difference between ||q$\Diamond$|| and ||K$\Diamond$|| helps explain why rules such as (B) fail to express their corresponding conditions on frames. Since ||q$\Diamond$|| is weaker, a rule like $A \vdash \Box\Diamond A$, says "less" than what would express were ||K$\Diamond$|| to hold.

Working out what rules involving $\Diamond$ actually do express is an interesting area for future research. It is of course a straightforward matter to write out semantical conditions corresponding to various rules by merely unpacking the truth conditions for the modal operators using $\|\Box\|$ and $\|q\Diamond\|$. For example, doing so yields the following for (B).

(B?) If $v(A)=t$, then for all u in V, if vR_Vu, then

for all v' in V, if $u\leq v'$, then

for some v'' in V, $v'R_Vv''$ and $v''(A)=qT$.

However, this exercise is fruitless. What we want in correspondence theory for modal logic are the conditions *on frames* that correspond to the various rules. Such conditions do not mention the truth-value of the formulas A on various valuations, but are expressed entirely in terms of V and R_V alone. In is an interesting and open question whether "second-order" conditions such as (B?) can be expressed without mentioning the truth value of any formula. Therefore, a completely new set of questions in correspondence theory are raised in natural semantics, where $\Diamond$ has the quasi-truth reading.

So far, we have been assuming that $\Diamond$ is defined from $\Box$ using $\|\text{Def }\Diamond\|$. However, an inferentialist account of $\Diamond$ would be better served by exploring what the rules for $\Diamond$ express about the reading for $\Diamond$. The problem with this idea is to identify a suitable set of introduction and elimination rules for $\Diamond$. The closest that I can think of is the following variant of (K).

$(\Diamond K)$ $\quad \dfrac{H, A \vdash B}{\Box H, \Diamond A \vdash \Diamond B}$

But this rule involves $\Box$ as well as $\Diamond$. The difficulty is that we have no rules that are formulated in the spirit of natural deduction systems. Even K was defined using (K) rather than with a pair of natural deduction rules that introduce and eliminate $\Box$ from proofs. In an attempt to overcome this failing, a full-fledged natural deduction system for modal logics will be explored in Section 16.5. However, this will require a generalization of the notion of validity for modal logic, and as we will see, the project faces serious problems.

16.4 The natural semantics of quantified modal logic

A pleasant feature of propositional modal logics is the modularity of their completeness results. For the most part, when one has proven the completeness of logic S with respect to a property of frames $\|F\|$, and the

completeness of logic S' with respect to frame property ‖F'‖, then completeness for the sum of the two systems S+S' with respect to the conjunction of F
and F' can be given by "pasting together" the reasoning of the original pair
of completeness proofs. For example, from the proof that S4 (which is K +
(M) + (4)) is complete for reflexive transitive frames, and the proof that B
(which is K + (M) + (B)) is complete for reflexive symmetric frames, we may
obtain a proof that S4+B=S5 is complete for reflexive, transitive, and symmetric frames.

The completeness problem for quantified modal logic (QML) is complicated by the fact that this kind of modularity may fail. In general, one may
not obtain completeness for a quantified modal logic Q+M, composed of a
quantifier system Q and a propositional modal logic M, by combining the
reasoning used in the completeness proofs for Q with those for M. For
example, classical quantificational logic QL is complete for the substitution
and objectual interpretations, and S4 is complete for reflexive transitive
frames, but when the semantical conditions from the two systems are
combined in the obvious way, the resulting semantics ‖QL+S4‖ validates
the Barcan formula (BF), which is not provable in QL+S4.

(BF) $\forall x \Box A \rightarrow \Box \forall x A$

(The objectual version of the combined semantics we are discussing has a
single domain of quantification, rather than a separate one for each possible
world.) The situation is oddly asymmetrical, since the converse Barcan
formula (CBF) is provable in QL+S4.

(CBF) $\Box \forall x A \rightarrow \forall x \Box A$

Even in systems that restore symmetry by adopting BF, modularity may fail.
For example, for the propositional modal logic S4.1 is complete, but QL+BF
+S4.1 is not complete (Cresswell, 1995).

Chapter 14 (Sections 14.3 and 14.4) has shown that the sentential interpretation, which is what the quantifier rules express, differs from the
substitution and objectual interpretations. That difference emerges even
more clearly in a modal setting. Theorem 16.1.2 assures us that both intuitionistic and classical quantified modal logics based on K are complete, for
by the ‖S‖ Completeness Theorem of Section 12.1, a system S is complete for
a semantics ‖S‖ that it expresses.

Theorem 16.1.2 IQ+K expresses ‖IQ+K‖ the conjunction of ‖IQ‖ with ‖□‖, and QL+K expresses ‖QL+K‖, the conjunction of ‖QL‖ with ‖□‖.

‖S‖ **Completeness Theorem.** If H ⊨$_{‖S‖}$ C, then H ⊢$_S$ C.

Furthermore, by Theorem 16.2.1, these results extend to systems (such as S4) that include the rules (M) and (4).

Theorem 16.2.1 If V obeys ‖□‖, then (M) expresses reflexivity of <V, R$_V$>, and (4) expresses the transitivity of <V, R$_V$>.

So let the system QM be IQ+K (intuitionistic QML) or QL+K (classical QML) together with any (or none) of the two rules (M) and (4), and let ‖QM‖ be the corresponding semantics. Completeness of QM for ‖QM‖ follows immediately.

QM Completeness Theorem. QM is complete for ‖QM‖.

In general, the method of natural semantics provides resources for establishing modular completeness results in quantified modal logic, at least where the relevant frame properties are expressed. In fact it was the recognition that natural semantics would provide a tool for obtaining modular completeness results in QML that first prompted my research in the area.

The outcome for QL+S4 is that it is complete (and in fact adequate) for the natural semantics ‖QL+S4‖, which uses the sentential interpretation of the quantifier. Therefore, we can predict that BF and CBF are treated asymmetrically in ‖QL+S4‖. It is not difficult to show directly that BF (which is not provable in QL+S4) is ‖QL+S4‖-invalid (even though CBF is ‖QL+S4‖-valid). This contrasts with the symmetrical results obtained when the substitution or objectual interpretations are used, for in those cases, both BF and CBF are validated. The explanation is that the sentential interpretation is a weaker reading of the quantifier that leaves room for counterexamples to BF.

It is well known that the "asymmetrical" quantified modal logic that accepts CBF and rejects BF can be shown to be adequate for a semantics where the domains of quantification vary from one possible world w to another, and where one stipulates that the domains expand, that is, when wRw', the domain of w is a subset of the domain of w'. (For more details see, for example, Garson (2006, Section 13.10).) My own view is that the expanding domains stipulation is ad hoc. It has no intuitive attractions, but seems motivated purely by a desire to cobble together a semantics for which the combination of QL and S4 is adequate. In the natural semantics ||QL+S4||, however, there are no domains, and no need to make any adjustments to obtain an adequacy result. The sentential interpretation is a new and more "natural" way to interpret the quantifier in a modal setting that provides a semantics adequate for straightforward combinations of quantification and modality.

These reflections provide an explanation for the non-modularity in QML completeness results. The substitution and objectual readings of the quantifier are stronger than what the quantifier rules actually express. In a modal setting, this reveals itself in the validation of BF, which is in fact invalid on the natural reading. An inferentialist strategy for designing the semantics for QML starts with the weaker natural readings that are expressed by the standard QL rules. A technical advantage of that strategy is that failures of modularity simply cannot arise.

Working in the natural semantics paradigm does not require that we abandon quantified modal logics with the more familiar treatments of the quantifier. Remember that Theorem 14.9 demonstrated that $S\forall\infty$, the system that uses the omega rule ($\forall\infty$) in place of ($\forall$ Introduction), expresses the substitution interpretation of the quantifier. By the ||S|| Completeness Theorem, it follows that $QL\infty+S4$ must be complete for that semantics. Since (BF) is valid there, it follows that the omega rule removes the asymmetry found in QL+S4, since it yields a proof of (BF). It is easy enough to construct the proof directly.

1. $\{A^y/x: y \text{ is in Var}\} / \forall xA$		($\forall\infty$)
2. $\square\{A^y/x: y \text{ is in Var}\} / \square\forall xA$		(K)
3. $\forall x\square A / \square A^y/x$ for each y in Var		($\forall$ Elimination)
4. $\forall x\square A / \square\forall xA$		2, 3 (Cut∞)

So $QL\infty+S4$ is stronger than QL+S4, and that added strength reflects the difference between the substitution and sentential readings of the quantifiers. The Barcan formula must be added to QL+S4 to fill the gap between the sentential interpretation, where it would not be required, and the substitution reading, which validates it. The omega rule eliminates this weakness in

QL+S4 by restoring the "intended" interpretation of the quantifier, and opening the way for modular completeness.

This is just a first taste of the ways in which natural semantics may be useful in understanding the complexities that emerge in quantified modal logic. Much more can be done to investigate the full range of systems, including those where the semantics allows varying the domain across the possible worlds. The natural semantics for systems based on the rules of free logic is an interesting field for further exploration. For example, it promises to yield an explanation (on analogy with the case of (BF)) for why it is necessary to "modalize" the rule of universal introduction (G∀In) in Thomason's (1970) system Q3 in order to obtain completeness.

(G∀In): $\underline{A_1 \rightarrow \Box(A_2 \rightarrow \ldots \Box(A_n{}^y/x) \ldots)}$

$A_1 \rightarrow \Box(A_2 \rightarrow \ldots \Box(\forall xA_n) \ldots)$ no y free in the conclusion

Here again, the effect of adding the omega rule to Q3 is to eliminate these complications by restoring modular completeness. A careful study of these matters is left for another occasion.

16.5 Variations on the definition of validity

The study of modal logic presented so far lies outside the main focus of this book, namely to investigate what natural deduction (ND) systems express. The modal logics discussed are built around a single rule (K), rather than introduction and elimination rules typical of ND systems. There are ND formulations of modal logic where one introduces special (boxed) subproofs for the introduction and elimination of the modal operator $\Box$. However, their use requires that we generalize the notion of logical consequence to take account of the semantic content of these new subproof structures. Garson (2006, pp. 174ff.) shows how this can be accomplished by providing a new definition of validity for "arguments" whose premises are indicated by ancillary hypotheses and occurrences of boxed subproofs. Here is a brief description of some details.

In horizontal format, the rules for a ND modal system can be defined over L-arguments L/C, where L is a sequence $\ldots H_n, \Box, H_{n-1}, \Box, \ldots, \Box, H_1$ of lists H_i of wffs separated by occurrences of $\Box$. The occurrences of $\Box$ indicate the point at which boxed subproofs are opened. The ND modal logic K_{ND} results from adding the following two rules to the generalizations of those for propositional logic PL, where sequences L are replaced for sets of hypotheses H in those rules.

K_{ND}: ($\Box$ In)   ($\Box$ Out)

$$\frac{L, \Box \vdash A}{L \vdash \Box A} \qquad \frac{L \vdash \Box A}{L, \Box \vdash A}$$

Validity for generalized arguments L / C is defined for a frame model <V, R> as follows, where R is any binary relation over V. $L \vDash_{<V, R>} C$ iff for all v in V if v(L)=t, then v(C)=t. However, we need to explain what v(L)=t means. This is defined recursively by the structure of L.

(Def v(L)) For a set of wffs H, v(H)=t iff v(B)=t for every B in H.

For a sequence L, $\Box$, H, v(L, $\Box$, H)=t iff for some u in V, uRv, v(H)=t and u(L)=t.

Given these definitions, we can say that S expresses a condition P iff for all frame models <V, R> the rules of S preserve <V, R> validity iff <V, R> obeys P.

An attractive feature of this new definition of expression is that the relation R is not defined by the truth behavior of the valuations in V. Since it is antecedently given, potential circularity problems for truth conditions involving R are nipped in the bud. On the other hand, it is hard to independently motivate the definition (Def v(L)), apart from saying that its use in the definition of validity amounts to generalizing over valuations in the ancestral of the R relation. Whether that is good or bad seems to me to be an open question.

Nevertheless, the new approach to validity has its attractions. Exploration of expression results for K_{ND} suggests that it express a truth condition $\|\Box \leq\|$, which includes specific mention for the extension relation as well as R.

$\|\Box \leq\|$ v($\Box$A)=t iff for all u in V, if v$\leq$u, then for all w in V, if uRw, then w(A)=t.

The result is that it is easy to show the $\leq$ Lemma, which in turn promises to guarantee that $\|\Box \leq\|$ is a functional truth condition.

Unfortunately, there is a serious problem in making progress with this project. To show the soundness of rules that involve arguments with sequences of sets L in place of sets H, it is necessary to have the result that when v$\leq$v' and v(L)=t then v'(L)=t. Unfortunately, this conditions fails unless further conditions on the interaction between $\leq$ and R hold, such as the following.

$$\text{If } vRv' \text{ and } v' \leq v'', \text{ then } vRv''.$$

Faced with what is essentially the same problem, Humberstone (1981, p. 324, (P1)) stipulates this principle. However, a model-theoretic inferentialist is in no position to adopt such a principle unless it is expressed by the rules. As far as I can see, no modal logic rule could have that desired effect. For the moment then, the L-argument strategy for accommodating ND systems for modal logic is a failed project. I hope some reader will be inspired to find a way to overcome the problems just described. (The reader is warned that revising the definition of $v(L)=t$ to match the "doubly intensional" nature of $\|\Box \leq \|$, will still require a condition relating R to $\leq$.)

Let me close this section by mentioning some other ways in which the definition of validity could be modified so as to open promising territory to the natural semantics research program. An idea worth exploring in the case of the quantifiers is to allow models V to contain valuations over different languages. The result promises a more direct expression result for system S∀/, where there is no need for an ancillary rule (Sub). However, the reader is warned that that project is also hampered, this time, by a need for principles governing the interaction between $\leq$ and $\leq_x$.

Two other projects appear on the horizon. The approach in this book is essentially bivalent, but there is no reason why truth conditions could not be defined over three values or more. It might also be worth exploring bilateral truth conditions with separate clauses for truth (or assertion) and falsity (or denial). Finally, the definition of validity in this book automatically accepts the standard structural rules such as Weakening and Contraction. However variations on that definition could open the natural semantics paradigm to substructural logics (Restall, 2000), where standard structural rules are rejected. For example, a treatment of validity appropriate for a relevance logic could be fashioned by requiring that H / C be relevantly V-valid only if no subset of H is V-valid. That way, notions of expressive power for relevance logics can be explored where Weakening fails. (See Garson (1989) where that idea is exploited to delineate relationships between logic programming and relevance logics.) While these suggestions for varying the definition of validity will provide ample opportunities for future research, the reader is encouraged to devise even more.

Summary

It is time to draw this book to a close, and to reflect on what has been accomplished. I hope its main contribution will be to spark future research on what logics mean. So far, only a few excursions have been taken in a vast landscape of questions about natural semantics and its philosophical applications. A handful of answers have been given to the main question that is posed by this book, namely how or whether inferential rules governing an expression fix its truth conditions. However, we have just scratched the surface. For example, more needs to be done to fully understand classical quantification. Results for free logics and systems for generalized quantifiers have not even been attempted. Exploring rules in the logic programming tradition and the concept of negation as failure could be very fruitful. Modal logics and their quantified extensions are also promising territory for new results, to say nothing of tense logics, multi-modal logics, dynamic logic, and inquisitive logic. Despite the fact that natural semantics seems wedded to standard structural rules, it is still possible to obtain some results for relevance logic (Garson, 1990, Section 5). Modifications to the definition of validity mentioned in Section 16.5 promise to allow application of the ideas of natural semantics to a wider range of systems including substructural logics. Function symbols, descriptions, the lambda calculus, set theory, and arithmetic all remain to be explored. Furthermore, there is no reason why natural semantics has to be limited to the domain of logic. The inferential roles set up within a natural language provide a much richer field of investigation. There promise to be a wide range of applications to philosophical problems as well, at the very least to areas such as truth paradoxes and presupposition where supervaluations have been deployed in the past.

Given results obtained so far, what conclusions should be drawn concerning model-theoretic (MT) inferentialism? Those of an intuitionist persuasion may take heart at the fact that the rules for conjunction,

271

the conditional, and intuitionistic negation express exactly their intuition-istic readings in Kripke semantics. Furthermore, if the position taken in Section 8.9 is adopted, one will conclude that the reading of the rules for classical negation is intuitionist as well.

However, MT inferentialists may still worry that many results found in this book are not in their favor. Two different kinds of concern arise. First, some of the readings expressed are unexpected or unfamiliar. For example, Section 7.2 showed that the natural deduction (ND) disjunction rules express an unusual path bundle interpretation, and Chapter 14 revealed that the natural semantics for the ND quantifier rules is the sentential interpretation, a reading that differs from both the objectual and substitu-tion interpretations, and one where the existential quantifier does not have existential import.

My view is that MT inferentialists worth their salt can weather such worries about novelty in natural semantics. Novelty need not count as a defect; it makes the project all the more interesting. At the outset, there was no guarantee that MT inferentialism would vindicate truth conditions for the connectives that are widely known. The failure of natural semantics to match our expectations is not a reason to abandon MT inferentialism; it is instead one of the view's contributions to our understanding of what connectives mean. One who finds novelty a sufficient reason for rejecting the view is simply narrow-minded.

A second concern about MT inferentialism appears more telling. In some cases, there were reasons for thinking that the ND rules for a connective do not actually express any meaning at all. The most worrisome example of this is disjunction, where the condition expressed is not functional (Section 7.6). Similar worries arise for the sentential interpretation, partic-ularly for the existential quantifier (Section 14.8). Furthermore, what is expressed by the quantifier rules does not guarantee that models are refer-ential (Section 14.7). That means that the way that wffs are ruled true or false by the valuations of a model may be incompatible with the idea that those values (implicitly) are determined by an assignment of objects in a domain to the terms of the language.

There are two tactics the MT inferentialist may use to deal with this challenge. One is to cite isomorphism results of this book (for example, those in Sections 7.5 and 14.5) to argue that what is expressed counts as a correctly formed truth condition after all, so that the loss of functionality is tolerable. However, this response only goes so far, since it will not resolve the worry about non-referentiality.

Luckily there is a fall-back tactic. If the conclusion we are to draw from what we know about what rules say is that they do not determine a meaning, then so be it. MT inferentialism will then have accomplished something, by showing which rules underdetermine an interpretation. Take disjunction, for example. If its natural semantics ‖∨‖ does not qualify as a truth condition, then the rules S∨ fail to determine a reading for ∨. Under these circumstances we can stipulate a reading (for example the Beth reading ‖B∨‖ or the classical one ‖C∨‖), but which one we take is not determined by S∨. So the result is that meaning is underdetermined by inferential role. It wouldn't be the first time that a system of rules fails to fix a meaning. Is this a reason to give up on MT inferentialism and retreat to a proof-theoretic brand in its place? I think not. The proof-theoretic tradition includes several different accounts for disjunction, and on some of these disjunction fails to define a connective meaning there as well. (For example, Weir (1986) provides a definition where the harmony of S∨ fails.) So that tradition has no better resources for fixing the underdetermination. Part of the reason is that unlike the case of natural semantics, it provides no clear benchmark for calibrating success in defining the relation of logical consequence. So there is no device that provides a fact of the matter about which of several alternatives counts as the distinguished reading.

Does this mean that we must give up on inferentialism *tout court*? Again, I think not. If it turns out that the disjunction rules S∨ underdetermine a meaning, that is the fault of S∨ not inferentialism. The doctrine that inferential roles fix an expression's meaning does not entail that *every* inferential role fixes a meaning. That was, after all, the lesson of *tonk*. MT inferentialism is the view that inferential roles fix connective meaning *when meaning is fixed*. So the MT inferentialist can cheerfully accept the idea that S∨ underdetermines a meaning for ∨. While this outcome may appear radical, one may retreat to the view that while no interpretation for disjunction is provided by the logical rules alone, an interpretation may still be provided by the richer inferential relations set up for the use of 'or' in natural language. In the same way, the MT inferentialist need not worry about the non-referentiality of some models of predicate logic. Truth-value semantics underdetermines referential semantics. That is an important lesson to be learned about what quantifier rules say. It speaks to a weakness in those rules, but not in MT inferentialism. That we are able to prove that result within the MT inferentialist paradigm is not a fault, but a tribute to its fecundity.

The Alpha Centaurian anthropologists have no problem with MT inferentialism, as it is the guiding light for their study of inference in alien cultures. Since they are widely travelled, they have seen just about everything. Their study is profoundly empirical, so the occasional discovery that the inferential roles of a certain culture underdetermine a meaning for some of its sentential "connectives" is not a cause for dismay. It is all the more reason to press on with an exploration of the inferential varieties found among the intelligent beings of our galaxy. After all, MT inferentialism is not a theory of theirs; it is their discipline's necessary precondition. What better tools could they possibly forge for coming to understand what logics mean?

References

Azzouni, J. (2000) *Knowledge and Reference in Empirical Science*, Routledge, New York.

Baldwin, T. (1979) "Interpretations of Quantifiers," *Mind*, 88, 215–240.

Beall, J. C. and Restall, G. (2006) *Logical Pluralism*, Oxford University Press.

Beaver, D. (1997) "Presupposition," in J. van Bentham and A. ter Meulen (eds.), *Handbook of Logic and Language*, North Holland, Amsterdam, 939–1008.

Belnap, N. (1962) "Tonk, Plonk and Plink," in S. Cahn, R. Tallise, and S. Aikin (eds.), *Thinking About Logic*, Westview Press 2011, originally published in *Analysis*, 22, 130–134.

  (2005) "Branching Histories Approach to Indeterminism and Free Will," in B. Brown and F. Lepage (eds.), *Truth and Probability, Essays in Honour of Hugues Leblanc*, College Publishing, London, 197–211.

Belnap, N. and Dunn, J. (1968) "The Substitution Interpretation of the Quantifiers," *Nous*, 2, 177–185.

Belnap, N. and Massey, G. (1990) "Semantic Holism," *Studia Logica*, 49, 67–82.

Belnap, N., Perloff, M., and Xu, M. (2001) *Facing the Future*, Oxford University Press, New York.

Blackburn, P., de Rijke, M., and Venema, Y. (2002) *Modal Logic*, Cambridge University Press.

Boolos, G. (1993) *The Logic of Provability*, Cambridge University Press.

Boolos, G. and Jeffrey, R. (1974) *Computability and Logic*, Cambridge University Press.

Brandom, R. (1994) *Making it Explicit: Reasoning, Representation and Discursive Content*, Harvard University Press, Cambridge, MA.

  (2001) *Articulating Reasons: An Introduction to Inferentialism*, Harvard University Press, Cambridge, MA.

Brown, J. D. K. and Garson, J. (in preparation) "The Logic of Vagueness (and Everything Else , Too)."

Carnap, R. (1943) *Formalization of Logic*, Harvard University Press, Cambridge, MA.

Cresswell, M. J. (1995) "Incompleteness and the Barcan Formulas," *Journal of Philosophical Logic*, 24, 379–403.

Cummins, R. (1989) *Meaning and Mental Representation*, MIT Press, Cambridge, MA.

Davis, R. and Lenat, D. (1982) *Knowledge-Based Systems in Artificial Intelligence*, McGraw-Hill, New York.

de Campos Sanz, W., Piecha, T., and Schroeder-Heister, P. (forthcoming) "Constructive Semantics and the Validity of Peirce's Law."

Dennett, D. (1984) *Elbow Room: The Varieties of Free Will Worth Wanting*, MIT Press, Cambridge, MA.

Dosen, K. (1989) "Logical Constants as Punctuation Marks," *Notre Dame Journal of Formal Logic*, 30, 262–381.

Dummett, M. (1978) "The Philosophical Basis of Intuitionistic Logic," in M. Dummett, *Truth and Other Enigmas*, Harvard University Press, Cambridge, MA, 215–247.

(1991) *The Logical Basis of Metaphysics*, Harvard University Press, Cambridge, MA.

Fitting, M. (1969) *Intuitionistic Logic, Model Theory and Forcing*, North Holland, Amsterdam.

Fodor, J. (1988) *Psychosemantics*, MIT Press, Cambridge, MA.

Garson, J. (1979) "The Substitution Interpretation and the Expressive Power of Intensional Logics," *Notre Dame Journal of Formal Logic*, 20, 858–864.

(1989) "Modularity and Relevant Logic," *Notre Dame Journal of Formal Logic*, 30, 207–223.

(1990) "Categorical Semantics," in J. M. Dunn and A. Gupta (eds.), *Truth or Consequences*, Kluwer, Dordrecht, 155–175.

(2001) "Natural Semantics: Why Natural Deduction is Intuitionistic," *Theoria*, 67, 114–137.

(2006) *Modal Logic for Philosophers*, Cambridge University Press.

(2010) "Expressive Power and Incompleteness of Propositional Logics," *Journal of Philosophical Logic*, 39, #2, 159–171.

(2013) "Open Futures in the Foundations of Propositional Logic" in T. Mueller, (ed.), *Nuel Belnap on Indeterminism and Free Action*, Springer, New York.

Gentzen, G. (1969) "Investigations into Logical Deduction," in M. E. Szabo (trans.), *The Collected Papers of Gerhard Gentzen*, North Holland, Amsterdam, 68–131.

Haack, S. (1996) *Deviant Logic, Fuzzy Logic*, University of Chicago Press.

Hacking, I. (1979) "What is Logic?" *Journal of Philosophy*, 76, 285–319.

Hand, M. (1993) "Negations in Conflict," *Erkenntnis*, 38, 115–129.

Hart, W. (1982) "Prior and Belnap," *Theoria*, 47, 127–138.

Humberstone, L. (1981) "From Worlds to Possibilities," *Journal of Philosophical Logic*, 10, 313–339.

(1996) "Valuational Semantics of Rule Derivability," *Journal of Philosophical Logic*, 25, 451–461.

(2011) *The Connectives*, MIT Press, Cambridge, MA.

Kripke, S. (1963) "Semantical Analysis of Intuitionistic Logic I," in J. Crossley and M. Dummett (eds.), *Formal Systems and Recursive Systems*, North Holland, Amsterdam, 92–129.

Leblanc, H. (1976) *Truth Value Semantics*, North Holland, Amsterdam.

Lepore, E. and Ludwig, K. (2005) *Donald Davidson*, Oxford University Press.

Lyons, J. (1968) *Introduction to Theoretical Linguistics*, Cambridge University Press, London.

MacFarlane, J. (2009) "Logical Constants," in *Stanford Encyclopedia of Philosophy*, http://plato.stanford.edu/.

Mares, E. (2004) *Relevant Logic*, Cambridge University Press.

Massey, G. (1990) "Semantic Holism is Seriously False," *Studia Logica*, 49, 83–86.

McCawley, J. (1993) *Everything that Linguists Have Always Wanted to Know About Logic*, 2nd edition, University of Chicago Press.

Prawitz, D. (1965) *Natural Deduction*, Almqvist & Wiksell, Stockholm.

(1971) "Meaning and Proofs: On the Conflict Between Classical and Intuitionistic Logic," *Theoria*, 43, 2–40.

Prior, A. N. (1960) "The Runabout Inference-Ticket," *Analysis*, 21, 38–39.

Quine, W. V. O. (1953) "On What There Is," in *From a Logical Point of View*, Harvard University Press, Cambridge, MA.

(1960) *Word and Object*, MIT Press, Cambridge, MA.

Read, S. (2010) "General-Elimination Harmony and the Meaning of the Logical Constants," *Journal of Philosophical Logic*, 39, 557–576.

Restall, G. (1999) "Negation in Relevant Logics (How I Stopped Worrying and Learned to Love the Routley Star)," in D. Gabbay and H. Wansing (eds.), *What is Negation?*, Kluwer, Dordrecht, 53–76.

(2000) *An Introduction to Substructural Logics*, Routledge, London.

(2005) "Multiple Conclusions," in P. Hajek, L. Valdez-Villanueva, and D. Westerthal (eds.), *Logic, Methodology and the Philosophy of Science: Proceedings of the 12th International Congress*, King's College Publications, London, 237–309.

Sahlqvist, H. (1975). "Completeness and Correspondence in the First and Second Order Semantics for Modal Logic," in S. Kanger (ed.), *Proceedings of the Third Scandinavian Logic Symposium*, North Holland, Amsterdam, 110–143.

Sandqvist, T. (2009) "Classical Logic Without Bivalence," *Analysis*, 69, 211–217.

Schroeder-Heister, P. (2006) "Validity Concepts in Proof-Theoretic Semantics," *Synthese*, 148, 525–571.

(forthcoming) "Proof-Theoretic Semantics," *Stanford Encyclopedia of Philosophy*, http://plato.stanford.edu/.

Searle, J. (1980) "Minds, Brains and Programs," *The Behavioral and Brain Sciences*, 3, 63–73.

Shank, R. and Abelson, R. (1977) *Scripts, Plans, Goals and Understanding*, Erlbaum, Hillsdale, NJ.

Shapiro, S. (2008) "Reasoning with Slippery Predicates," *Studia Logica*, 90, 313–336.

Shoesmith, D. J., and Smiley, T. J. (1978) *Multiple-Conclusion Logic*, Cambridge University Press.

Smullyan, R. (1968) *First-Order Logic*, Springer-Verlag, New York.

Smullyan, R. and Fitting, M. (1996) *Set Theory and the Continuum Problem*, Clarendon Press, Oxford.

Steinberger, F. (2011) "Why Conclusions Should Remain Single," *Journal of Philosophical Logic*, 40, 333–355.

Strawson, P. (1967) "On Referring," in I. Copi and J. Gould (eds.), *Contemporary Readings in Logical Theory*, Macmillan, New York, 105–127.

Sundholm, G. (1981) "Hacking's Logic," *Journal of Philosophy*, 78, 160–168.

(1986) "Proof Theory and Meaning," in D. Gabbay and F. Guenthner (eds.), *Handbook of Philosophical Logic*, D. Reidel, Dordrecht, Chapter 8, 471–506.

Taylor, R. (1962) "Fatalism," *The Philosophical Review*, 71, 56–66, also in S. Cahn, R. Talise, and S. Aikin (eds.), *Thinking about Logic*, Westview Press, Boulder, Colorado. (Page numbers cited here are to the latter volume.)

Tennant, N. (1979) *Natural Logic*, Edinburgh University Press.

(1997) *The Taming of the True*, Oxford University Press.

(forthcoming) "Inferentialism, Logicism, Harmony, and a Counterpoint," in A. Miller (ed.), *Essays for Crispin Wright*, Oxford University Press.

Thomason, R. H. (1970) "Some Completeness Results for Modal Predicate Calculi," in K. Lambert (ed.), *Philosophical Problems in Logic*, D. Reidel, Dordrecht, 56–76.

Troelstra, A. and van Dalen, D. (1988) *Constructivism in Mathematics*, North-Holland, Amsterdam.

van Bentham, J. (1984) "Correspondence Theory," in D. Gabbay and F. Guenthner (eds.), *Handbook of Philosophical Logic*, Volume II, 167–247.

van Dalen, D. (1986) "Intuitionistic Logic," in D. Gabbay and F. Guenthner (eds.), *Handbook of Philosophical Logic*, Volume III, 225–339.

van Fraassen, B. (1969) "Presuppositions, Supervaluations and Free Logic," in K. Lambert (ed.), *The Logical Way of Doing Things*, Yale University Press, New Haven, 67–91.

Wagner, S. (1981) "Tonk," *Notre Dame Journal of Formal Logic*, 22, 289–300.

Weir, A. (1986) "Classical Harmony," *Notre Dame Journal of Formal Logic*, 27, 459–482.

Williams, C. J. F. (1980) "Misinterpretations of Quantifiers," *Mind*, 89, 420–422.

Williamson, T. (1994) *Vagueness*, Routledge, New York.

Wittgenstein, L. (1961) *Tractatus Logico-Philosophicus*, Routledge & Kegan Paul, New York.

(1969) *Philosophical Investigations*, 3rd edition, McMillan, New York.

Woods, J. (2013) "Failures of Categoricity and Compositionality for Intuitionistic Disjunction," *Thought*, DOI: 10.1002/tht3.45. Online at http://onlinelibrary.wiley.com/doi/10.1002/tht3.45/abstract;jsessionid=AAD31973A0B18DB497C39F1F3FD96090.d02t02

Index

Printed in Great Britain
by Amazon